THE WALLFLOWER

YAMATONADESHIKO SHICHIHENGE

9

Tomoko Hayakawa

TRANSLATED AND ADAPTED BY
David Ury

LETTERED BY
Dana Hayward

DEL
REY

BALLANTINE BOOKS • NEW YORK

The Wallflower, volume 9 is a work of fiction. Names, characters, places, and incidents are the products of the author's imagination or are used fictitiously. Any resemblance to actual events, locales, or persons, living or dead, is entirely coincidental.

A Del Rey Trade Paperback Original

Published in the United States by Del Rey Books, an imprint of The Random House Publishing Group, a division of Random House Inc., New York.

Publication rights arranged through Kodansha, Ltd.

First published in Japan in 2004 by Kodansha Ltd., Tokyo, as *Yamatonadeshiko Shichihenge.*

ISBN 0-345-48527-0

Printed in the United States of America

www.delreymanga.com

9 8 7 6 5 4 3

Translator and adaptor—David Ury

Lettering and touchup—Dana Hayward

Cover Design—David Stevenson

Contents

A Note from the Author

♥ This is "Ten," the cutest little fella in the whole wide world. His full name is Tennosuke Hayakawa. He's a male Scottish Field Cat. He's a bit naughty and he has a knack for getting into trouble, but he's still a good boy.♥ Thanks to Ten, every day is full of love and happiness. Even scooping up his poop brings me joy.♥

—Tomoko Hayakawa

Honorifics

Throughout the Del Rey Manga books, you will find Japanese honorifics left intact in the translations. For those not familiar with how the Japanese use honorifics, and more important, how they differ from American honorifics, we present this brief overview.

Politeness has always been a critical facet of Japanese culture. Ever since the feudal era, when Japan was a highly stratified society, use of honorifics—which can be defined as polite speech that indicates relationship or status—has played an essential role in the Japanese language. When addressing someone in Japanese, an honorific usually takes the form of a suffix attached to one's name (example: "Asuna-san"), or as a title at the end of one's name or in place of the name itself (example: "Negi-sensei," or simply "Sensei!").

Honorifics can be expressions of respect or endearment. In the context of manga and anime, honorifics give insight into the nature of the relationship between characters. Many English translations leave out these important honorifics, and therefore distort the feel of the original Japanese. Because Japanese honorifics contain nuances that English honorifics lack, it is our policy at Del Rey not to translate them. Here, instead, is a guide to some of the honorifics you may encounter in Del Rey Manga.

-san: This is the most common honorific, and is equivalent to Mr., Miss, Ms., Mrs. It is the all-purpose honorific and can be used in any situation where politeness is required.

-sama: This is one level higher than "-san" and is used to confer great respect.

-dono: This comes from the word "tono," which means "lord." It is an even higher level than "-sama," and confers utmost respect.

-kun: This suffix is used at the end of boys' names to express familiarity or endearment. It is also sometimes used by men amongst friends, or when addressing someone younger or of a lower station.

-chan: This is used to express endearment, mostly toward girls. It is also used for little boys, pets, and even amongst lovers. It gives a sense of childish cuteness.

Bozu: This is an informal way to refer to a boy, similar to the English terms "kid" or "squirt."

Sempai/senpai: This title suggests that the addressee is one's "senior" in a group or organization. It is most often used in a school setting, where underclassmen refer to their upperclassmen as "sempai." It can also be used in the workplace, such as when a newer employee addresses an employee who has seniority in the company.

Kohai: This is the opposite of "sempai," and is used toward underclassmen in school or newcomers in the workplace. It connotes that the addressee is of a lower station.

Sensei: Literally meaning "one who has come before," this title is used for teachers, doctors, or masters of any profession or art.

[blank]:   This is usually forgotten in these lists, but it is perhaps the most significant difference between Japanese and English. The lack of honorific means that the speaker has permission to address the person in a very intimate way. Usually, only family, spouses, or very close friends have this kind of permission. Known as *yobisute,* it can be gratifying when someone who has earned the intimacy starts to call one by one's name without an honorific. But when that intimacy hasn't been earned, it can be very insulting.

THE wallflower

YAMATONADESHIKO SHICHIHENGE

ヤマトナデシコ七変化♡

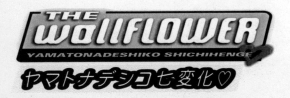

CONTENTS

WALLFLOWER'S BEAUTIFUL CAST OF CHARACTERS (?)

KYOHEI TAKANO—
A STRONG FIGHTER, "I'M THE KING."
RANMARU MORII—
A TRUE LADIES' MAN.
TAKENAGA ODA—
A CARING FEMINIST.
YUKINOJO TOYAMA—
A GENTLE, CHEERFUL AND VERY EMOTIONAL GUY.
SUNAKO NAKAHARA

SUNAKO IS A DARK LONER WHO LOVES HORROR MOVIES. WHEN HER AUNT, THE LANDLADY OF A BOARDINGHOUSE, LEAVES TOWN WITH HER BOYFRIEND, SUNAKO IS FORCED TO LIVE WITH FOUR HANDSOME GUYS. SUNAKO'S AUNT MAKES A DEAL WITH THE BOYS, WHICH CAUSES NOTHING BUT HEADACHES FOR SUNAKO. "MAKE SUNAKO INTO A LADY, AND YOU CAN LIVE RENT FREE."

SUNAKO CONTINUES TO SEEK SHELTER IN THE DARK RECESSES OF HER ROOM. EVERYTHING WILL BE FINE, AS LONG AS THE LANDLADY DOESN'T FIND OUT.

Chapter 35

The Journey to Becoming a Lady [Part 1]

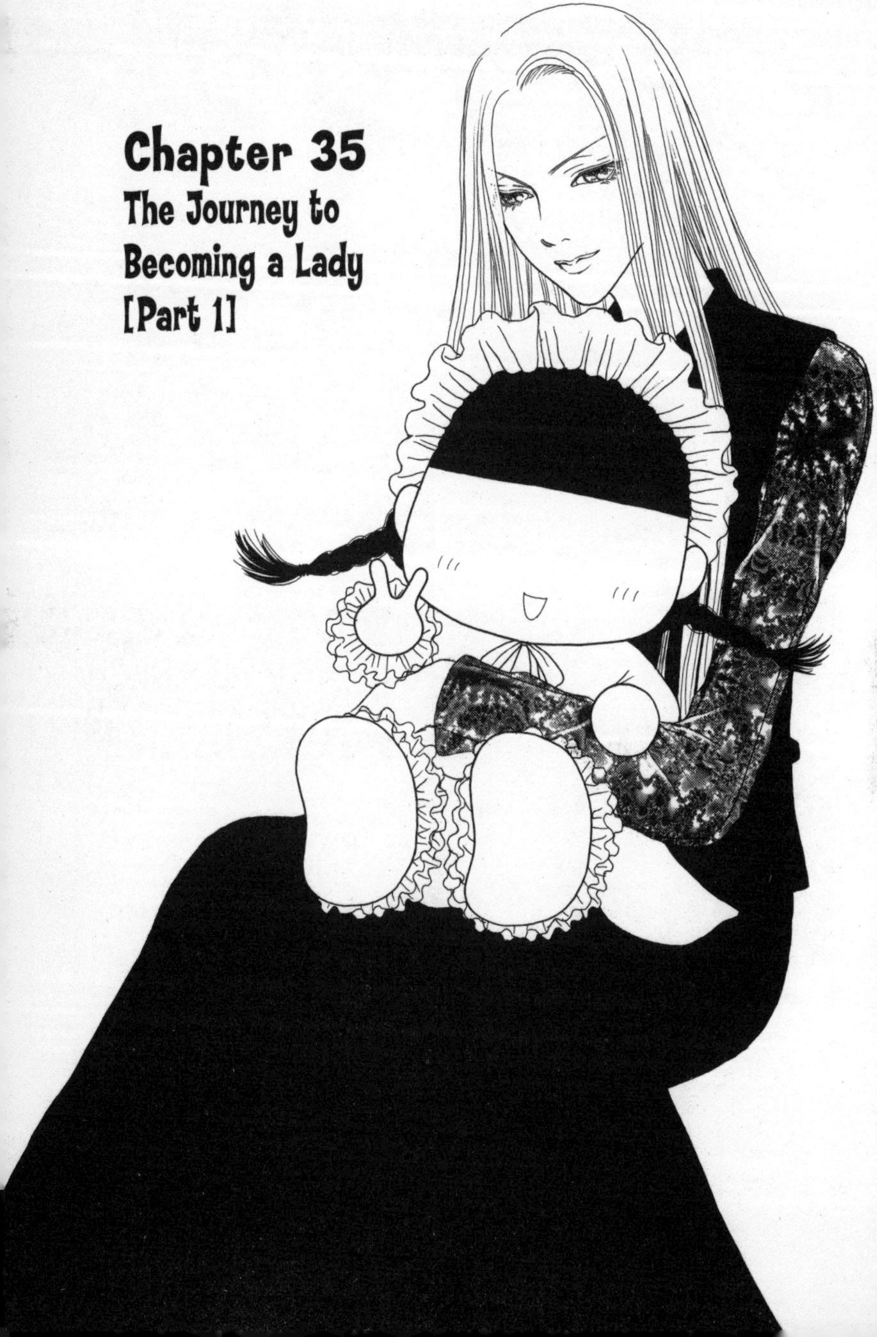

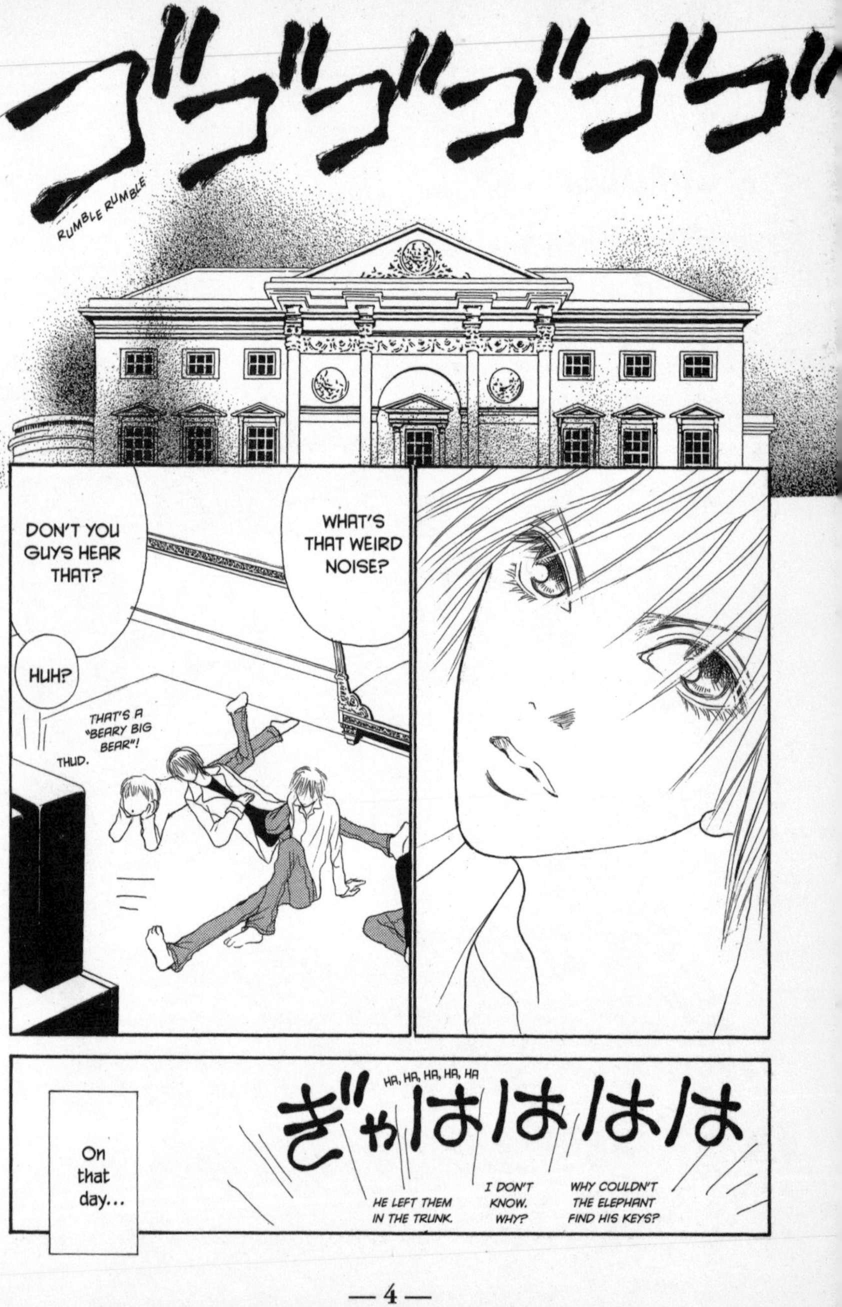
ゴゴゴゴゴ
RUMBLE RUMBLE
WHAT'S THAT WEIRD NOISE?
DON'T YOU GUYS HEAR THAT?
HUH?
THAT'S A "BEARY BIG BEAR"!
THUD.
ぎゃはははは
HA, HA, HA, HA, HA
WHY COULDN'T THE ELEPHANT FIND HIS KEYS?
I DON'T KNOW. WHY?
HE LEFT THEM IN THE TRUNK.
On that day...

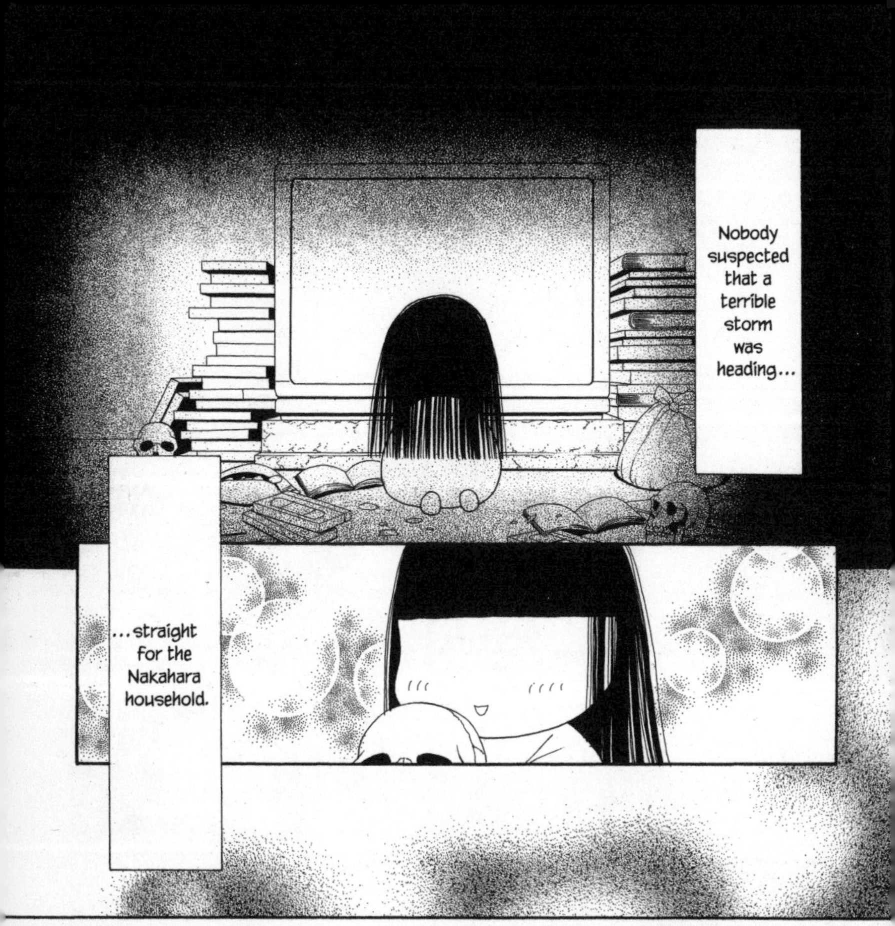
Nobody suspected that a terrible storm was heading...
...straight for the Nakahara household.

BEHIND THE SCENES

YOSSUI, WHOM I WROTE ABOUT IN BOOK 7, CAME BY TO HELP OUT THE OTHER DAY. ♥ (HIS NAME USED TO BE YOSHII.) (I KNEW HE WAS BUSY WITH HIS JOB, SO I STOPPED ASKING HIM TO WORK FOR ME, BUT THEN I FOUND OUT THAT HE QUIT. I CALLED HIM RIGHT AWAY. ♥) FROM NOW ON, YOSHII IS GONNA HELP ME ALL THE TIME. HE'S SO HELPFUL. ♥

AND GET THIS! HE WAS THE FIRST ONE TO STAY IN THE SPARE ROOM IN MY NEW APARTMENT. YOSHII WAS LIKE, "THERE'S A GHOST IN YOUR SPARE ROOM! A GHOST!" I HADN'T EVEN NOTICED. IT WAS JUST LIFE AS USUAL FOR ME.... ACTUALLY, IT STILL IS! I GOT KIND OF SCARED, SO EVERY TIME I HAD SOMEBODY OVER, I'D ASK IF THEY COULD FEEL THE PRESENCE OF A GHOST, BUT EVERYBODY WAS LIKE, "HOW SHOULD I KNOW?" COULD IT REALLY BE HAUNTED?

I USED TO ALWAYS SLEEP IN THAT SPARE ROOM.

AHH! BUT IT'S A NEW BUILDING.

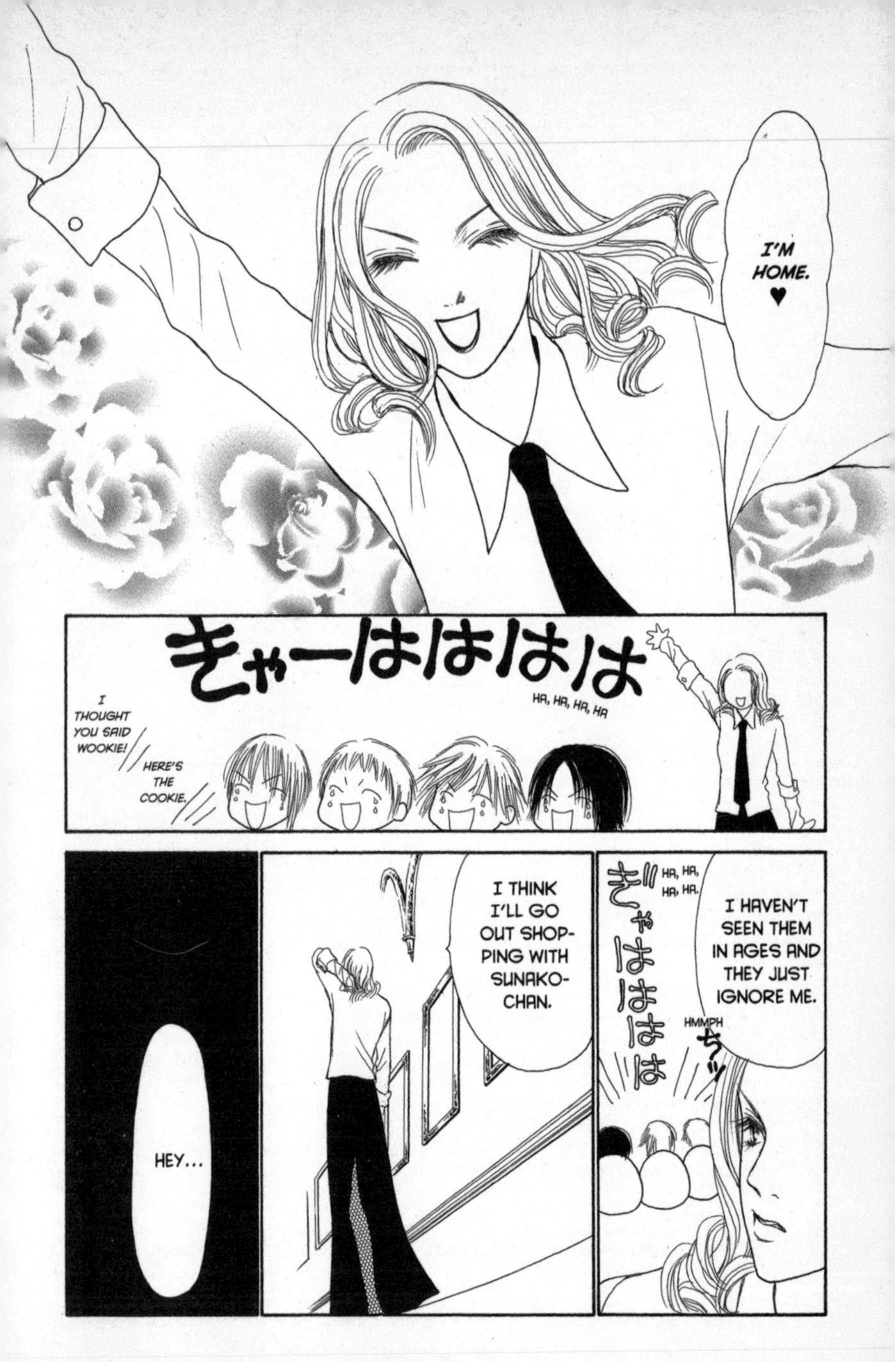
I'M HOME. ♥
きゃーはははは
HA, HA, HA, HA
HERE'S THE COOKIE.
I THOUGHT YOU SAID WOOKIE!
I HAVEN'T SEEN THEM IN AGES AND THEY JUST IGNORE ME.
ぎゃはははは
HA, HA, HA, HA.
ちッ
HMMPH
I THINK I'LL GO OUT SHOP-PING WITH SUNAKO-CHAN.
HEY...

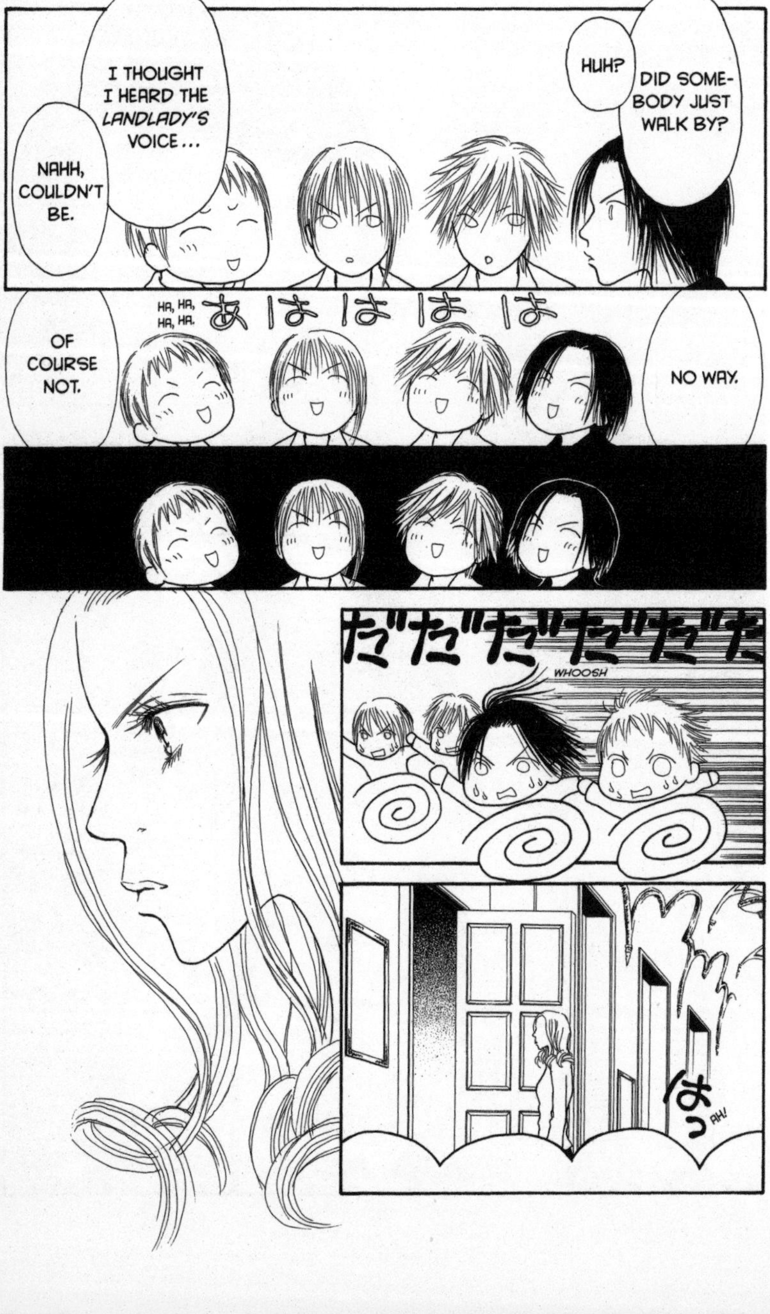
HUH?
DID SOME-BODY JUST WALK BY?
I THOUGHT I HEARD THE *LANDLADY'S* VOICE...
NAHH, COULDN'T BE.
NO WAY.
あははははは
HA, HA, HA, HA.
OF COURSE NOT.
だだだだだだ
WHOOSH
はっ
AH!

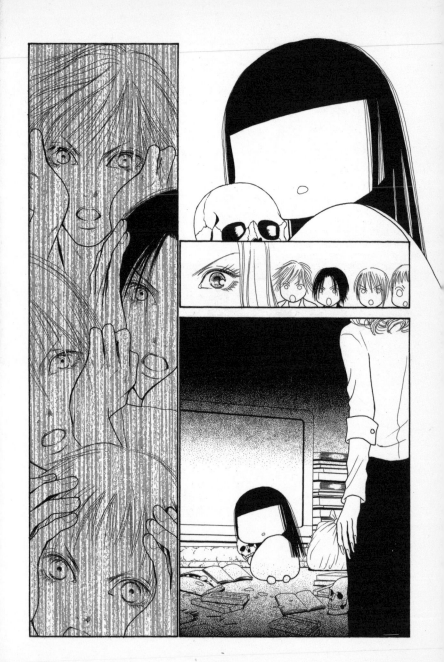

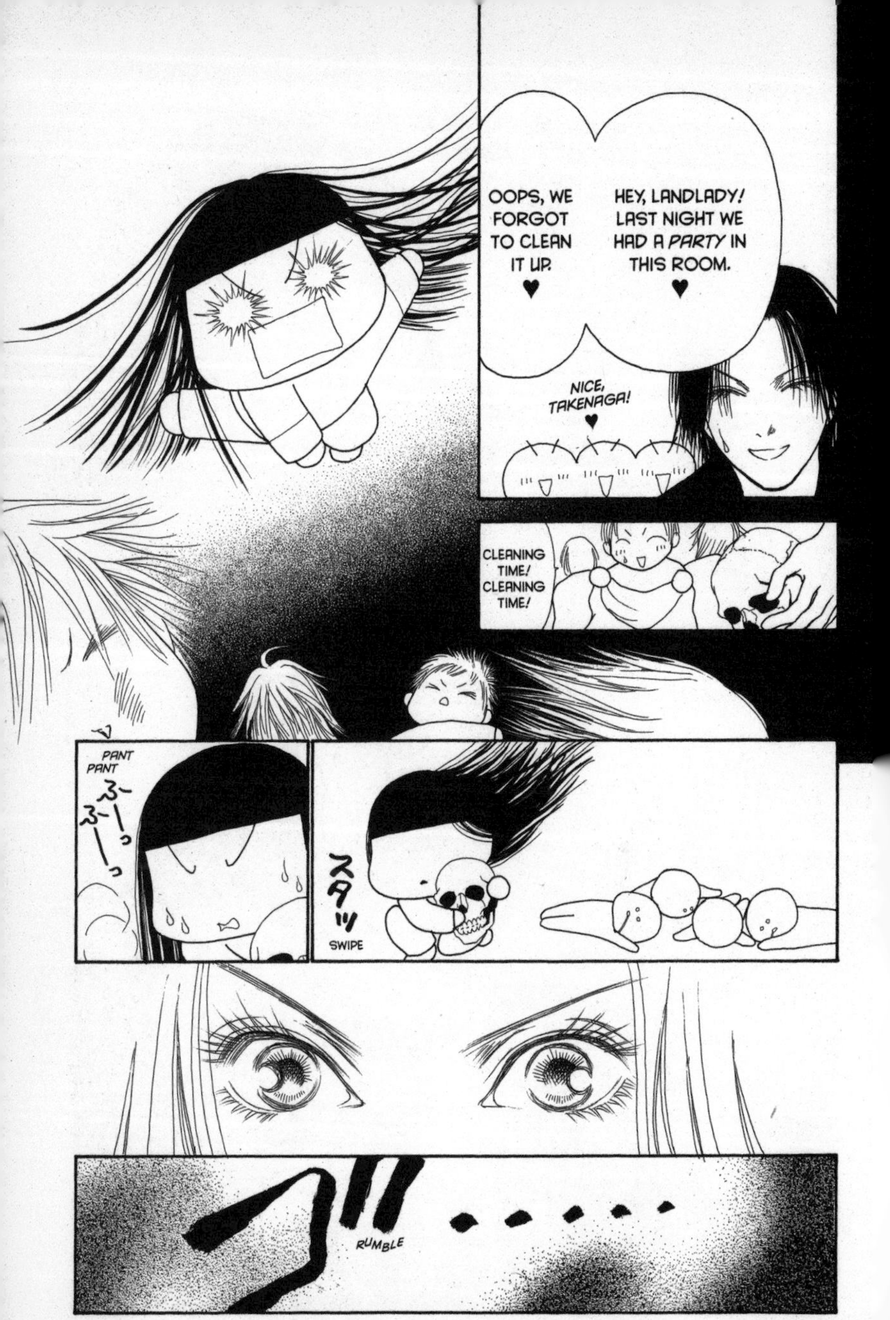
HEY, LANDLADY! LAST NIGHT WE HAD A PARTY IN THIS ROOM. ♥
OOPS, WE FORGOT TO CLEAN IT UP. ♥
NICE, TAKENAGA! ♥
CLEANING TIME! CLEANING TIME!
スタッ
SWIPE
PANT PANT
ふーっ ふーっ
RUMBLE

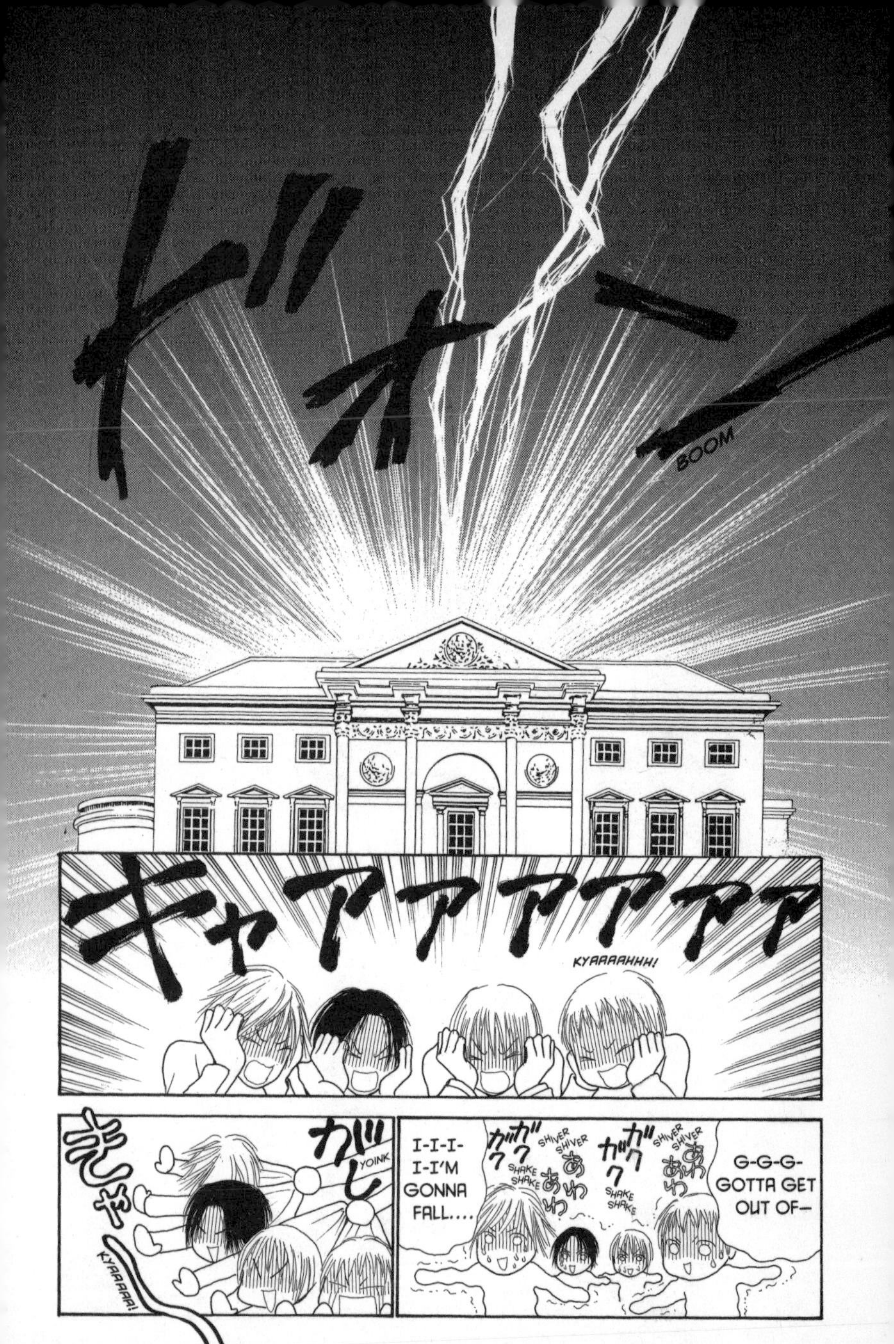
ドオーー
BOOM
キャアアアアア
KYAAAAHHH!
G-G-G-
GOTTA GET
OUT OF—
SHIVER
SHIVER
SHAKE
SHAKE
SHIVER
SHIVER
SHAKE
SHAKE
I-I-I-
I-I'M
GONNA
FALL....
YOINK
KYAAAAA!

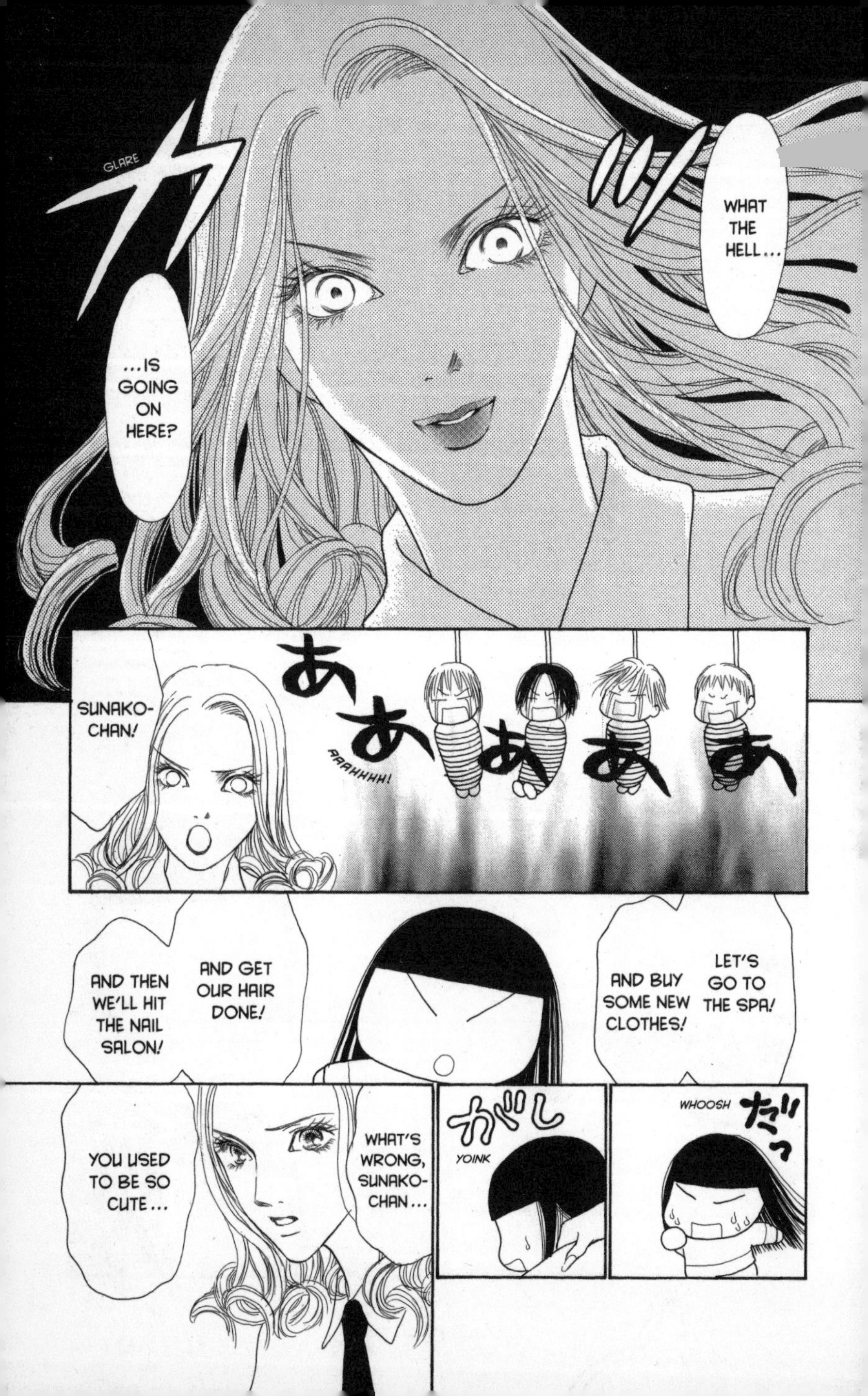
WHAT THE HELL...
GLARE
...IS GOING ON HERE?
ああああああ
AAAHHHH!
SUNAKO-CHAN!
LET'S GO TO THE SPA!
AND BUY SOME NEW CLOTHES!
AND GET OUR HAIR DONE!
AND THEN WE'LL HIT THE NAIL SALON!
だっ
WHOOSH
がし
YOINK
WHAT'S WRONG, SUNAKO-CHAN...
YOU USED TO BE SO CUTE...

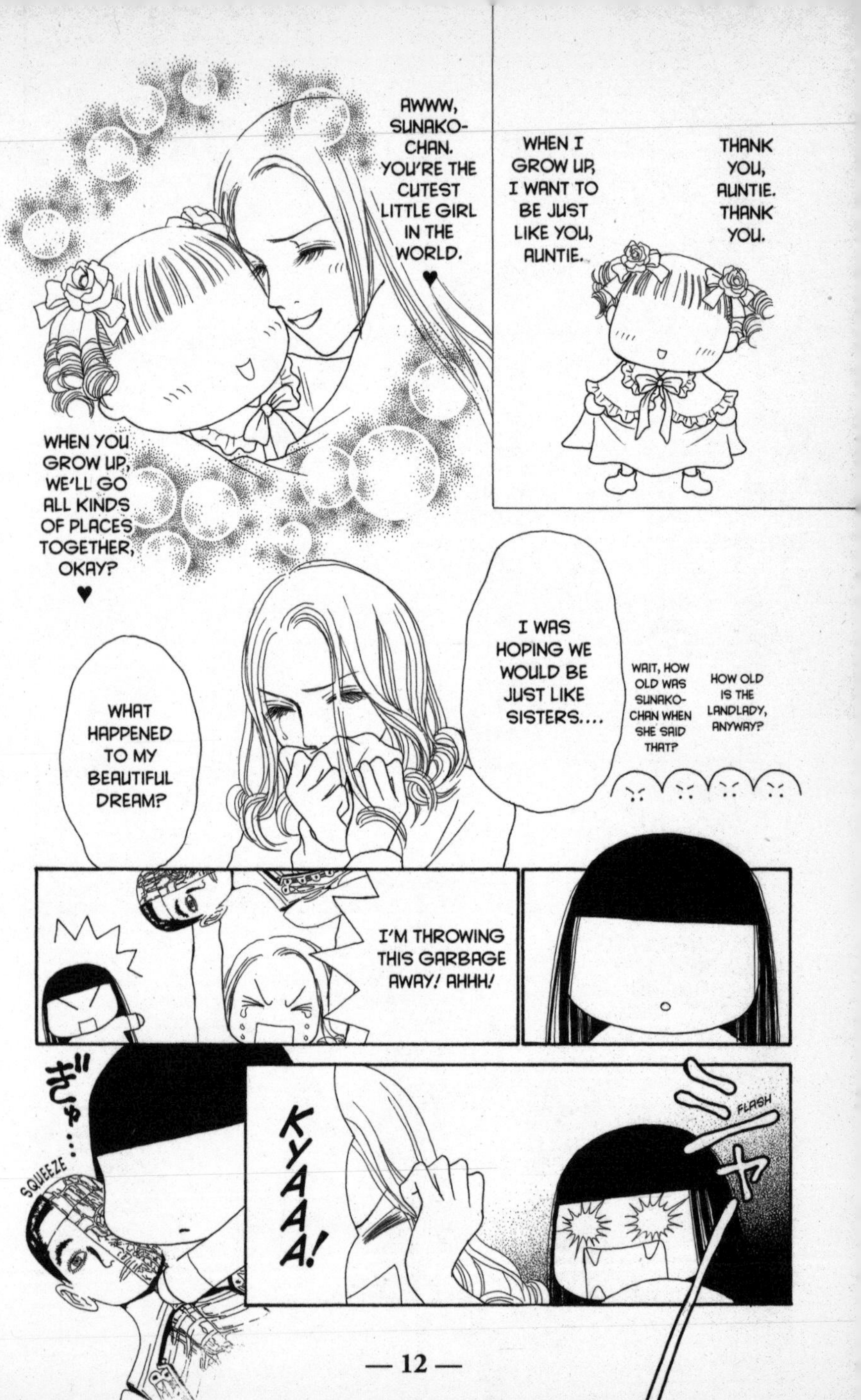
THANK YOU, AUNTIE. THANK YOU.
WHEN I GROW UP, I WANT TO BE JUST LIKE YOU, AUNTIE.
AWWW, SUNAKO-CHAN. YOU'RE THE CUTEST LITTLE GIRL IN THE WORLD. ♥
WHEN YOU GROW UP, WE'LL GO ALL KINDS OF PLACES TOGETHER, OKAY? ♥
I WAS HOPING WE WOULD BE JUST LIKE SISTERS....
HOW OLD IS THE LANDLADY, ANYWAY?
WAIT, HOW OLD WAS SUNAKO-CHAN WHEN SHE SAID THAT?
WHAT HAPPENED TO MY BEAUTIFUL DREAM?
I'M THROWING THIS GARBAGE AWAY! AHHH!
FLASH
KYAAAA!
SQUEEZE

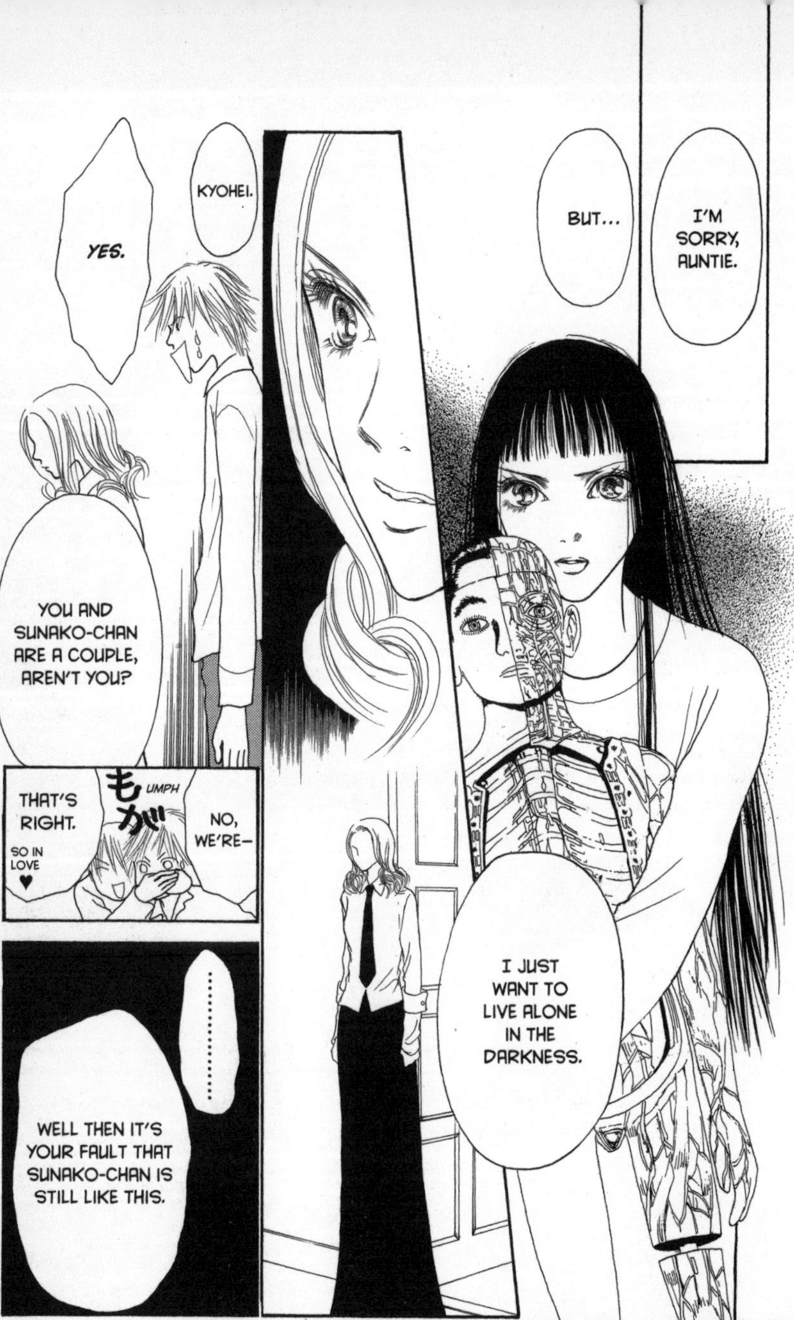
I'M SORRY, AUNTIE.
BUT...
I JUST WANT TO LIVE ALONE IN THE DARKNESS.
KYOHEI.
YES.
YOU AND SUNAKO-CHAN ARE A COUPLE, AREN'T YOU?
NO, WE'RE–
もが
UMPH
THAT'S RIGHT.
SO IN LOVE ♥
......
WELL THEN IT'S YOUR FAULT THAT SUNAKO-CHAN IS STILL LIKE THIS.

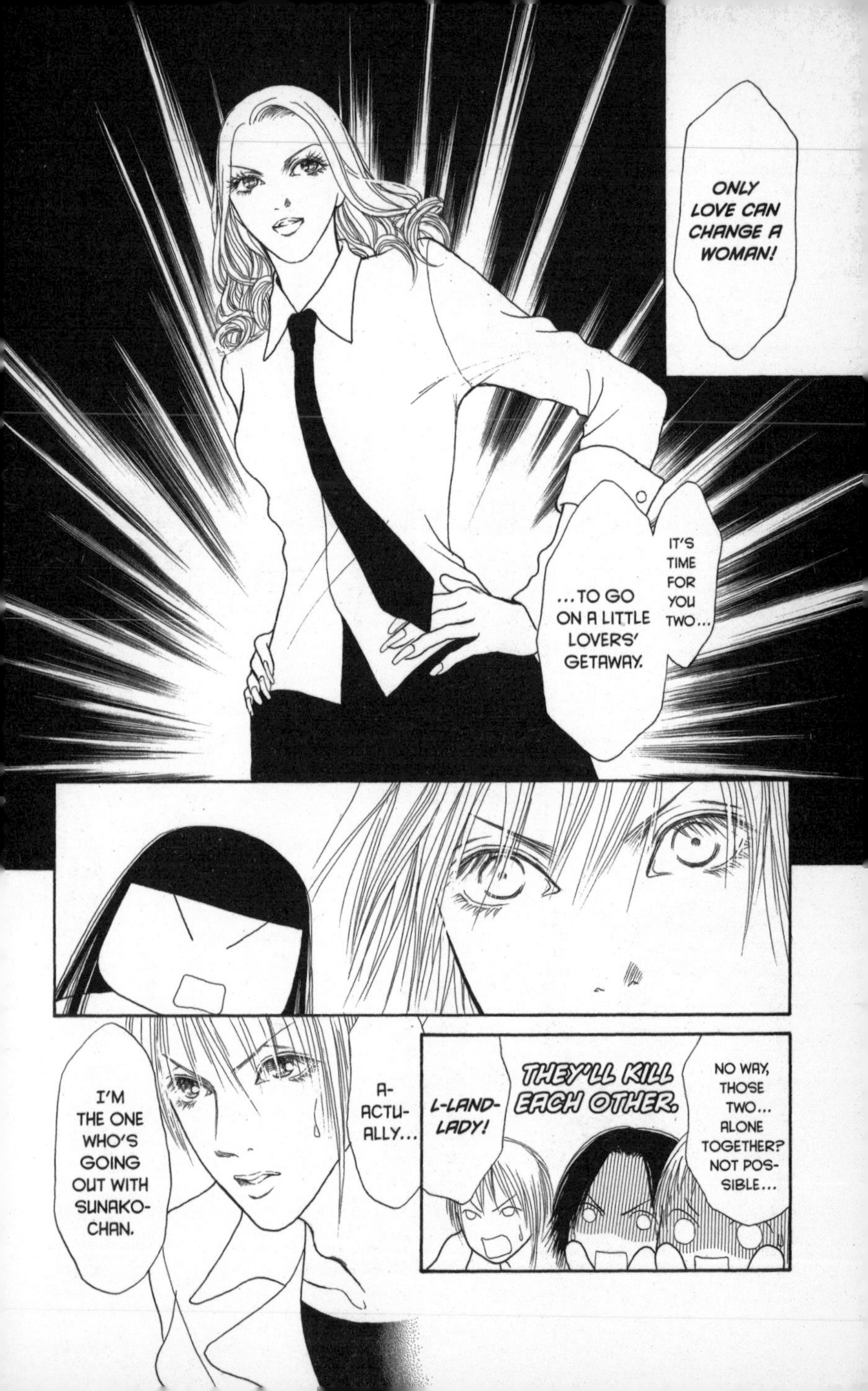
ONLY LOVE CAN CHANGE A WOMAN!
IT'S TIME FOR YOU TWO...
...TO GO ON A LITTLE LOVERS' GETAWAY.
NO WAY, THOSE TWO... ALONE TOGETHER? NOT POSSIBLE...
THEY'LL KILL EACH OTHER.
L-LANDLADY!
A-ACTUALLY...
I'M THE ONE WHO'S GOING OUT WITH SUNAKO-CHAN.

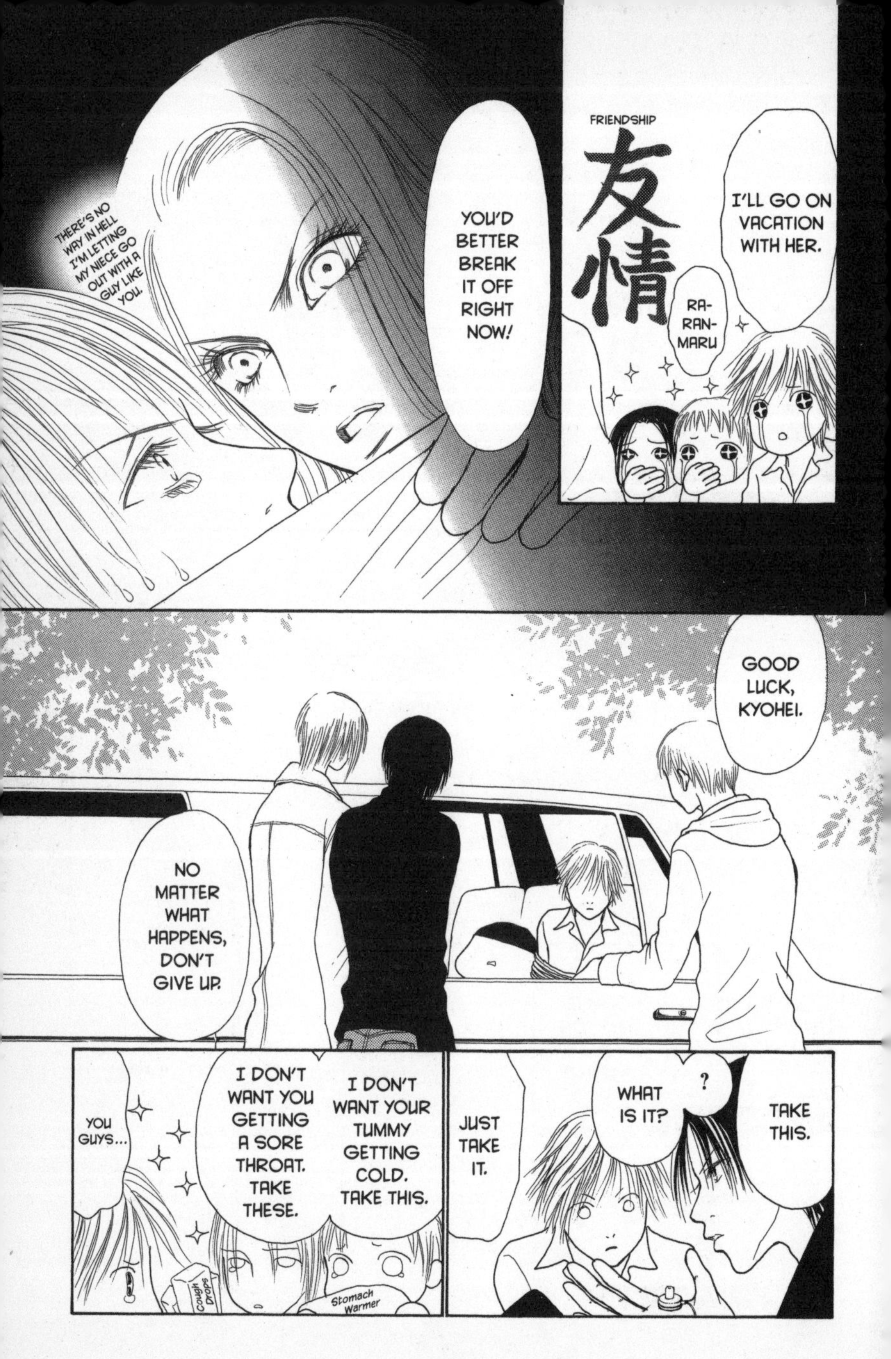

I'LL GO ON VACATION WITH HER.
RA-RAN-MARU
FRIENDSHIP
友情
YOU'D BETTER BREAK IT OFF RIGHT NOW!
THERE'S NO WAY IN HELL I'M LETTING MY NIECE GO OUT WITH A GUY LIKE YOU.
GOOD LUCK, KYOHEI.
NO MATTER WHAT HAPPENS, DON'T GIVE UP.
TAKE THIS.
?
WHAT IS IT?
JUST TAKE IT.
I DON'T WANT YOUR TUMMY GETTING COLD. TAKE THIS.
I DON'T WANT YOU GETTING A SORE THROAT. TAKE THESE.
YOU GUYS...
Cough Drops
Stomach Warmer

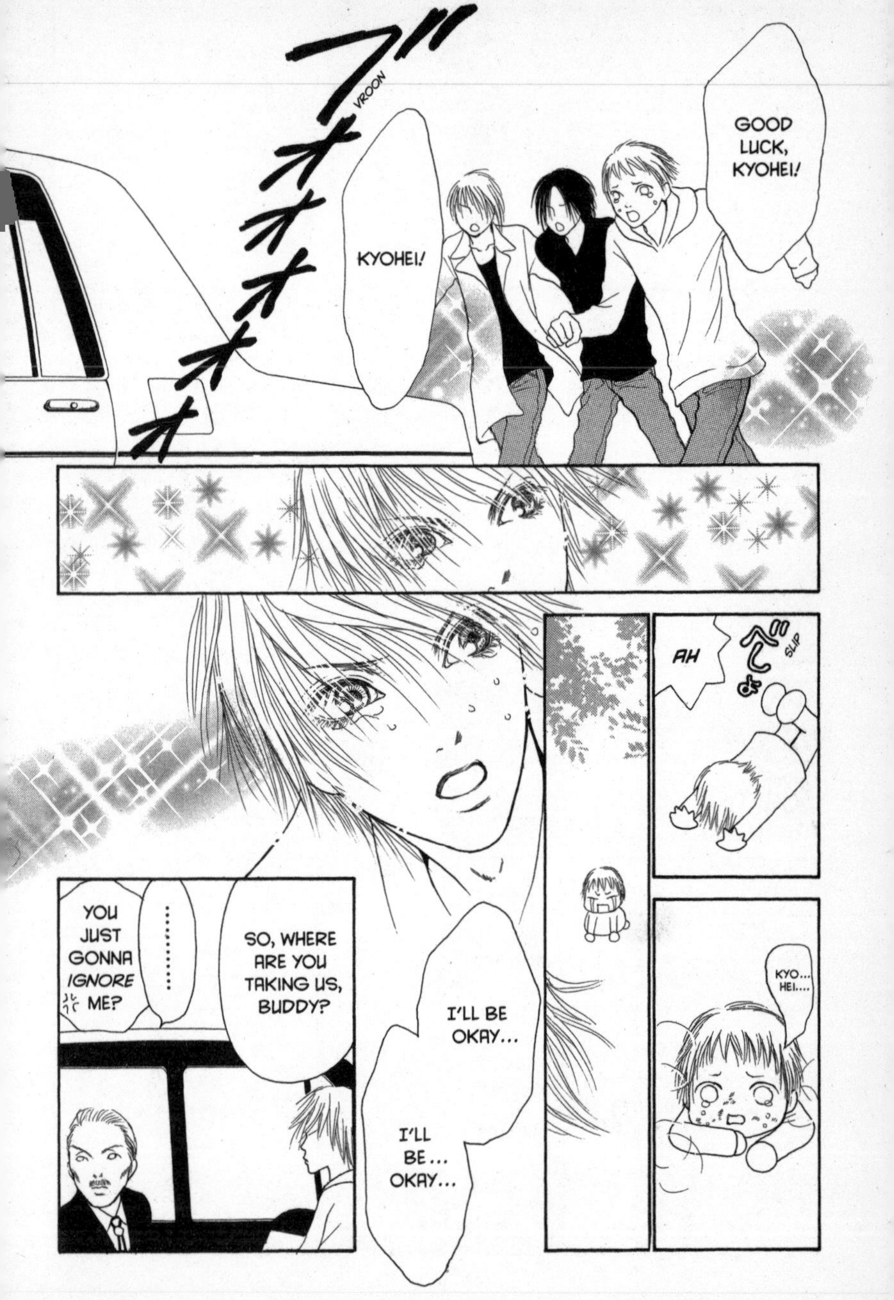
VROON
GOOD LUCK, KYOHEI!
KYOHEI!
AH
SLIP
KYO... HEI....
I'LL BE OKAY...
I'LL BE... OKAY...
SO, WHERE ARE YOU TAKING US, BUDDY?
....
YOU JUST GONNA *IGNORE* ME?

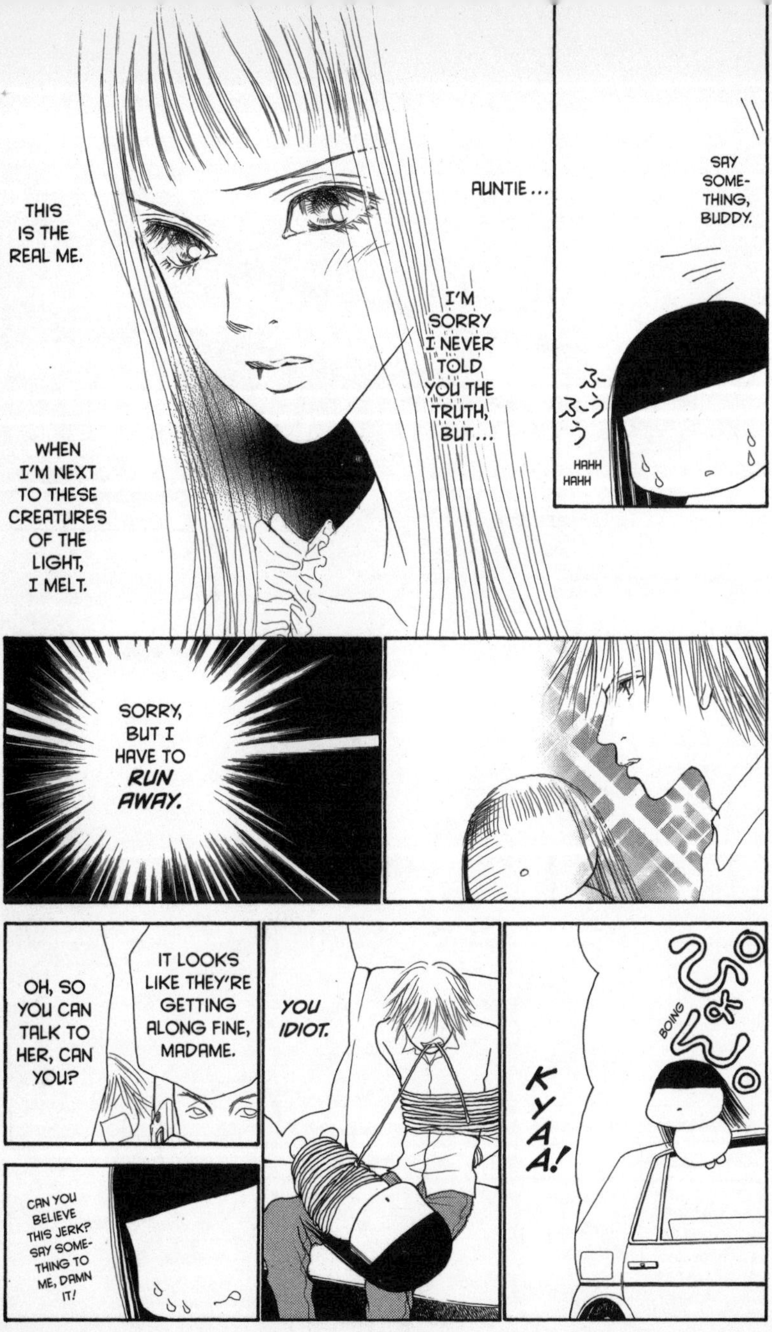
SAY SOMETHING, BUDDY.
ふうふう
HAHH HAHH
AUNTIE...
I'M SORRY I NEVER TOLD YOU THE TRUTH, BUT...
THIS IS THE REAL ME.
WHEN I'M NEXT TO THESE CREATURES OF THE LIGHT, I MELT.
SORRY, BUT I HAVE TO *RUN AWAY.*
KYAA!
BOING
YOU IDIOT.
IT LOOKS LIKE THEY'RE GETTING ALONG FINE, MADAME.
OH, SO YOU CAN TALK TO HER, CAN YOU?
CAN YOU BELIEVE THIS JERK? SAY SOMETHING TO ME, DAMN IT!

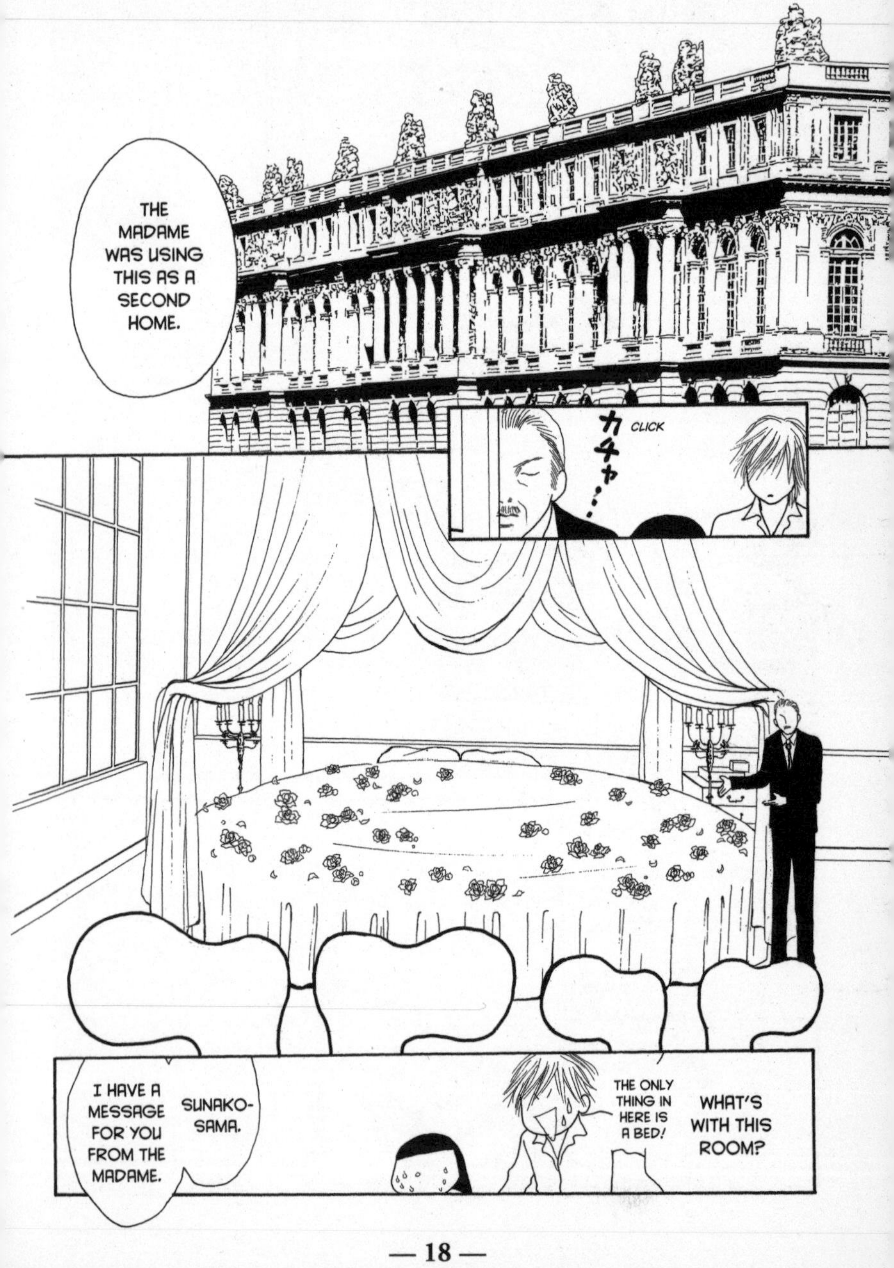
THE MADAME WAS USING THIS AS A SECOND HOME.
カチャ…
CLICK
WHAT'S WITH THIS ROOM?
THE ONLY THING IN HERE IS A BED!
SUNAKO-SAMA.
I HAVE A MESSAGE FOR YOU FROM THE MADAME.

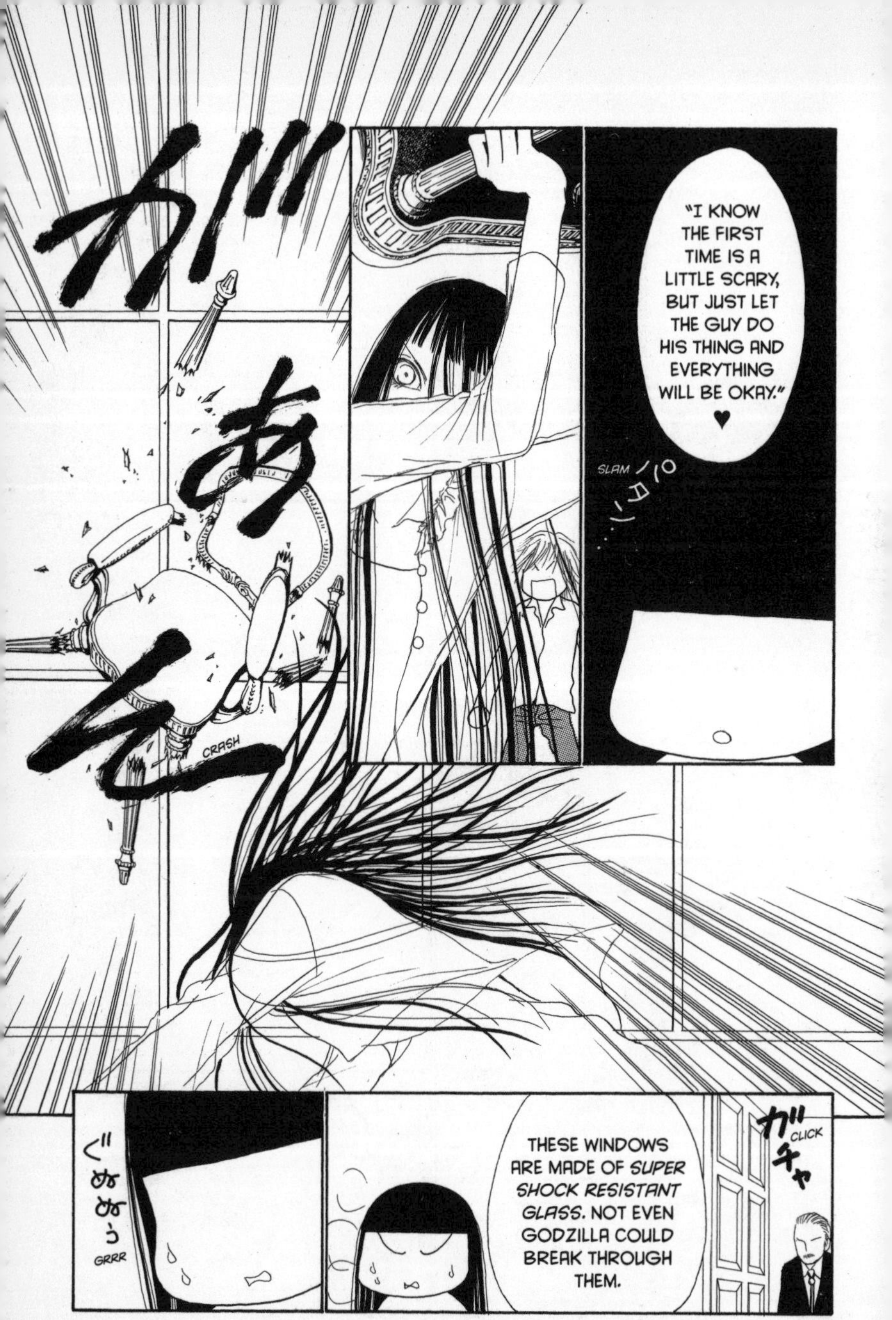
"I KNOW THE FIRST TIME IS A LITTLE SCARY, BUT JUST LET THE GUY DO HIS THING AND EVERYTHING WILL BE OKAY." ♥
SLAM
CRASH
CLICK
THESE WINDOWS ARE MADE OF *SUPER SHOCK RESISTANT GLASS*. NOT EVEN GODZILLA COULD BREAK THROUGH THEM.
GRRR

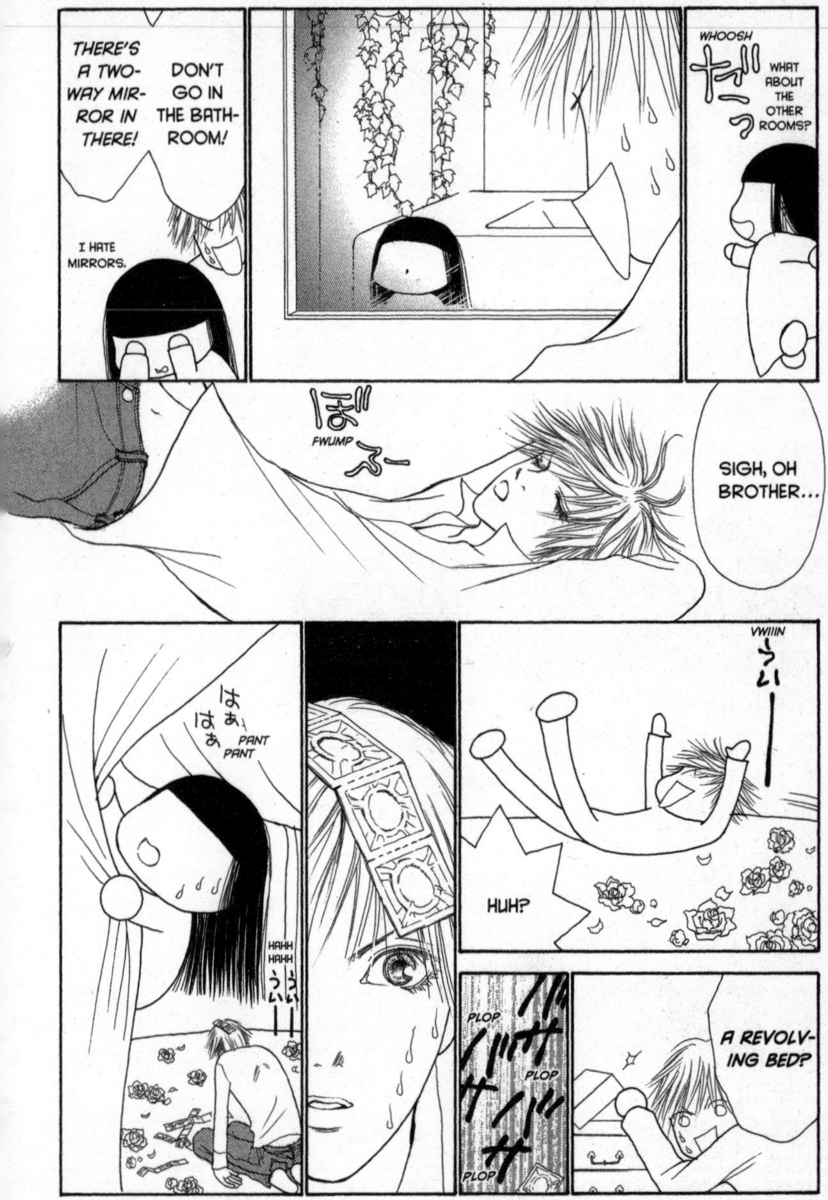
WHOOSH
たーっ
WHAT ABOUT THE OTHER ROOMS?
THERE'S A TWO-WAY MIR-ROR IN THERE!
DON'T GO IN THE BATH-ROOM!
I HATE MIRRORS.
SIGH, OH BROTHER...
ぼふー
FWUMP
VWIIIN
うぃーー
HUH?
A REVOLV-ING BED?
バサバサ
PLOP
PLOP
PLOP
はぁ はぁ
PANT PANT
HAHH HAHH
うぃーー

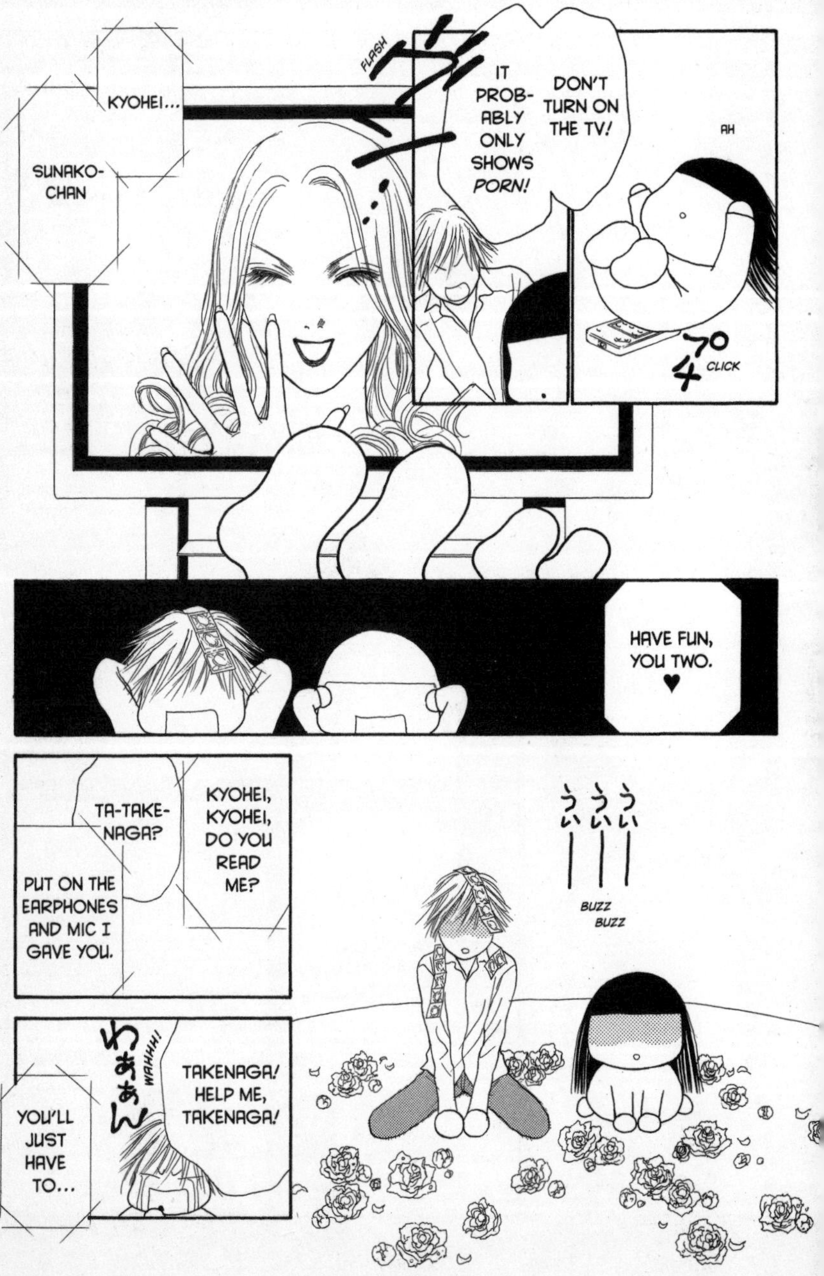
AH
CLICK
DON'T TURN ON THE TV!
IT PROBABLY ONLY SHOWS PORN!
FLASH
KYOHEI...
SUNAKO-CHAN
HAVE FUN, YOU TWO. ♥
うぃ うぃ うぃ
BUZZ BUZZ
KYOHEI, KYOHEI, DO YOU READ ME?
TA-TAKENAGA?
PUT ON THE EARPHONES AND MIC I GAVE YOU.
TAKENAGA! HELP ME, TAKENAGA!
わぁあん
WAHHH!
YOU'LL JUST HAVE TO...

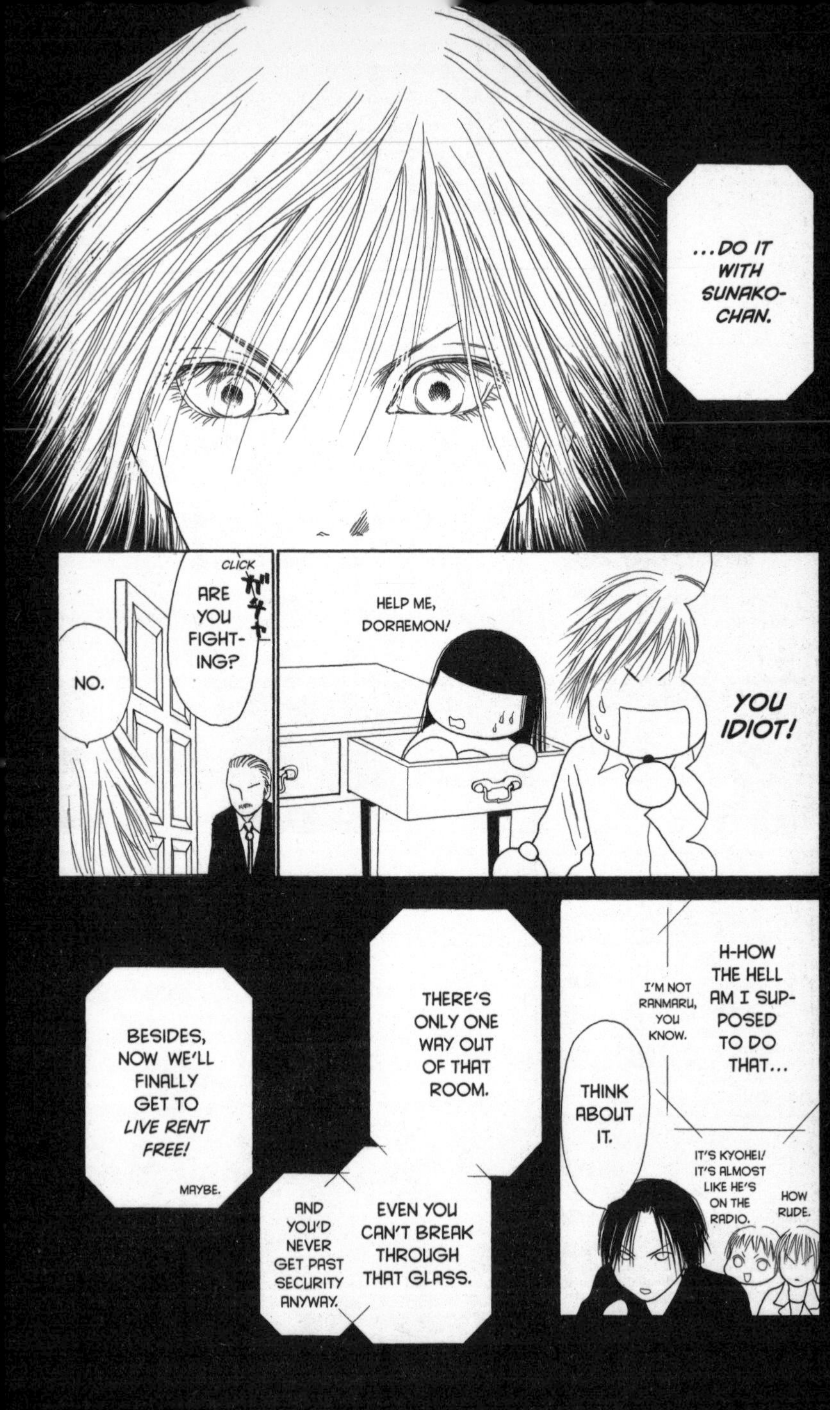
...DO IT WITH SUNAKO-CHAN.
YOU IDIOT!
HELP ME, DORAEMON!
CLICK
ARE YOU FIGHTING?
NO.
H-HOW THE HELL AM I SUPPOSED TO DO THAT...
I'M NOT RANMARU, YOU KNOW.
THINK ABOUT IT.
IT'S KYOHEI! IT'S ALMOST LIKE HE'S ON THE RADIO.
HOW RUDE.
THERE'S ONLY ONE WAY OUT OF THAT ROOM.
EVEN YOU CAN'T BREAK THROUGH THAT GLASS.
AND YOU'D NEVER GET PAST SECURITY ANYWAY.
BESIDES, NOW WE'LL FINALLY GET TO *LIVE RENT FREE!*
MAYBE.

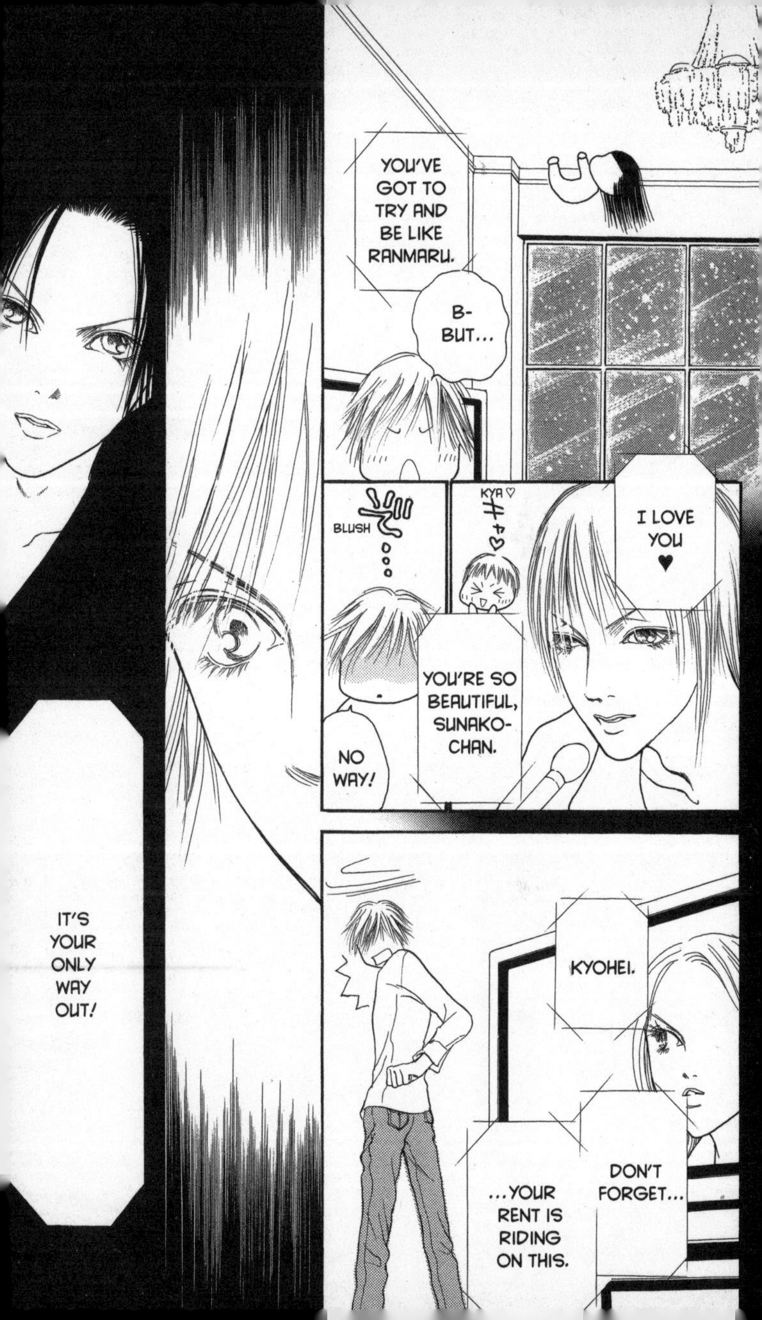
YOU'VE GOT TO TRY AND BE LIKE RANMARU.
B- BUT...
I LOVE YOU ♥
YOU'RE SO BEAUTIFUL, SUNAKO-CHAN.
KYA ♡
BLUSH
NO WAY!
KYOHEI.
DON'T FORGET...
...YOUR RENT IS RIDING ON THIS.
IT'S YOUR ONLY WAY OUT!

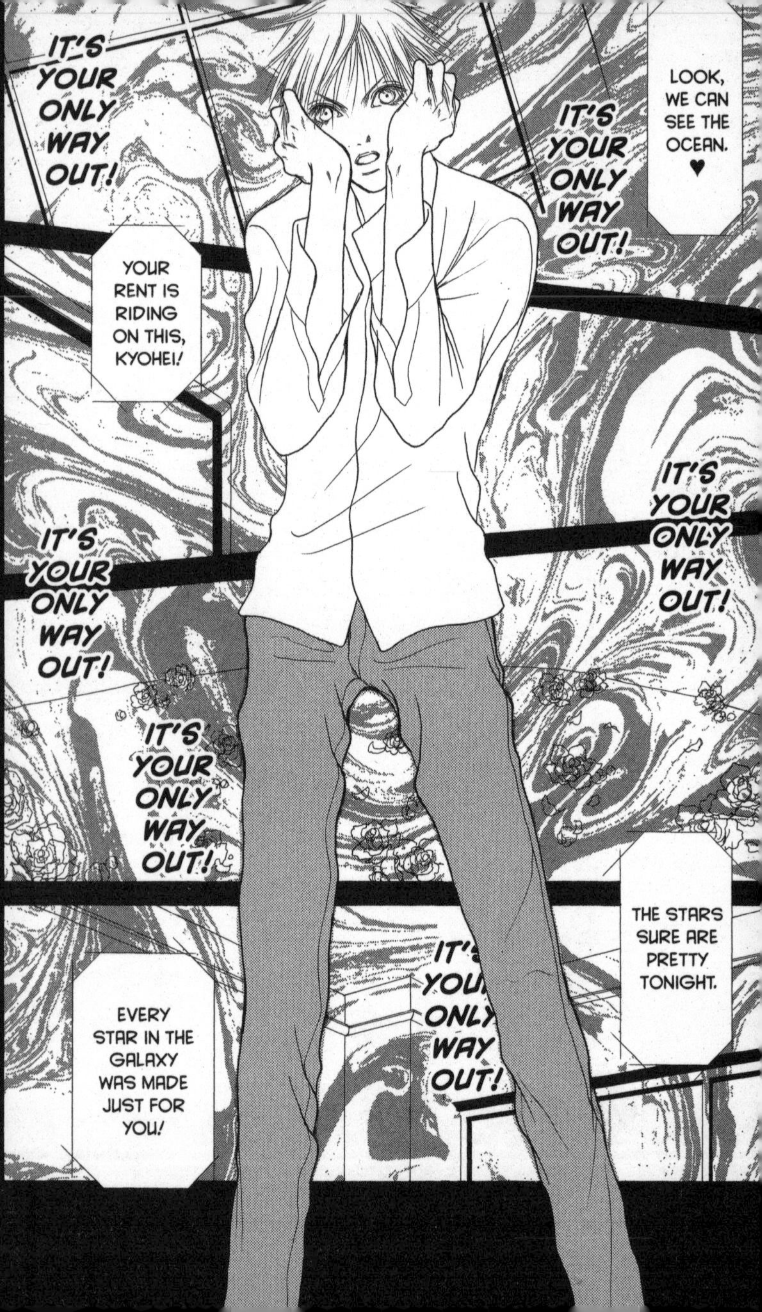
LOOK, WE CAN SEE THE OCEAN. ♥
IT'S YOUR ONLY WAY OUT!
IT'S YOUR ONLY WAY OUT!
YOUR RENT IS RIDING ON THIS, KYOHEI!
IT'S YOUR ONLY WAY OUT!
IT'S YOUR ONLY WAY OUT!
IT'S YOUR ONLY WAY OUT!
THE STARS SURE ARE PRETTY TONIGHT.
IT'S YOUR ONLY WAY OUT!
EVERY STAR IN THE GALAXY WAS MADE JUST FOR YOU!

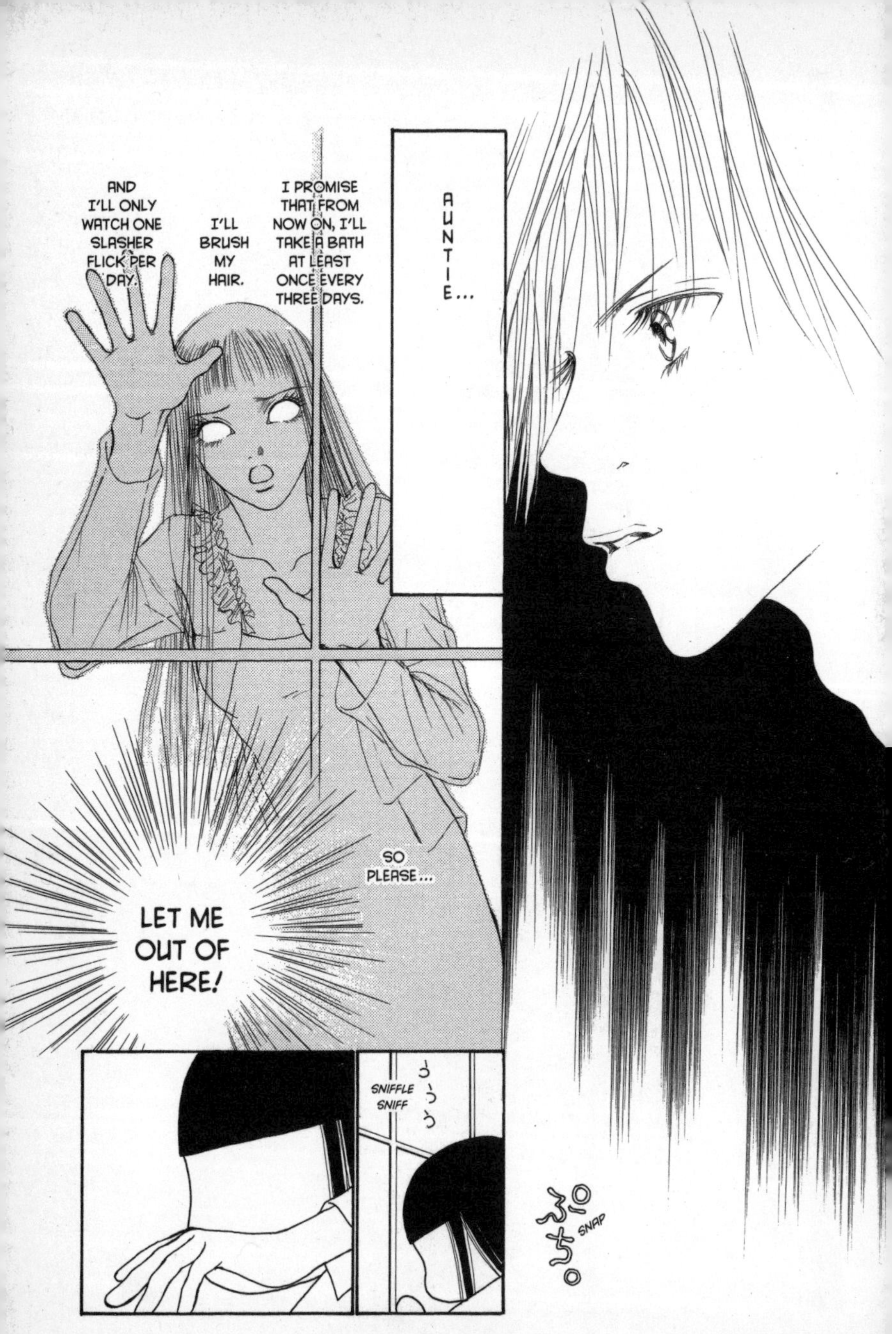
AUNTIE...
ぷち。
SNAP
I PROMISE THAT FROM NOW ON, I'LL TAKE A BATH AT LEAST ONCE EVERY THREE DAYS.
I'LL BRUSH MY HAIR.
AND I'LL ONLY WATCH ONE SLASHER FLICK PER DAY.
SO PLEASE...
LET ME OUT OF HERE!
うっう
SNIFFLE SNIFF

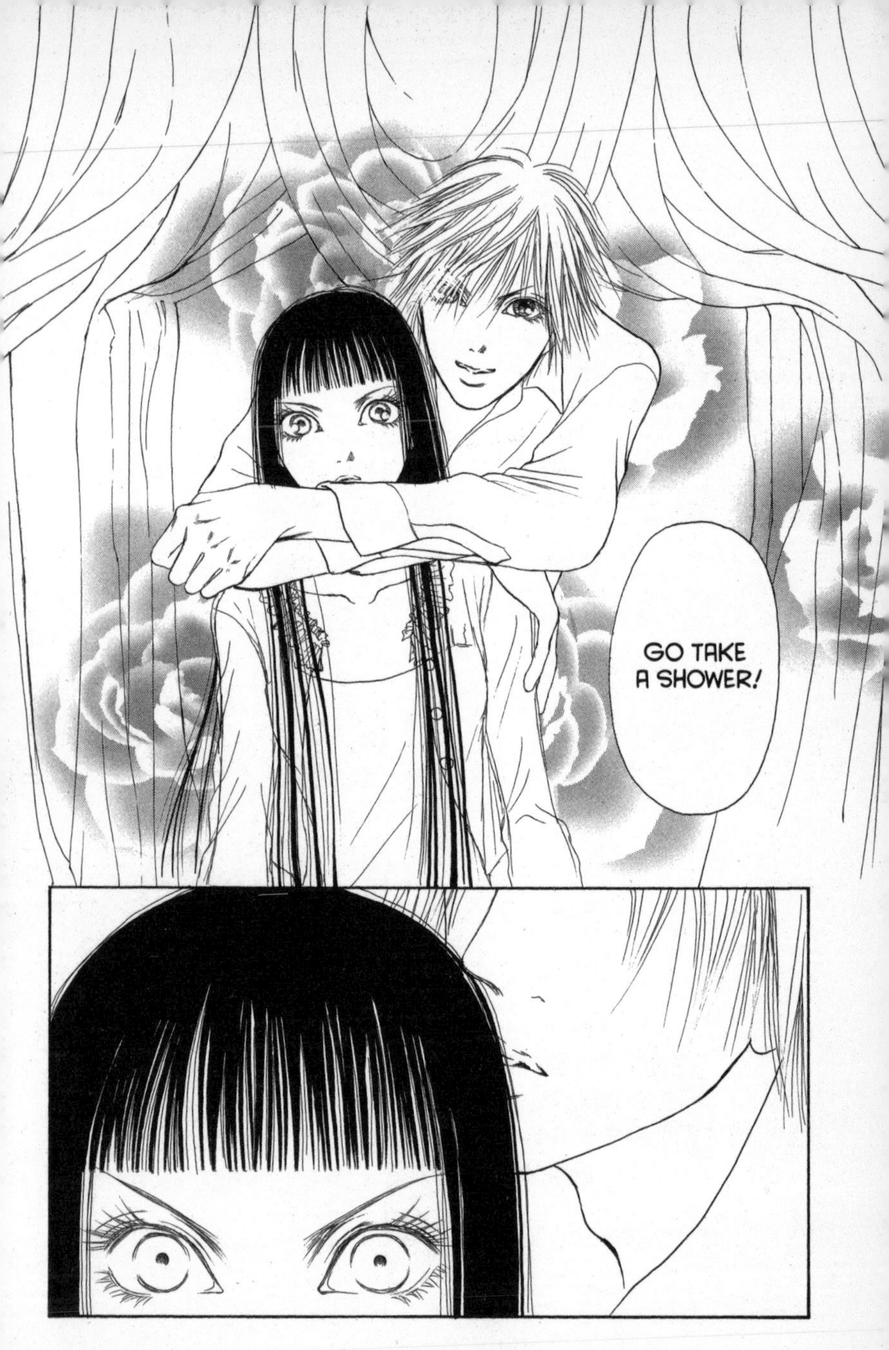
GO TAKE
A SHOWER!

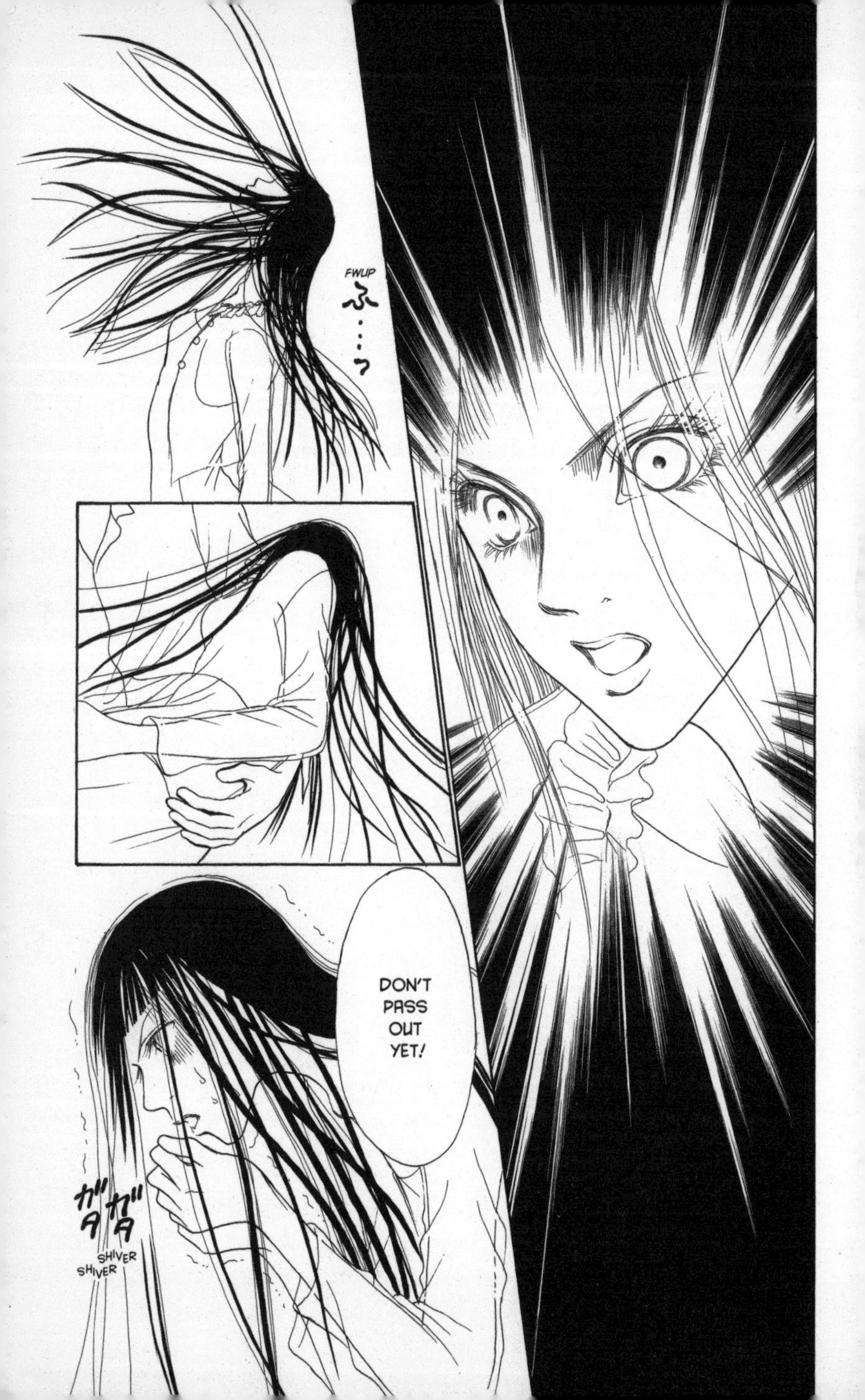
FWUP
ふ…っ
DON'T PASS OUT YET!
ガタガタ
SHIVER SHIVER

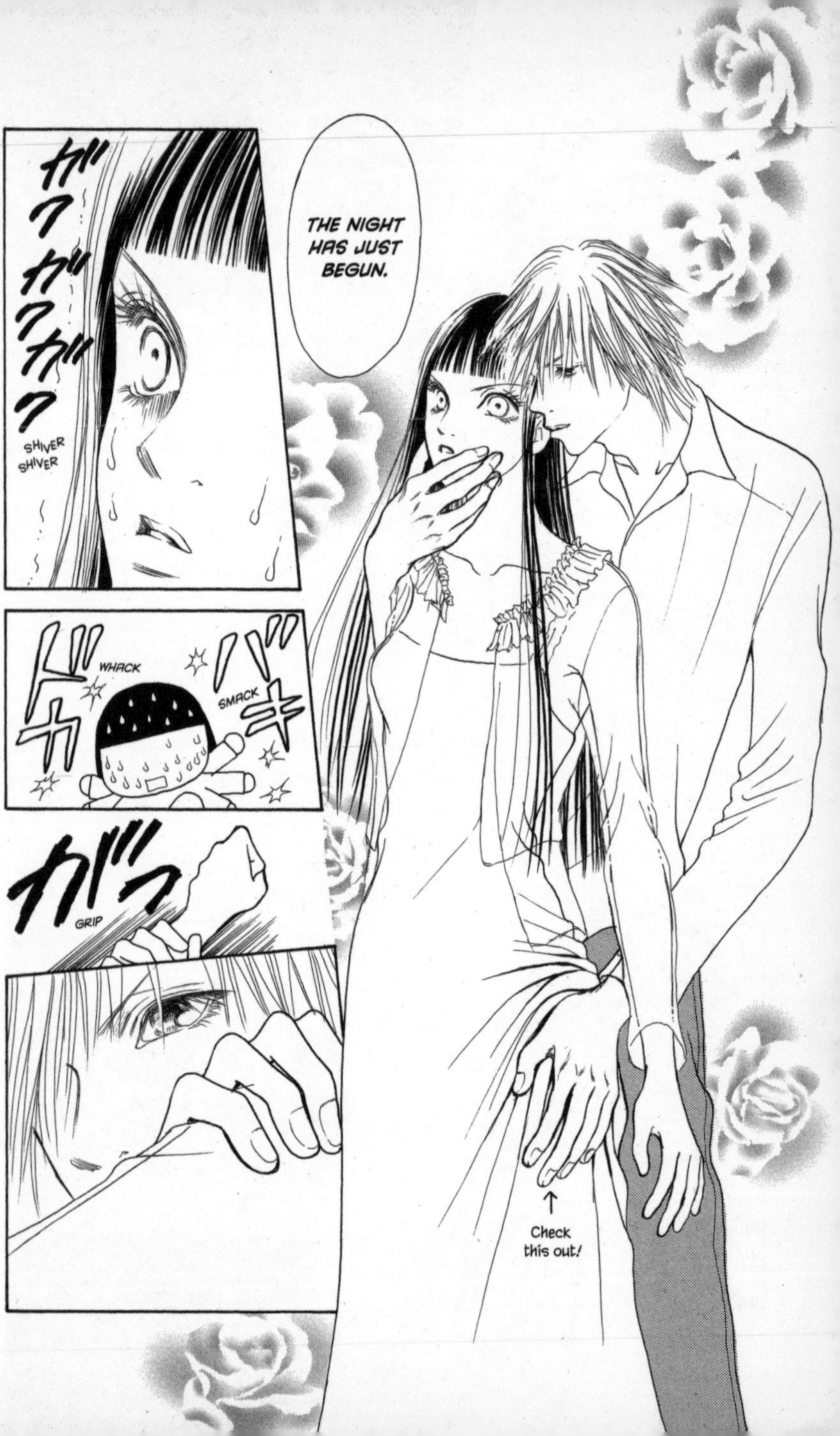
THE NIGHT HAS JUST BEGUN.
Check this out!
ガクガクガクガク
SHIVER SHIVER
バキ
SMACK
ドカ
WHACK
ガッ
GRIP

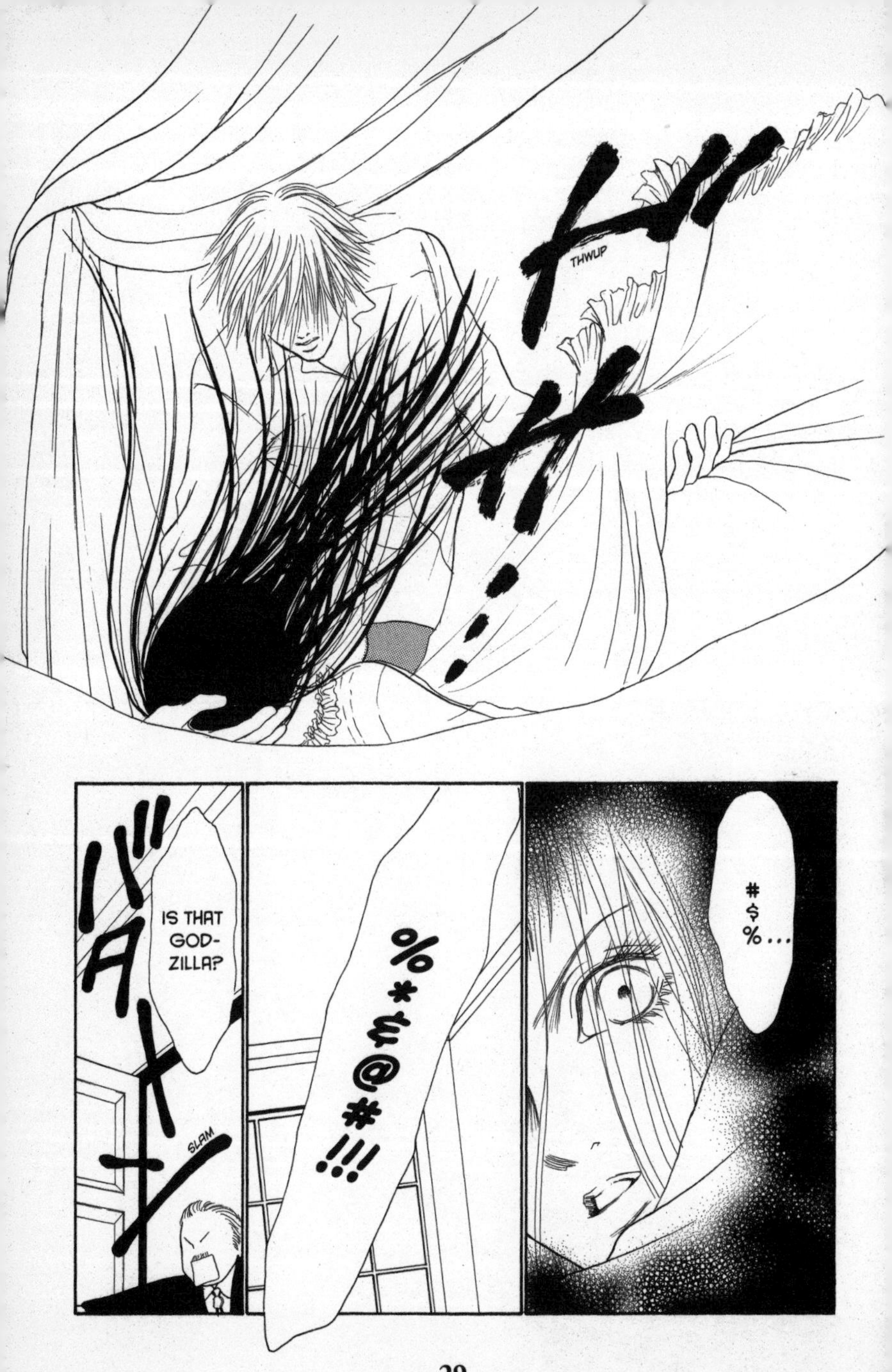
THWUP
#$%...
%*&@#!!!
IS THAT GOD-ZILLA?
SLAM

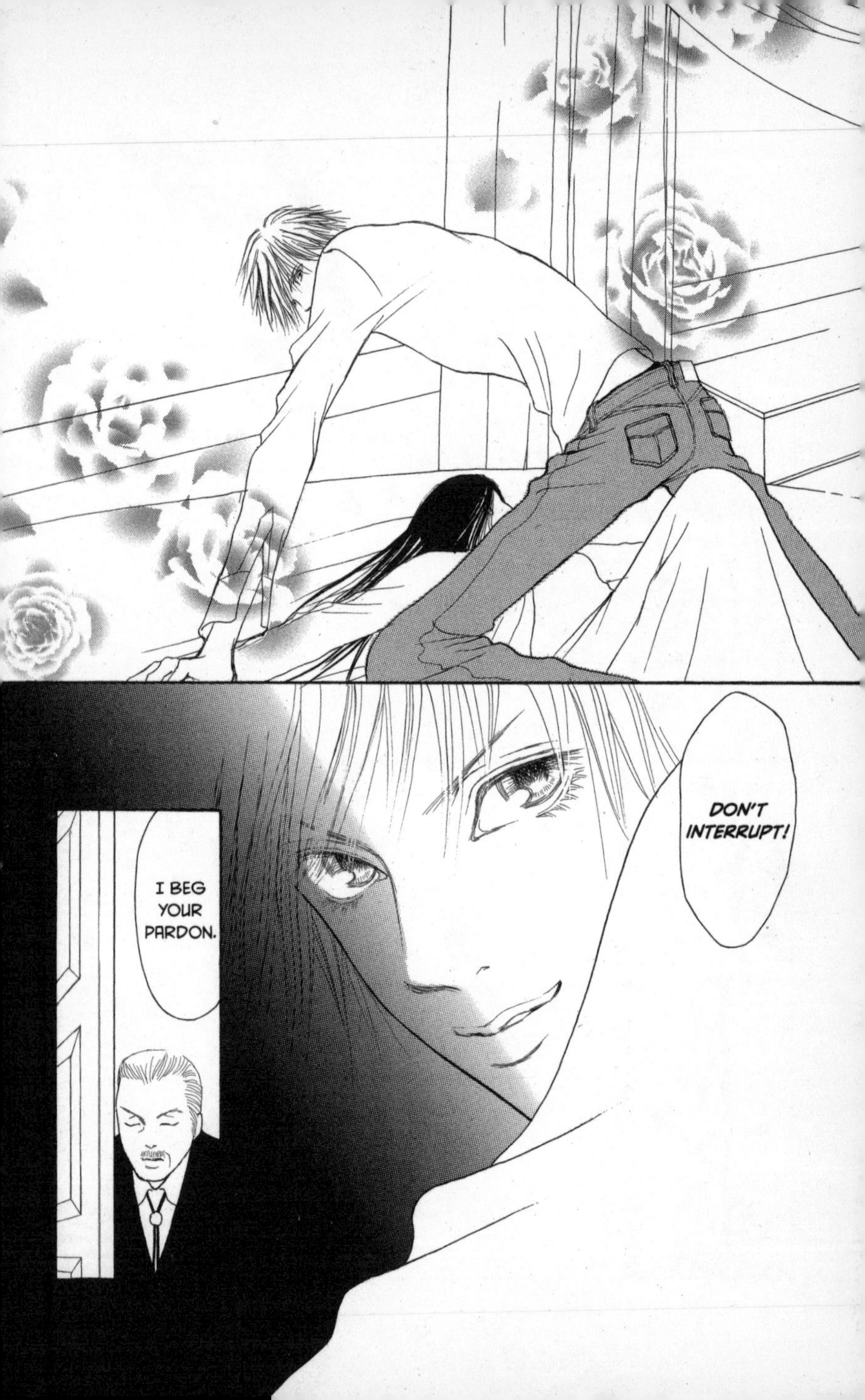
DON'T INTERRUPT!
I BEG YOUR PARDON.

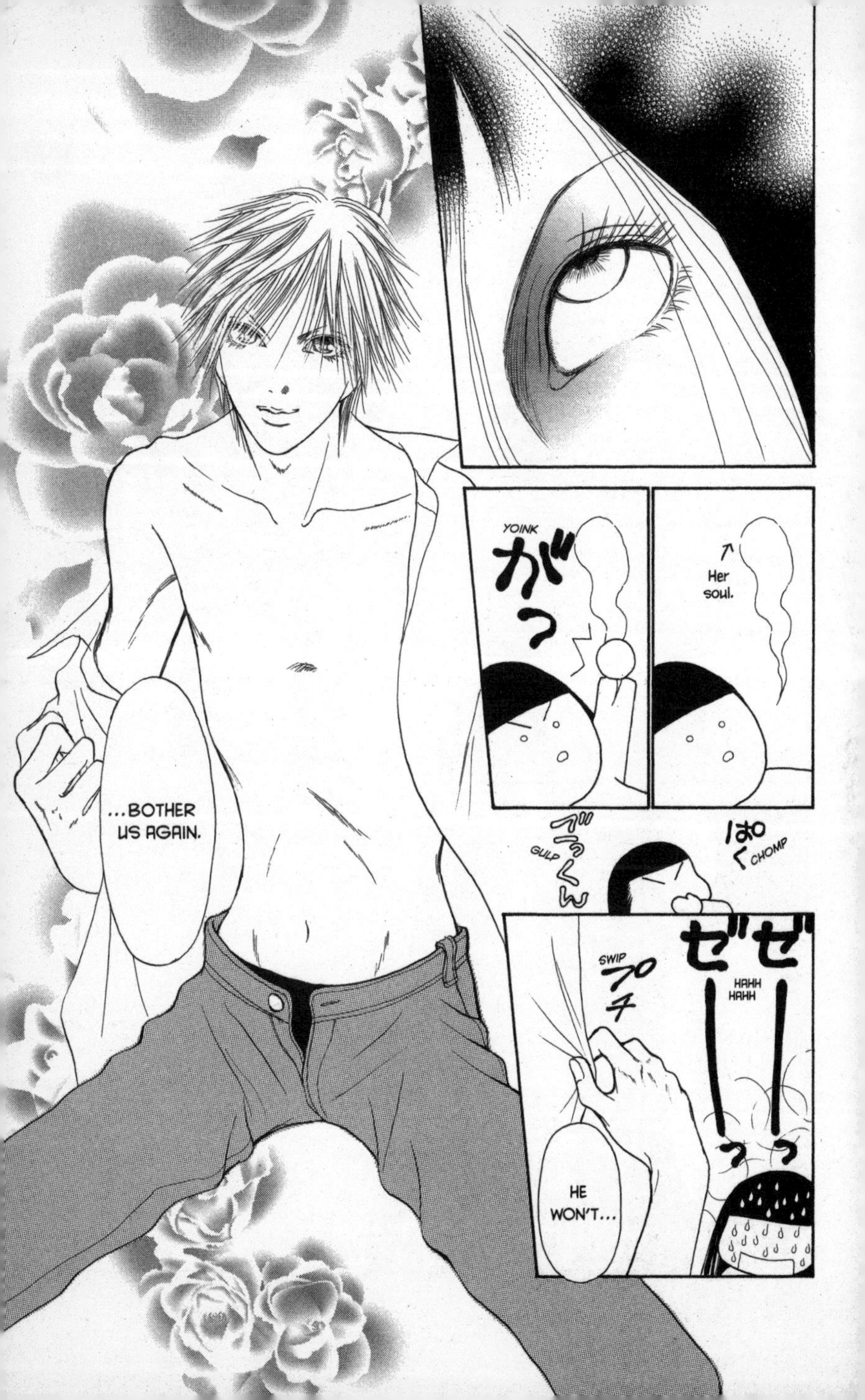

Her soul.
YOINK
がっ
ぱく
CHOMP
ごっくん
GULP
ぜーっ ぜーっ
HAHH HAHH
SWIP
プチ
HE WON'T...
...BOTHER US AGAIN.

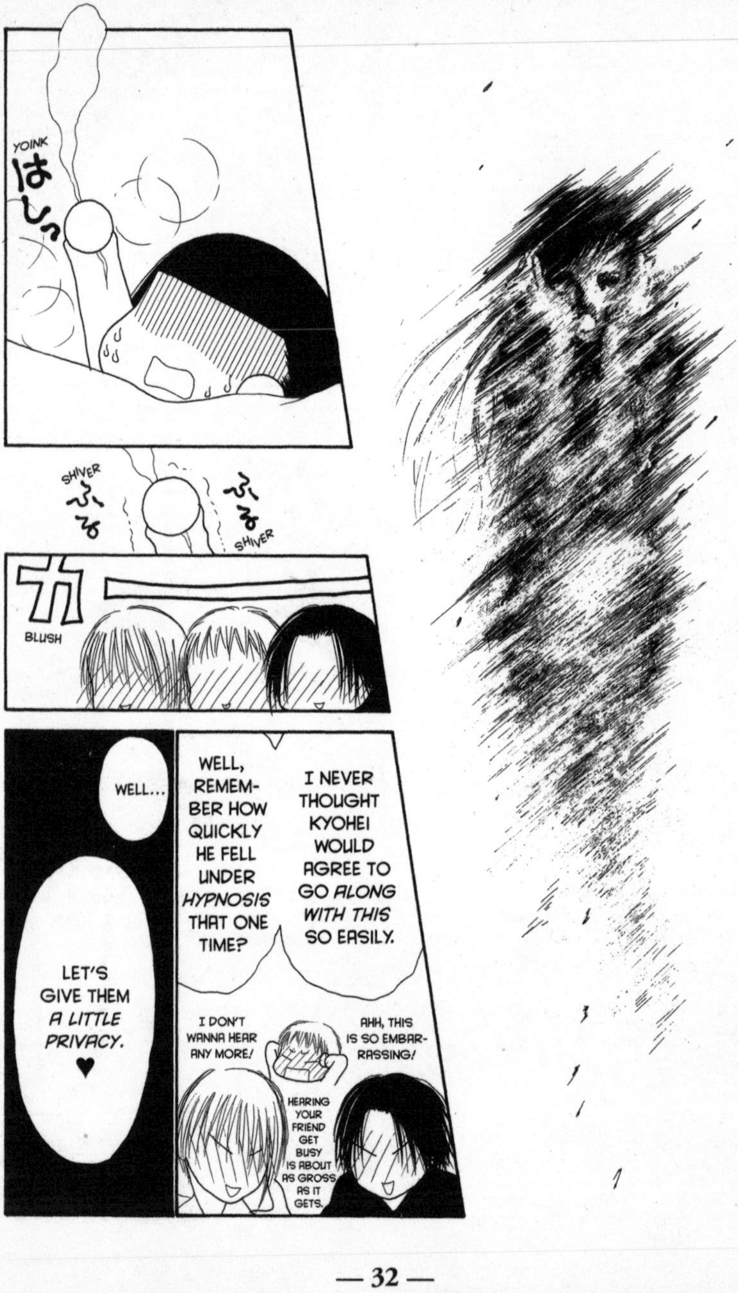
YOINK
はしっ
SHIVER
ふる
ふる
SHIVER
カー
BLUSH
I NEVER THOUGHT KYOHEI WOULD AGREE TO GO *ALONG WITH THIS* SO EASILY.
WELL, REMEMBER HOW QUICKLY HE FELL UNDER *HYPNOSIS* THAT ONE TIME?
AHH, THIS IS SO EMBARRASSING!
I DON'T WANNA HEAR ANY MORE!
HEARING YOUR FRIEND GET BUSY IS ABOUT AS GROSS AS IT GETS.
WELL...
LET'S GIVE THEM *A LITTLE PRIVACY.* ♥

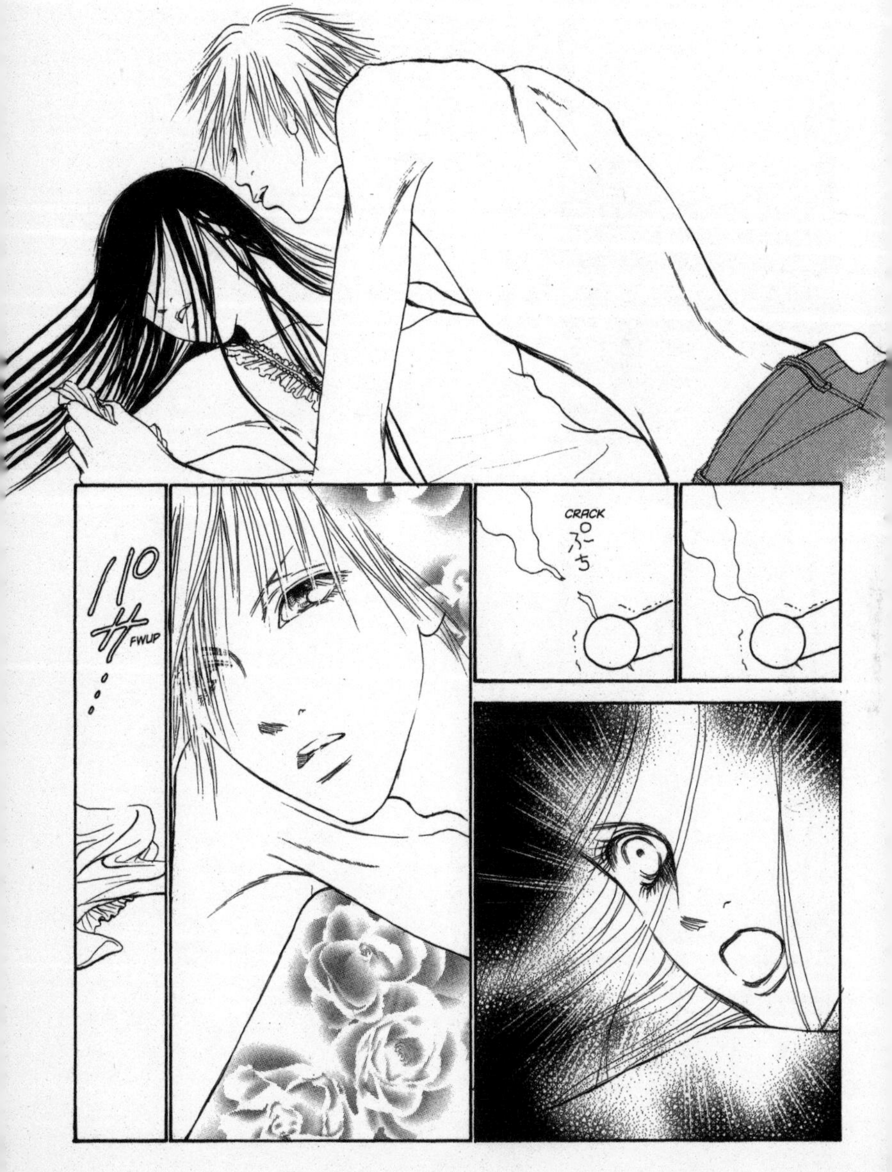
CRACK
ぷち
パサ…
FWUP

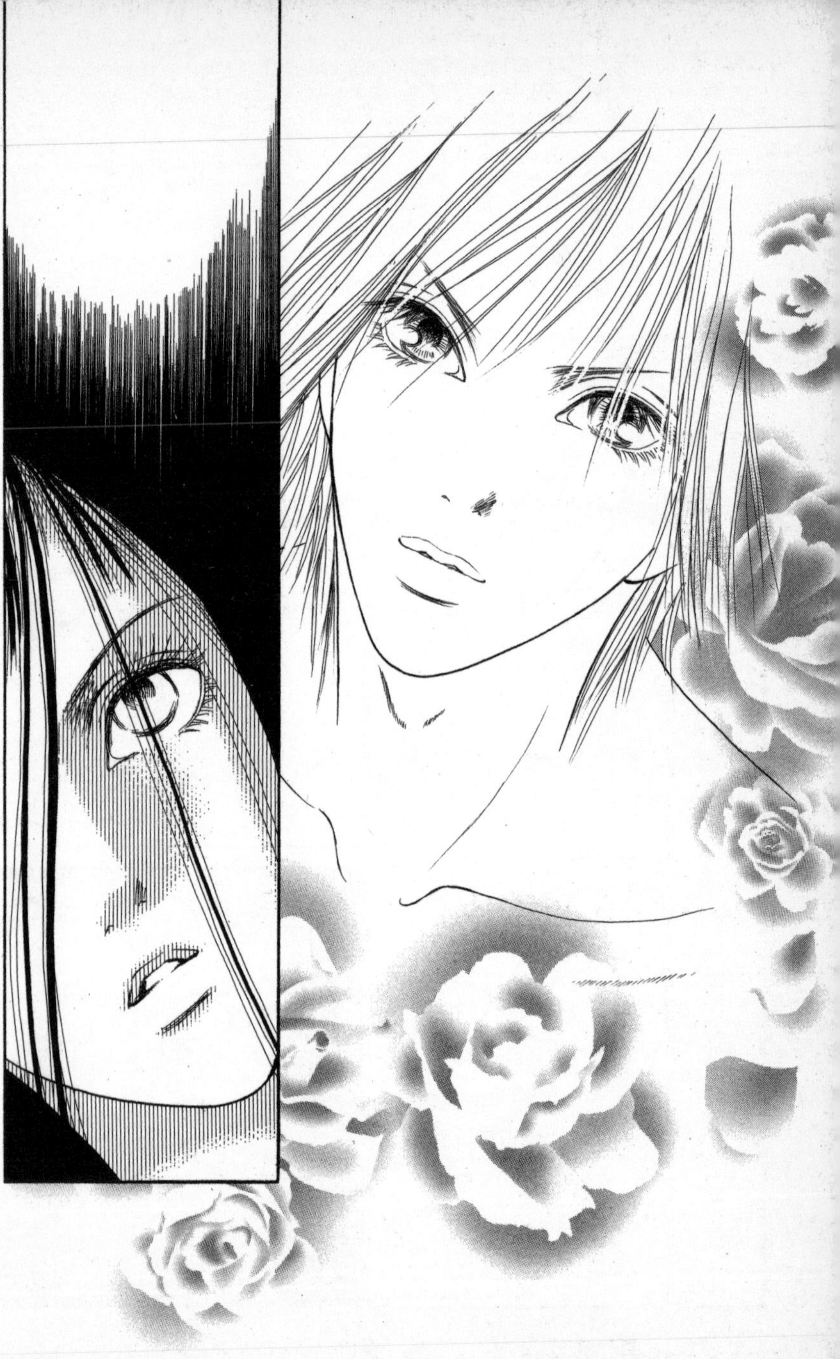

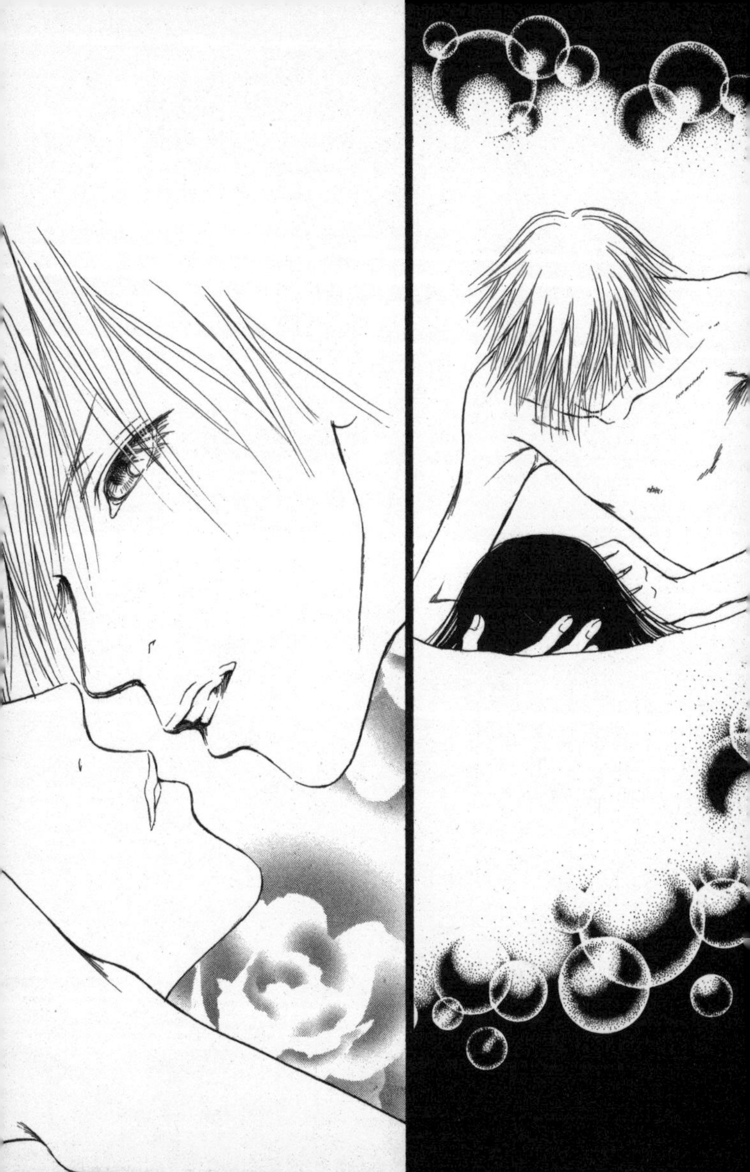

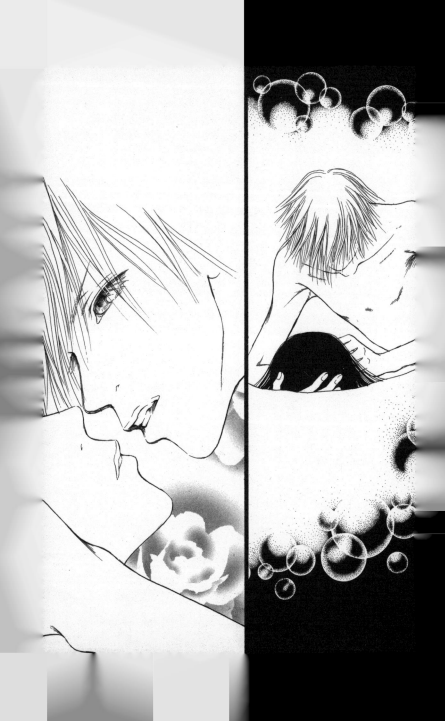

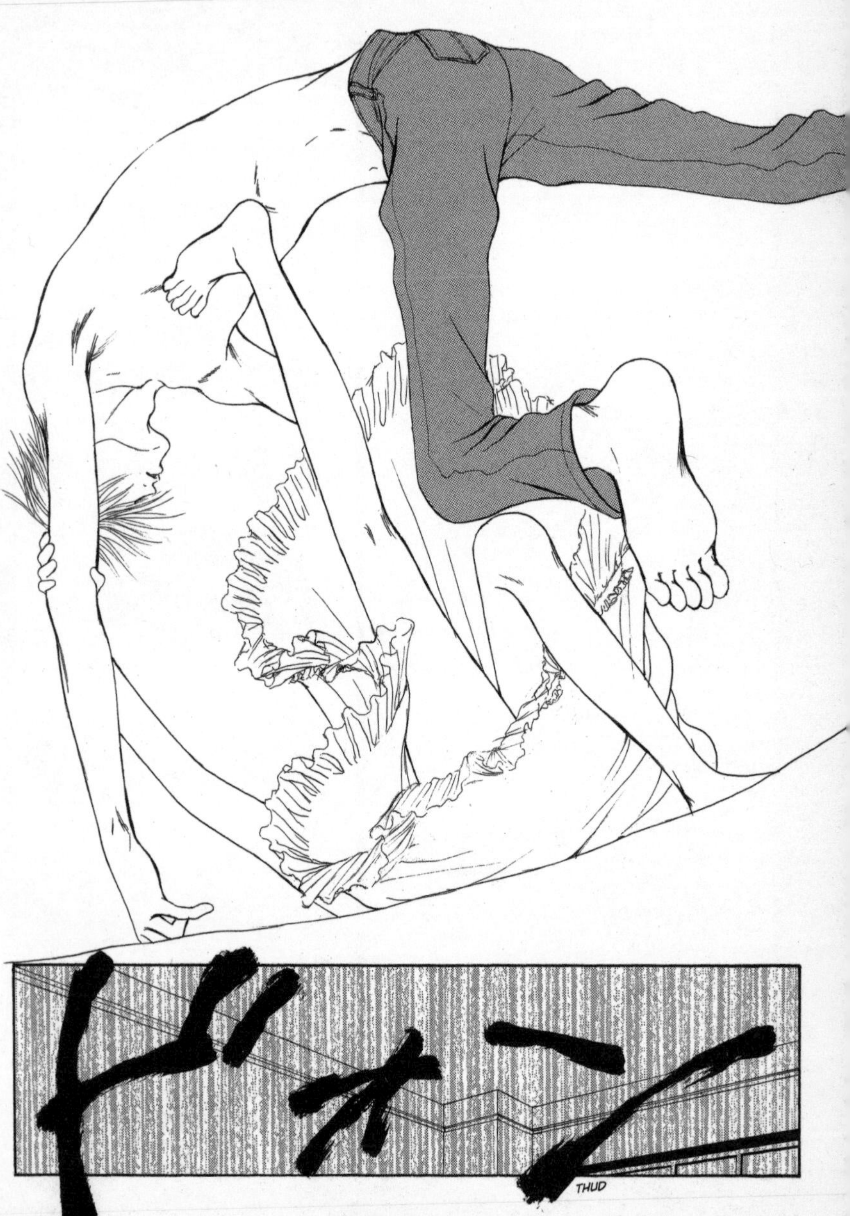
ドオーン
THUD

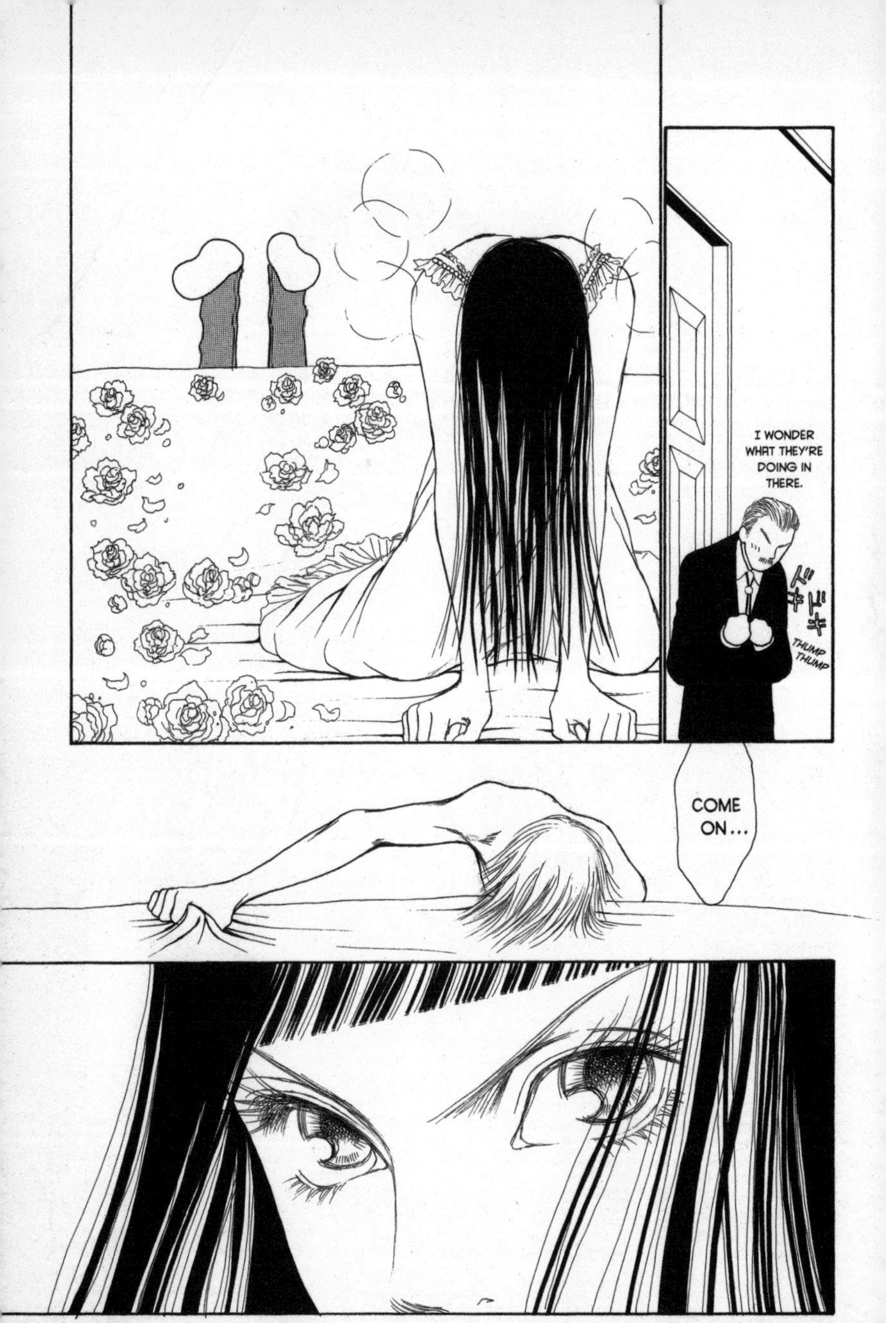
I WONDER WHAT THEY'RE DOING IN THERE.
ドキドキ
THUMP THUMP
COME ON...

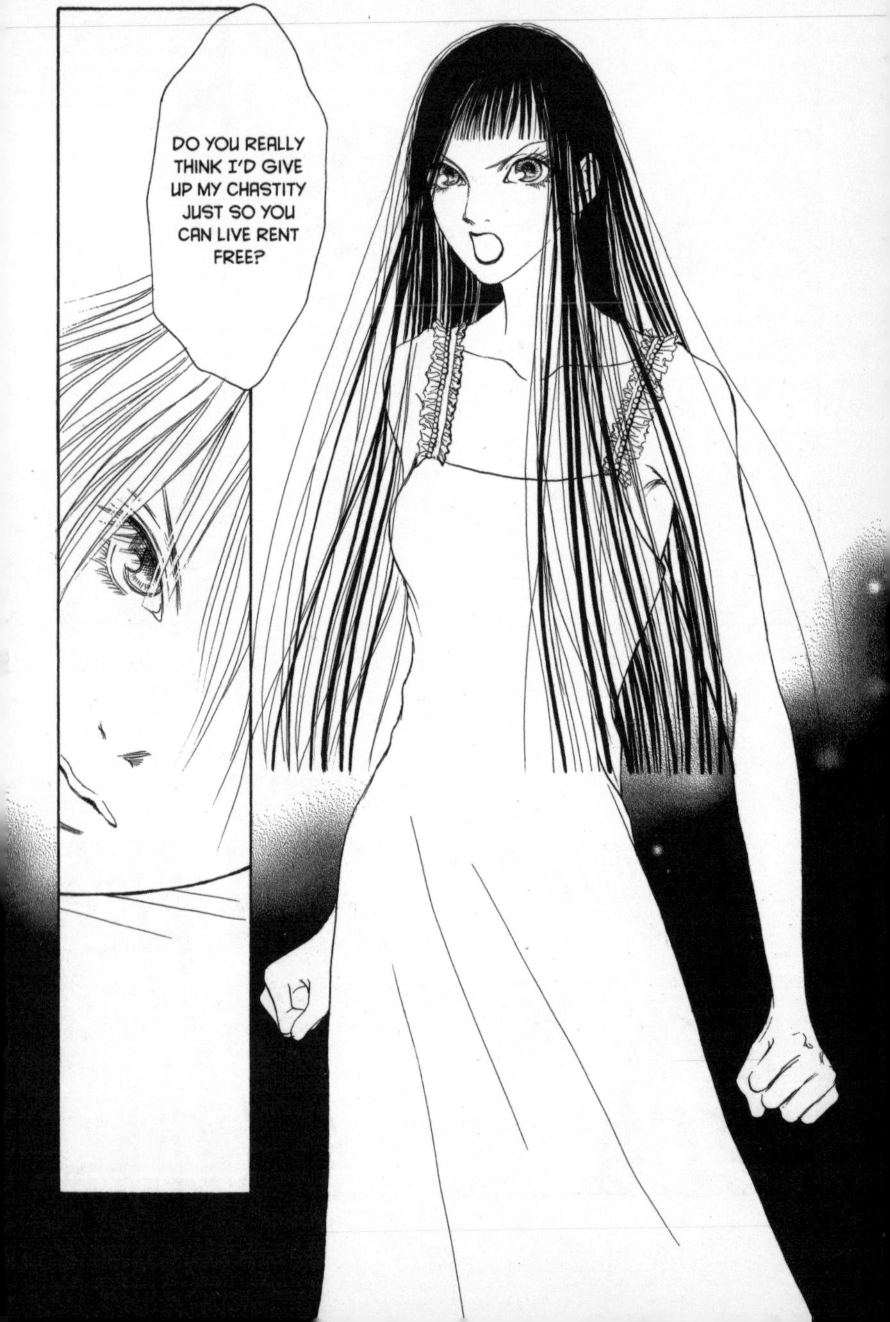
DO YOU REALLY THINK I'D GIVE UP MY CHASTITY JUST SO YOU CAN LIVE RENT FREE?

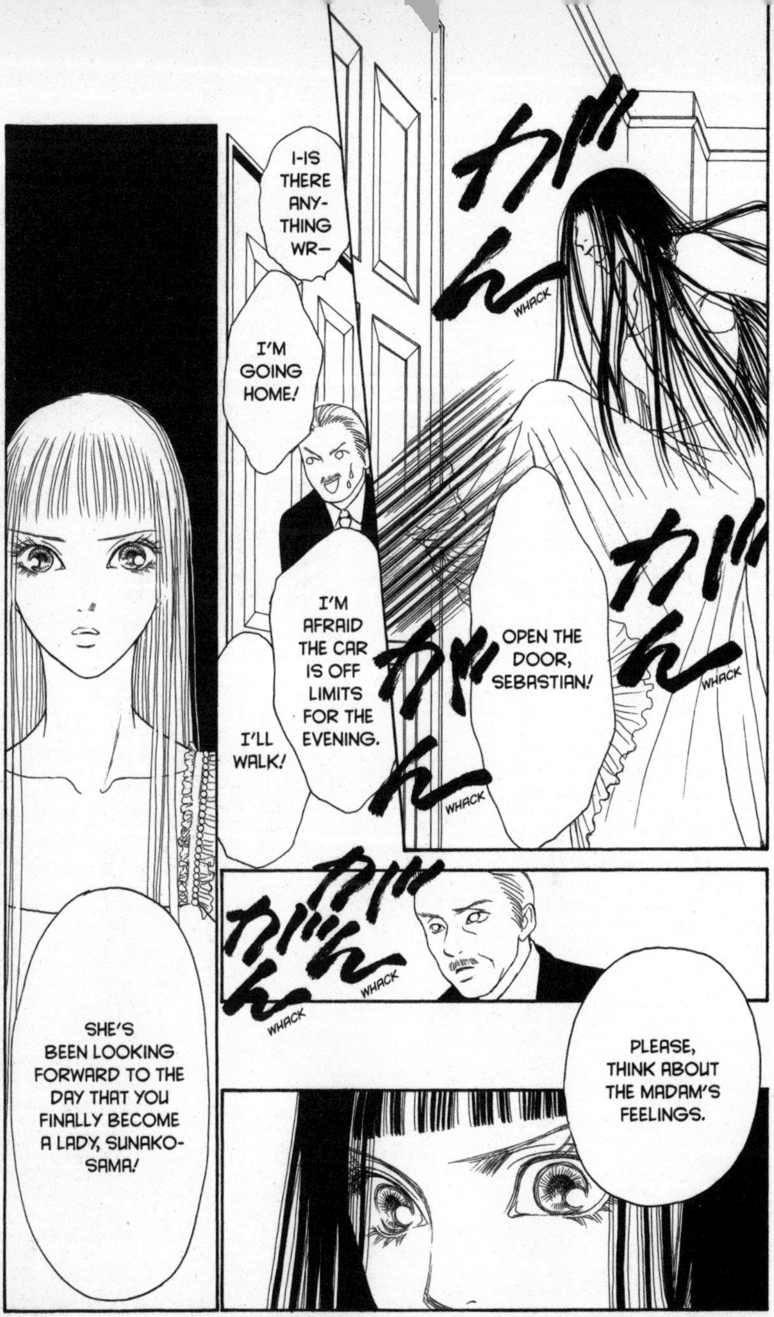
がん
WHACK
OPEN THE DOOR, SEBASTIAN!
がん
WHACK
I-IS THERE ANYTHING WR–
I'M GOING HOME!
がん
WHACK
I'M AFRAID THE CAR IS OFF LIMITS FOR THE EVENING.
I'LL WALK!
がん
WHACK
がん
WHACK
PLEASE, THINK ABOUT THE MADAM'S FEELINGS.
SHE'S BEEN LOOKING FORWARD TO THE DAY THAT YOU FINALLY BECOME A LADY, SUNAKO-SAMA!

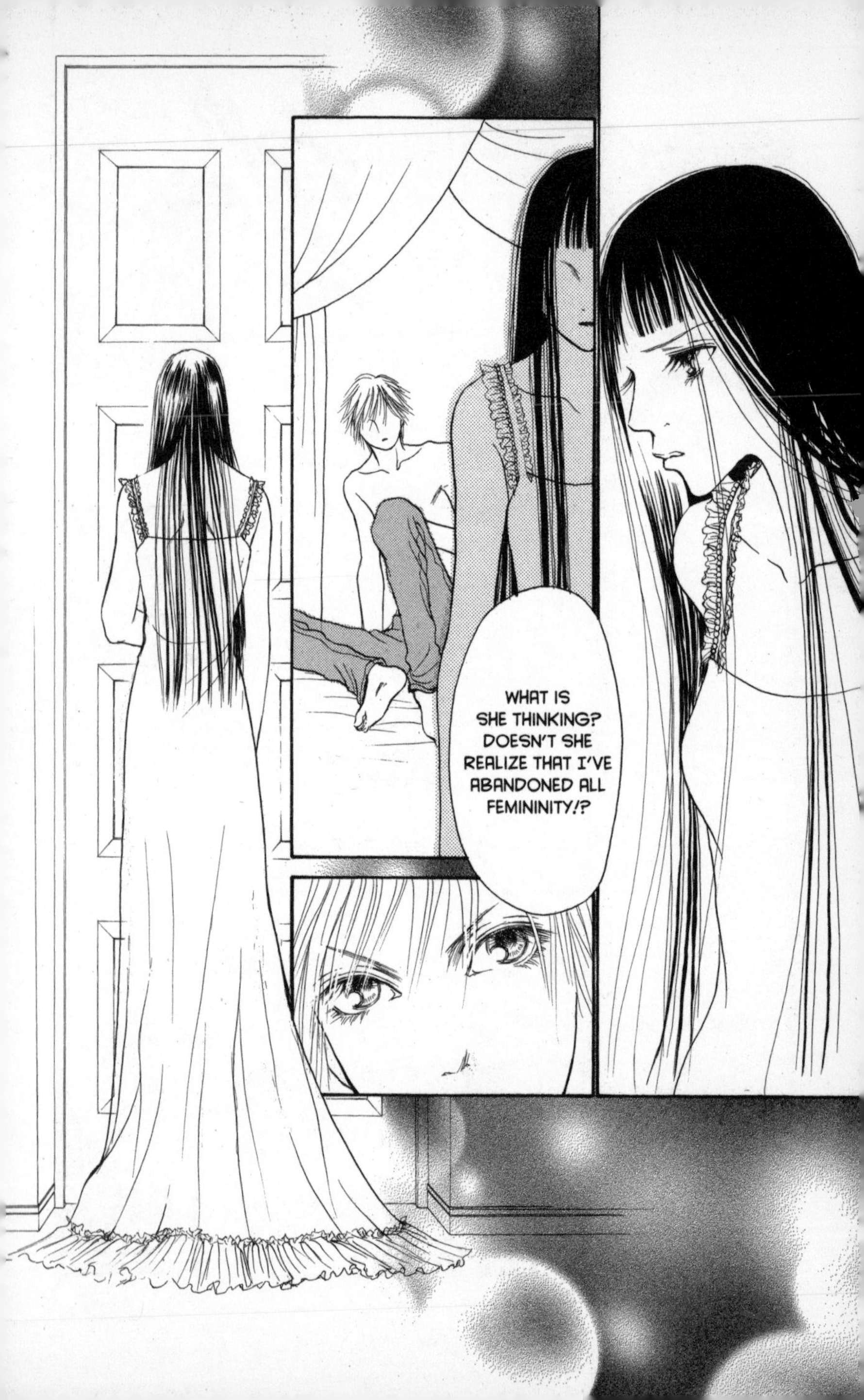
WHAT IS SHE THINKING? DOESN'T SHE REALIZE THAT I'VE ABANDONED ALL FEMININITY!?

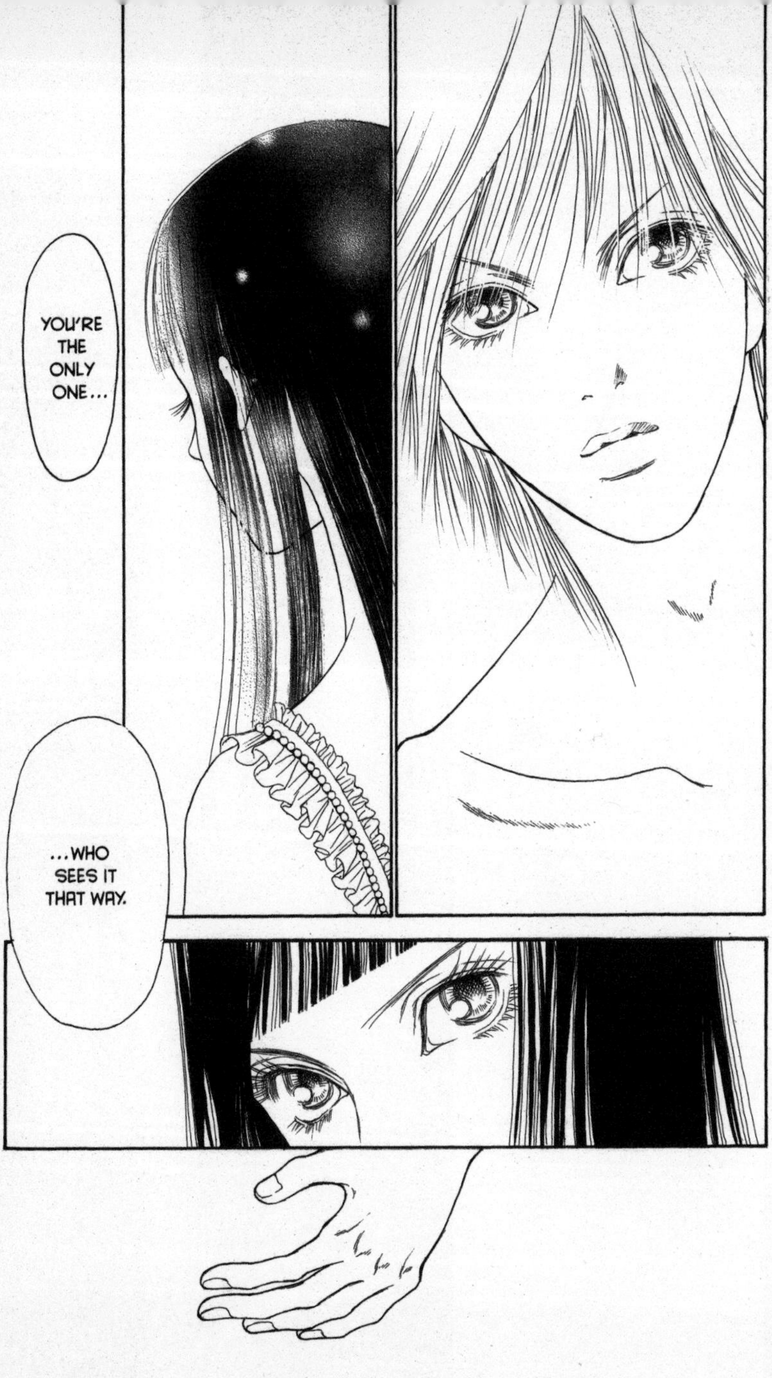
YOU'RE THE ONLY ONE...
...WHO SEES IT THAT WAY.

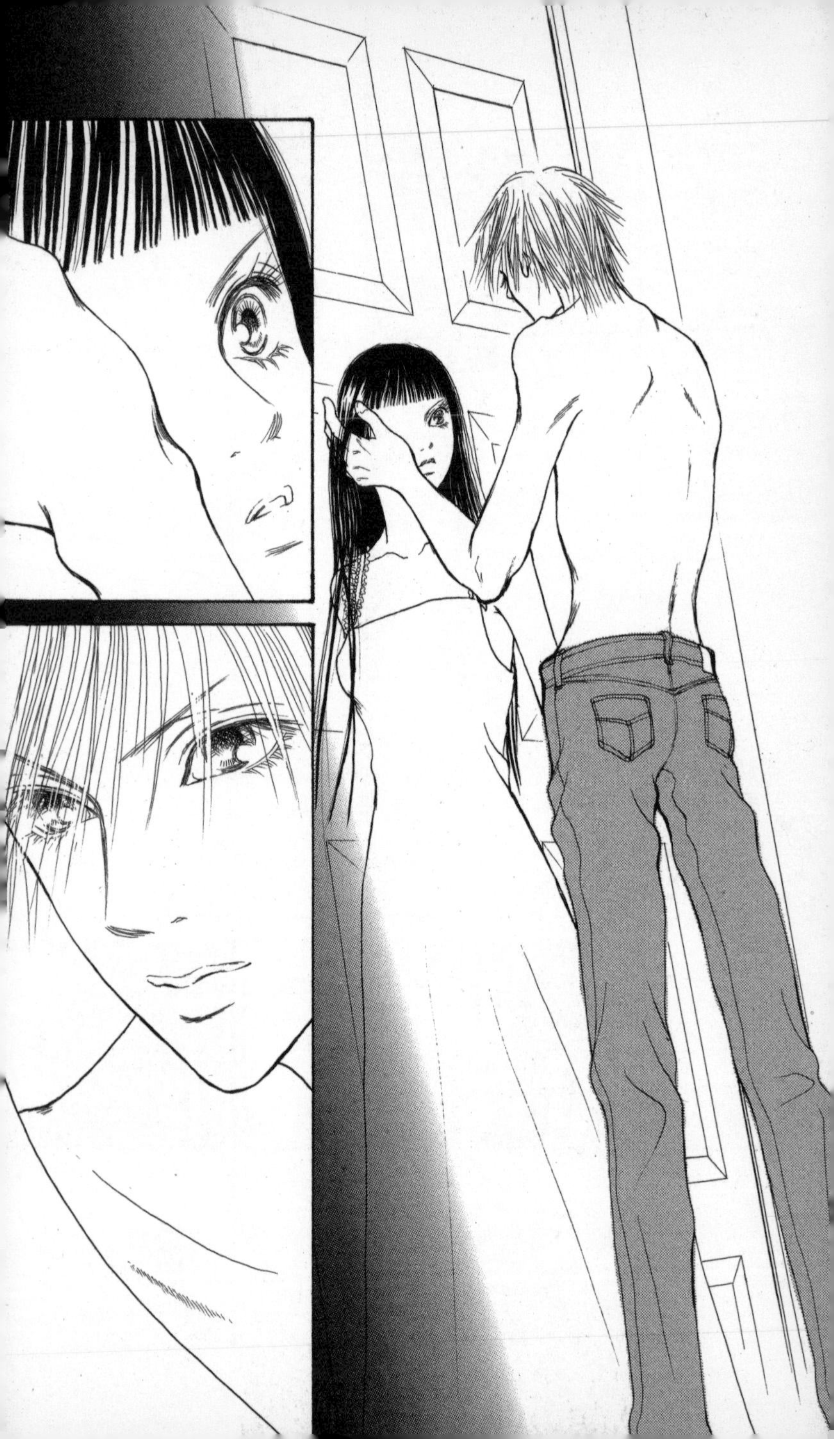

Chapter 36
The Journey to Becoming a Lady [Part 2]

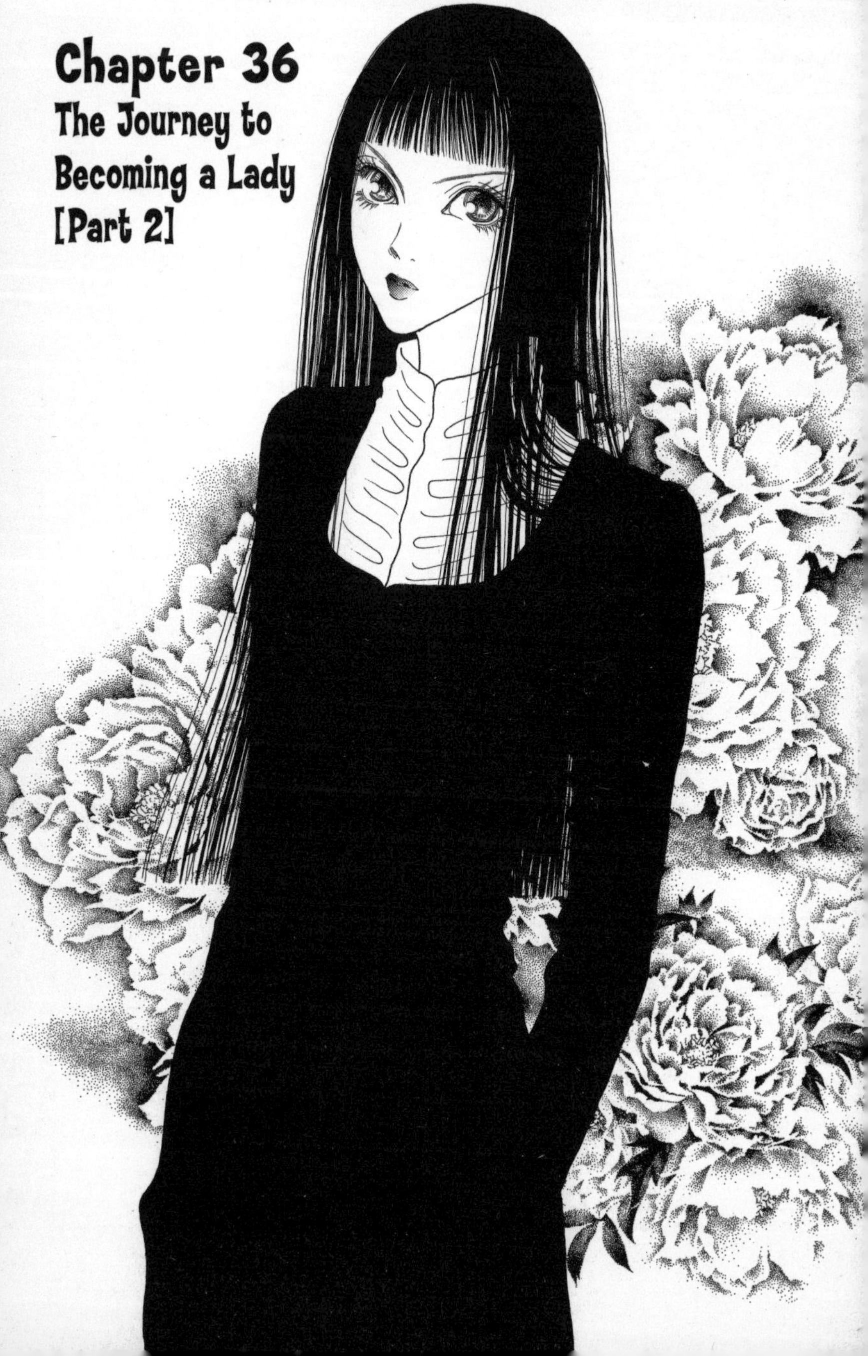

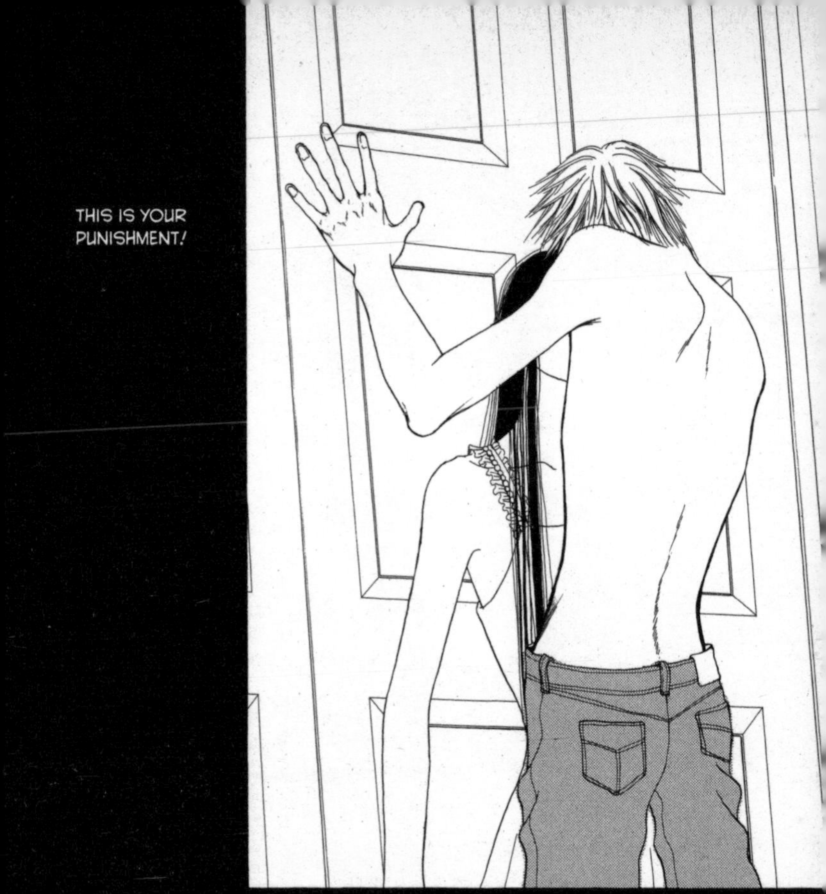
THIS IS YOUR PUNISHMENT!

BEHIND THE SCENES

MIZUHO AIMOTO-SENSEI (WHO'S CURRENTLY WORKING ON "BE LOVE") HELPED ME WITH THIS STORY ♥ (EVEN THOUGH SHE REALLY ONLY CAME BY TO VISIT).

AI-CHAN- SENSEI IS SO AMAZING. SHE CAN DRAW ANYTHING.

I ESPECIALLY LIKE HER DRAWINGS OF TRANSVESTITES. AREN'T THEY CUTE? ♥ AREN'T THEY CUTE? ♥

THE OKONOMIYAKI SHE MADE ME AT WORK WAS FABULOUS. ♥

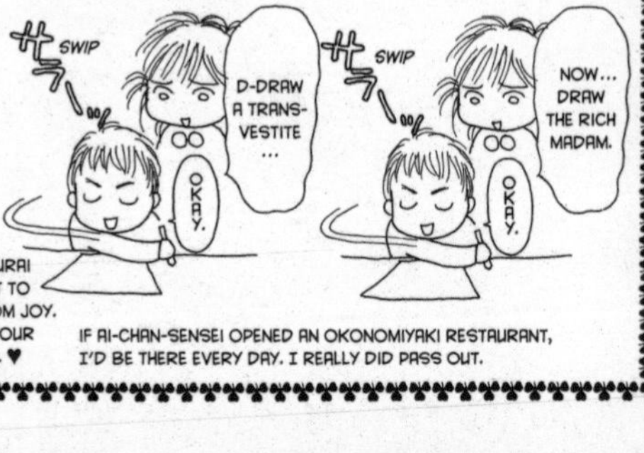
SWIP
NOW... DRAW THE RICH MADAM.
OKAY.
SWIP
D-DRAW A TRANS-VESTITE...
OKAY.

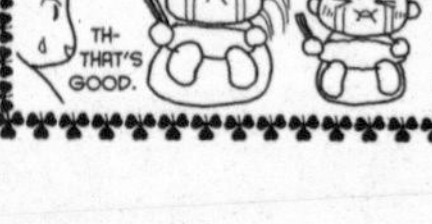
YUM.
TH-THAT'S GOOD.

MACHIKO SAKURAI AND ME ABOUT TO PASS OUT FROM JOY. THANKS FOR YOUR HELP, SAKURAI. ♥

IF AI-CHAN-SENSEI OPENED AN OKONOMIYAKI RESTAURANT, I'D BE THERE EVERY DAY. I REALLY DID PASS OUT.

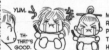

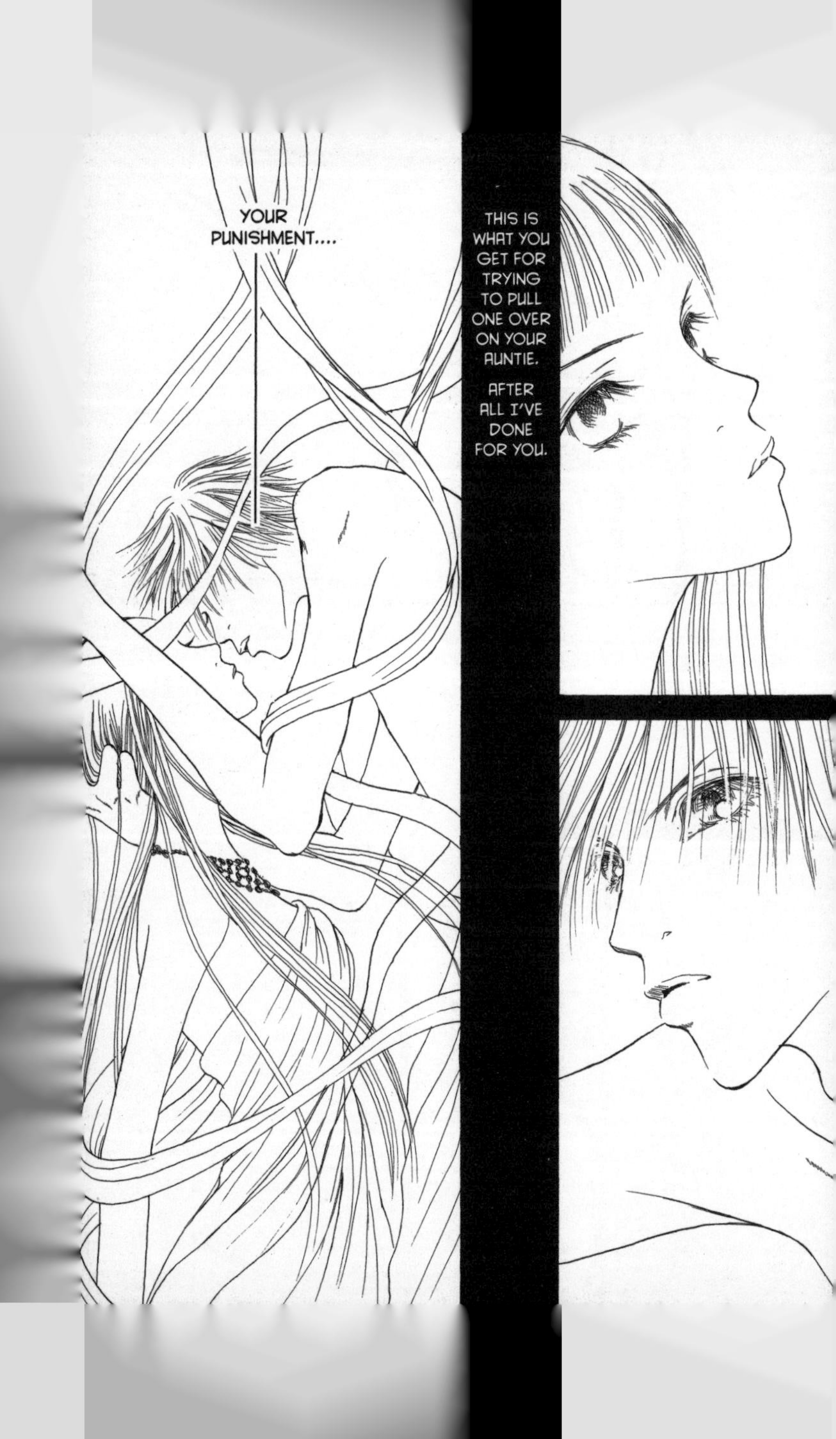
THIS IS WHAT YOU GET FOR TRYING TO PULL ONE OVER ON YOUR AUNTIE.
AFTER ALL I'VE DONE FOR YOU.
YOUR PUNISHMENT....

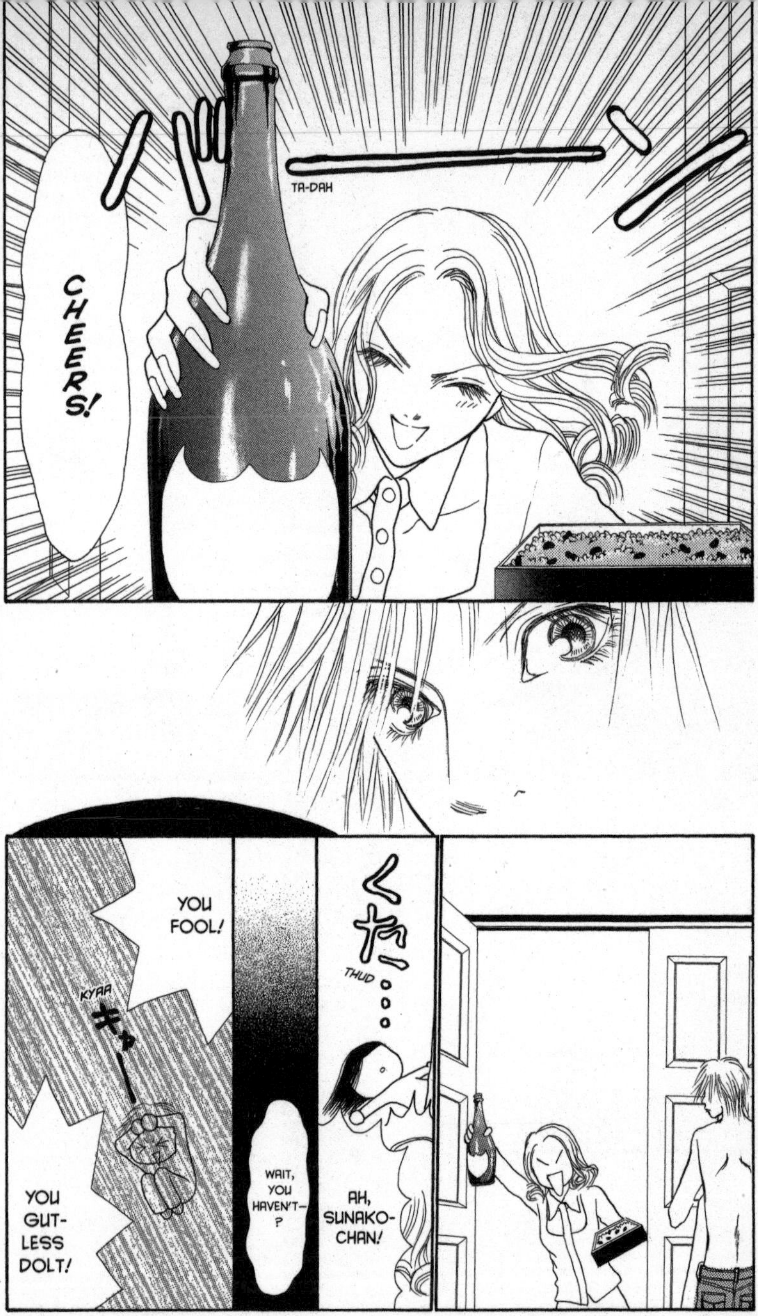
TA-DAH
CHEERS!
AH, SUNAKO-CHAN!
THUD
WAIT, YOU HAVEN'T-?
YOU FOOL!
KYAA
YOU GUT-LESS DOLT!

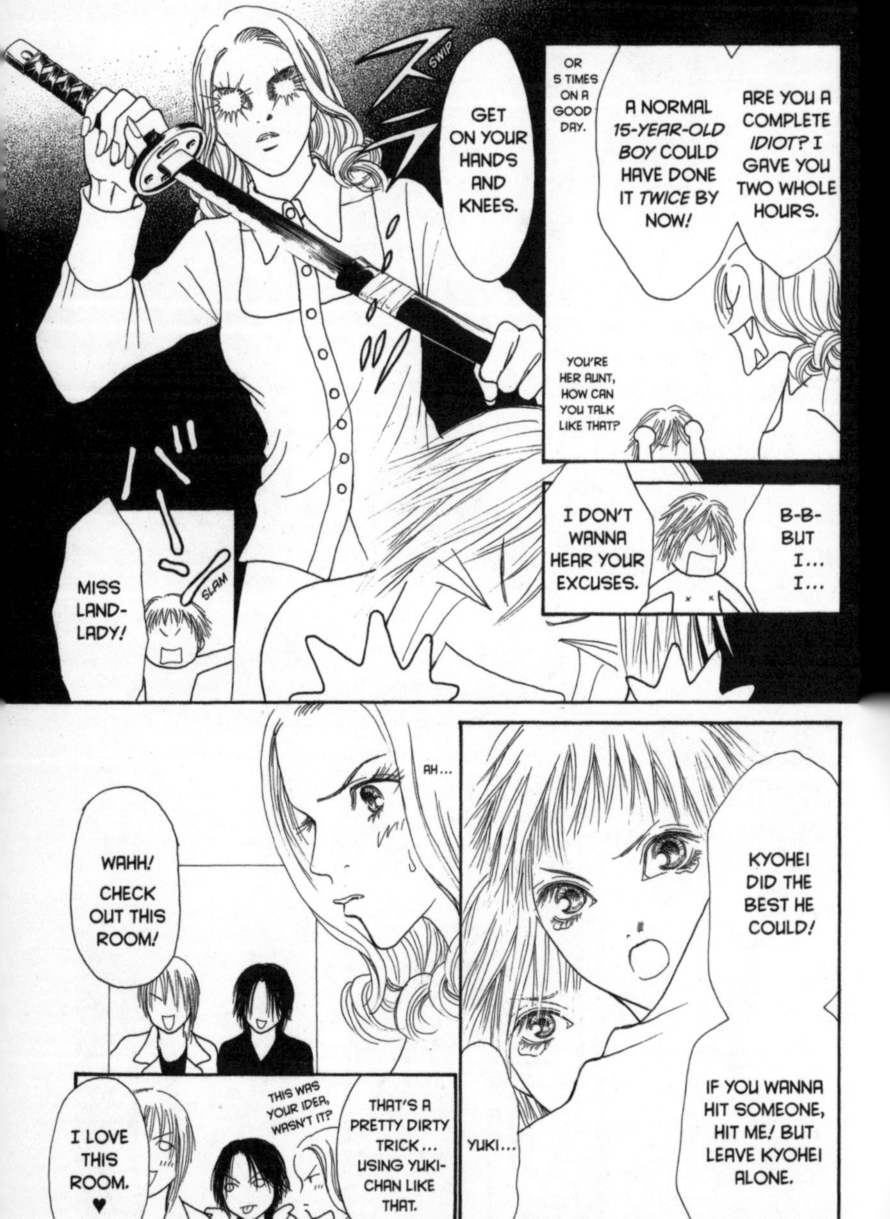
ARE YOU A COMPLETE IDIOT? I GAVE YOU TWO WHOLE HOURS.
A NORMAL 15-YEAR-OLD BOY COULD HAVE DONE IT TWICE BY NOW!
OR 5 TIMES ON A GOOD DAY.
YOU'RE HER AUNT, HOW CAN YOU TALK LIKE THAT?
B-B-BUT I... I...
I DON'T WANNA HEAR YOUR EXCUSES.
SWIP
GET ON YOUR HANDS AND KNEES.
SLAM
MISS LANDLADY!
KYOHEI DID THE BEST HE COULD!
IF YOU WANNA HIT SOMEONE, HIT ME! BUT LEAVE KYOHEI ALONE.
YUKI...
AH...
WAHH! CHECK OUT THIS ROOM!
THAT'S A PRETTY DIRTY TRICK... USING YUKI-CHAN LIKE THAT.
THIS WAS YOUR IDEA, WASN'T IT?
I LOVE THIS ROOM. ♥
The landlady has a soft spot for Yuki.

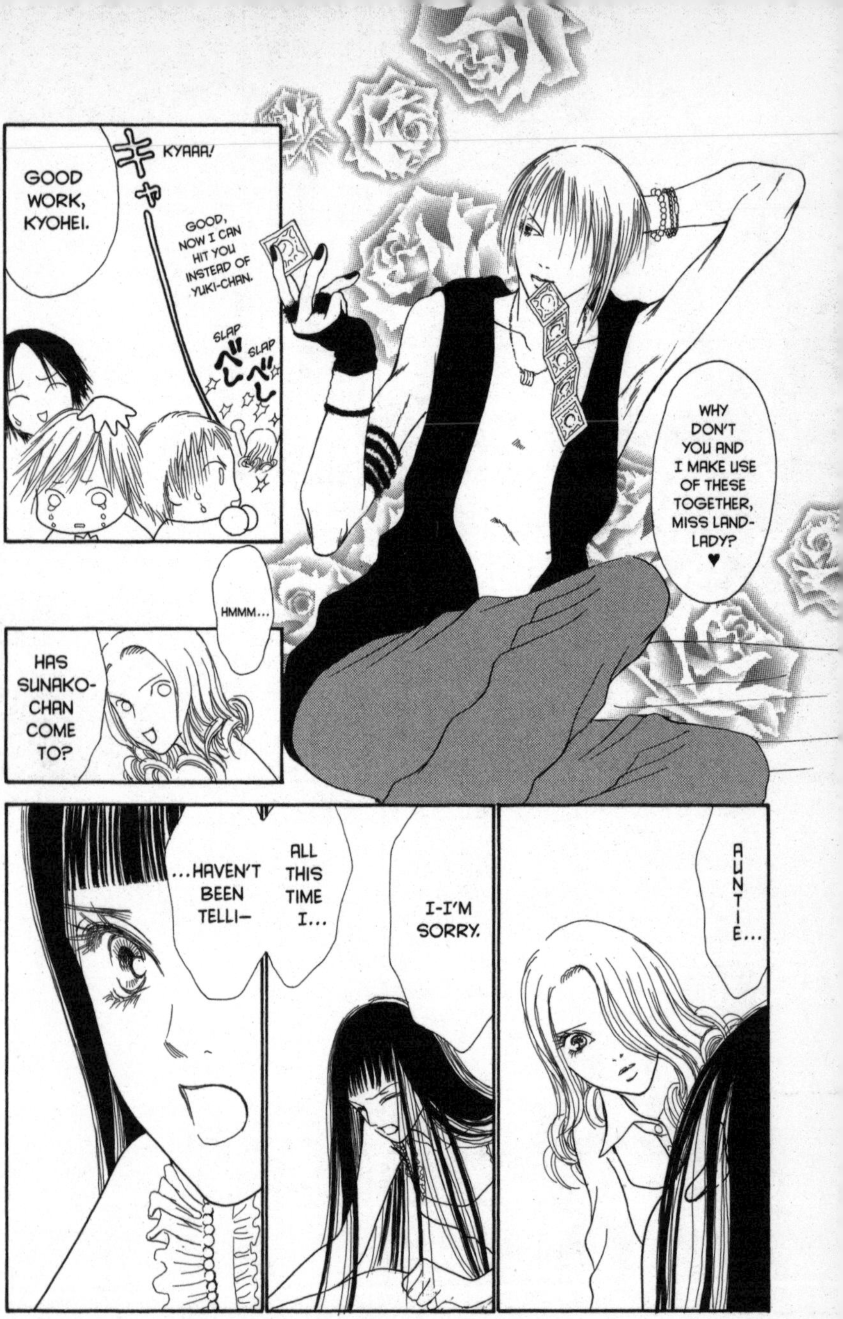
WHY DON'T YOU AND I MAKE USE OF THESE TOGETHER, MISS LAND-LADY? ♥
KYAAA!
GOOD WORK, KYOHEI.
GOOD, NOW I CAN HIT YOU INSTEAD OF YUKI-CHAN.
SLAP
SLAP
HMMM...
HAS SUNAKO-CHAN COME TO?
AUNTIE...
I-I'M SORRY.
ALL THIS TIME I...
...HAVEN'T BEEN TELLI—

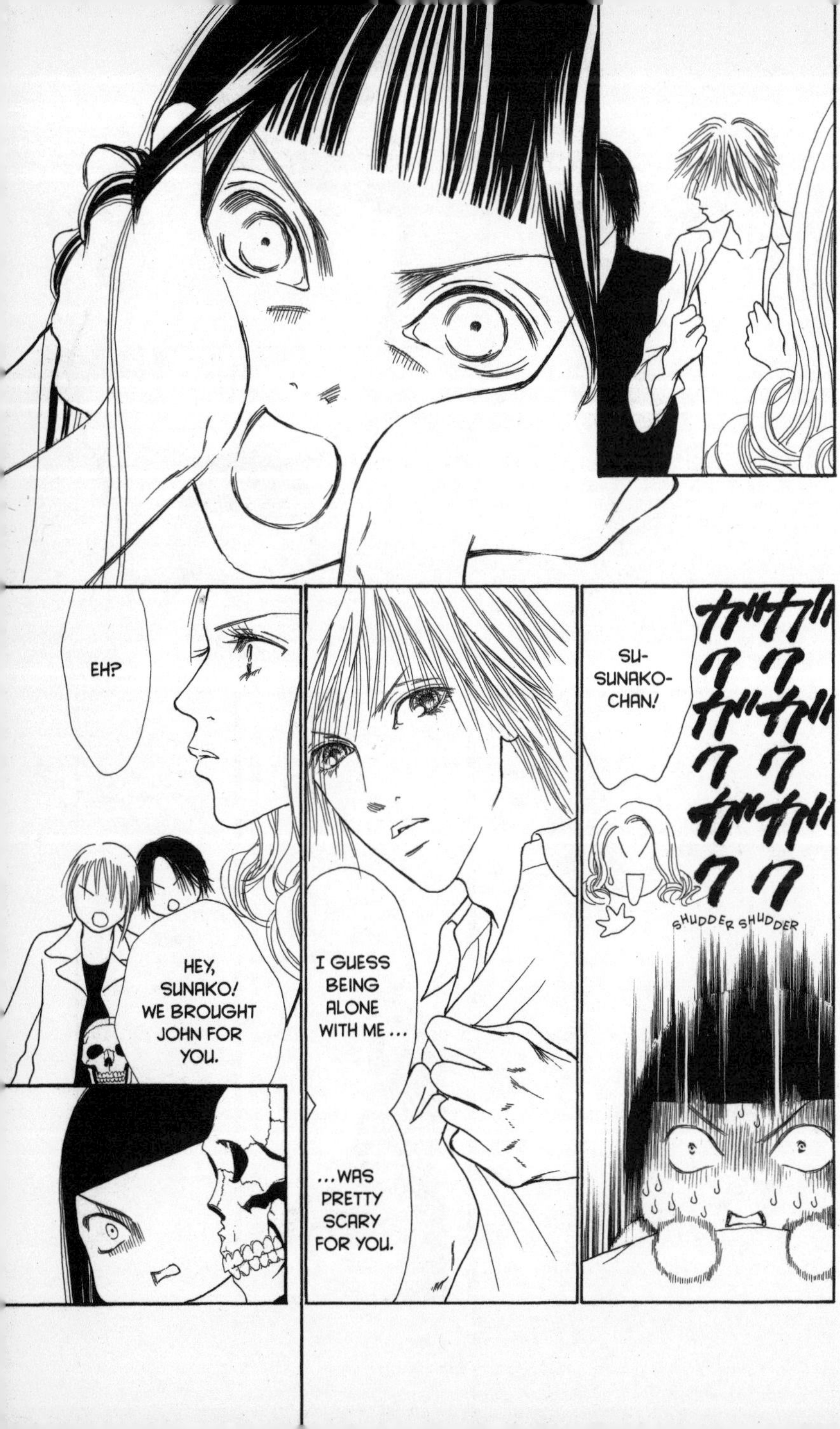
SU-SUNAKO-CHAN!
ガクガクガク
ガクガクガク
SHUDDER SHUDDER
I GUESS BEING ALONE WITH ME ...
...WAS PRETTY SCARY FOR YOU.
EH?
HEY, SUNAKO! WE BROUGHT JOHN FOR YOU.

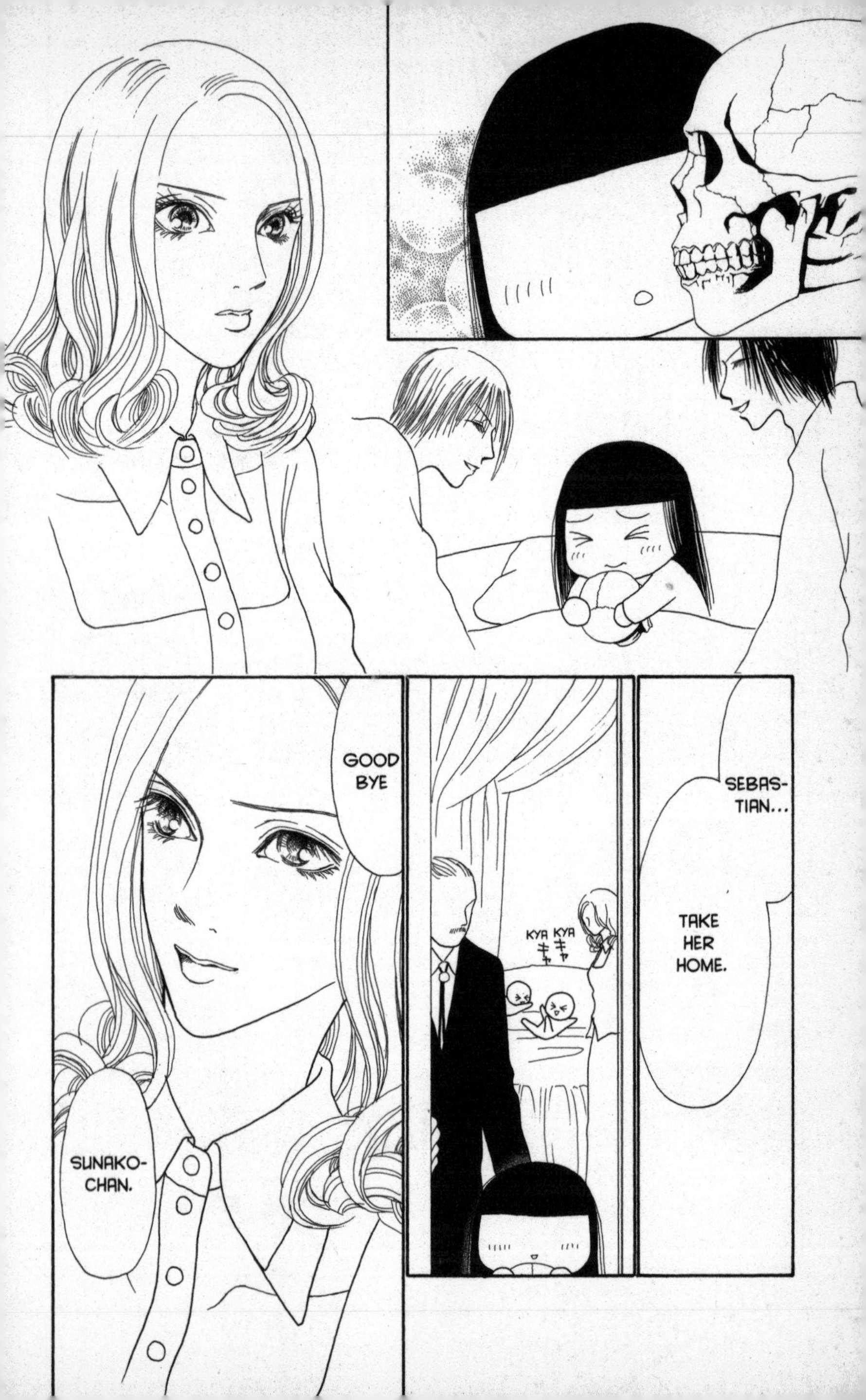
SEBAS-TIAN...
TAKE HER HOME.
KYA KYA
キャ キャ
GOOD BYE
SUNAKO-CHAN.

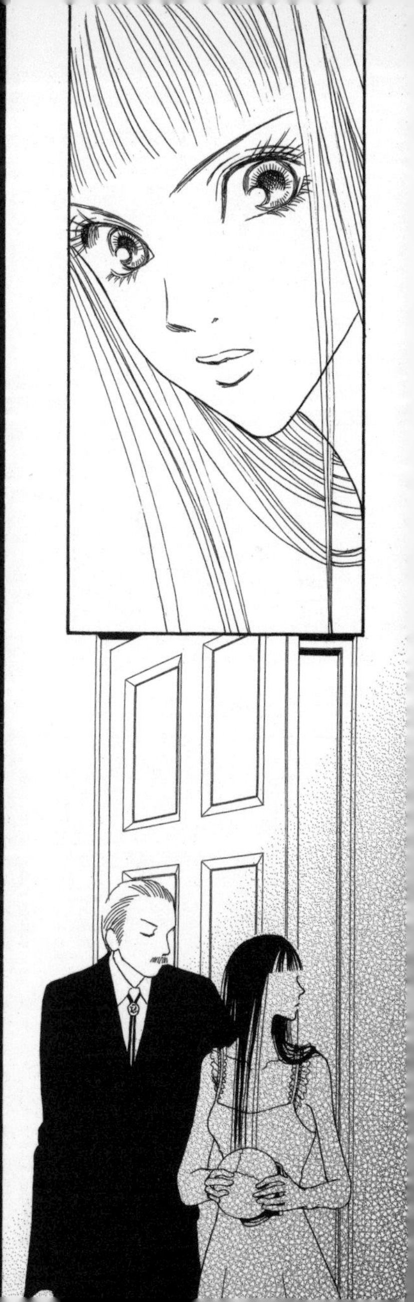

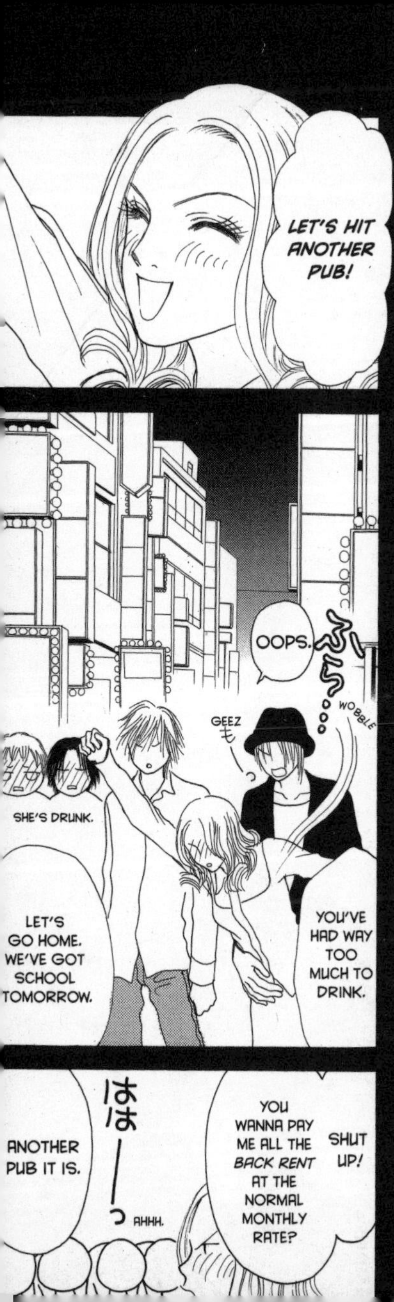
LET'S HIT ANOTHER PUB!
OOPS.
ふら〜〜
WOBBLE
GEEZ
もーっ
YOU'VE HAD WAY TOO MUCH TO DRINK.
SHE'S DRUNK.
LET'S GO HOME. WE'VE GOT SCHOOL TOMORROW.
SHUT UP!
YOU WANNA PAY ME ALL THE *BACK RENT* AT THE NORMAL MONTHLY RATE?
ははーっ
AHHH.
ANOTHER PUB IT IS.

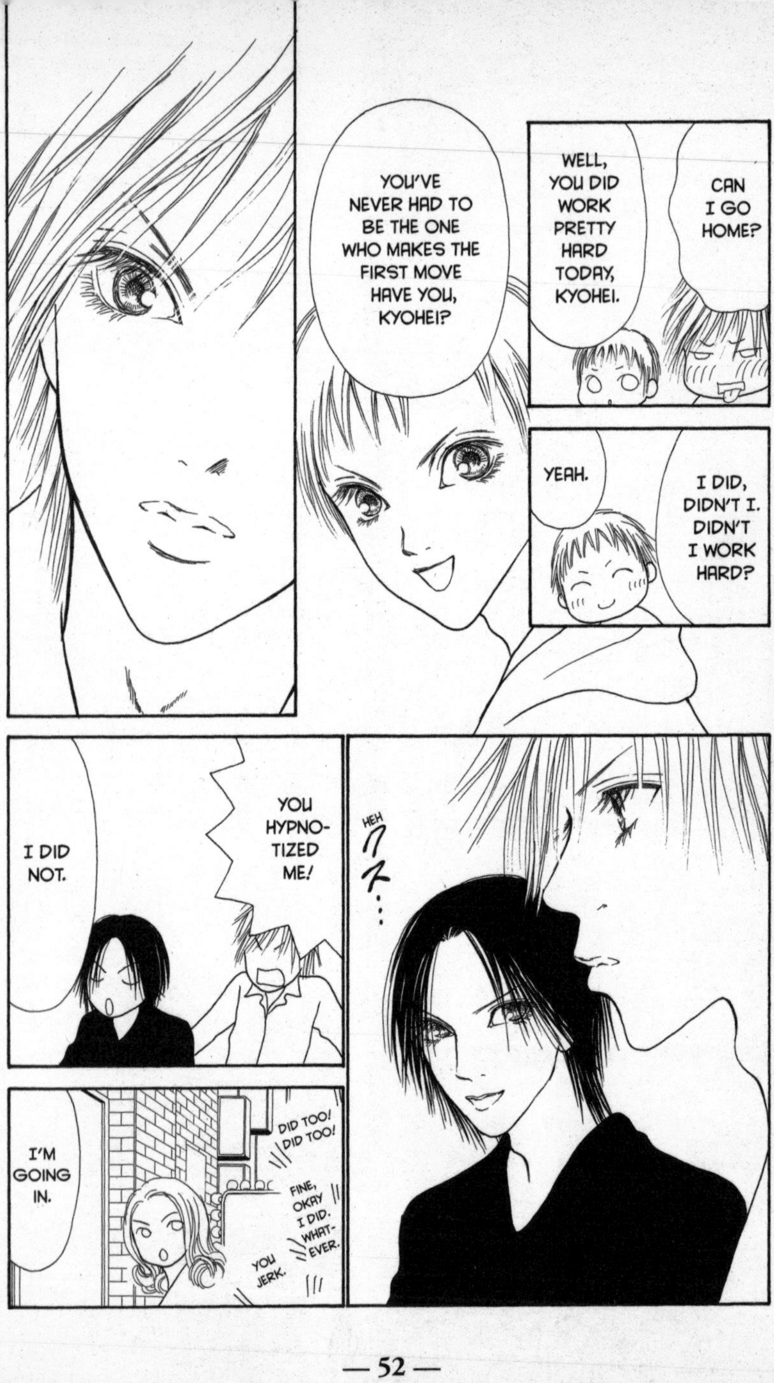
CAN I GO HOME?
WELL, YOU DID WORK PRETTY HARD TODAY, KYOHEI.
I DID, DIDN'T I. DIDN'T I WORK HARD?
YEAH.
YOU'VE NEVER HAD TO BE THE ONE WHO MAKES THE FIRST MOVE HAVE YOU, KYOHEI?
HEH
YOU HYPNO-TIZED ME!
I DID NOT.
DID TOO! DID TOO!
FINE, OKAY I DID. WHAT-EVER.
YOU JERK.
I'M GOING IN.

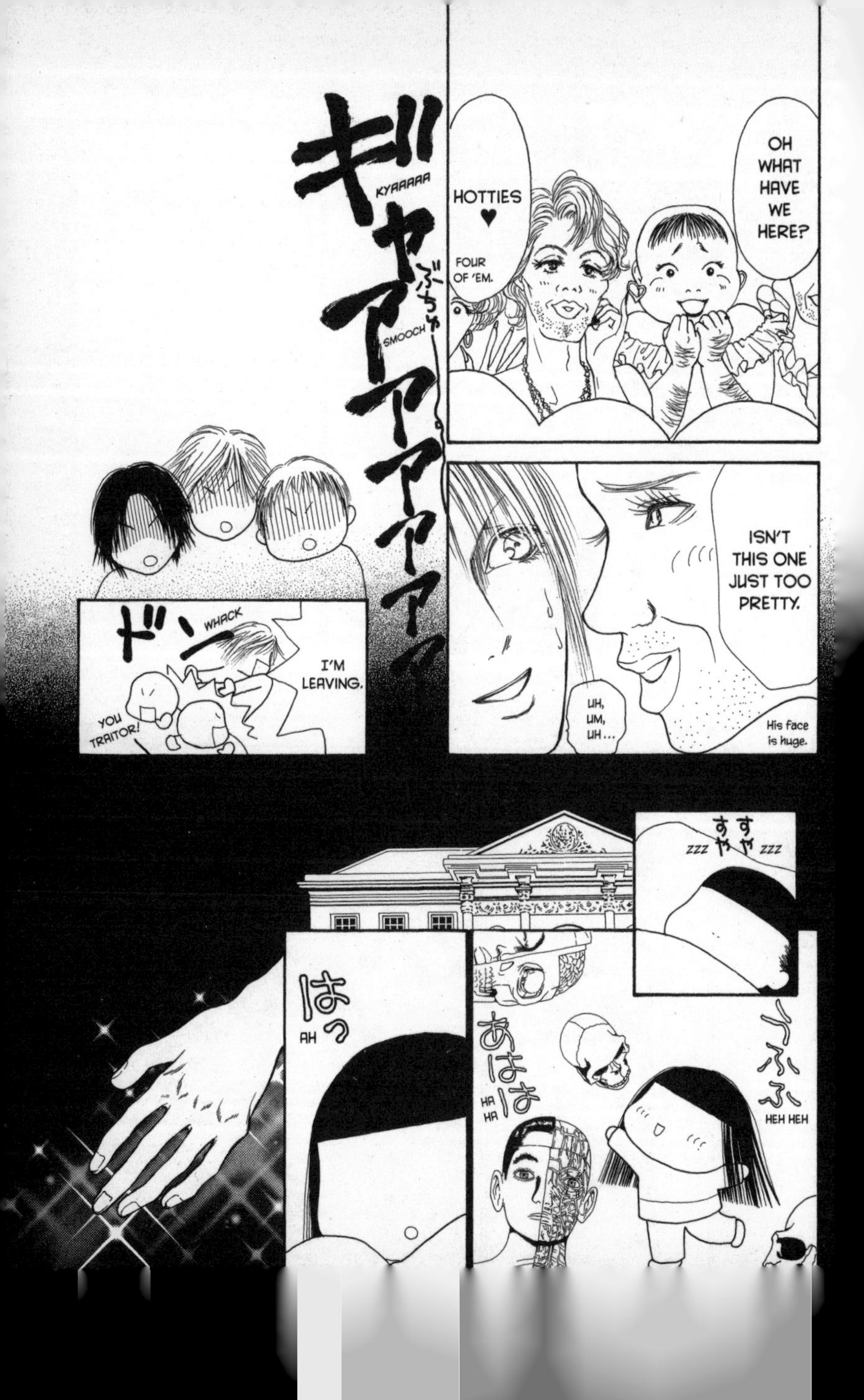

OH WHAT HAVE WE HERE?
HOTTIES ♥
FOUR OF 'EM.
キャアアアアア
KYAAAAAA
ぶちゅ
SMOOCH
ISN'T THIS ONE JUST TOO PRETTY.
UH, UM, UH...
His face is huge.
I'M LEAVING.
ドン
WHACK
YOU TRAITOR!
すやすや
ZZZ ZZZ
うふふ
HEH HEH
あはは
HA HA
はっ
AH

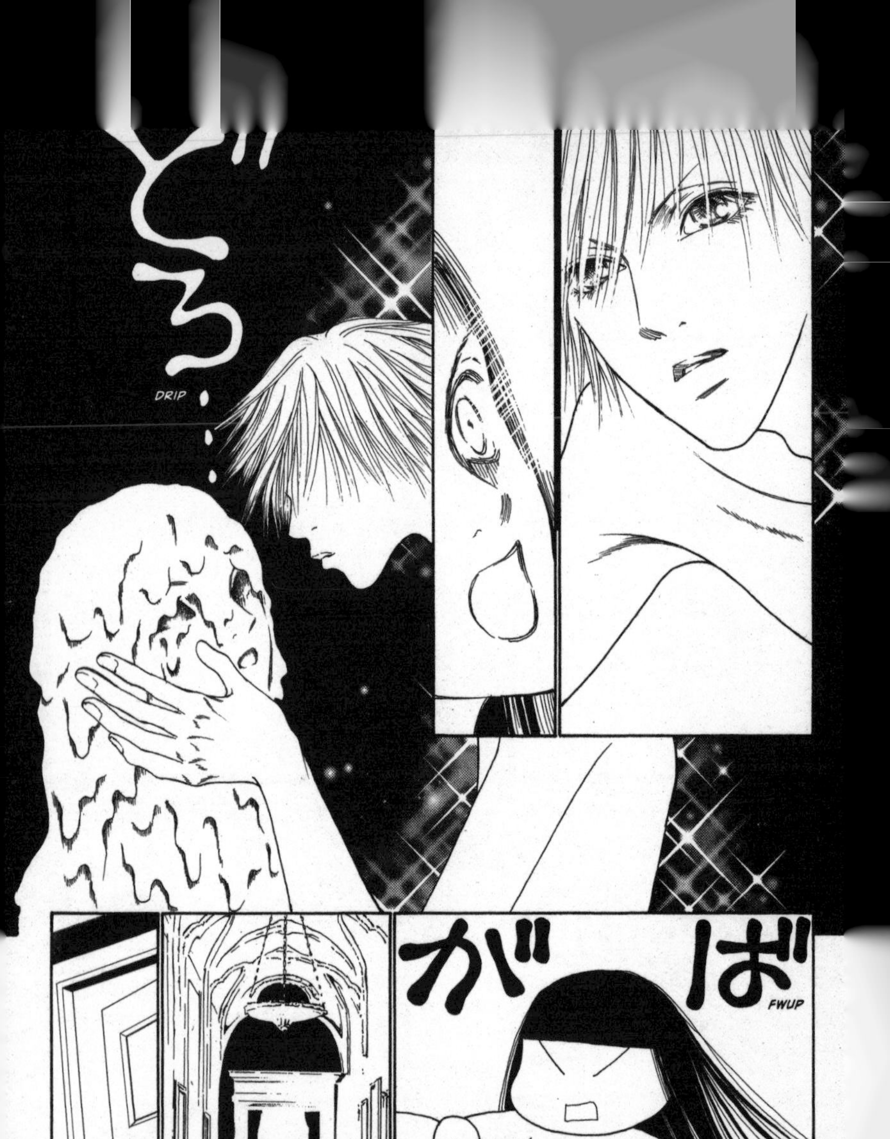
どろ
DRIP
がば
FWUP
HAHH
はぁっ
HAHH
はぁっ
HAHH
はぁっ
WATER...
CLICK
カチャ

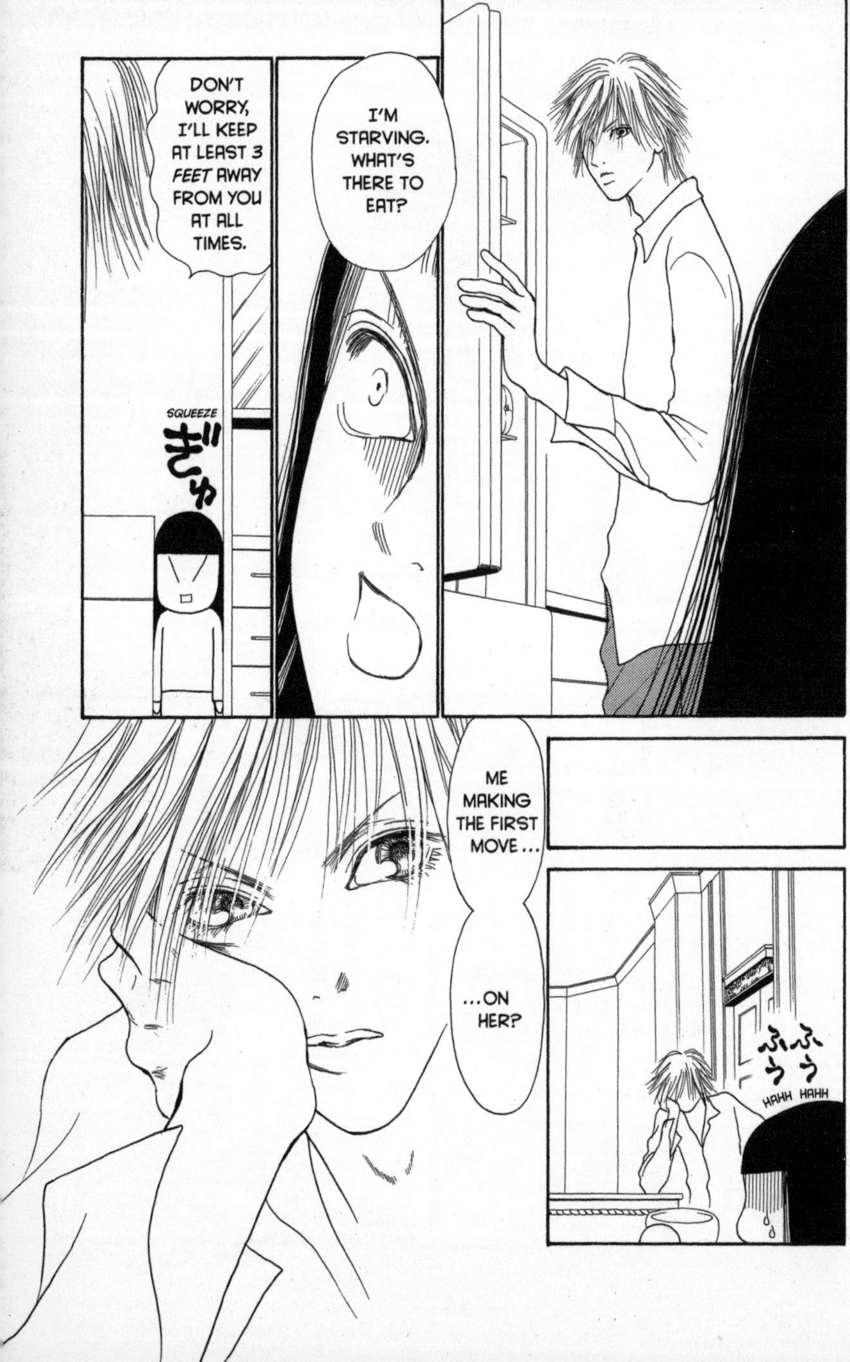
I'M STARVING. WHAT'S THERE TO EAT?
DON'T WORRY, I'LL KEEP AT LEAST 3 *FEET* AWAY FROM YOU AT ALL TIMES.
SQUEEZE
ぎゅ
ふう ふう
HAHH HAHH
ME MAKING THE FIRST MOVE...
...ON HER?

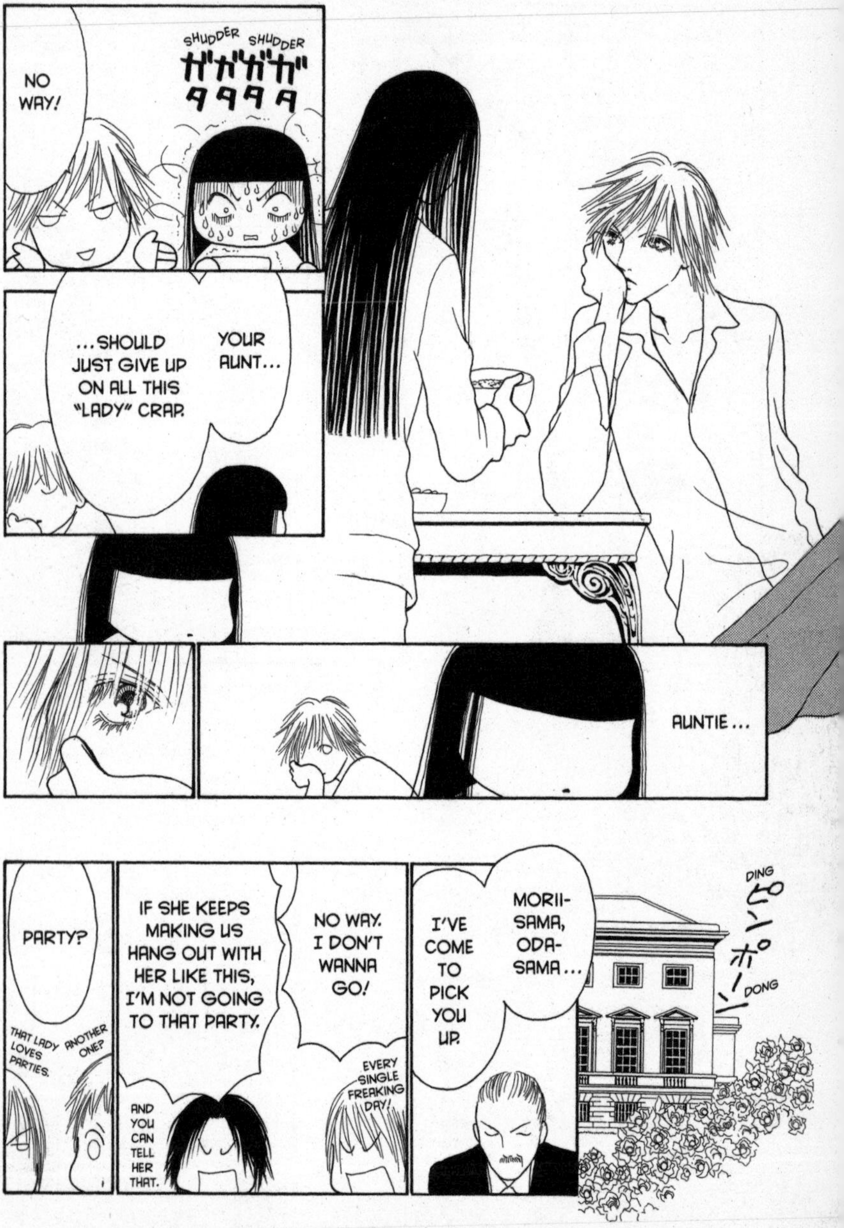
SHUDDER SHUDDER
NO WAY!
YOUR AUNT...
...SHOULD JUST GIVE UP ON ALL THIS "LADY" CRAP.
AUNTIE...
DING DONG
MORII-SAMA, ODA-SAMA...
I'VE COME TO PICK YOU UP.
NO WAY. I DON'T WANNA GO!
EVERY SINGLE FREAKING DAY!
IF SHE KEEPS MAKING US HANG OUT WITH HER LIKE THIS, I'M NOT GOING TO THAT PARTY.
AND YOU CAN TELL HER THAT.
PARTY?
ANOTHER ONE?
THAT LADY LOVES PARTIES.

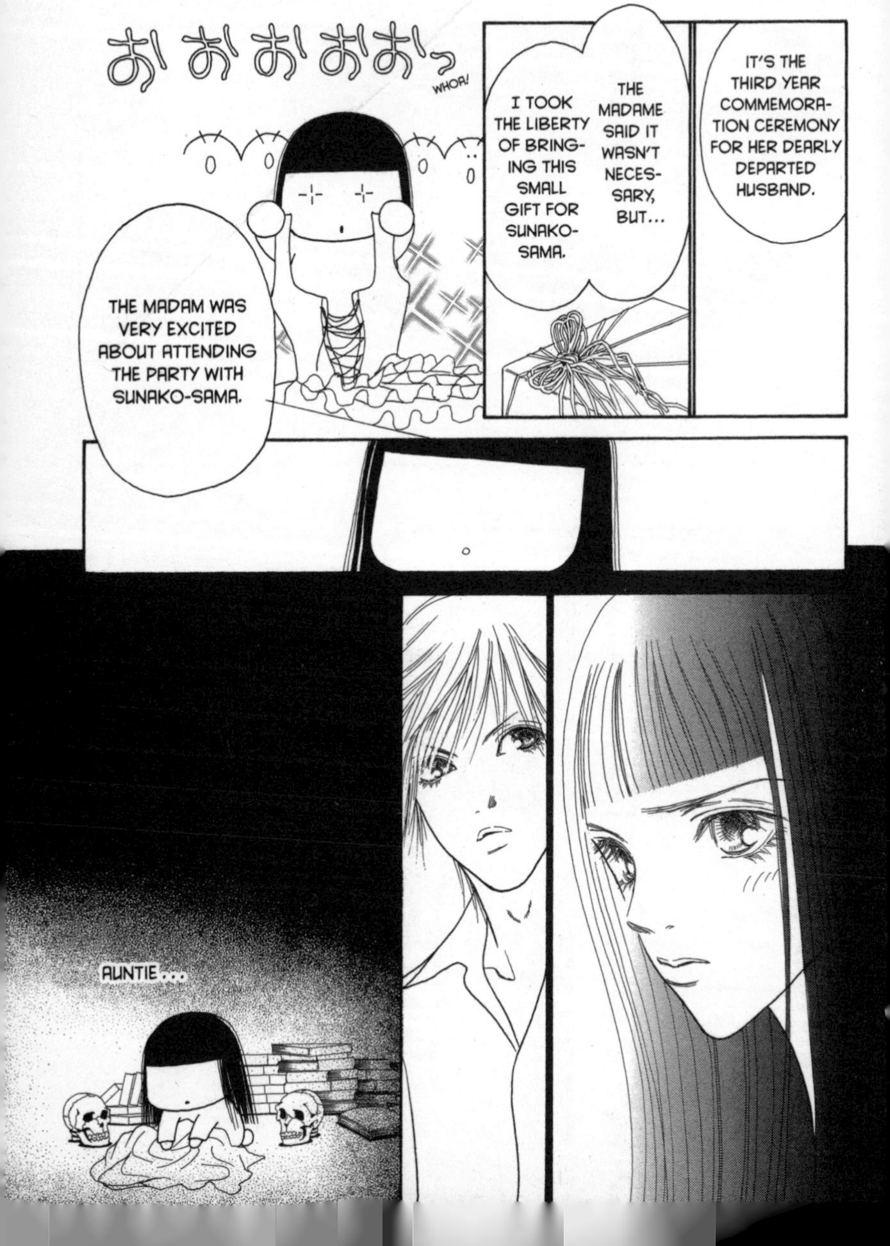
IT'S THE THIRD YEAR COMMEMORATION CEREMONY FOR HER DEARLY DEPARTED HUSBAND.
THE MADAME SAID IT WASN'T NECESSARY, BUT...
I TOOK THE LIBERTY OF BRINGING THIS SMALL GIFT FOR SUNAKO-SAMA.
おおおおおっ
WHOA!
THE MADAM WAS VERY EXCITED ABOUT ATTENDING THE PARTY WITH SUNAKO-SAMA.
AUNTIE...

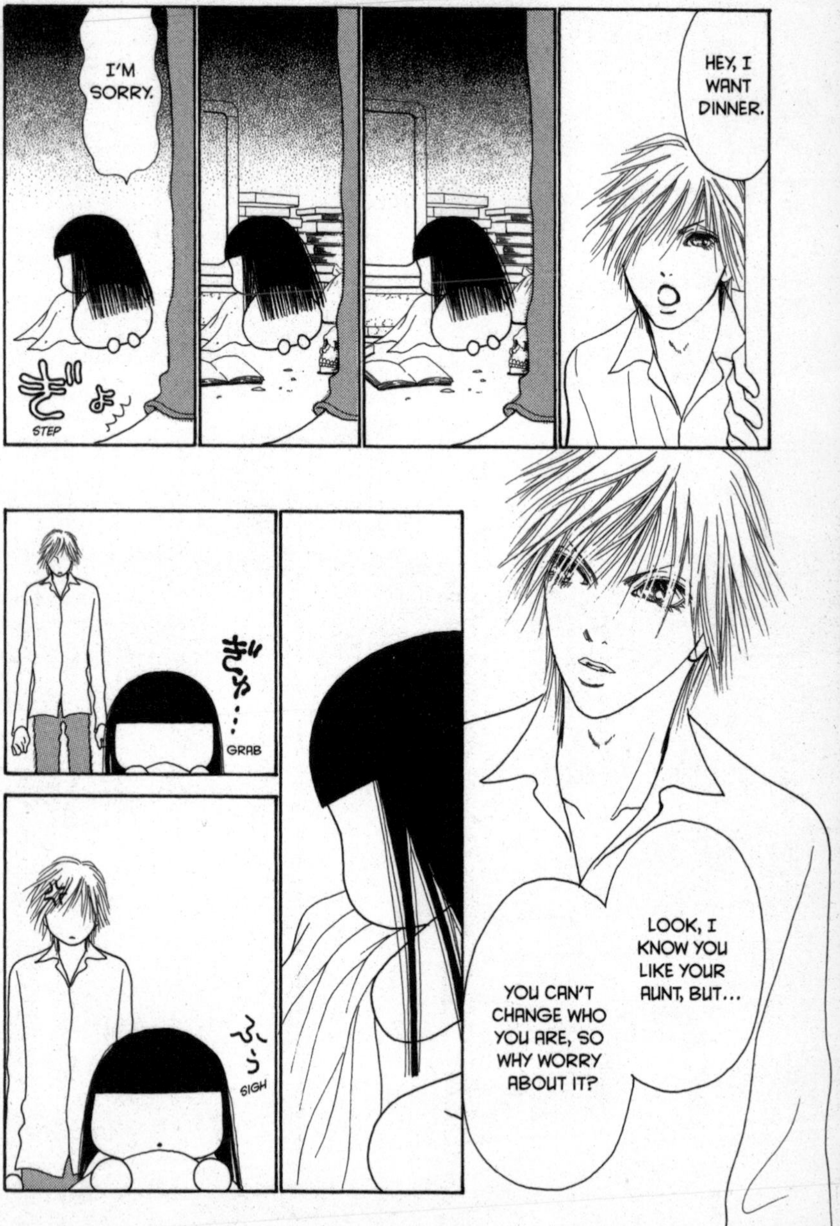
HEY, I WANT DINNER.
I'M SORRY.
ぞょ
STEP
LOOK, I KNOW YOU LIKE YOUR AUNT, BUT...
YOU CAN'T CHANGE WHO YOU ARE, SO WHY WORRY ABOUT IT?
ぎゅ...
GRAB
ふう
SIGH

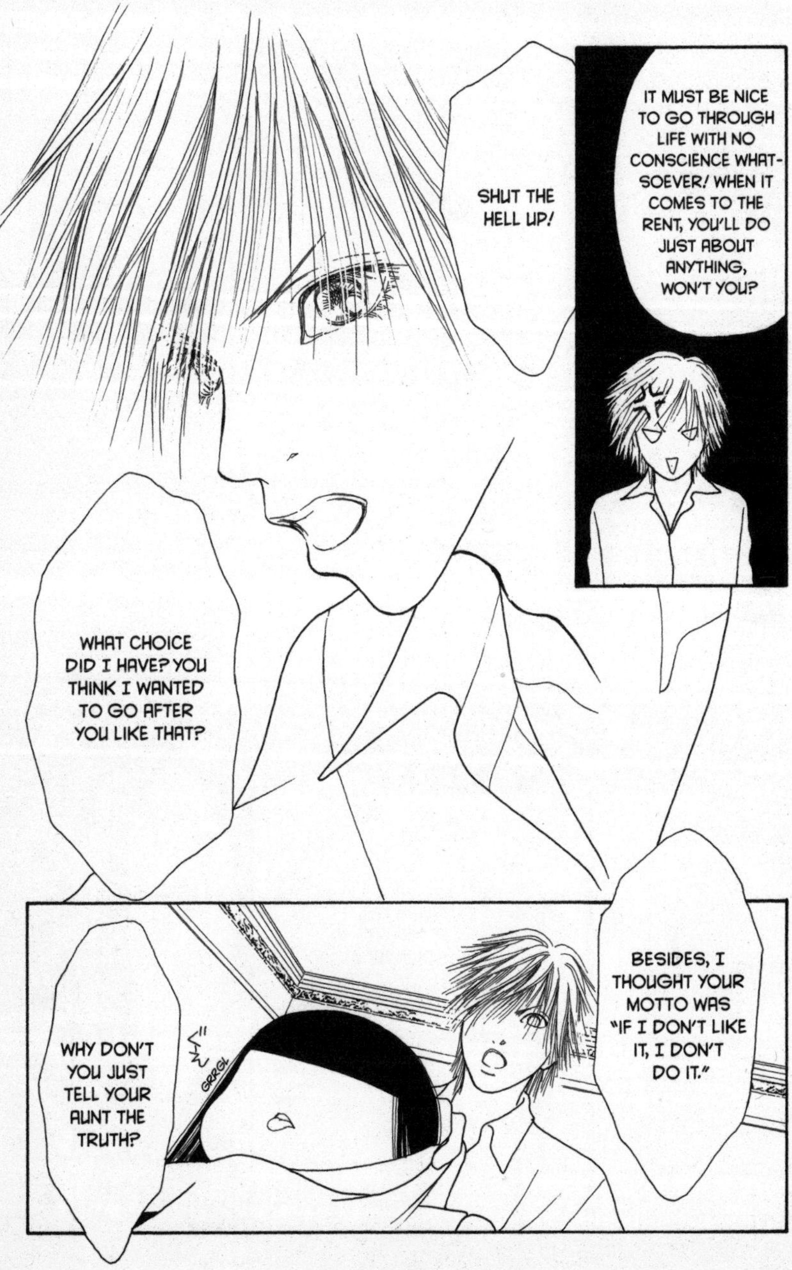
IT MUST BE NICE TO GO THROUGH LIFE WITH NO CONSCIENCE WHAT-SOEVER! WHEN IT COMES TO THE RENT, YOU'LL DO JUST ABOUT ANYTHING, WON'T YOU?
SHUT THE HELL UP!
WHAT CHOICE DID I HAVE? YOU THINK I WANTED TO GO AFTER YOU LIKE THAT?
BESIDES, I THOUGHT YOUR MOTTO WAS "IF I DON'T LIKE IT, I DON'T DO IT."
GRRGL
WHY DON'T YOU JUST TELL YOUR AUNT THE TRUTH?

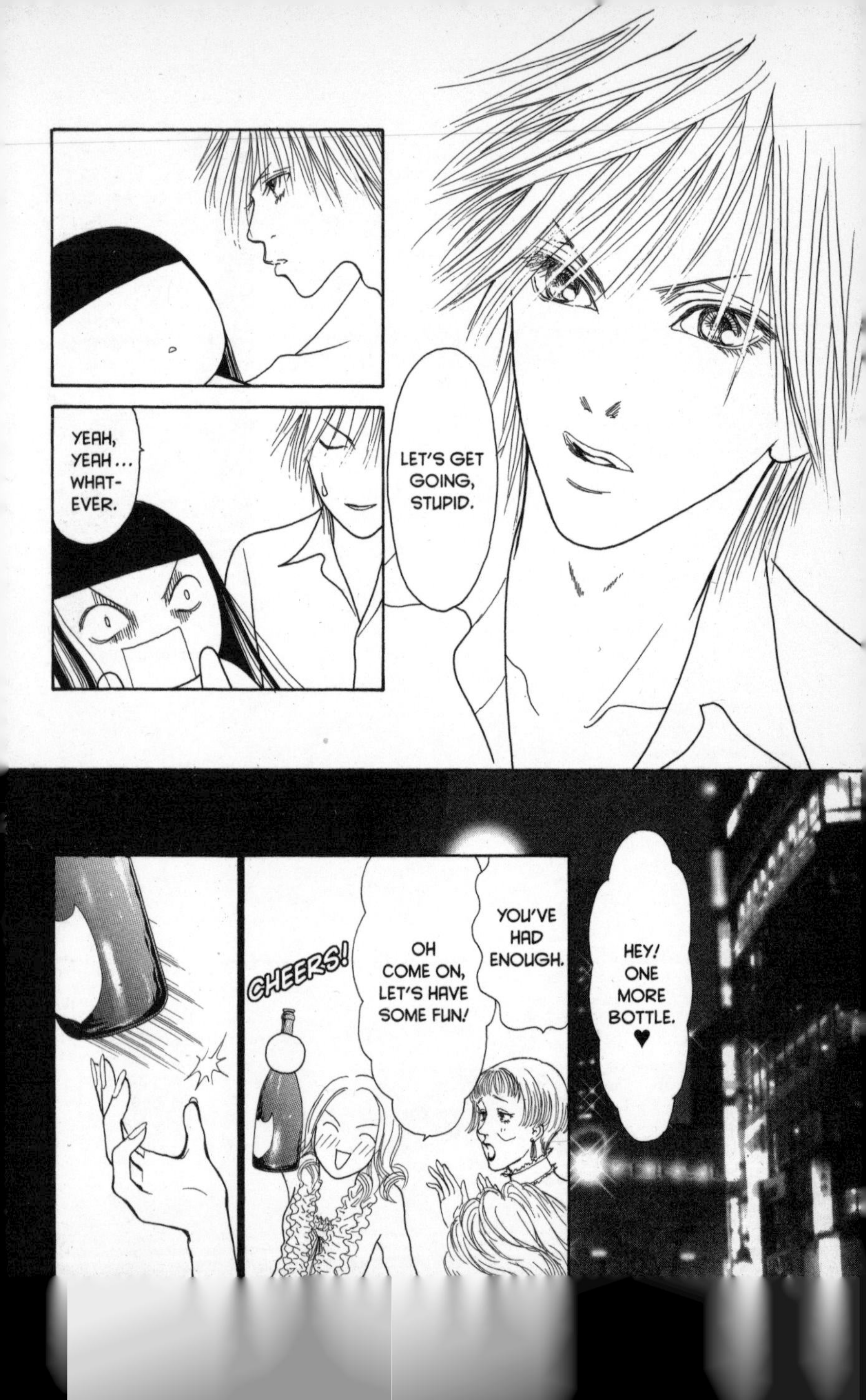
LET'S GET GOING, STUPID.
YEAH, YEAH... WHATEVER.
HEY! ONE MORE BOTTLE. ♥
YOU'VE HAD ENOUGH.
OH COME ON, LET'S HAVE SOME FUN!
CHEERS!

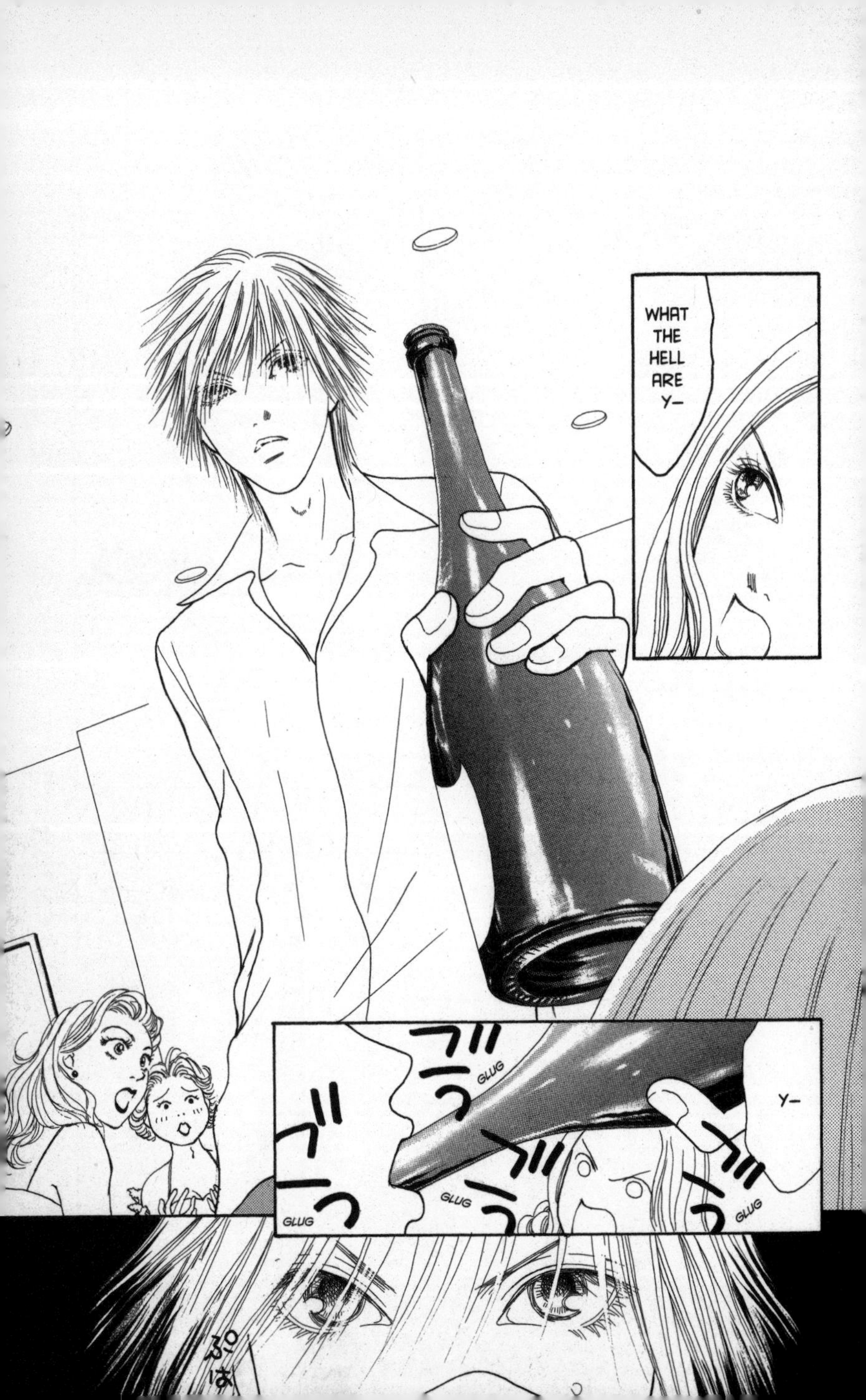
WHAT THE HELL ARE Y—
Y—
GLUG
GLUG
GLUG
GLUG

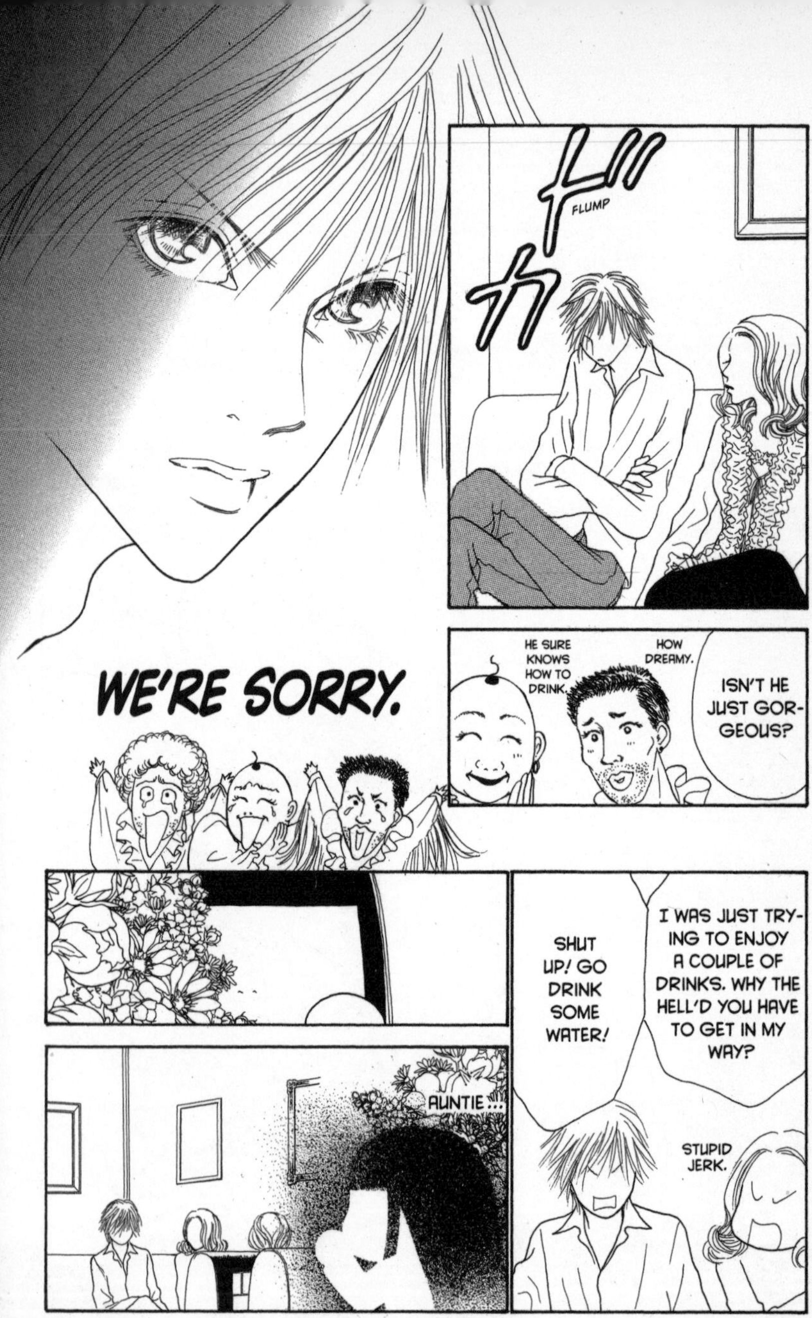
FLUMP
ISN'T HE JUST GORGEOUS?
HOW DREAMY.
HE SURE KNOWS HOW TO DRINK.
WE'RE SORRY.
I WAS JUST TRYING TO ENJOY A COUPLE OF DRINKS. WHY THE HELL'D YOU HAVE TO GET IN MY WAY?
SHUT UP! GO DRINK SOME WATER!
STUPID JERK.
AUNTIE...

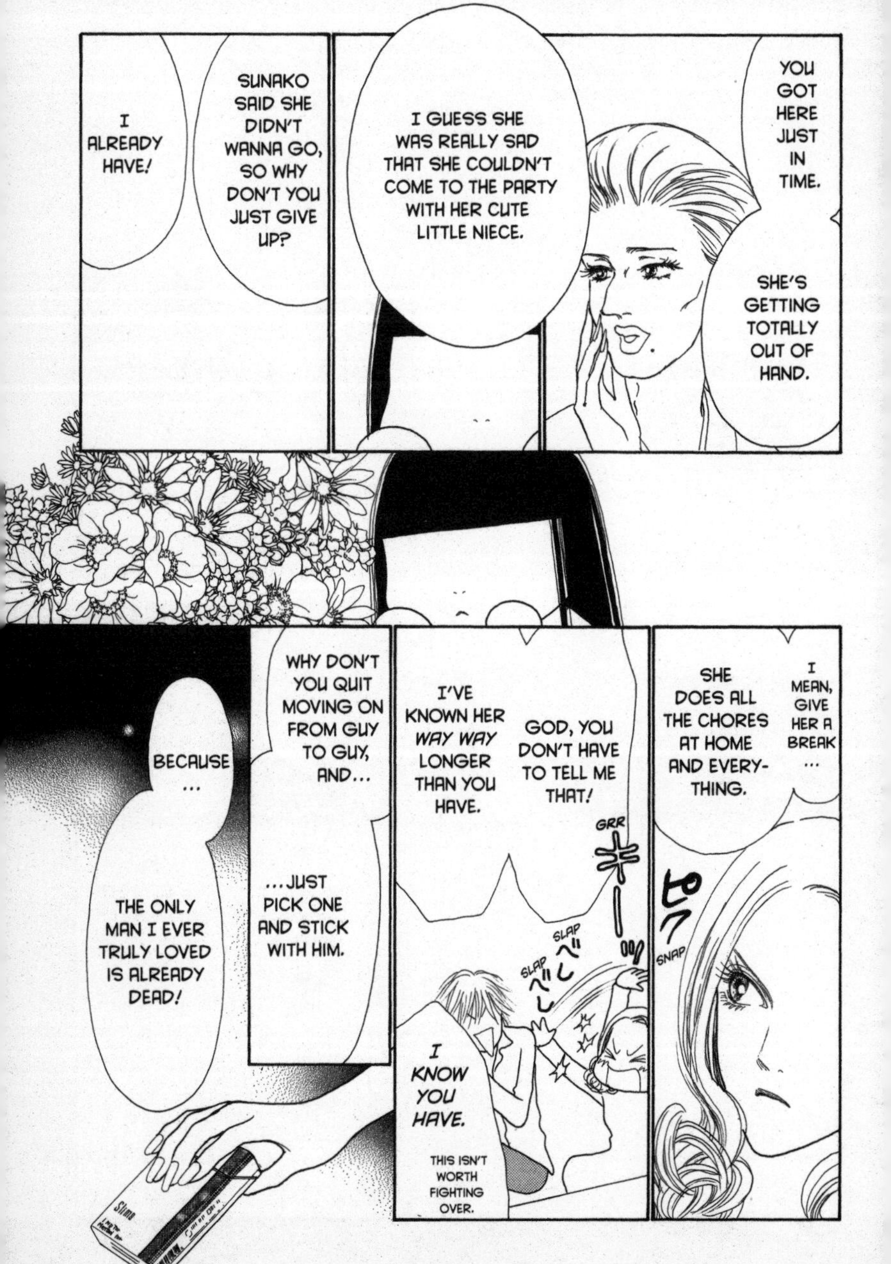

YOU GOT HERE JUST IN TIME.
SHE'S GETTING TOTALLY OUT OF HAND.
I GUESS SHE WAS REALLY SAD THAT SHE COULDN'T COME TO THE PARTY WITH HER CUTE LITTLE NIECE.
SUNAKO SAID SHE DIDN'T WANNA GO, SO WHY DON'T YOU JUST GIVE UP?
I ALREADY HAVE!
I MEAN, GIVE HER A BREAK...
SHE DOES ALL THE CHORES AT HOME AND EVERY-THING.
ピク SNAP
GOD, YOU DON'T HAVE TO TELL ME THAT!
I'VE KNOWN HER *WAY WAY* LONGER THAN YOU HAVE.
キー GRR
べし SLAP
べし SLAP
I KNOW YOU HAVE.
THIS ISN'T WORTH FIGHTING OVER.
WHY DON'T YOU QUIT MOVING ON FROM GUY TO GUY, AND...
...JUST PICK ONE AND STICK WITH HIM.
BECAUSE...
THE ONLY MAN I EVER TRULY LOVED IS ALREADY DEAD!

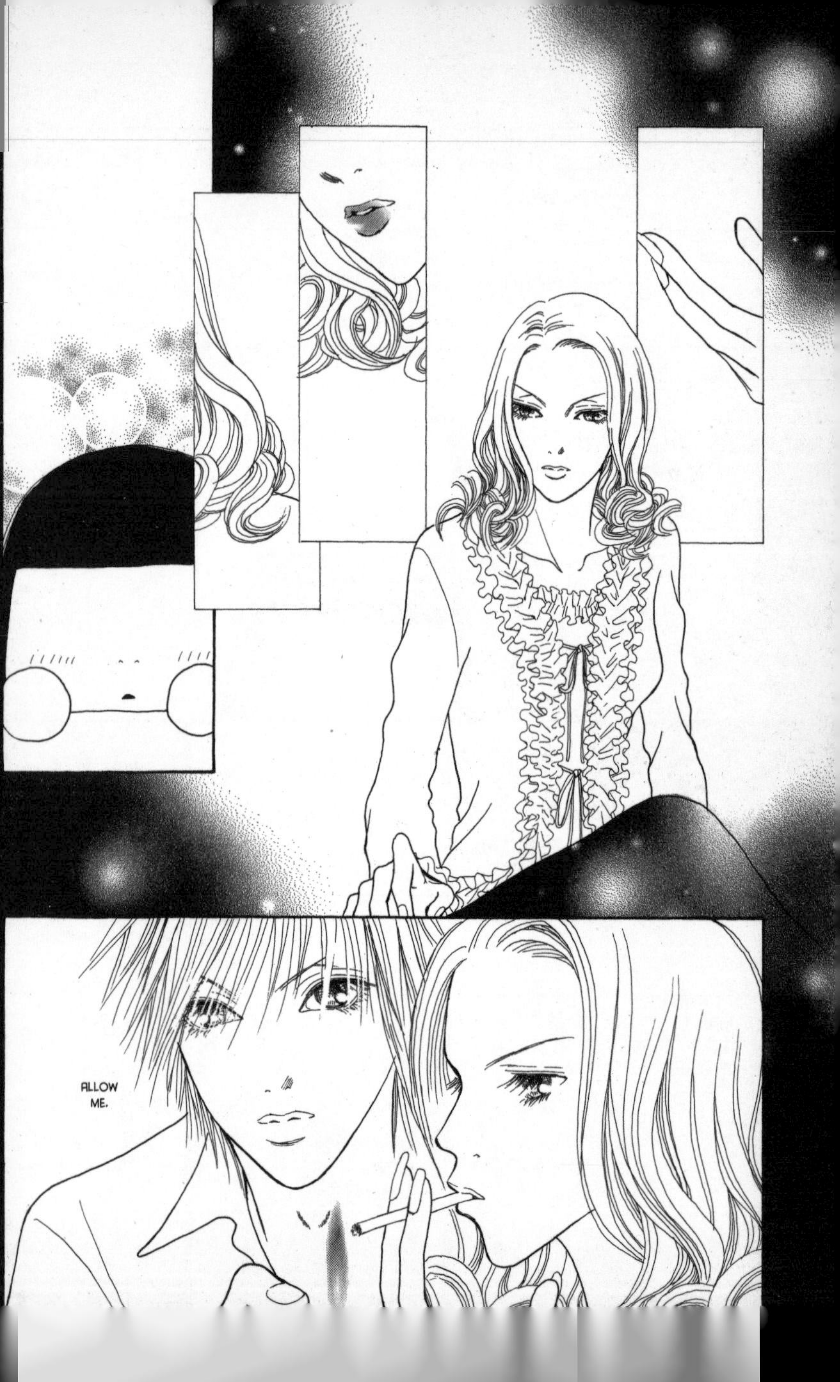
ALLOW ME.

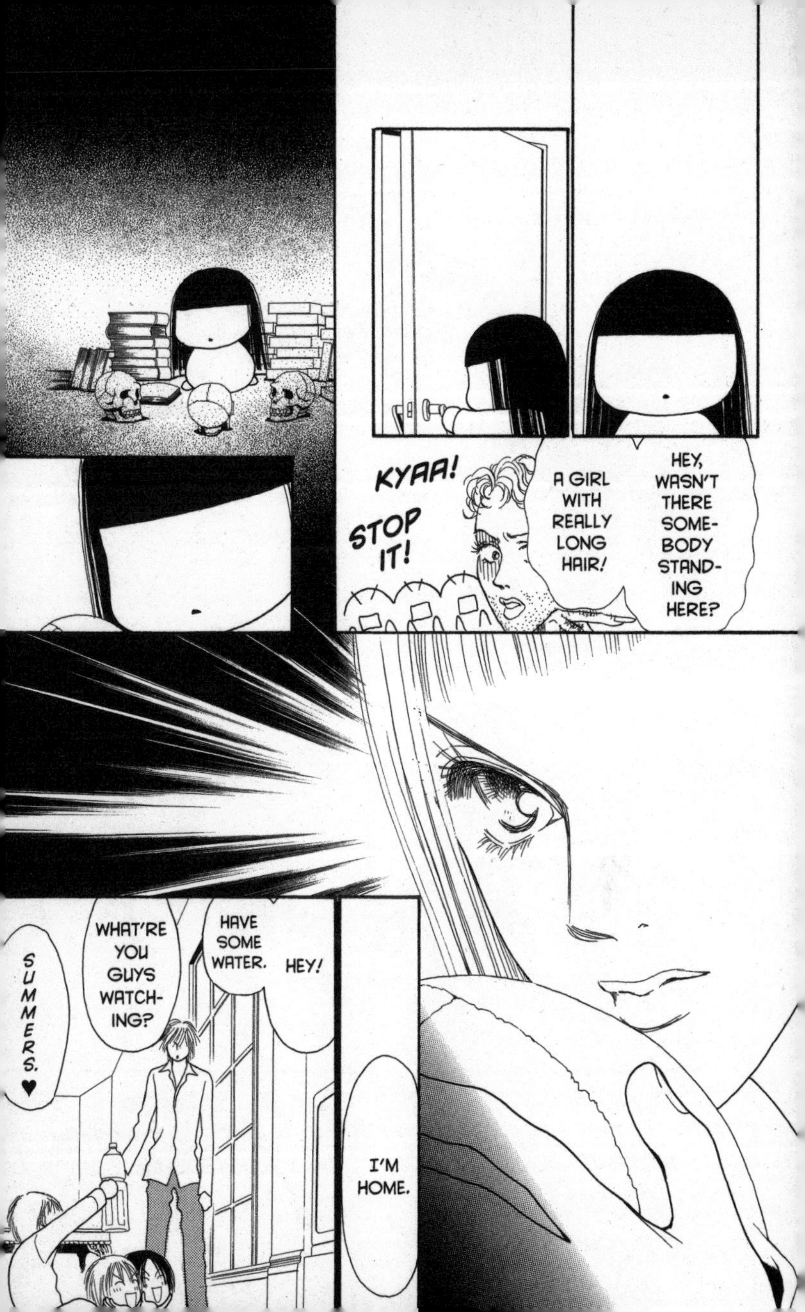

HEY, WASN'T THERE SOME-BODY STAND-ING HERE?
A GIRL WITH REALLY LONG HAIR!
KYAA!
STOP IT!
I'M HOME.
HEY!
HAVE SOME WATER.
WHAT'RE YOU GUYS WATCHING?
SUMMERS.♥

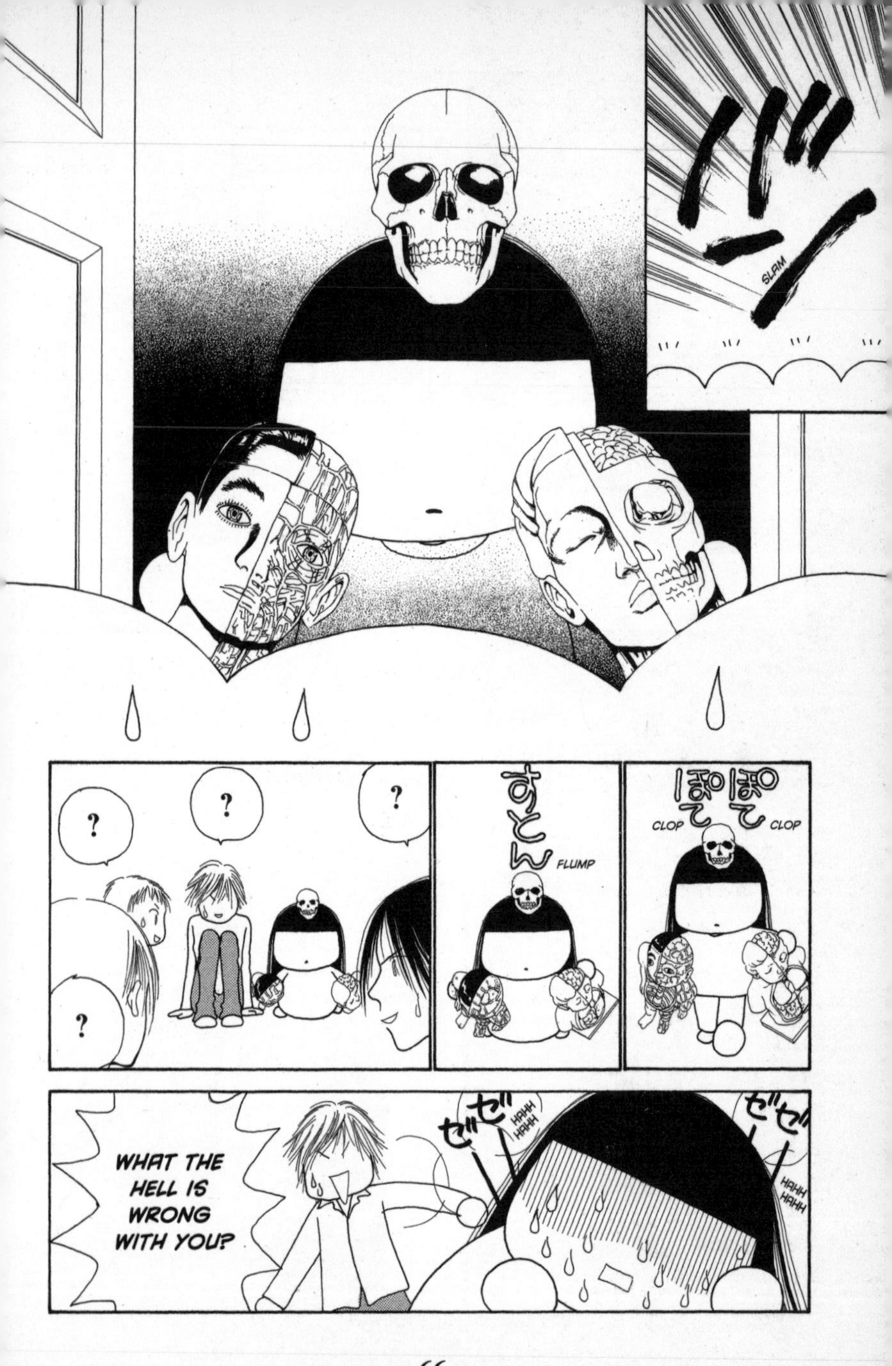
バン
SLAM
ぽてぽて
CLOP
CLOP
すとん
FLUMP
?
?
?
?
ぜぜ
HAHH HAHH
ぜぜ
HAHH HAHH
WHAT THE HELL IS WRONG WITH YOU?

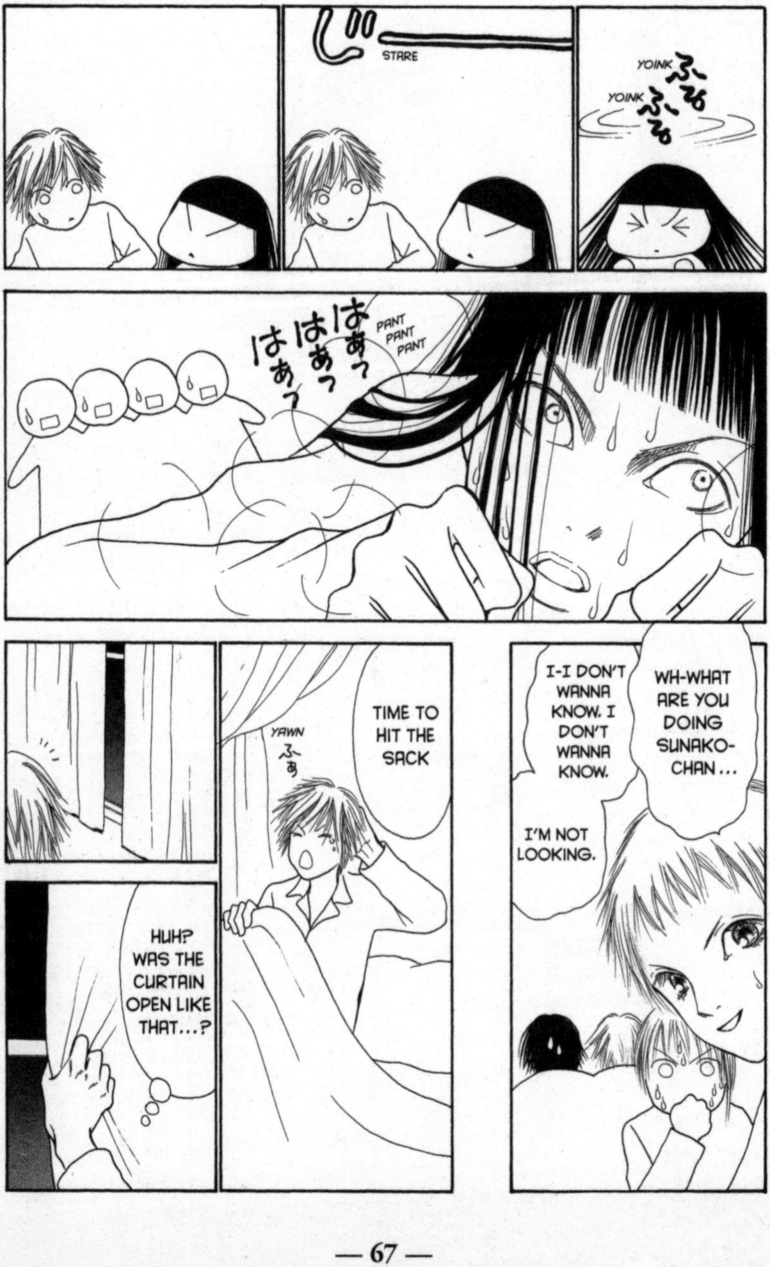
YOINK
YOINK
STARE
PANT PANT PANT
WH-WHAT ARE YOU DOING SUNAKO-CHAN...
I-I DON'T WANNA KNOW. I DON'T WANNA KNOW.
I'M NOT LOOKING.
YAWN
TIME TO HIT THE SACK
HUH? WAS THE CURTAIN OPEN LIKE THAT...?

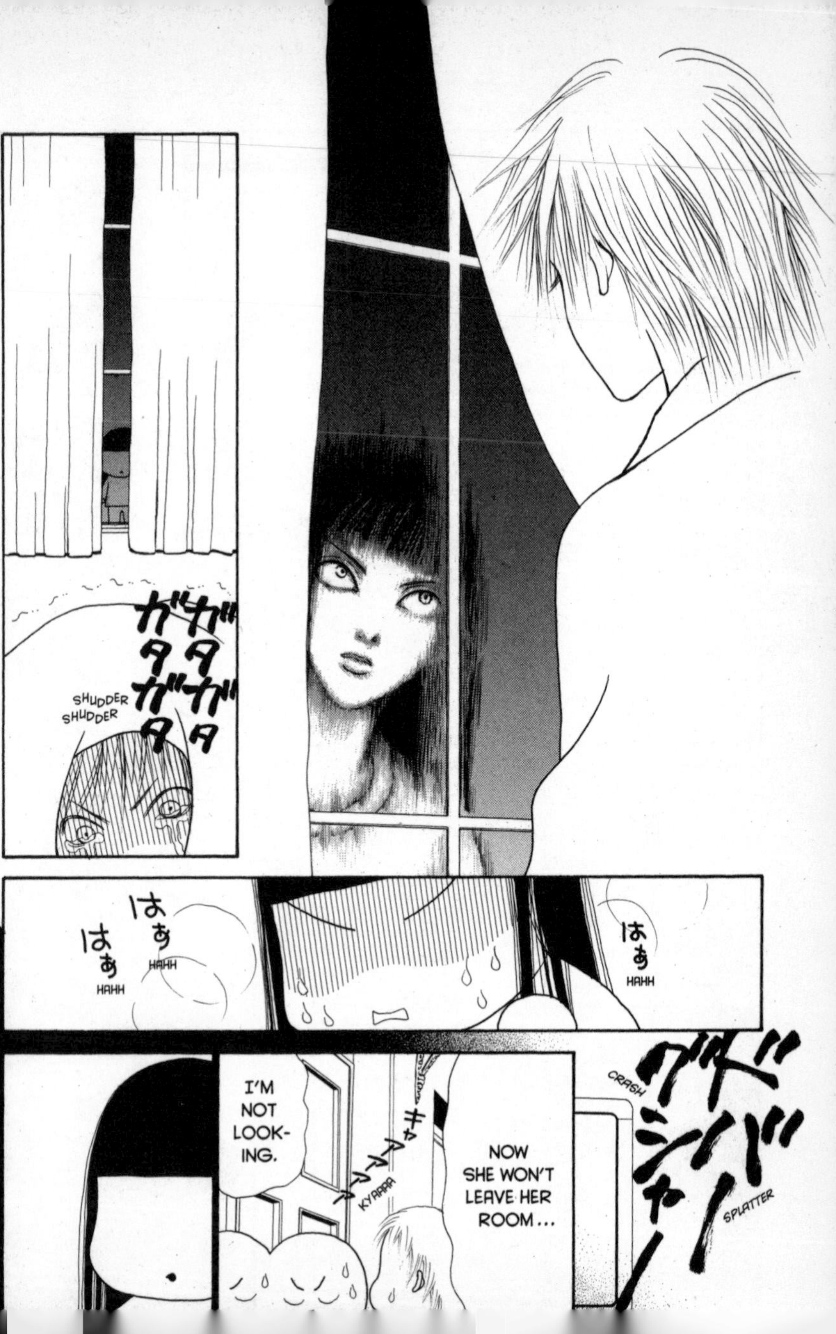
ガタガタ
ガタガタ
SHUDDER SHUDDER
はぁ
HAHH
はぁ
HAHH
はぁ
HAHH
CRASH
SPLATTER
NOW SHE WON'T LEAVE HER ROOM...
キャアアア
KYAAAA
I'M NOT LOOK-ING.

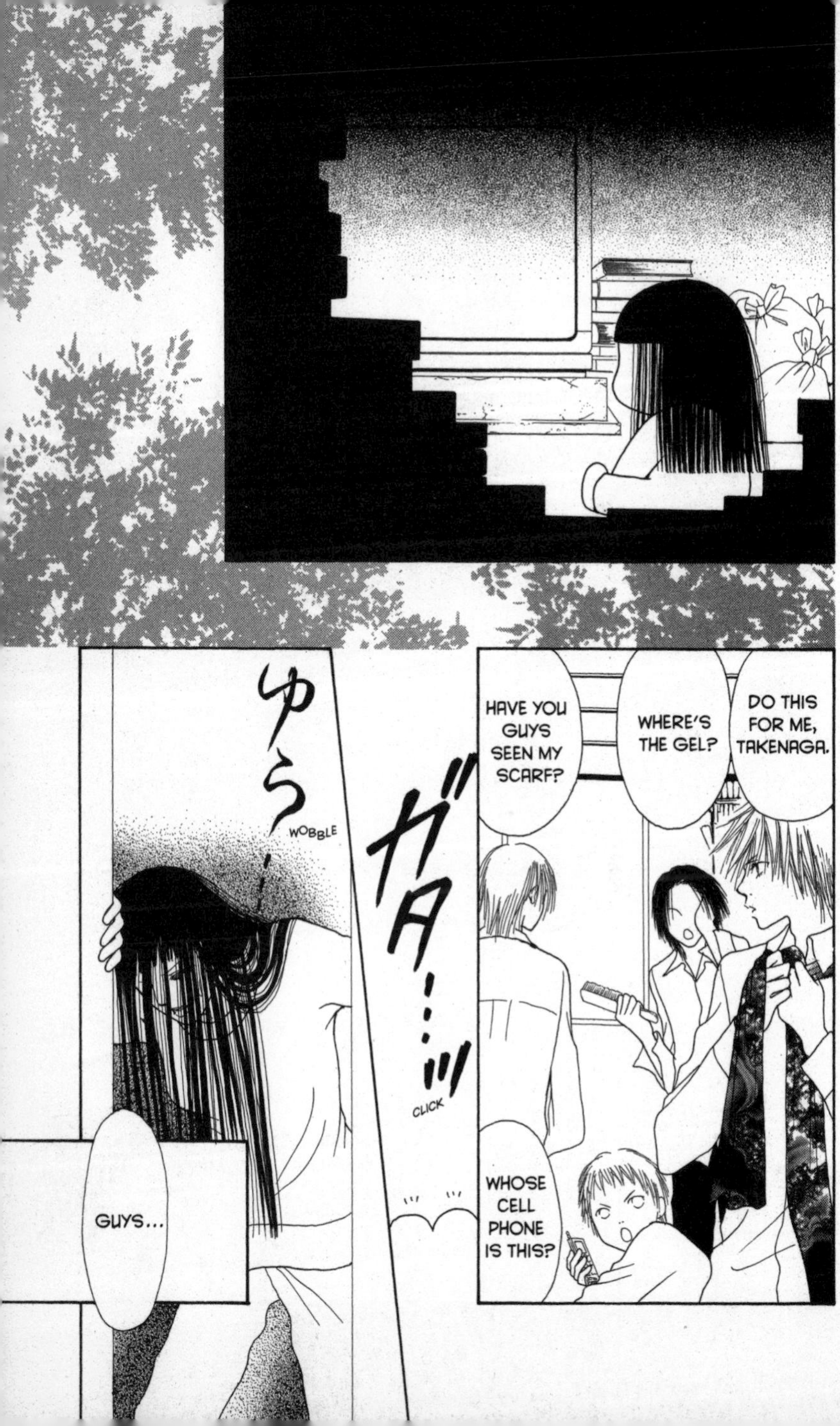

DO THIS FOR ME, TAKENAGA.
WHERE'S THE GEL?
HAVE YOU GUYS SEEN MY SCARF?
WHOSE CELL PHONE IS THIS?
ガタ…ッ
CLICK
ゆら
WOBBLE
GUYS...

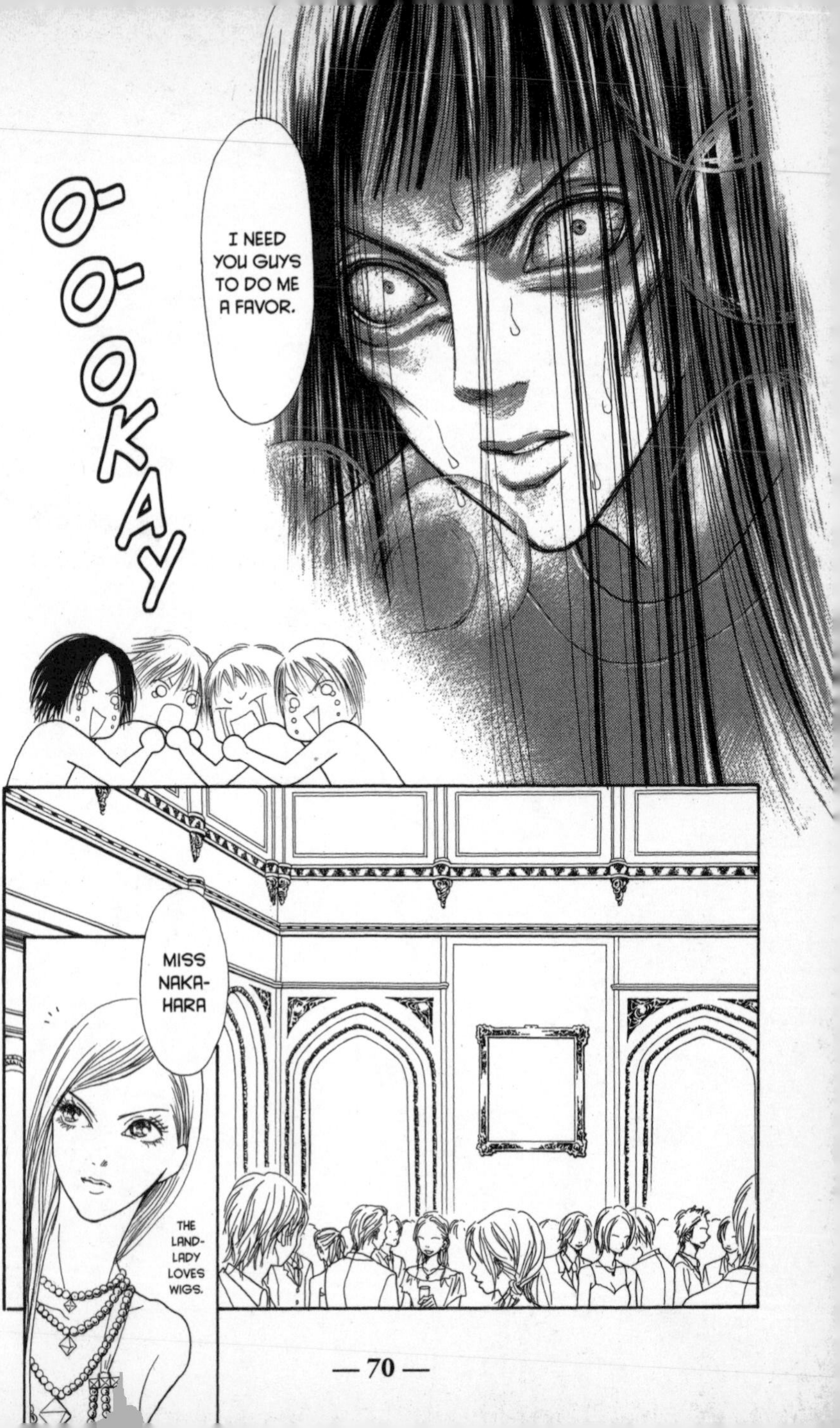
I NEED YOU GUYS TO DO ME A FAVOR.
O-O-OKAY
MISS NAKA-HARA
THE LAND-LADY LOVES WIGS.

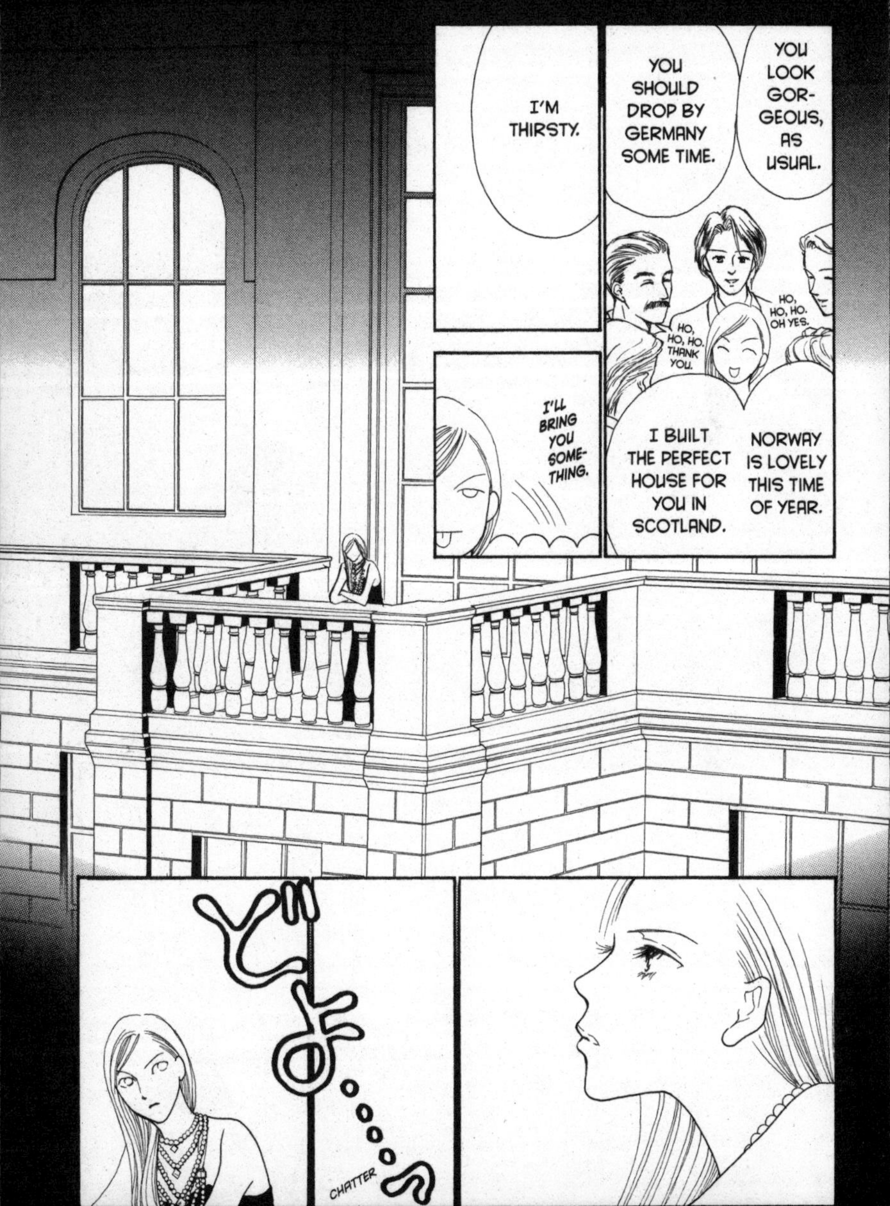
YOU LOOK GORGEOUS, AS USUAL.
YOU SHOULD DROP BY GERMANY SOME TIME.
HO, HO, HO. OH YES.
HO, HO, HO. THANK YOU.
NORWAY IS LOVELY THIS TIME OF YEAR.
I BUILT THE PERFECT HOUSE FOR YOU IN SCOTLAND.
I'M THIRSTY.
I'LL BRING YOU SOMETHING.
CHATTER

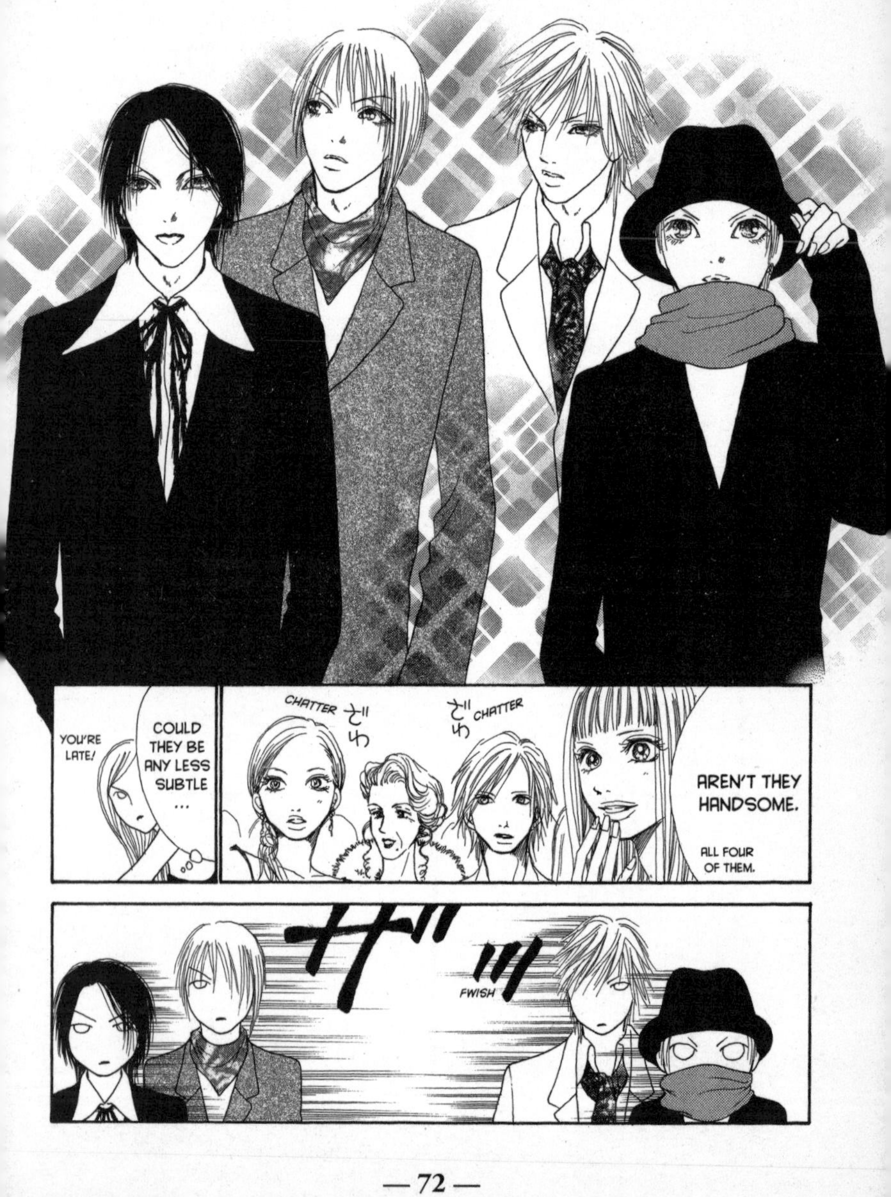
ざわ CHATTER
CHATTER ざわ
AREN'T THEY HANDSOME.
ALL FOUR OF THEM.
COULD THEY BE ANY LESS SUBTLE ...
YOU'RE LATE!
ザザッ
FWISH

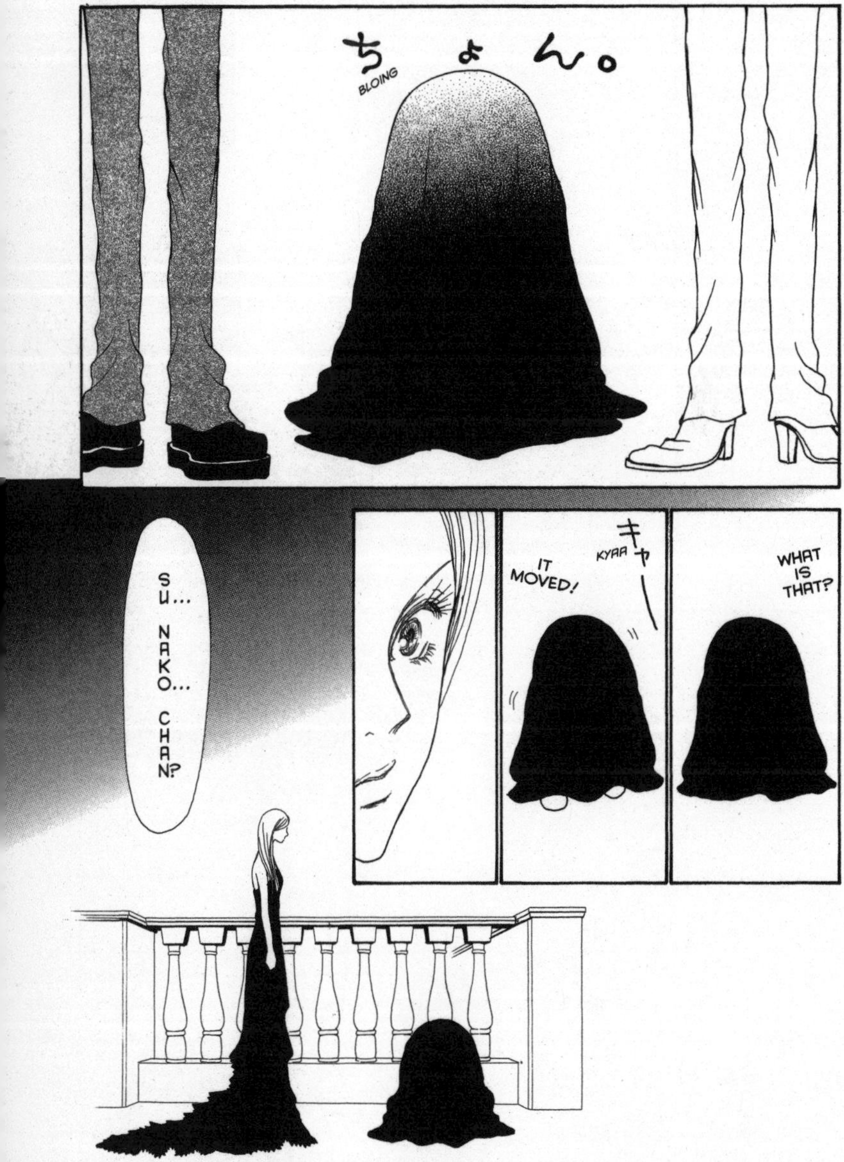
ちょん。
BLOING
WHAT IS THAT?
キャー
KYAA
IT MOVED!
SU... NAKO... CHAN?

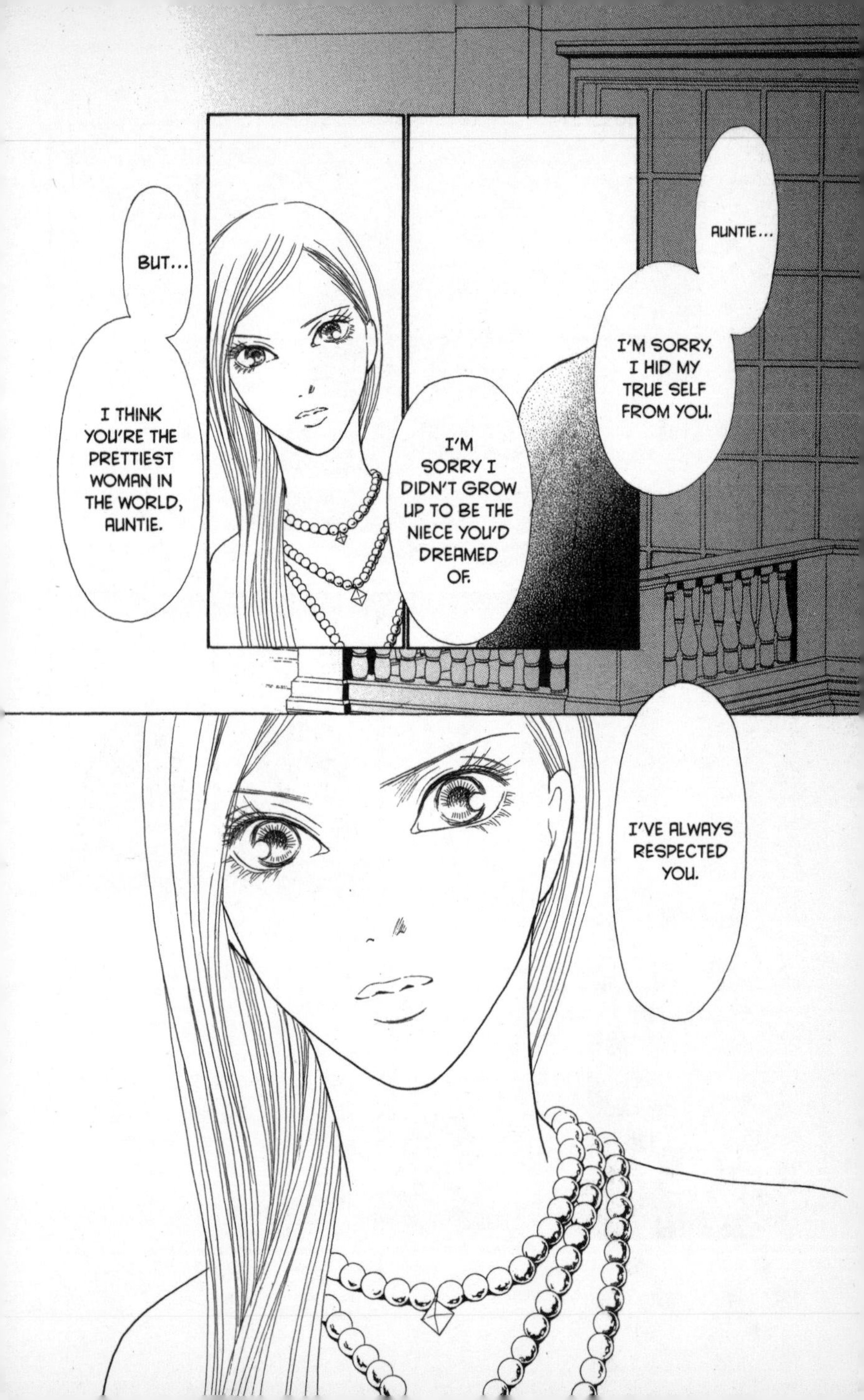
AUNTIE...
I'M SORRY, I HID MY TRUE SELF FROM YOU.
I'M SORRY I DIDN'T GROW UP TO BE THE NIECE YOU'D DREAMED OF.
BUT...
I THINK YOU'RE THE PRETTIEST WOMAN IN THE WORLD, AUNTIE.
I'VE ALWAYS RESPECTED YOU.

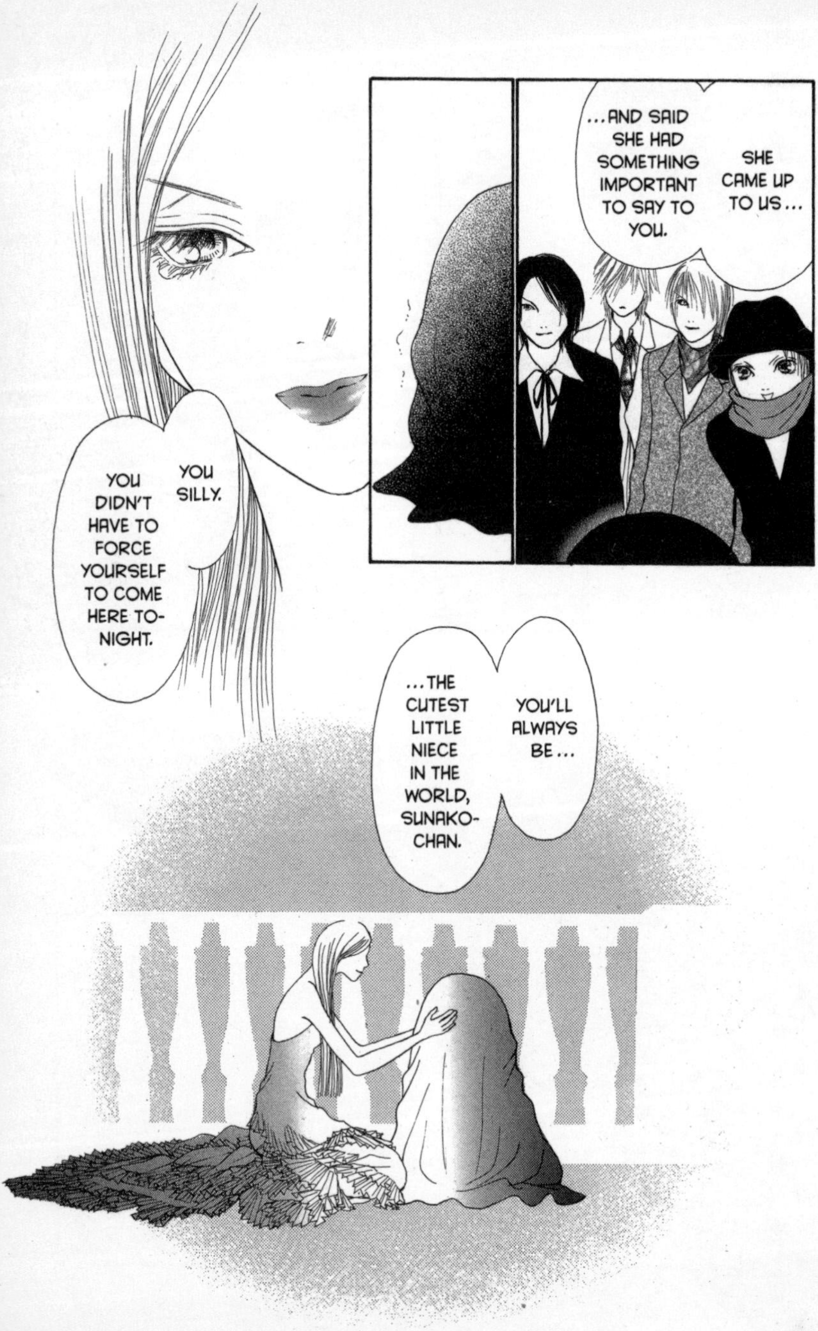
SHE CAME UP TO US...
...AND SAID SHE HAD SOMETHING IMPORTANT TO SAY TO YOU.
YOU SILLY.
YOU DIDN'T HAVE TO FORCE YOURSELF TO COME HERE TO-NIGHT.
YOU'LL ALWAYS BE...
...THE CUTEST LITTLE NIECE IN THE WORLD, SUNAKO-CHAN.

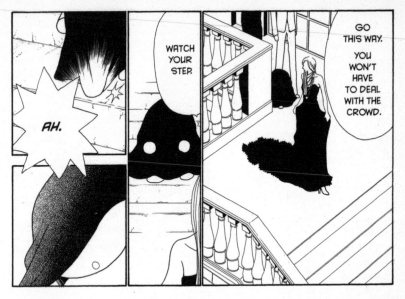

GO THIS WAY.
YOU WON'T HAVE TO DEAL WITH THE CROWD.
WATCH YOUR STEP.
AH.
はら…
FWUP

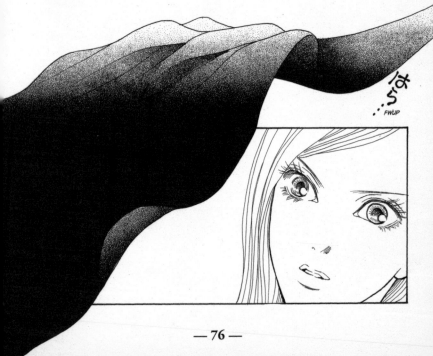

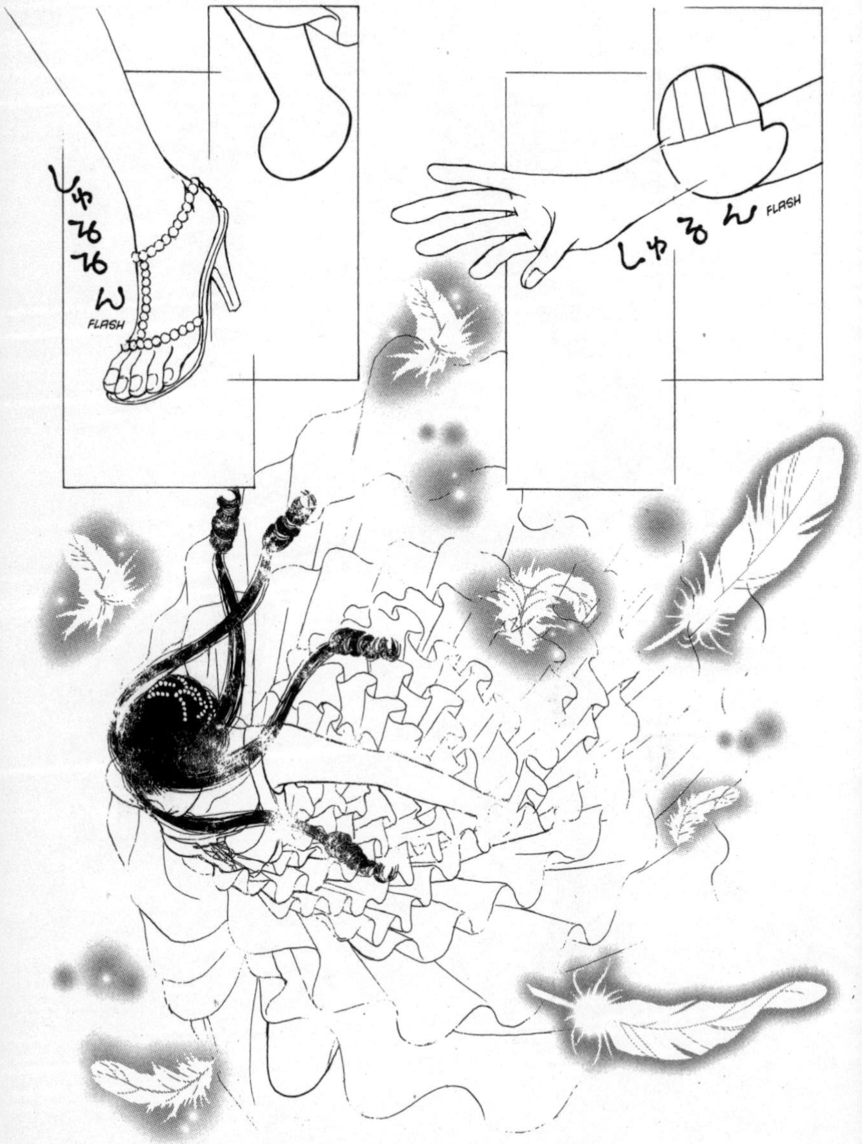
しゅるん
FLASH
しゅるるん
FLASH

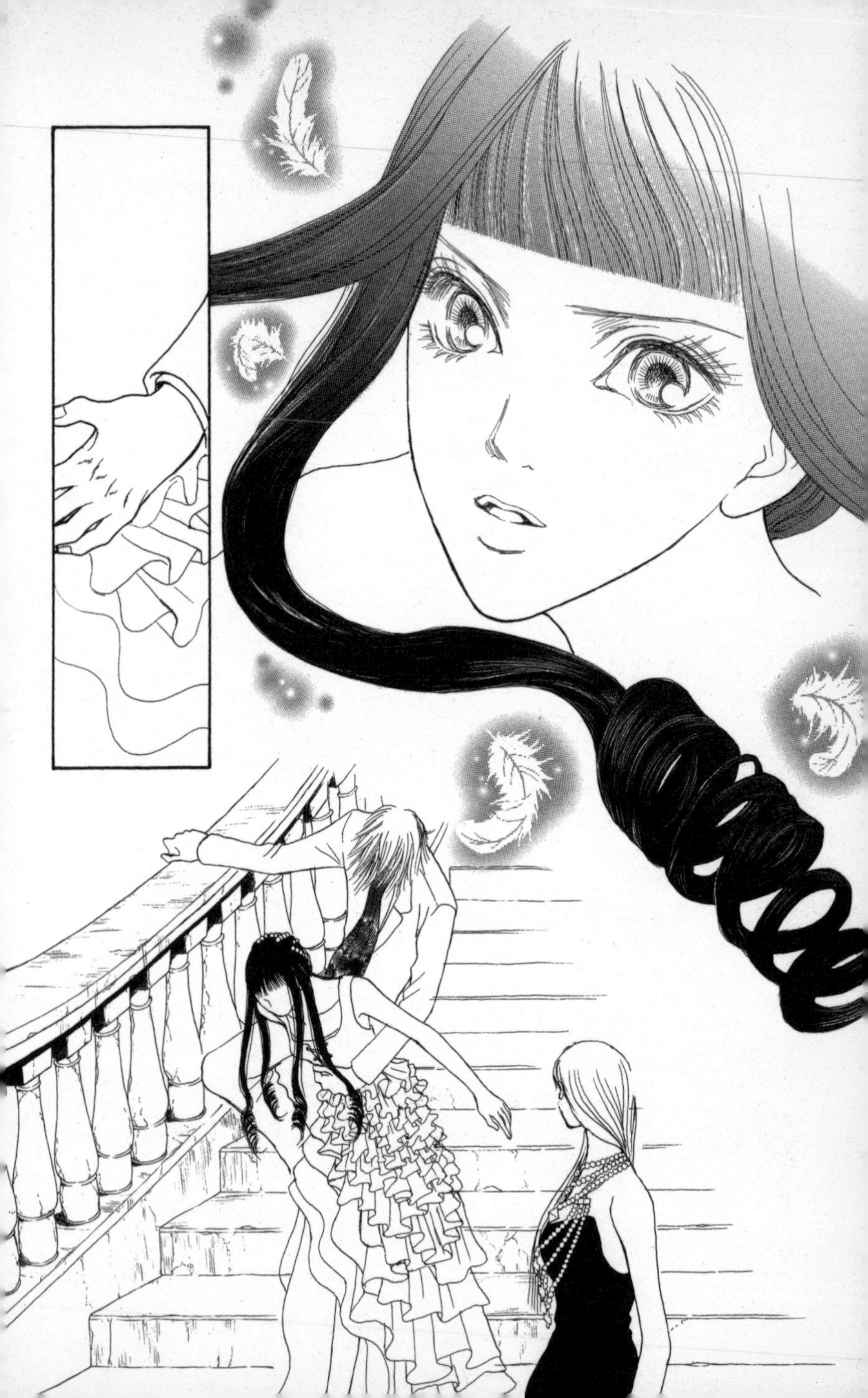

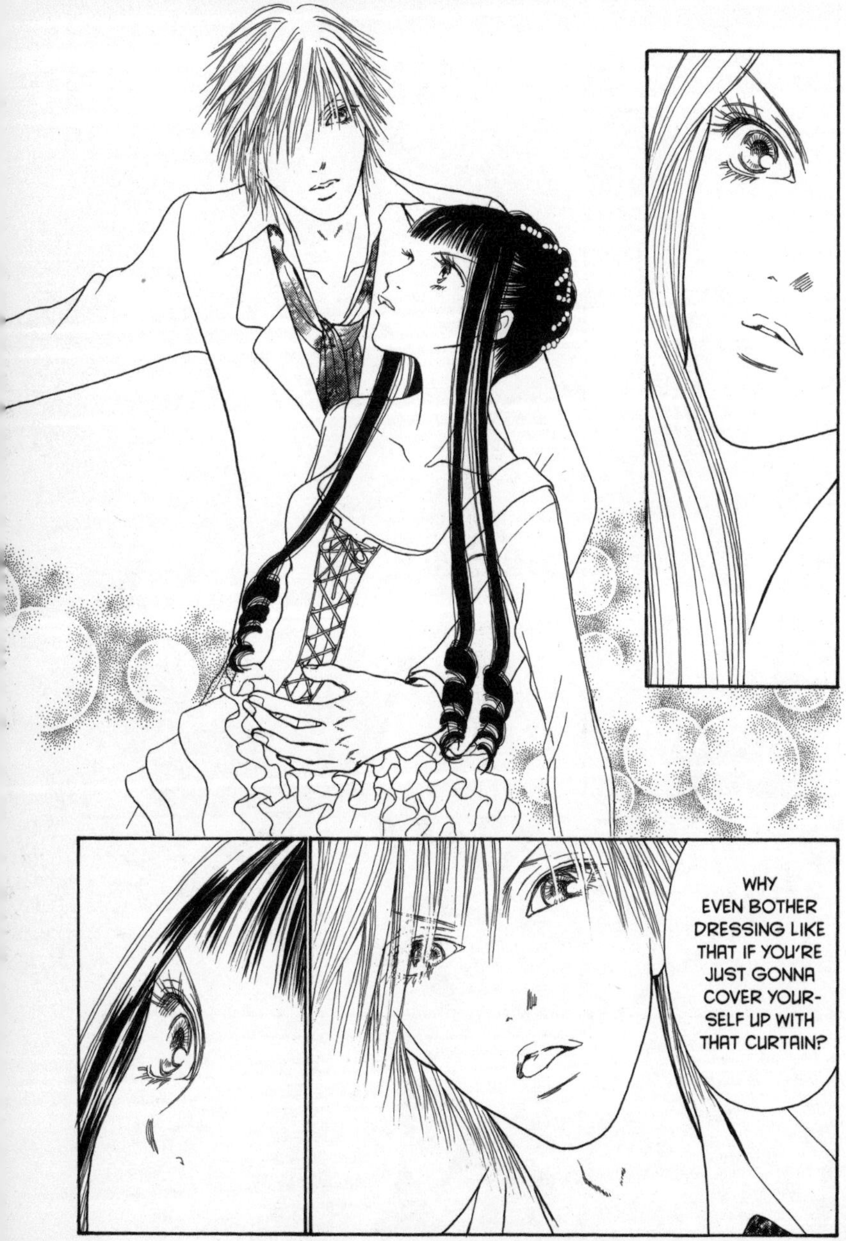
WHY EVEN BOTHER DRESSING LIKE THAT IF YOU'RE JUST GONNA COVER YOURSELF UP WITH THAT CURTAIN?

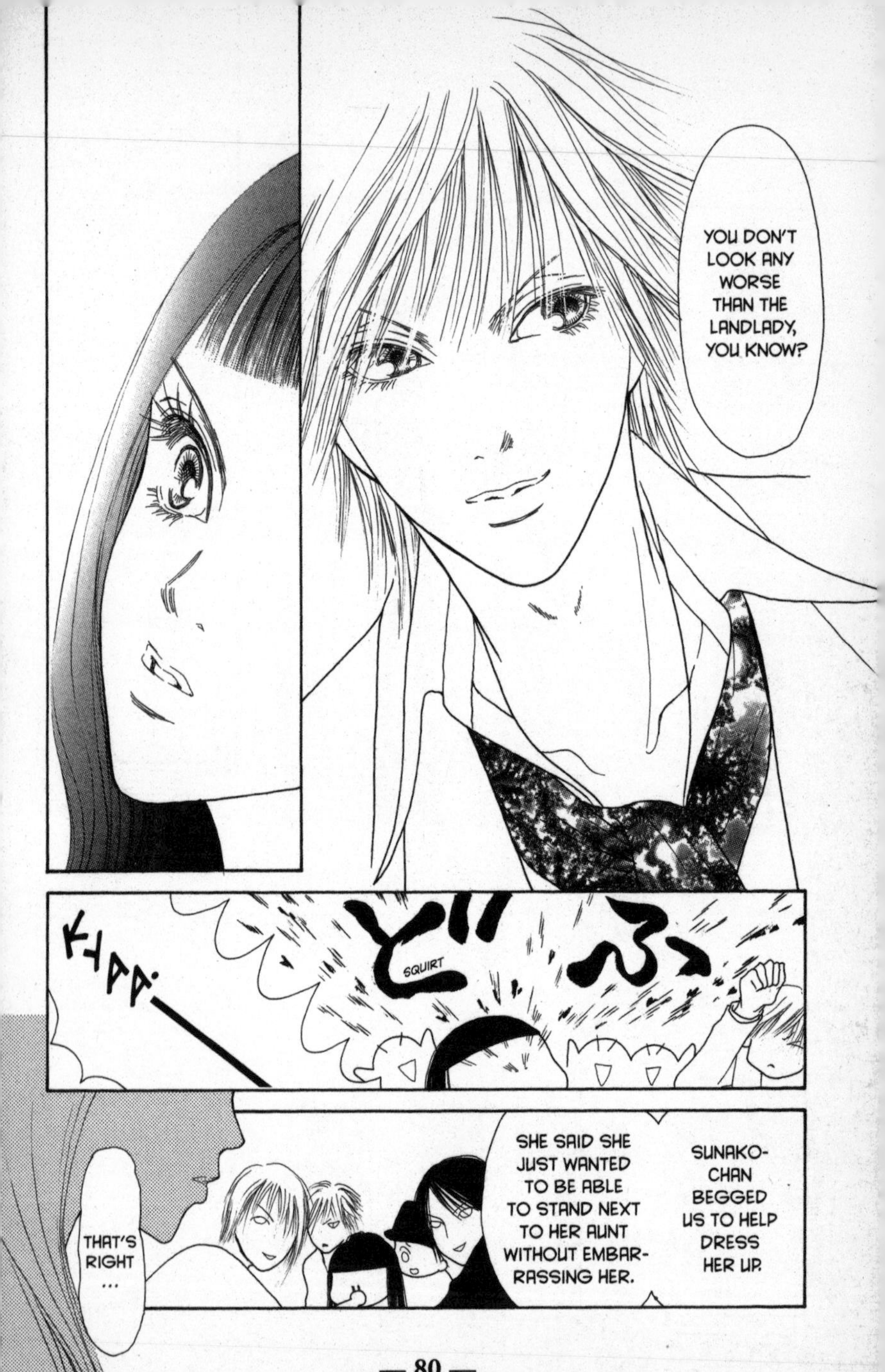
YOU DON'T LOOK ANY WORSE THAN THE LANDLADY, YOU KNOW?
SQUIRT
SUNAKO-CHAN BEGGED US TO HELP DRESS HER UP.
SHE SAID SHE JUST WANTED TO BE ABLE TO STAND NEXT TO HER AUNT WITHOUT EMBARRASSING HER.
THAT'S RIGHT ...

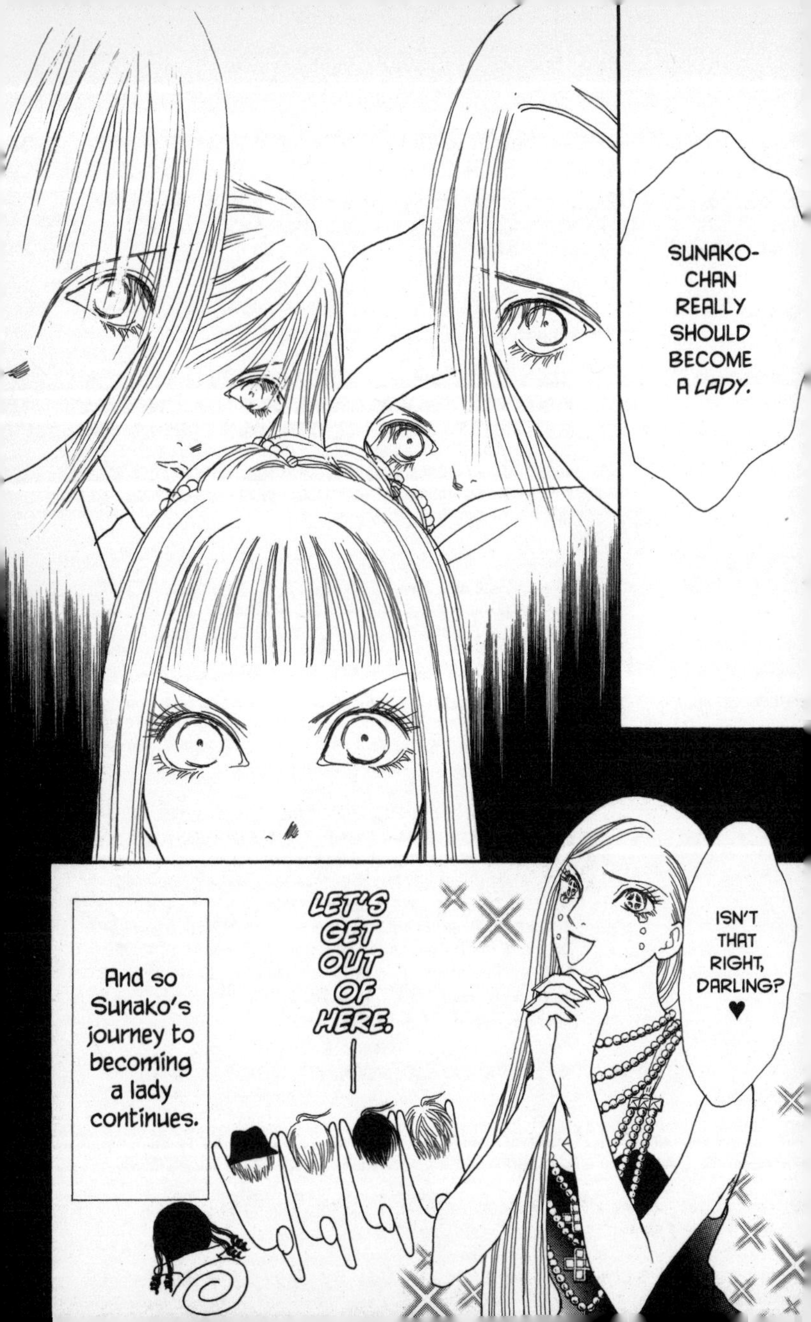
SUNAKO-CHAN REALLY SHOULD BECOME A *LADY*.
ISN'T THAT RIGHT, DARLING? ♥
LET'S GET OUT OF HERE.
And so Sunako's journey to becoming a lady continues.

HELLO, EVERYBODY. I'M TOMOKO HAYAKAWA.

HERE'S A LIST OF MY RECENT ACTIVITIES. IT'S ALL ABOUT CONCERTS, SO PLEASE FEEL FREE TO SKIP IT IF YOU'RE NOT INTERESTED. ACTUALLY, I HAVEN'T BEEN TO MANY CONCERTS LATELY ... I'M SURPRISED MYSELF.

SMAP
SEE CHAPTER 38. I HAD SO MUCH FUN. I'D LOVE TO GO AGAIN SOMETIME WITH AI-CHAN-SENSEI. ♥

BAROQUE
THEY HAD A CONCERT AT THE BUDOUKAN. ♥ WOW, THEY'VE REALLY MADE IT BIG! AS ALWAYS, BANSAKU-KUN (BASS) WAS TOO COOL! ♥ DURING THE INTERMISSION, I WAS TALKING TO REI-KUN'S (VOCALS) FRIEND, AND SHE WAS LIKE "I SAW YOU GIVE A PRESENT TO BANSAKU-KUN, GOOD FOR YOU. ♥" I GUESS SHE WAS WATCHING ME. I WAS SO EMBARRASSED... SHE SAID SHE READS MY MANGA ...

ZEN'S DEAD STOCK TOY
MY FRIEND YUKI-KUN (DRUMS) JOINED THIS BAND AS A BACK UP MEMBER, SO I WENT TO SEE THEM. ZEN-KUN (VOCALS) STARTED THIS BAND AFTER VANILLA BROKE UP. I HAD SO MUCH FUN. I HOPE THEY KEEP PLAYING TOGETHER. ♥

MICHIRU-KUN EVENT
I WENT TO SEE THIS EVENT BECAUSE TORU-SAN'S (MOI DIX MOIS, KIREEK) BAND AND HITOKI-KUN (EX KUROYUME ♥♥♥) WAS CO-HEADLINING, AND ALSO YUKI-KUN HAPPENED TO BE WORKING THE EVENT. I HAD LOTS OF FUN. ♥ THANKS, TORU-SAN, MICHIRU-KUN, AND YUKI-KUN.

MIYAVI
WOW, MASA-KUN IS SUCH A HOTTIE. HE'S TALL, AND HE'S CUTE EVEN WITHOUT MAKEUP. I GOT A LITTLE NERVOUS WHEN HE SHOOK MY HAND WITH HIS BIG HAND. I GOT TO SPEAK WITH PATA-SAN (EX X JAPAN) AND SHINYA-KUN (EX LUNA SEA) AT THE CONCERT. ♥ I WAS SO HAPPY, ALTHOUGH I WAS A LITTLE NERVOUS. ♥ SHINYA-KUN LOOKED EXACTLY LIKE HE DOES ON TV. ♥ PATA-SAN WAS SUCH A NICE PERSON. LOVE ♥ I SPOTTED DAIGO-KUN (DAIGO STARDUST) THERE TOO. HE WAS SO HOT THAT I COULDN'T STOP STARING AT HIM ... FROM A DISTANCE, OF COURSE.

HUH? IS THAT IT? NO WAY...WELL, I DID GO SEE SHOCKING LEMON AND GENTLE AS USUAL, BUT...

I GUESS I DIDN'T GO OUT MUCH BECAUSE I DIDN'T WANT TO LEAVE MY LOVELY KITTY ALONE IN THE HOUSE. (SEE BONUS PAGES.) I WAS REALLY BUSY WITH WORK TOO.

ACTUALLY, TOMORROW ♥♥♥ I'M GOING TO SEE *KIYOHARU-SAMA* AT *SHIBUYA KOUKAIDO* ♥♥♥ I'M SO EXCITED. ♥ KYAA. KYAA. KYAA.

I HOPE BAROQUE'S CONCERT SCHEDULE COMES OUT BY THE TIME THIS BOOK GOES ON SALE.

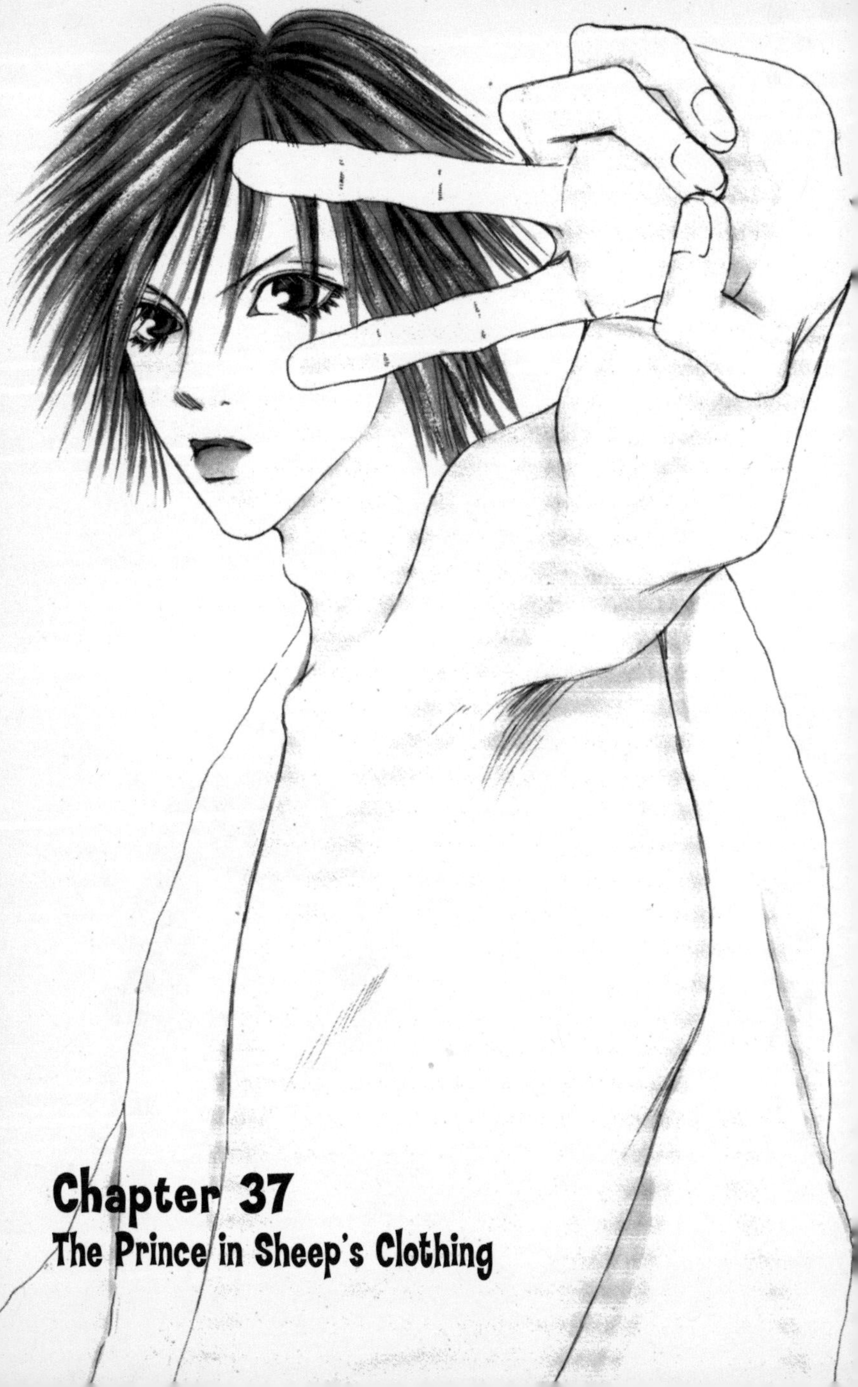

Chapter 37
The Prince in Sheep's Clothing

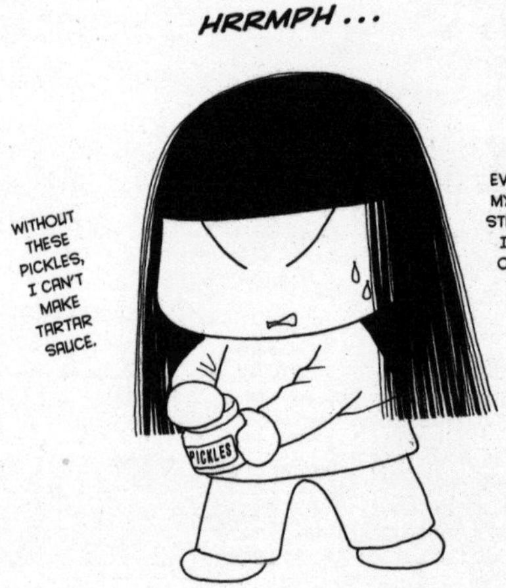
HRRMPH ...
EVEN WITH MY SUPER STRENGTH, I CAN'T OPEN IT.
WITHOUT THESE PICKLES, I CAN'T MAKE TARTAR SAUCE.
PICKLES

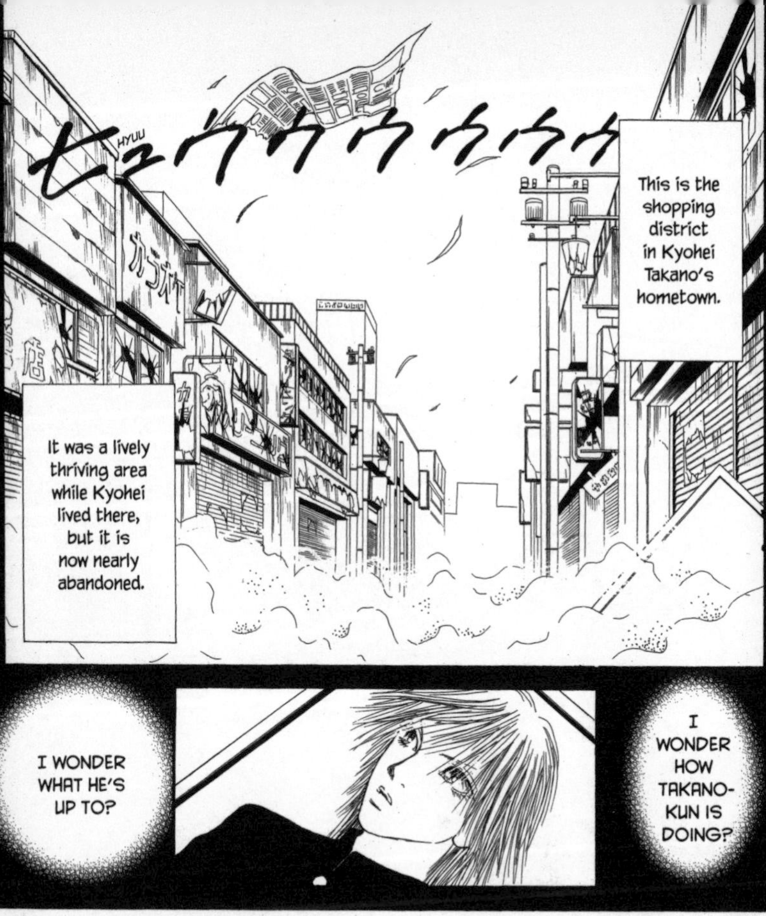
This is the shopping district in Kyohei Takano's hometown.
ヒュウウウウウウ
HYUU
It was a lively thriving area while Kyohei lived there, but it is now nearly abandoned.
I WONDER HOW TAKANO-KUN IS DOING?
I WONDER WHAT HE'S UP TO?

BEHIND THE SCENES

A FEW DAYS BEFORE MY DEADLINE, I WENT TO JUDGE A MODELING AUDITION FOR THE H.NAOTO CLOTHING LINE. I'M HORRIBLE AT TALKING IN FRONT OF PEOPLE (I JUST CAN'T DO IT). IT WAS A VERY LAID-BACK ENVIRONMENT, BUT I WAS STILL TOTALLY NERVOUS. HOW LAME.

THE MODELS WERE ALL SO CUTE. ♥ THEY WERE DEFINITELY THE MODELS OF THE FUTURE. ♥ AND THEY WERE ALL SO NICE. ♥♥♥ THEY WERE PROBABLY EVEN MORE NERVOUS THAN I WAS, BUT THEY REALLY HELPED CALM ME DOWN. THANKS. ♥ I WAS SO HAPPY TO GET TO TALK TO NAOTO-SAN (I'M A HUGE FAN. ♥). THANKS FOR EVERYTHING. AND THANKS TO THE STYLIST AND THE PHOTOGRAPHER. I ONLY GOT TO TALK TO THE GUESTS FOR A LITTLE BIT, BUT I WAS STILL REALLY HAPPY...

A WEEK BEFORE MY DEADLINE, I WENT TO MY FRIEND'S WEDDING. IT WAS SO FUN. ♥ CONGRATULATIONS, HEE-SAN. ♥ GOOD LUCK WITH YOUR NEW BRIDE. ♥

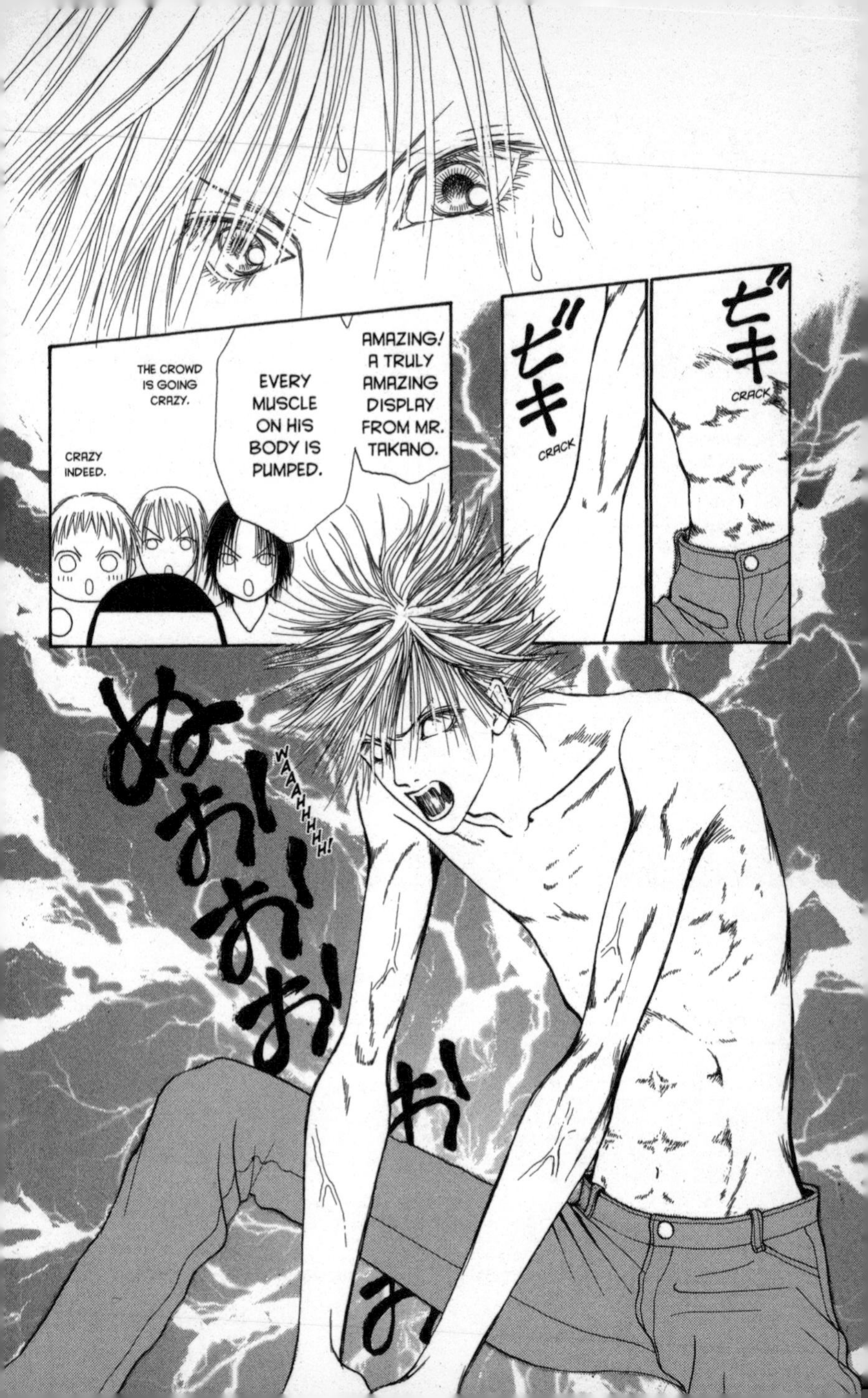
ビキ
CRACK
ビキ
CRACK
AMAZING! A TRULY AMAZING DISPLAY FROM MR. TAKANO.
EVERY MUSCLE ON HIS BODY IS PUMPED.
THE CROWD IS GOING CRAZY.
CRAZY INDEED.
ぬおおおおお
WAAAHHHHH!

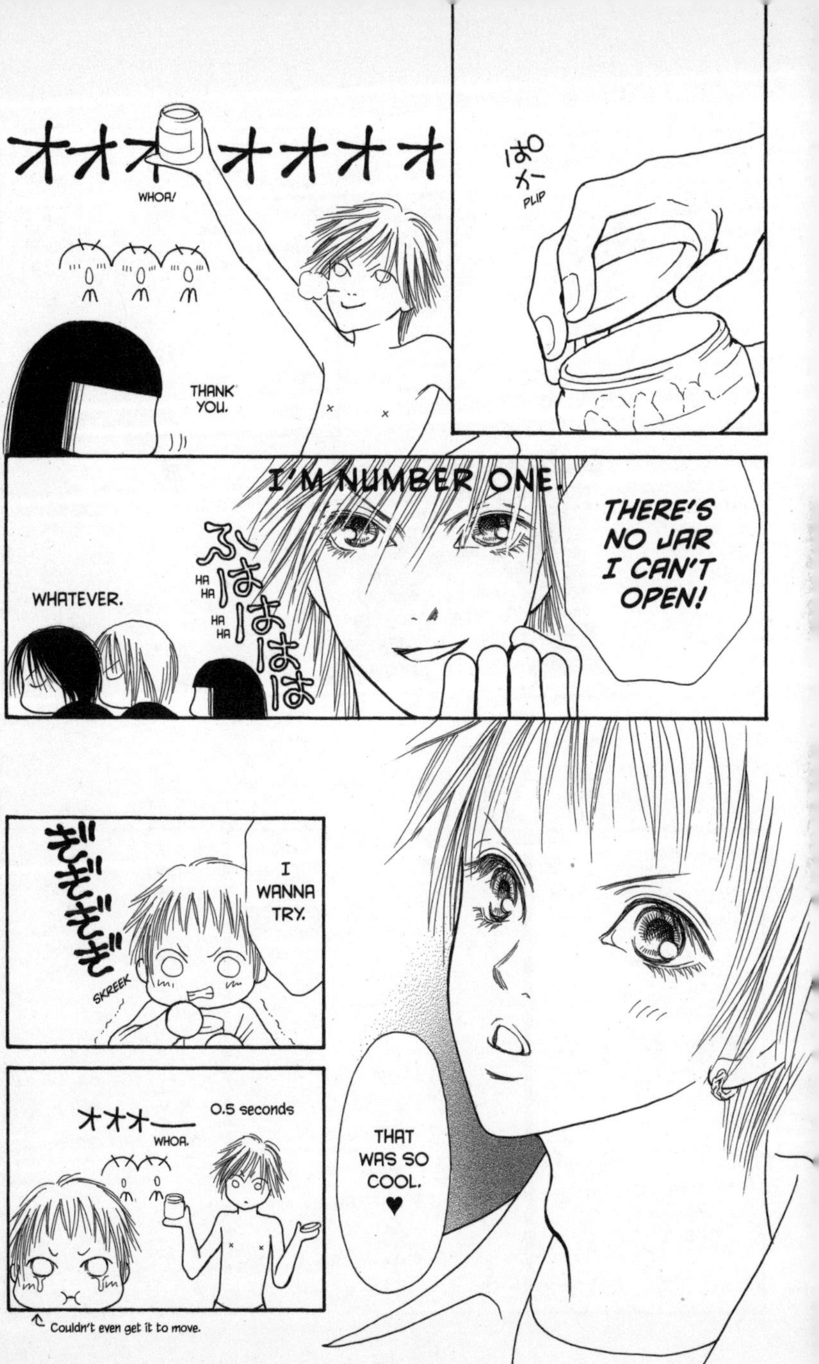
ぱか
PLIP
オオオオオオオ
WHOA!
THANK YOU.
I'M NUMBER ONE.
THERE'S NO JAR I CAN'T OPEN!
ふはははは
HA HA HA HA
WHATEVER.
THAT WAS SO COOL. ♥
ぎぎぎぎ
SKREEK
I WANNA TRY.
オオオー
WHOA.
0.5 seconds
Couldn't even get it to move.

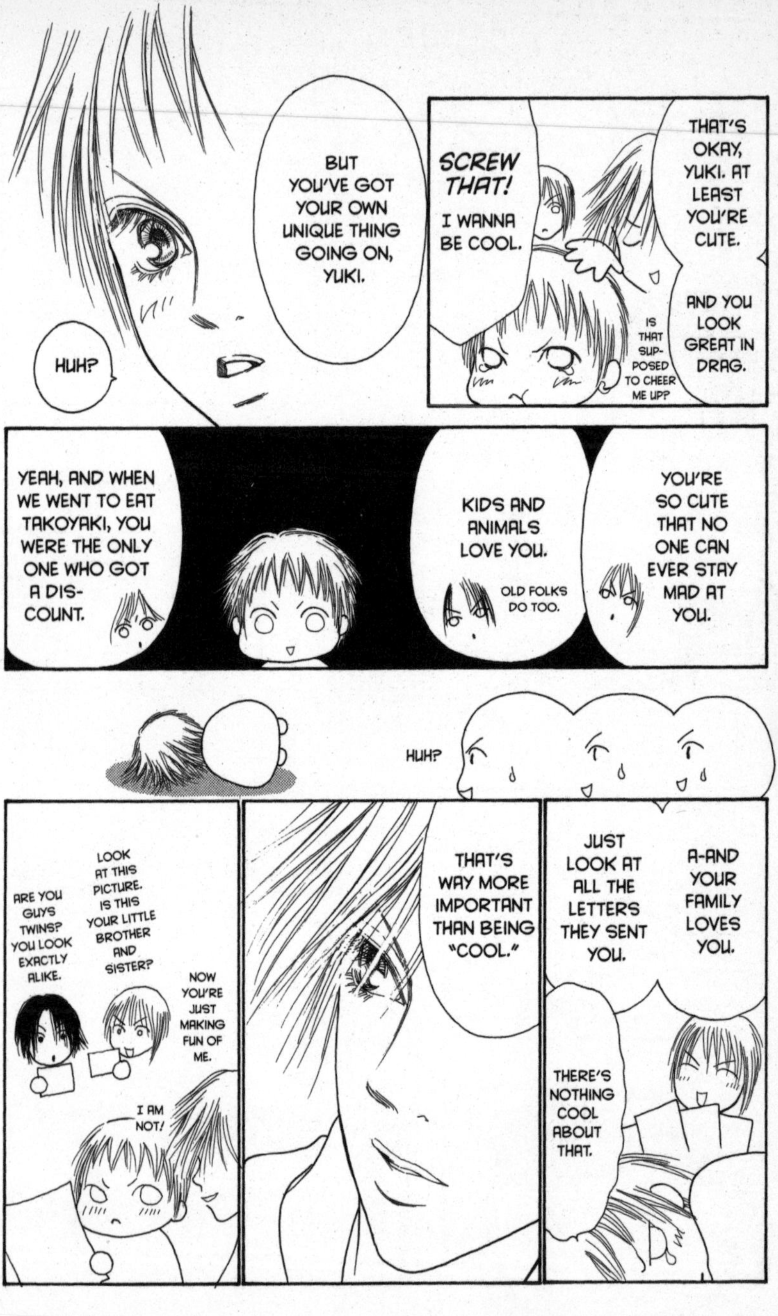
THAT'S OKAY, YUKI. AT LEAST YOU'RE CUTE.
AND YOU LOOK GREAT IN DRAG.
IS THAT SUP-POSED TO CHEER ME UP?
SCREW THAT! I WANNA BE COOL.
BUT YOU'VE GOT YOUR OWN UNIQUE THING GOING ON, YUKI.
HUH?
YOU'RE SO CUTE THAT NO ONE CAN EVER STAY MAD AT YOU.
KIDS AND ANIMALS LOVE YOU.
OLD FOLKS DO TOO.
YEAH, AND WHEN WE WENT TO EAT TAKOYAKI, YOU WERE THE ONLY ONE WHO GOT A DIS-COUNT.
HUH?
A-AND YOUR FAMILY LOVES YOU.
JUST LOOK AT ALL THE LETTERS THEY SENT YOU.
THERE'S NOTHING COOL ABOUT THAT.
THAT'S WAY MORE IMPORTANT THAN BEING "COOL."
LOOK AT THIS PICTURE. IS THIS YOUR LITTLE BROTHER AND SISTER?
ARE YOU GUYS TWINS? YOU LOOK EXACTLY ALIKE.
NOW YOU'RE JUST MAKING FUN OF ME.
I AM NOT!

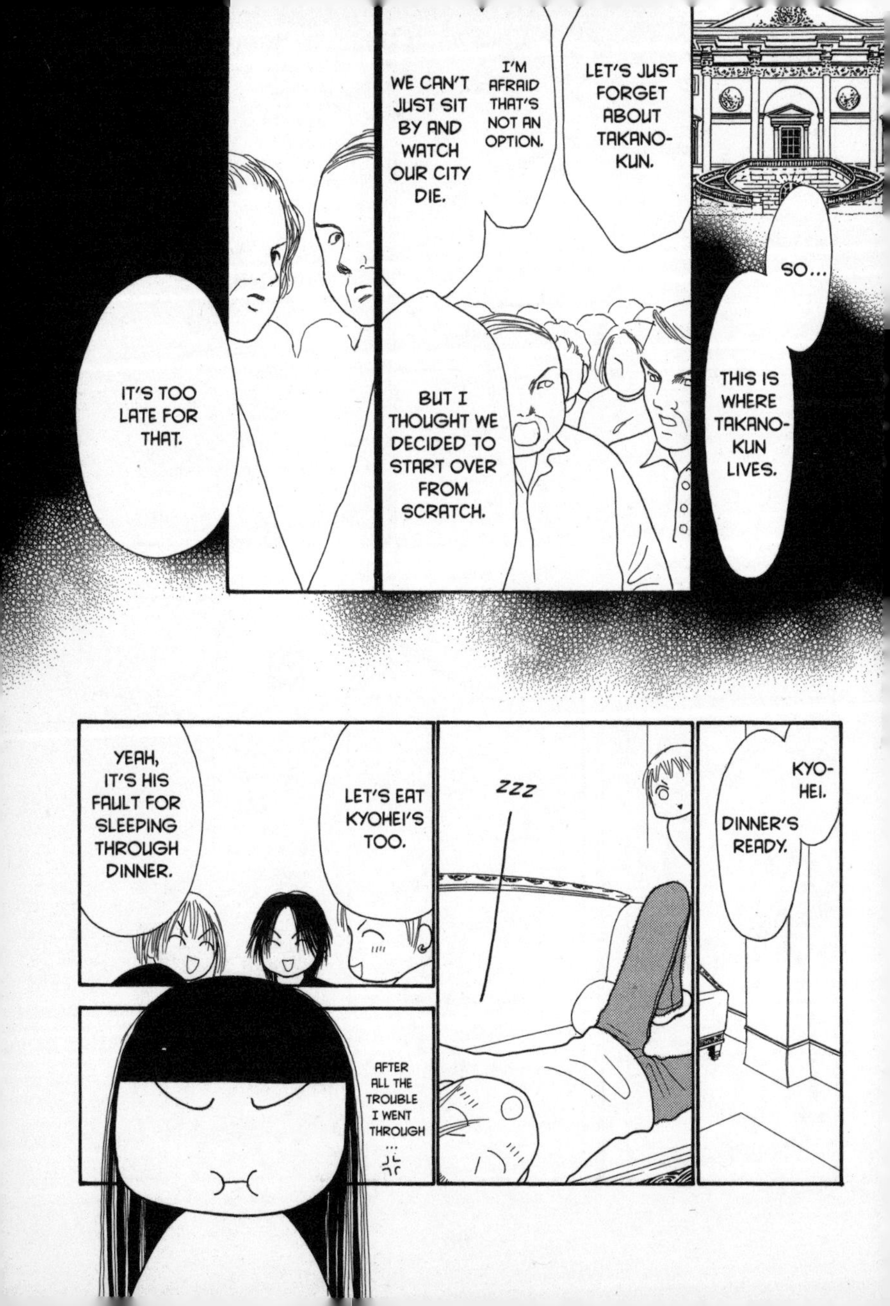
SO...
THIS IS WHERE TAKANO-KUN LIVES.
LET'S JUST FORGET ABOUT TAKANO-KUN.
I'M AFRAID THAT'S NOT AN OPTION.
BUT I THOUGHT WE DECIDED TO START OVER FROM SCRATCH.
WE CAN'T JUST SIT BY AND WATCH OUR CITY DIE.
IT'S TOO LATE FOR THAT.
KYO-HEI.
DINNER'S READY.
ZZZ
LET'S EAT KYOHEI'S TOO.
YEAH, IT'S HIS FAULT FOR SLEEPING THROUGH DINNER.
AFTER ALL THE TROUBLE I WENT THROUGH...

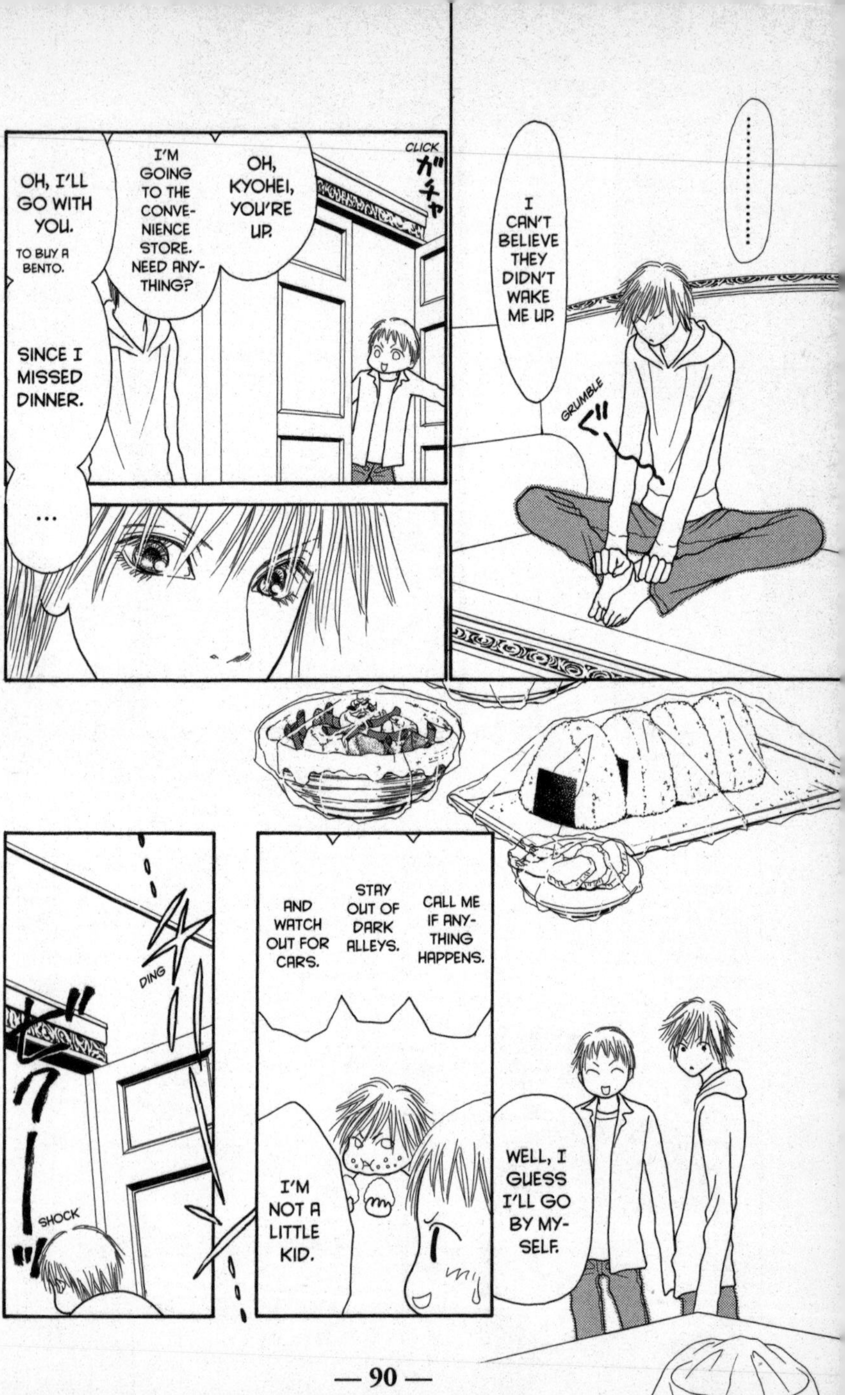
……
I CAN'T BELIEVE THEY DIDN'T WAKE ME UP.
GRUMBLE
CLICK
OH, KYOHEI, YOU'RE UP.
I'M GOING TO THE CONVENIENCE STORE. NEED ANYTHING?
OH, I'LL GO WITH YOU.
TO BUY A BENTO.
SINCE I MISSED DINNER.
...
WELL, I GUESS I'LL GO BY MYSELF.
CALL ME IF ANYTHING HAPPENS.
STAY OUT OF DARK ALLEYS.
AND WATCH OUT FOR CARS.
I'M NOT A LITTLE KID.
DING
SHOCK

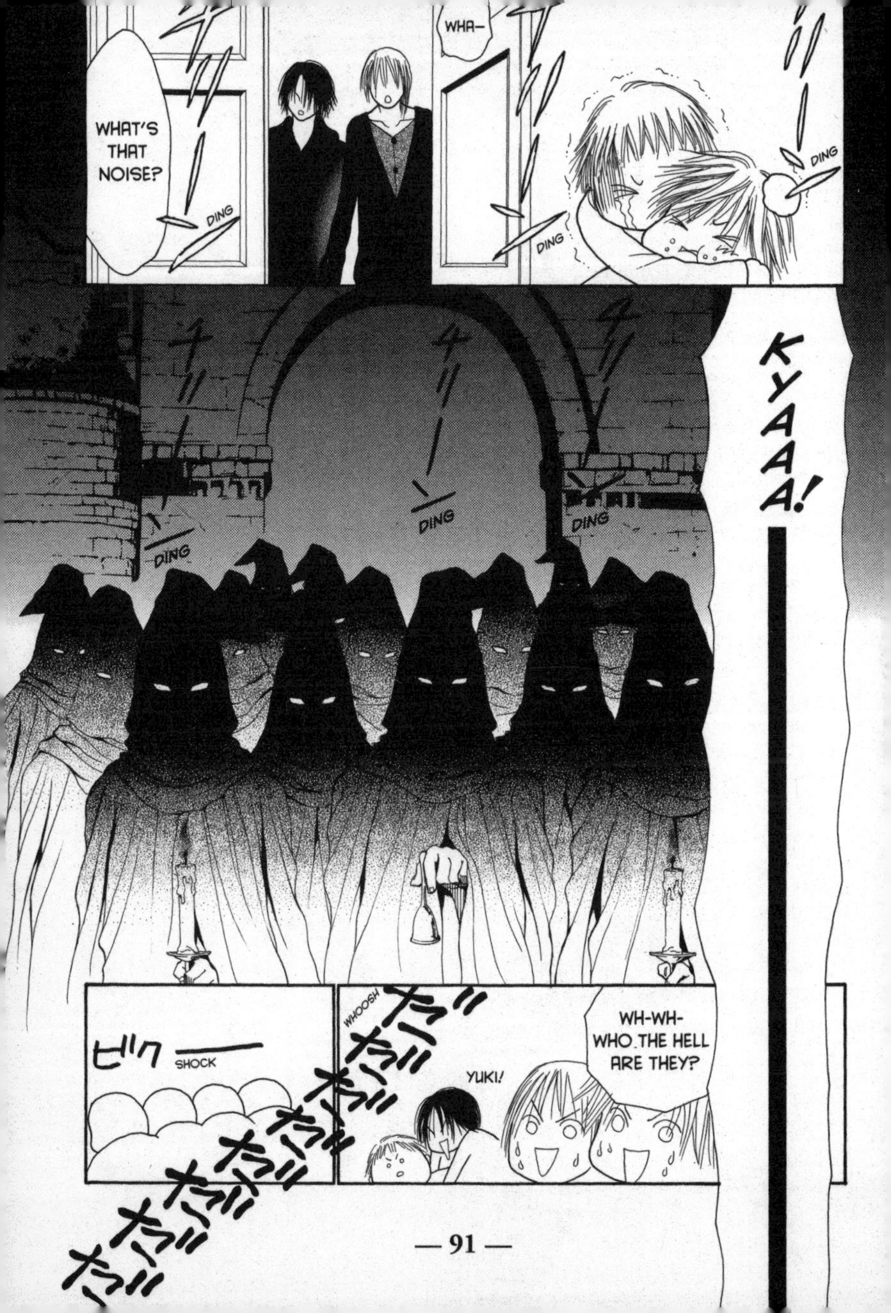
DING
DING
WHA–
DING
WHAT'S THAT NOISE?
KYAAAA!
DING
DING
DING
WH-WH-WHO THE HELL ARE THEY?
YUKI!
WHOOSH
ビク
SHOCK

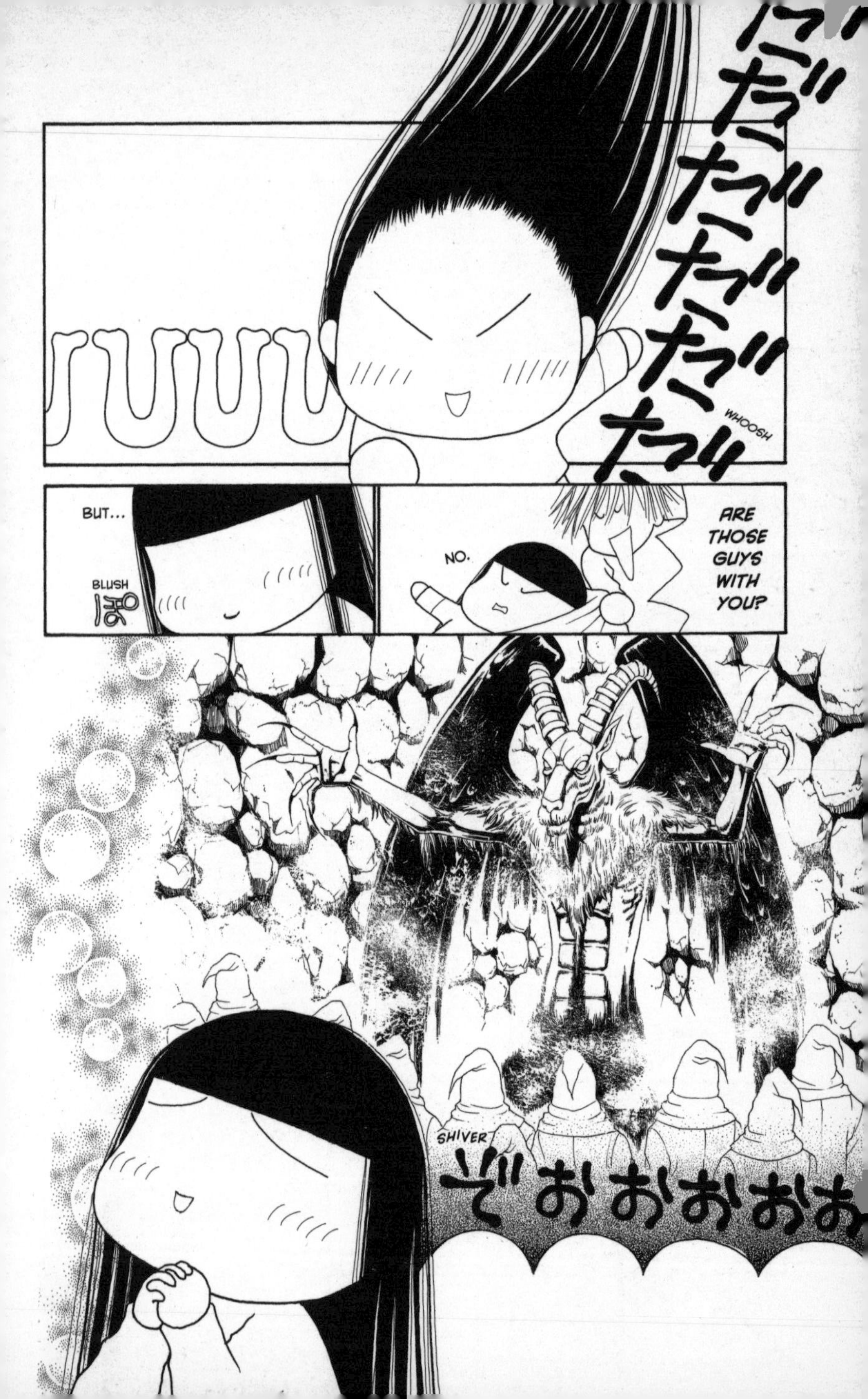
だだだだだっ
WHOOSH
ARE THOSE GUYS WITH YOU?
NO.
BUT...
BLUSH
ぽ
SHIVER
ぞおおおおお

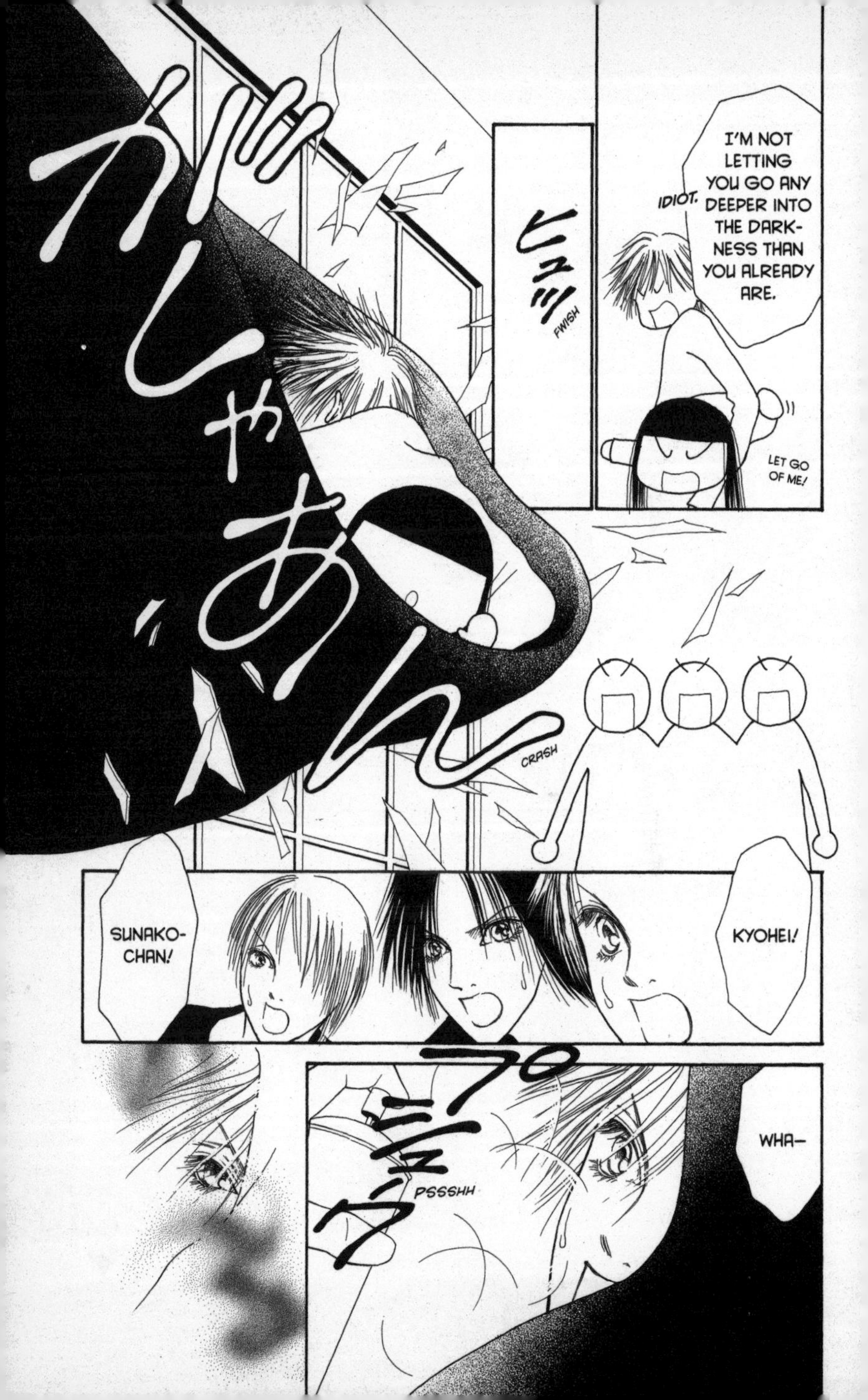

IDIOT.
I'M NOT LETTING YOU GO ANY DEEPER INTO THE DARKNESS THAN YOU ALREADY ARE.
LET GO OF ME!
ヒュッ
FWISH
がしゃあん
CRASH
KYOHEI!
SUNAKO-CHAN!
WHA-
プシュウ
PSSSHH

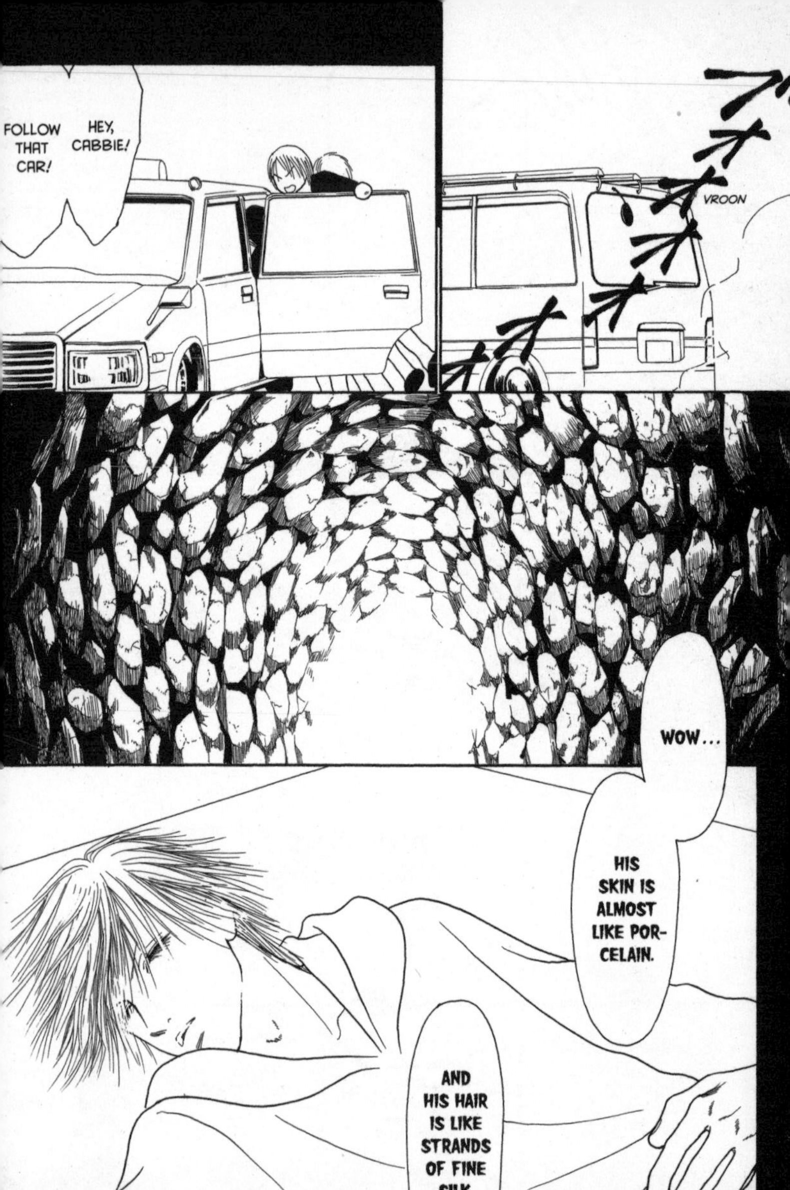
VROON
HEY, CABBIE!
FOLLOW THAT CAR!
WOW...
HIS SKIN IS ALMOST LIKE POR-CELAIN.
AND HIS HAIR IS LIKE STRANDS OF FINE SILK.

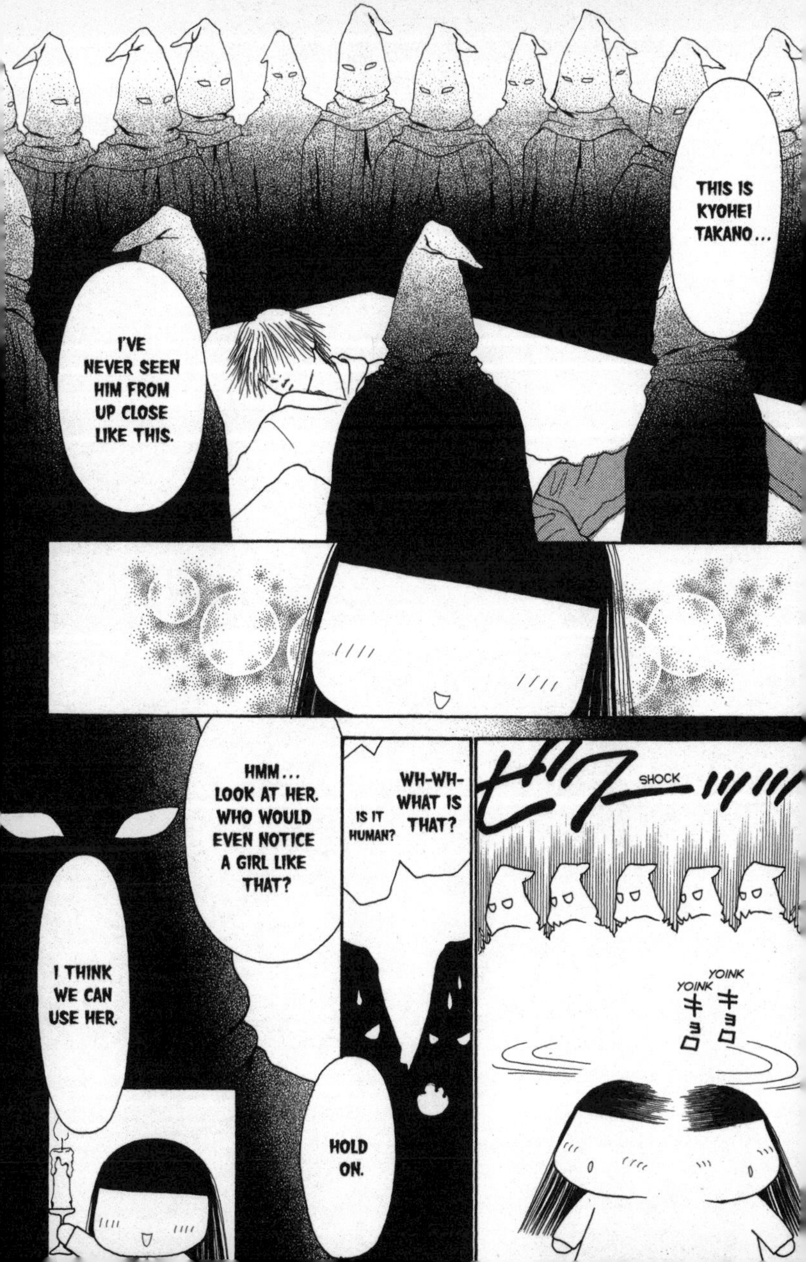
THIS IS KYOHEI TAKANO...
I'VE NEVER SEEN HIM FROM UP CLOSE LIKE THIS.
SHOCK
キョロ YOINK
キョロ YOINK
WH-WH- WHAT IS THAT?
IS IT HUMAN?
HMM... LOOK AT HER. WHO WOULD EVEN NOTICE A GIRL LIKE THAT?
HOLD ON.
I THINK WE CAN USE HER.

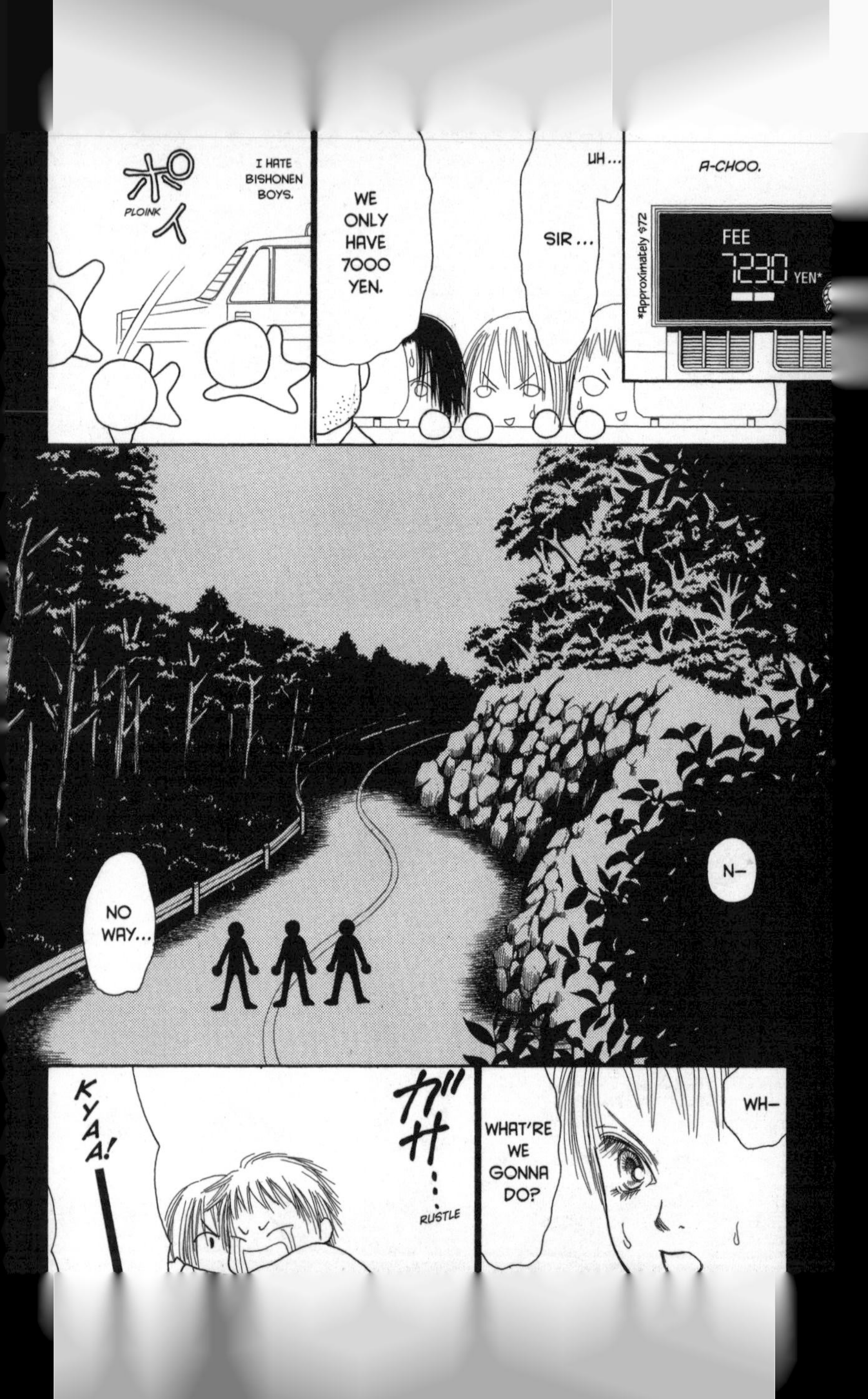
A-CHOO.
FEE
7230 YEN*
*Approximately $72
UH...
SIR...
WE ONLY HAVE 7000 YEN.
I HATE BISHONEN BOYS.
ポイ
PLOINK
N—
NO WAY...
WH—
WHAT'RE WE GONNA DO?
ガサ...
RUSTLE
KYAA!

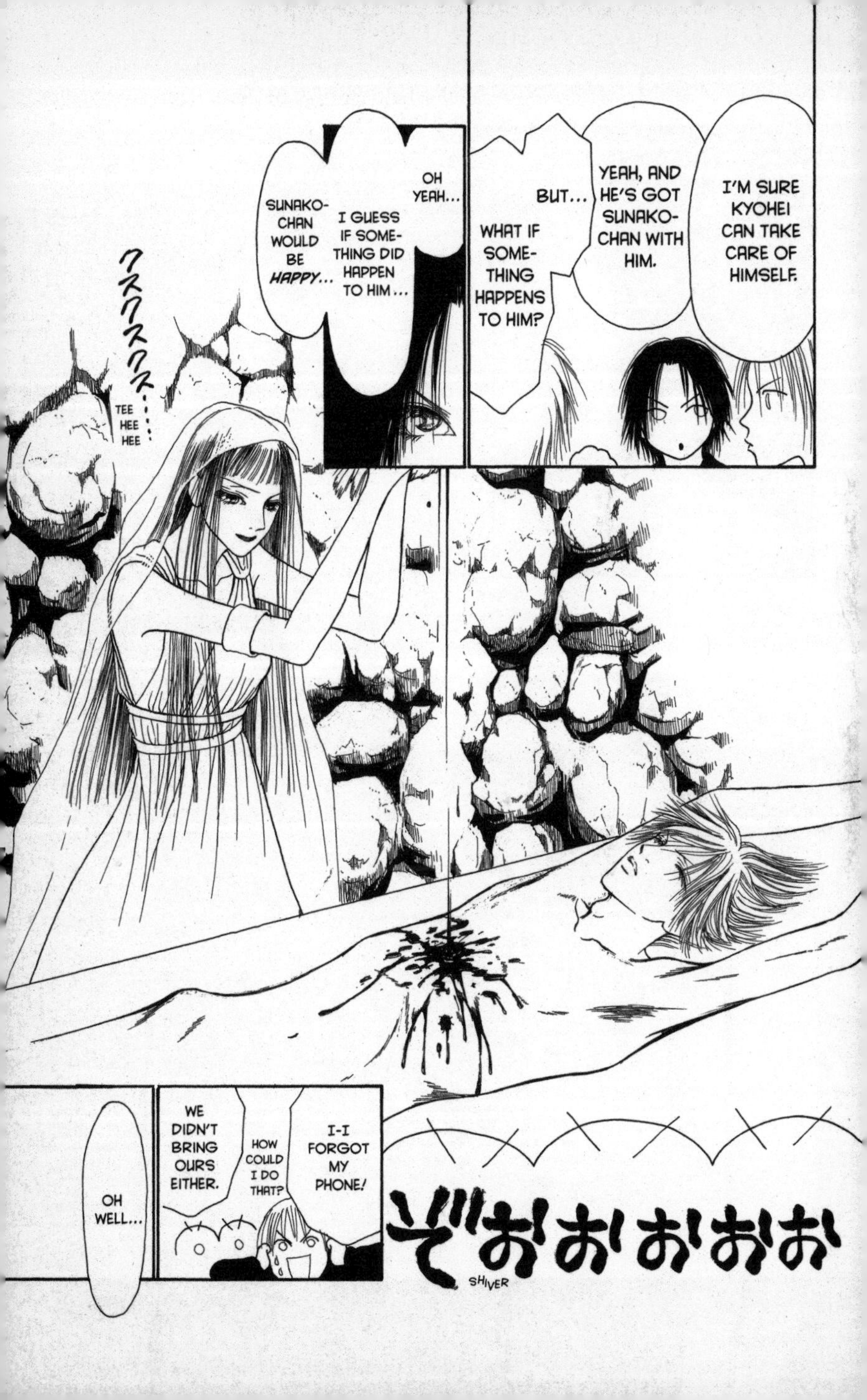

I'M SURE KYOHEI CAN TAKE CARE OF HIMSELF.
YEAH, AND HE'S GOT SUNAKO-CHAN WITH HIM.
BUT... WHAT IF SOMETHING HAPPENS TO HIM?
OH YEAH... I GUESS IF SOMETHING DID HAPPEN TO HIM...
SUNAKO-CHAN WOULD BE *HAPPY*...
クスクスクス...
TEE HEE HEE
ぞおおおお
SHIVER
I-I FORGOT MY PHONE!
HOW COULD I DO THAT?
WE DIDN'T BRING OURS EITHER.
OH WELL...

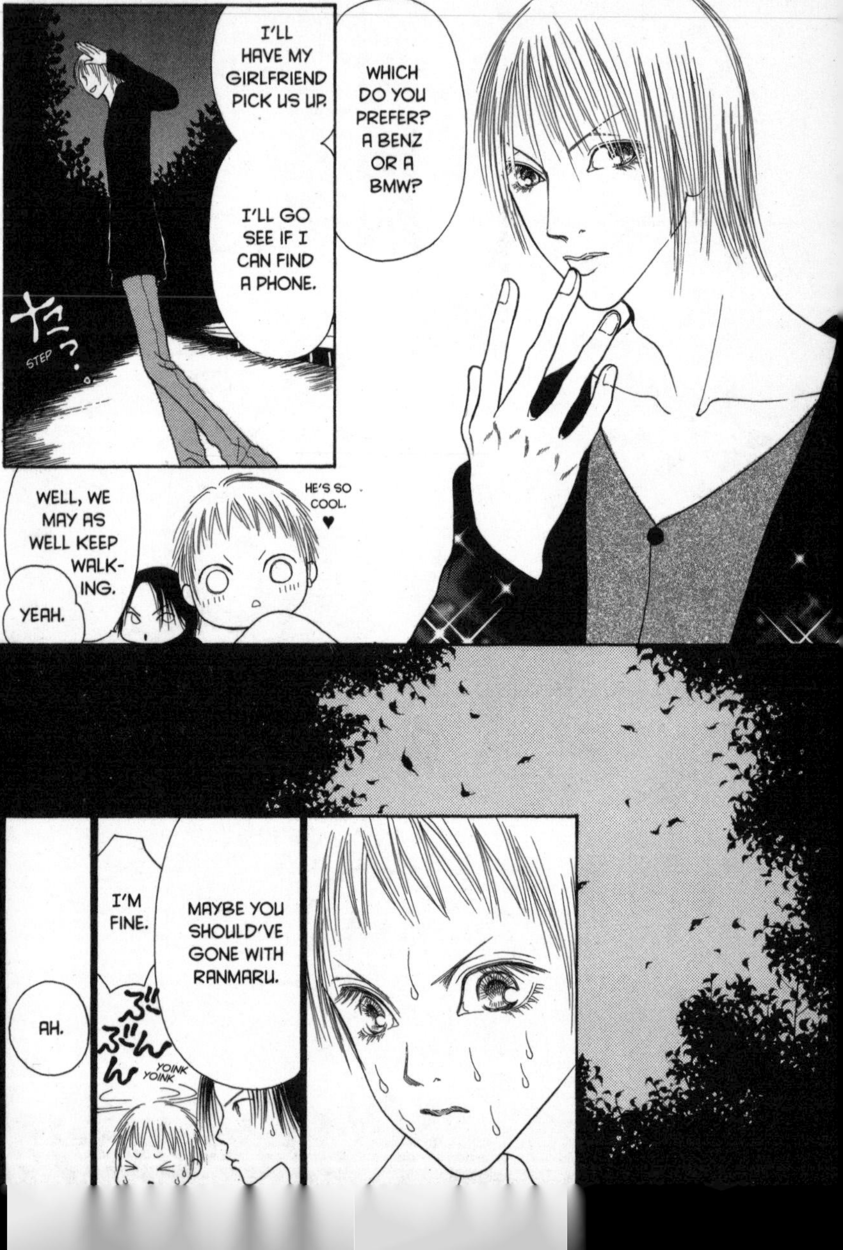
WHICH DO YOU PREFER? A BENZ OR A BMW?
I'LL HAVE MY GIRLFRIEND PICK US UP.
I'LL GO SEE IF I CAN FIND A PHONE.
STEP
HE'S SO COOL. ♥
WELL, WE MAY AS WELL KEEP WALKING.
YEAH.
MAYBE YOU SHOULD'VE GONE WITH RANMARU.
I'M FINE.
YOINK YOINK
AH.

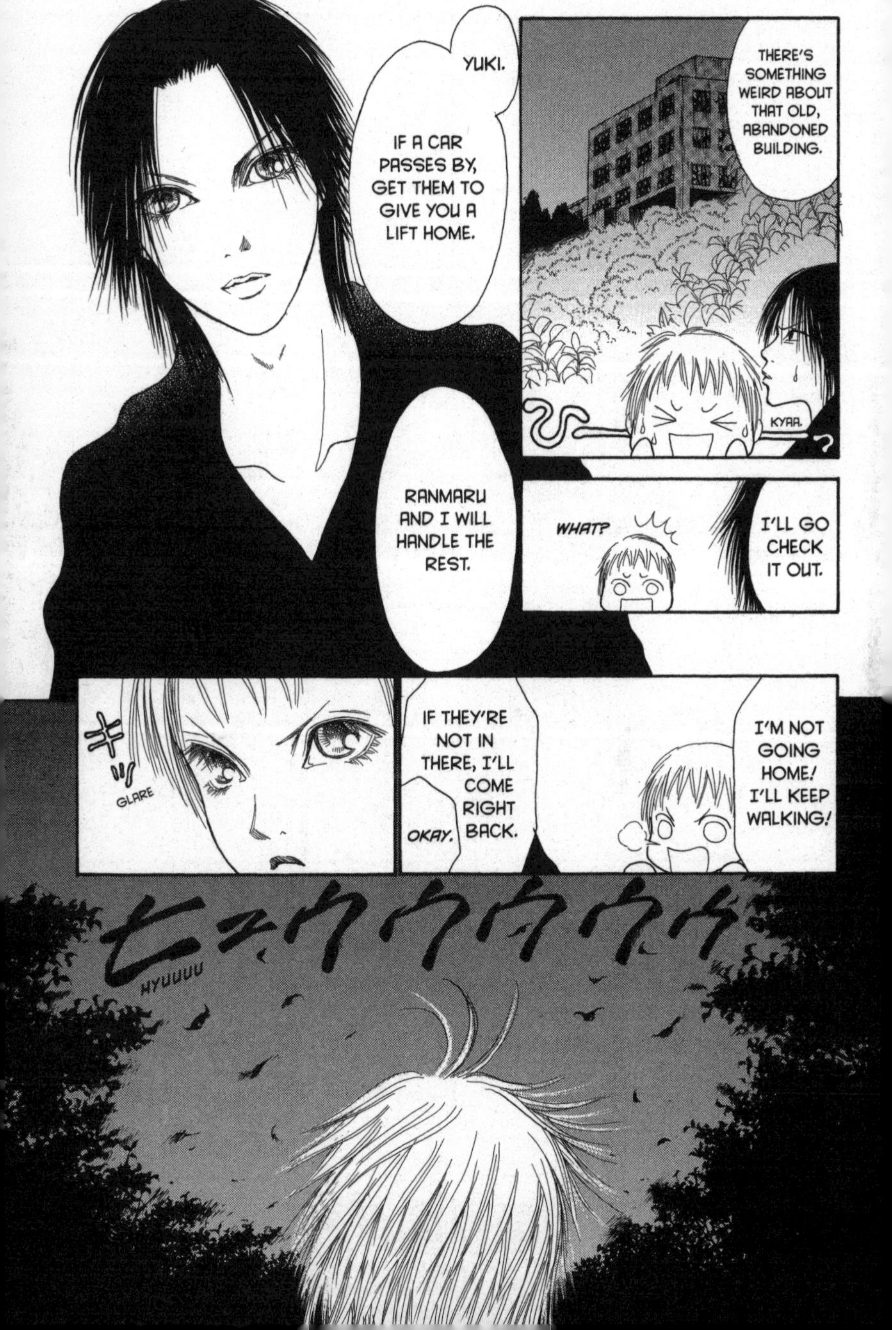
THERE'S SOMETHING WEIRD ABOUT THAT OLD, ABANDONED BUILDING.
KYAA.
I'LL GO CHECK IT OUT.
WHAT?
YUKI.
IF A CAR PASSES BY, GET THEM TO GIVE YOU A LIFT HOME.
RANMARU AND I WILL HANDLE THE REST.
I'M NOT GOING HOME! I'LL KEEP WALKING!
IF THEY'RE NOT IN THERE, I'LL COME RIGHT BACK.
OKAY.
ギ
GLARE
ヒュウウウウウ
HYUUUU

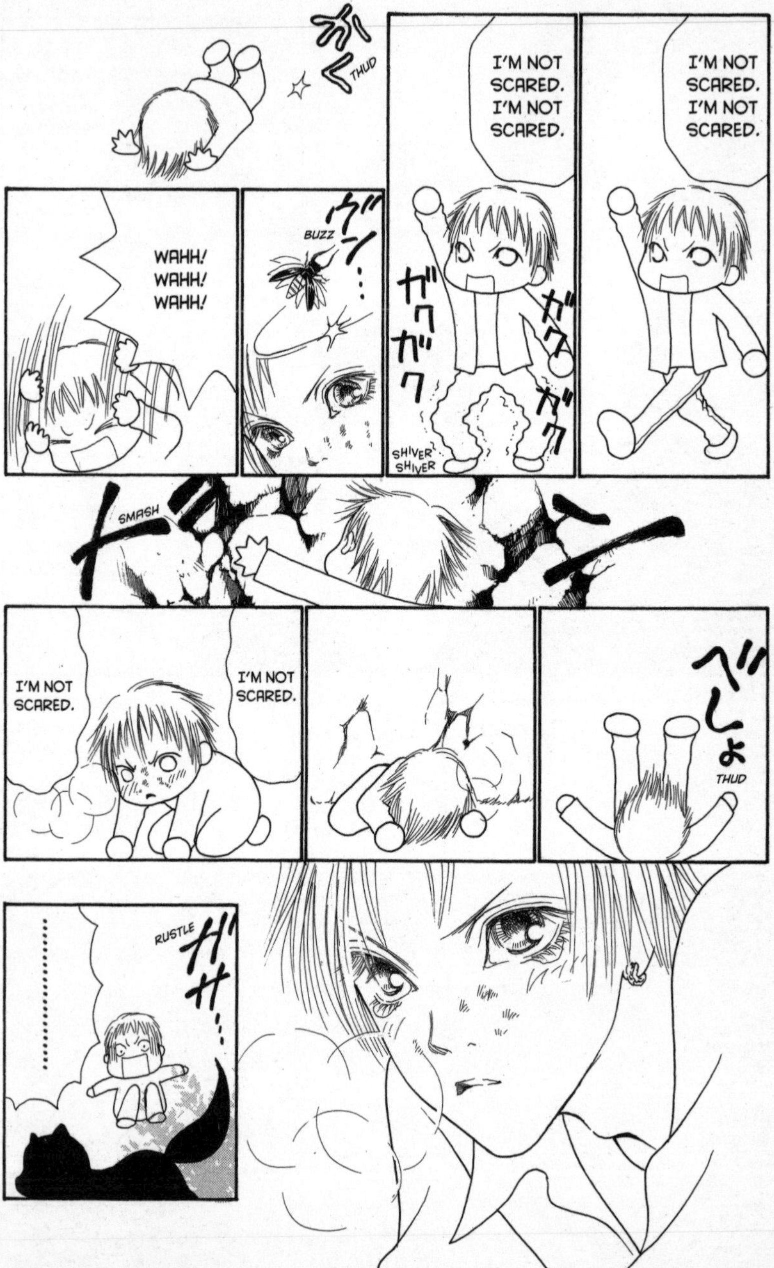

I'M NOT SCARED. I'M NOT SCARED.
I'M NOT SCARED. I'M NOT SCARED.
ガクガク
ガクガク
SHIVER SHIVER
THUD
ヴン…
BUZZ
WAHH! WAHH! WAHH!
SMASH
べしょ
THUD
I'M NOT SCARED.
I'M NOT SCARED.
ガサ…
RUSTLE
……………

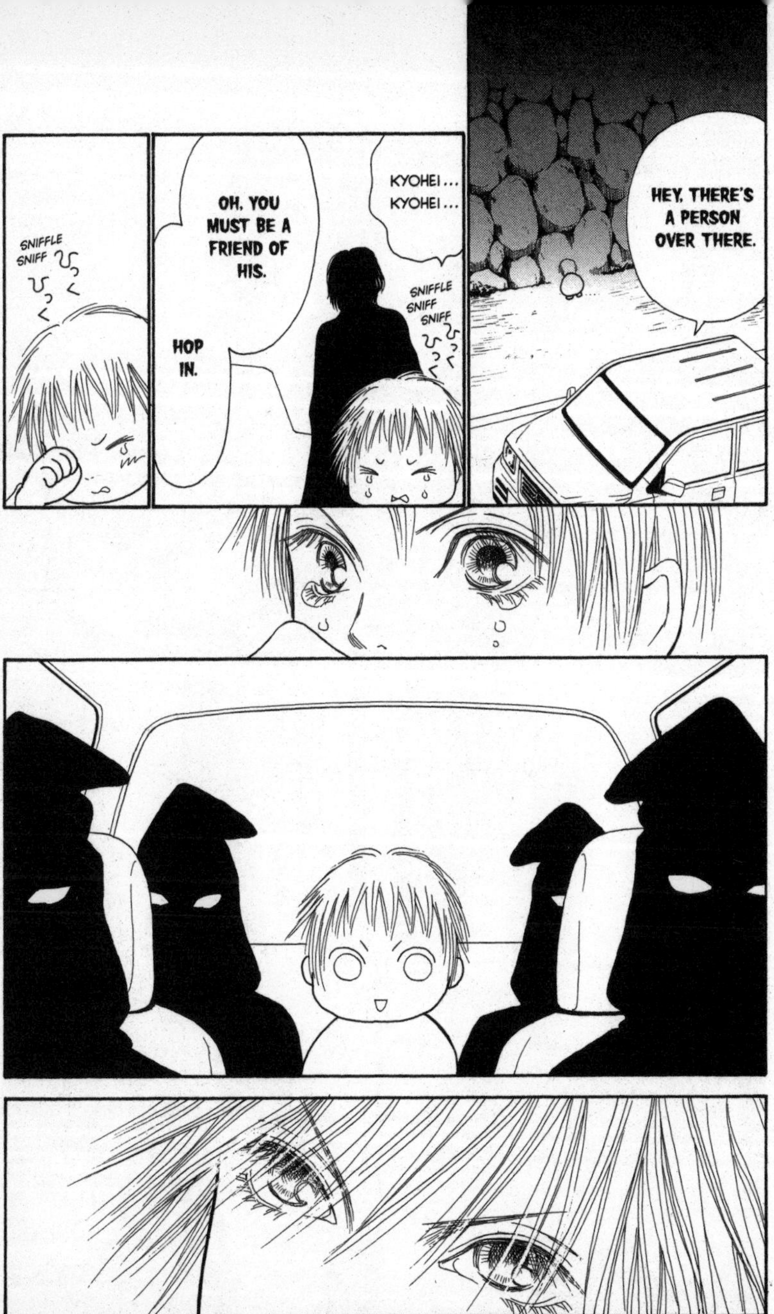
HEY, THERE'S A PERSON OVER THERE.
KYOHEI... KYOHEI...
OH, YOU MUST BE A FRIEND OF HIS.
SNIFFLE SNIFF SNIFF
HOP IN.
SNIFFLE SNIFF

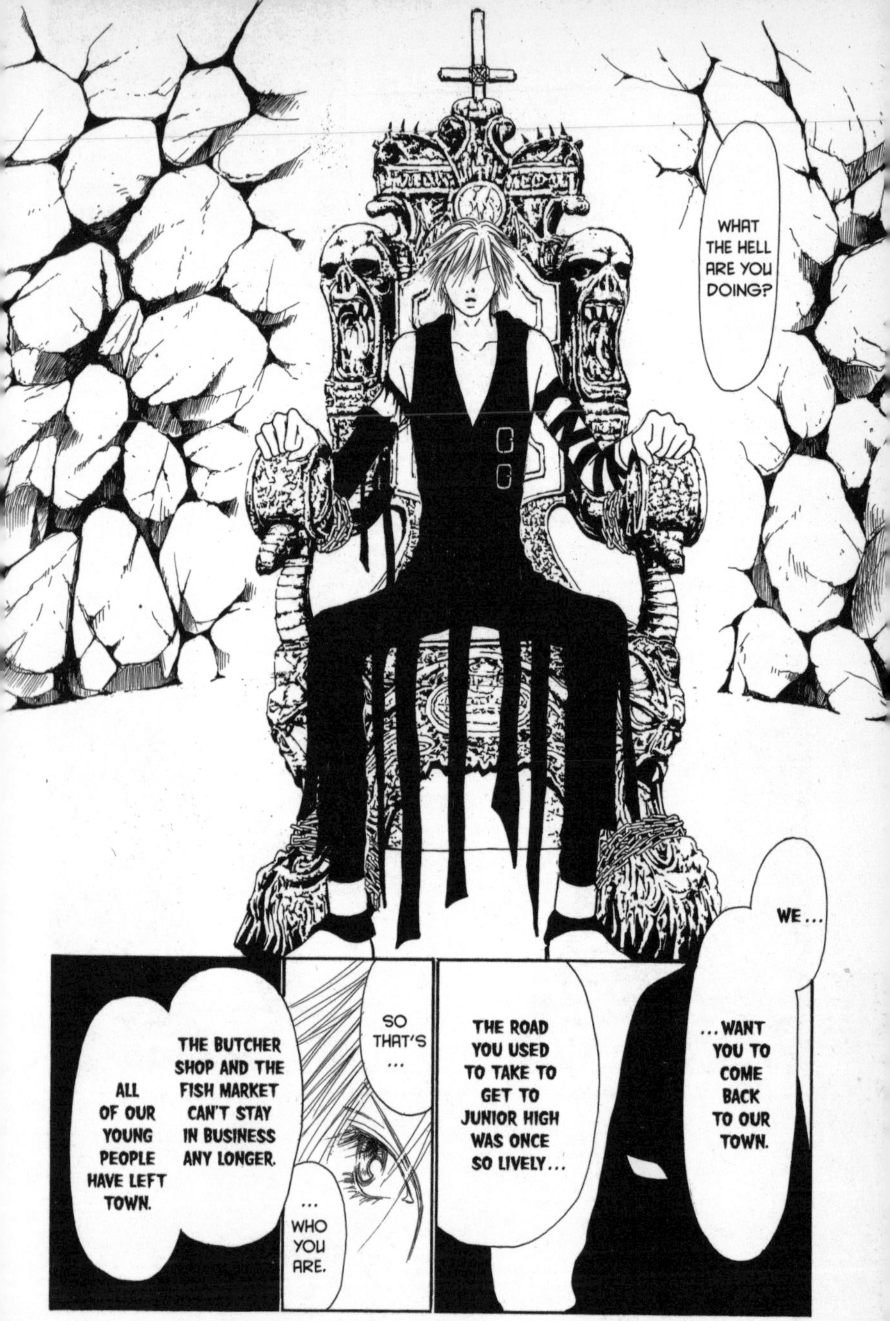
WHAT THE HELL ARE YOU DOING?
WE...
...WANT YOU TO COME BACK TO OUR TOWN.
THE ROAD YOU USED TO TAKE TO GET TO JUNIOR HIGH WAS ONCE SO LIVELY...
SO THAT'S...
...WHO YOU ARE.
THE BUTCHER SHOP AND THE FISH MARKET CAN'T STAY IN BUSINESS ANY LONGER.
ALL OF OUR YOUNG PEOPLE HAVE LEFT TOWN.

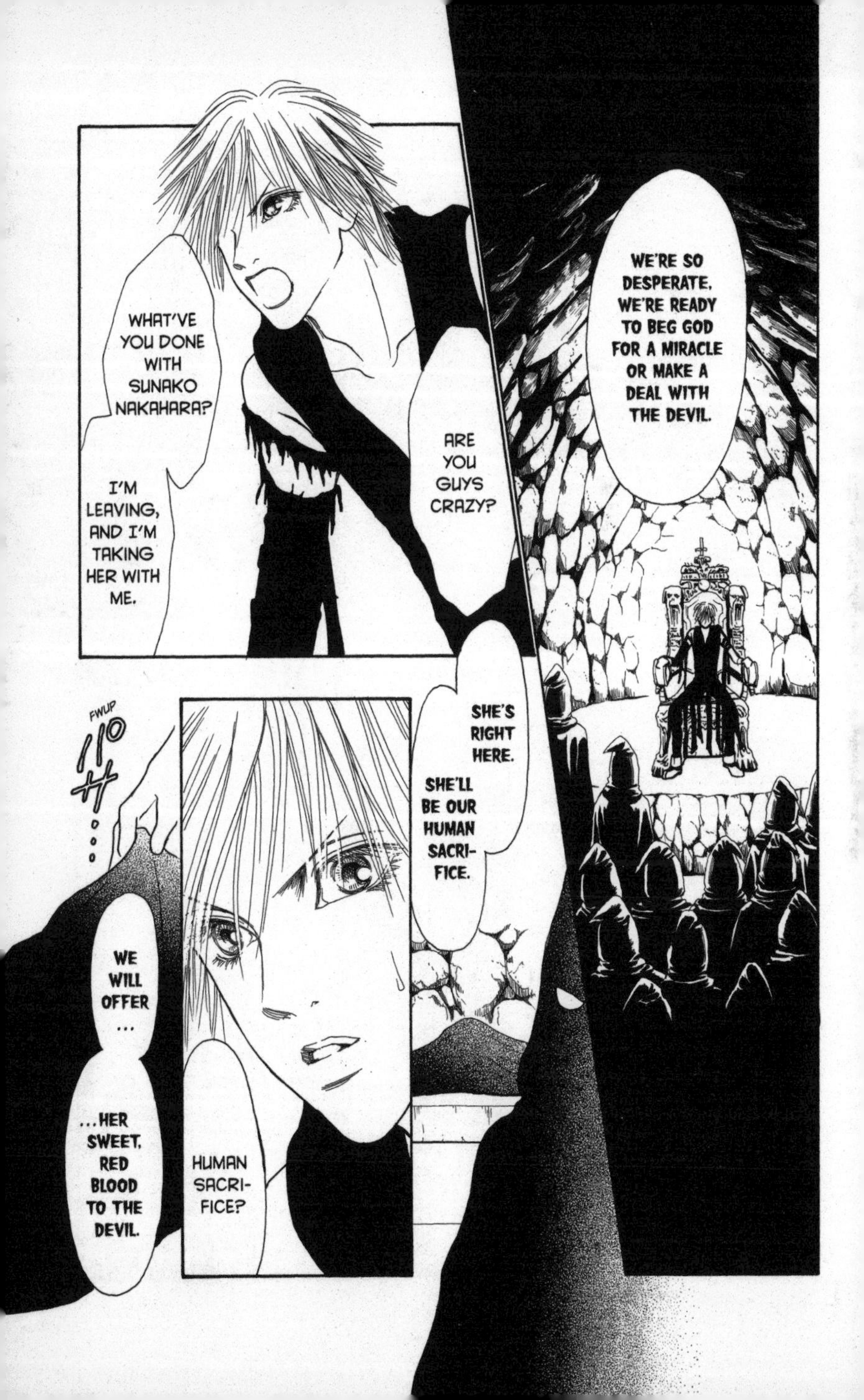
WE'RE SO DESPERATE, WE'RE READY TO BEG GOD FOR A MIRACLE OR MAKE A DEAL WITH THE DEVIL.
WHAT'VE YOU DONE WITH SUNAKO NAKAHARA?
ARE YOU GUYS CRAZY?
I'M LEAVING, AND I'M TAKING HER WITH ME.
SHE'S RIGHT HERE.
SHE'LL BE OUR HUMAN SACRI-FICE.
FWUP
HUMAN SACRI-FICE?
WE WILL OFFER ...
...HER SWEET, RED BLOOD TO THE DEVIL.

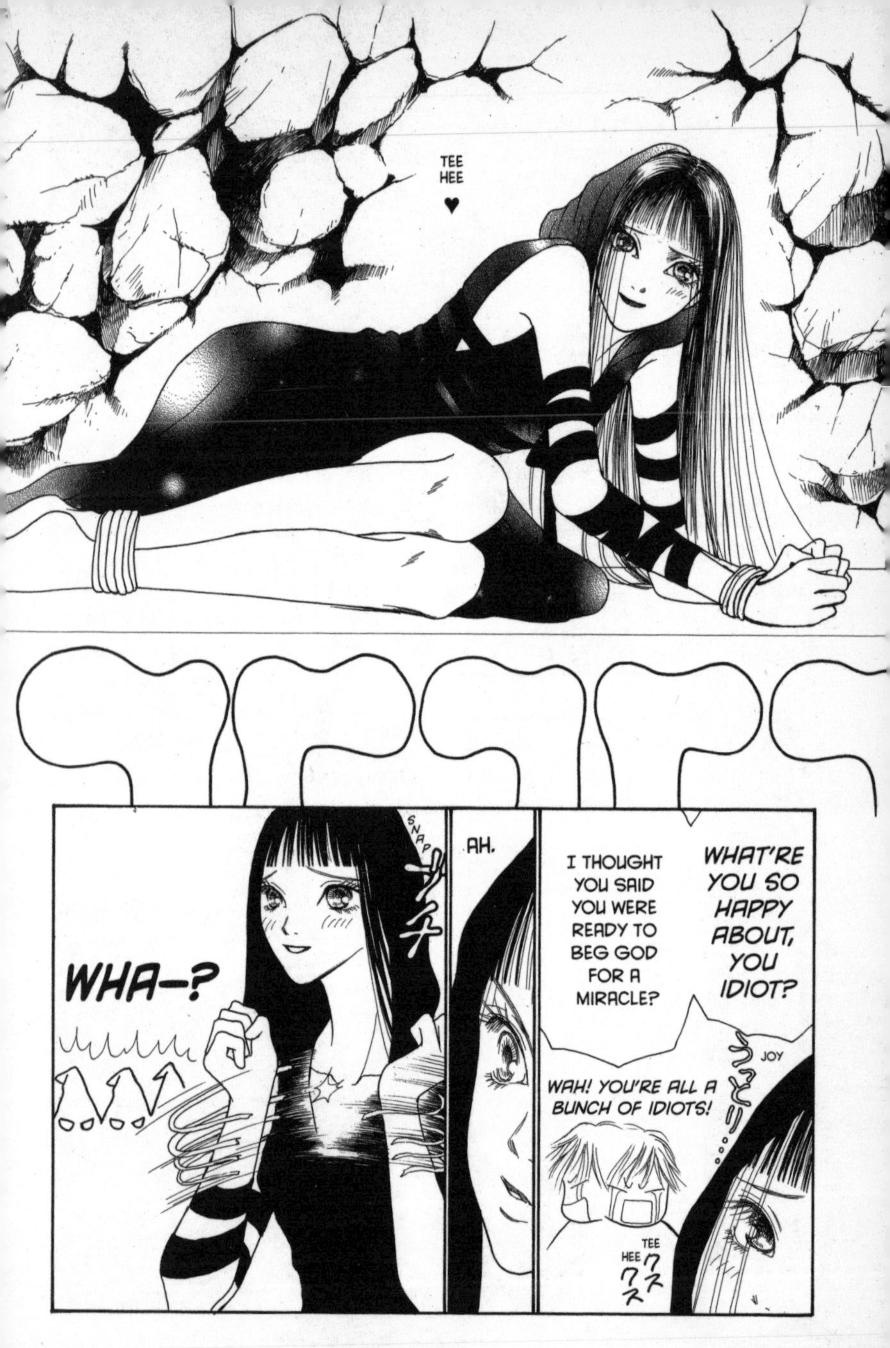
TEE HEE ♥
WHAT'RE YOU SO HAPPY ABOUT, YOU IDIOT?
I THOUGHT YOU SAID YOU WERE READY TO BEG GOD FOR A MIRACLE?
JOY
WAH! YOU'RE ALL A BUNCH OF IDIOTS!
TEE HEE
AH.
SNAP
WHA-?

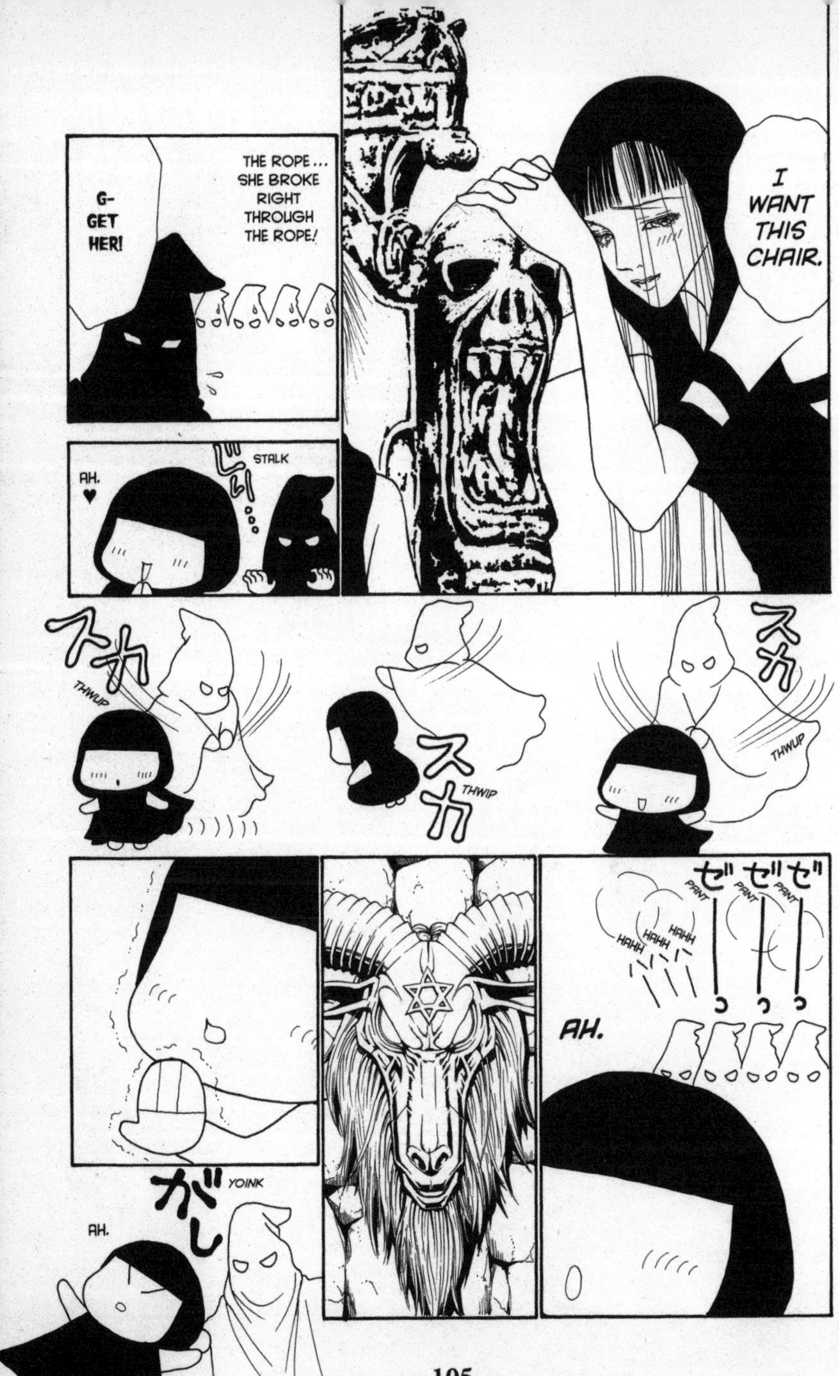
I WANT THIS CHAIR.
THE ROPE... SHE BROKE RIGHT THROUGH THE ROPE!
G-GET HER!
STALK
AH. ♥
スカ
THWUP
スカ
THWIP
スカ
THWUP
ゼ ゼ ゼ
PANT PANT PANT
HAHH HAHH HAHH
AH.
がし
YOINK
AH.

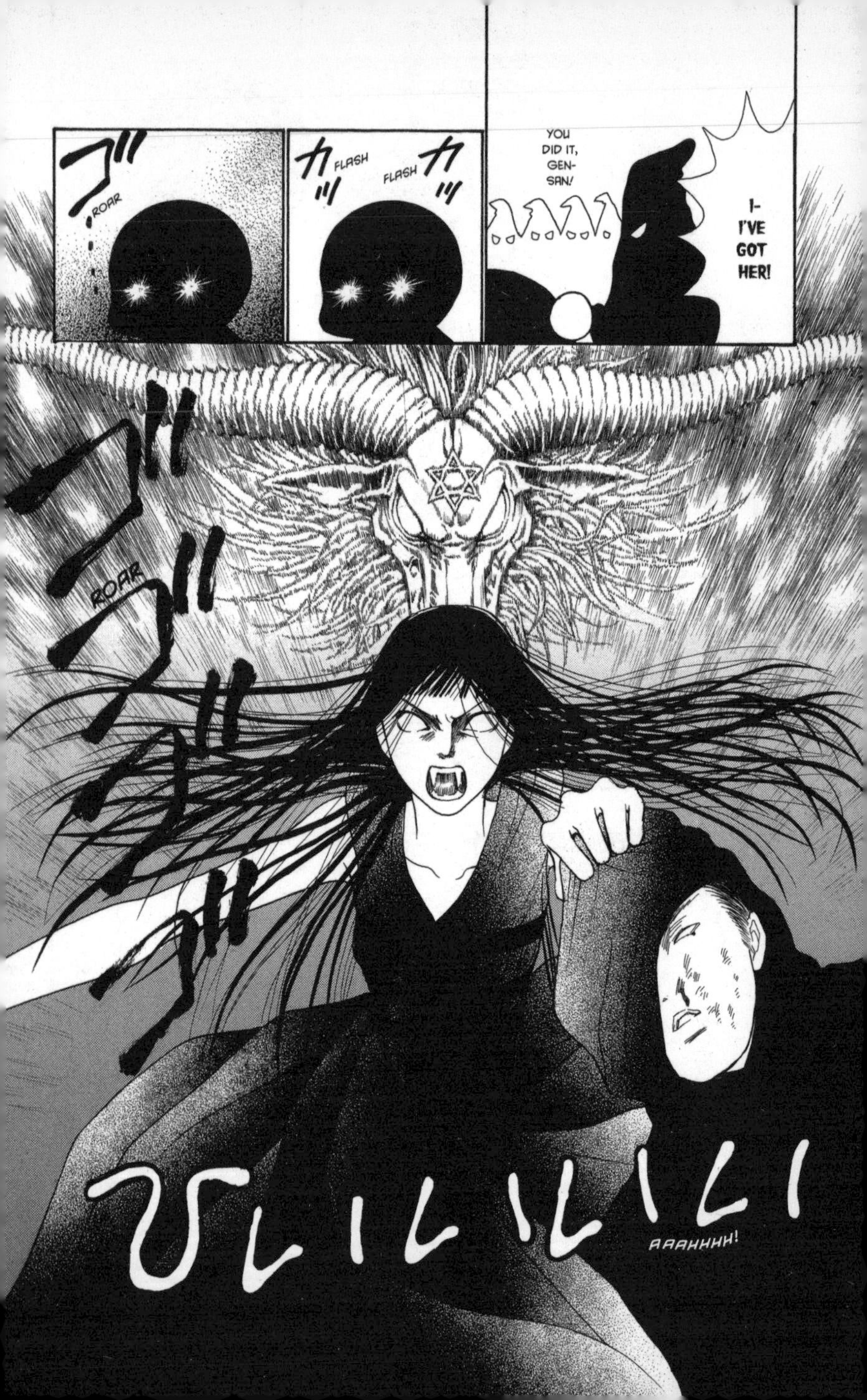
I- I'VE GOT HER!
YOU DID IT, GEN-SAN!
FLASH
FLASH
ROAR
ROAR
AAAHHHH!

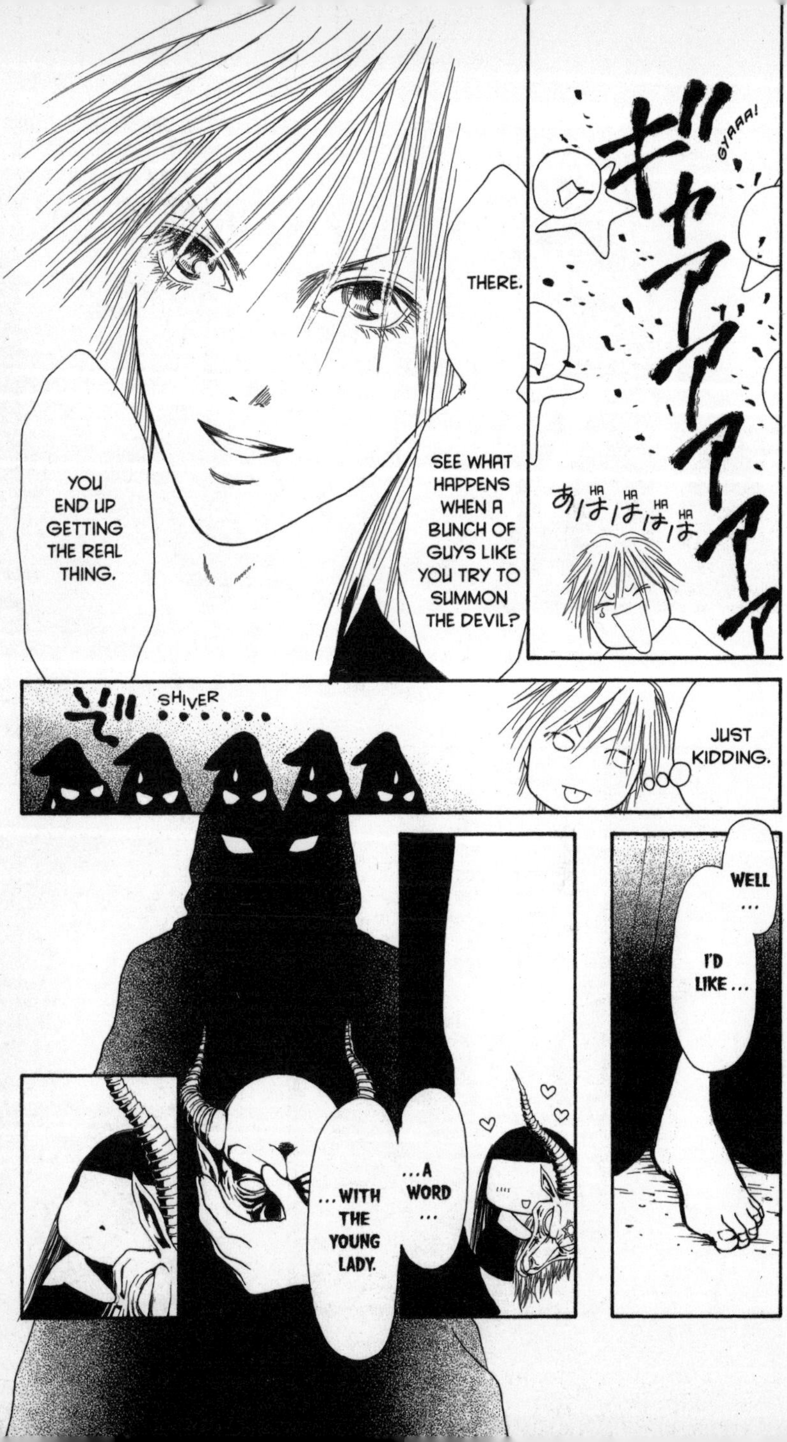
ギャアアアアアア
GYAAA!
あははははは
HA HA HA HA
THERE.
SEE WHAT HAPPENS WHEN A BUNCH OF GUYS LIKE YOU TRY TO SUMMON THE DEVIL?
YOU END UP GETTING THE REAL THING.
JUST KIDDING.
ぞ!!
SHIVER
......
WELL ...
I'D LIKE ...
... A WORD ...
... WITH THE YOUNG LADY.

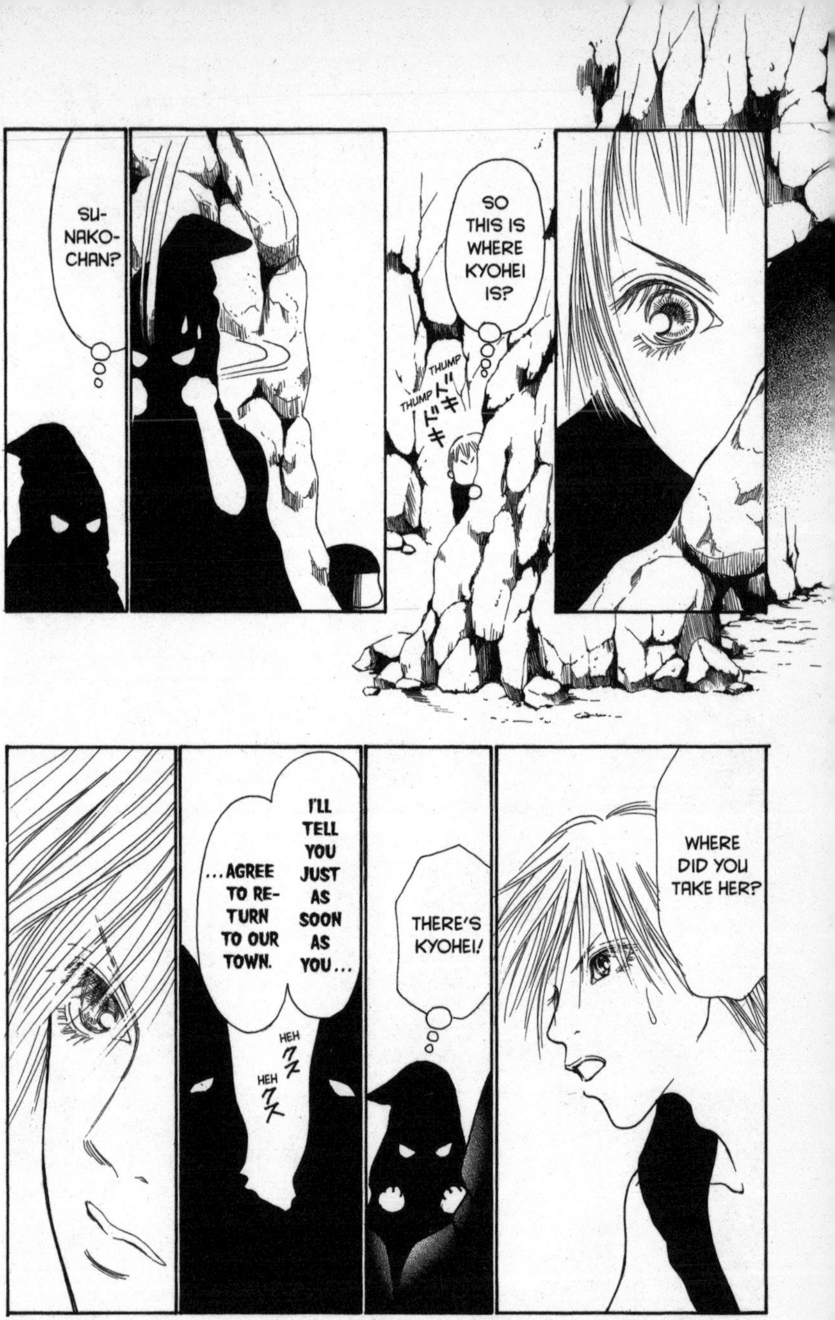
SO THIS IS WHERE KYOHEI IS?
THUMP THUMP
ドキドキ
SU-NAKO-CHAN?
WHERE DID YOU TAKE HER?
THERE'S KYOHEI!
I'LL TELL YOU JUST AS SOON AS YOU...
...AGREE TO RE-TURN TO OUR TOWN.
HEH HEH
クク クク

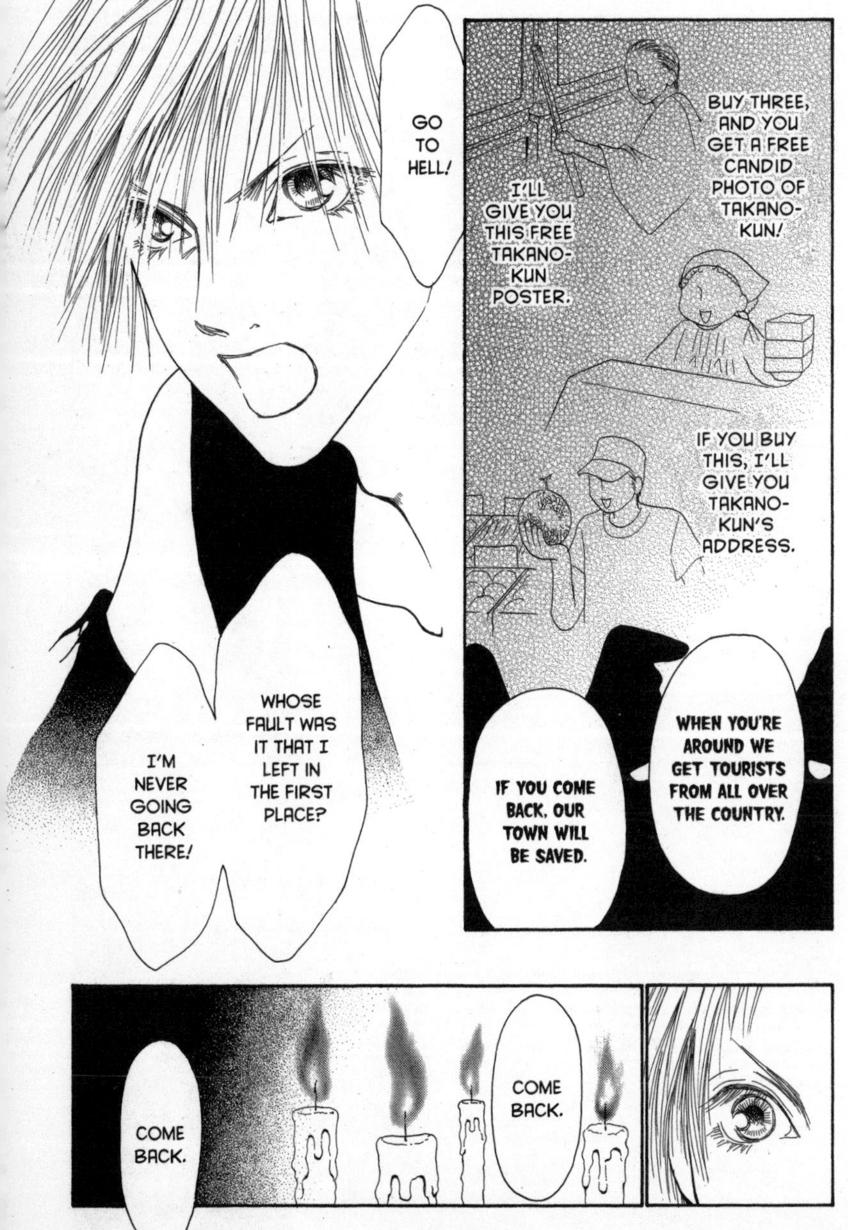
BUY THREE, AND YOU GET A FREE CANDID PHOTO OF TAKANO-KUN!
I'LL GIVE YOU THIS FREE TAKANO-KUN POSTER.
IF YOU BUY THIS, I'LL GIVE YOU TAKANO-KUN'S ADDRESS.
WHEN YOU'RE AROUND WE GET TOURISTS FROM ALL OVER THE COUNTRY.
IF YOU COME BACK, OUR TOWN WILL BE SAVED.
GO TO HELL!
WHOSE FAULT WAS IT THAT I LEFT IN THE FIRST PLACE?
I'M NEVER GOING BACK THERE!
COME BACK.
COME BACK.

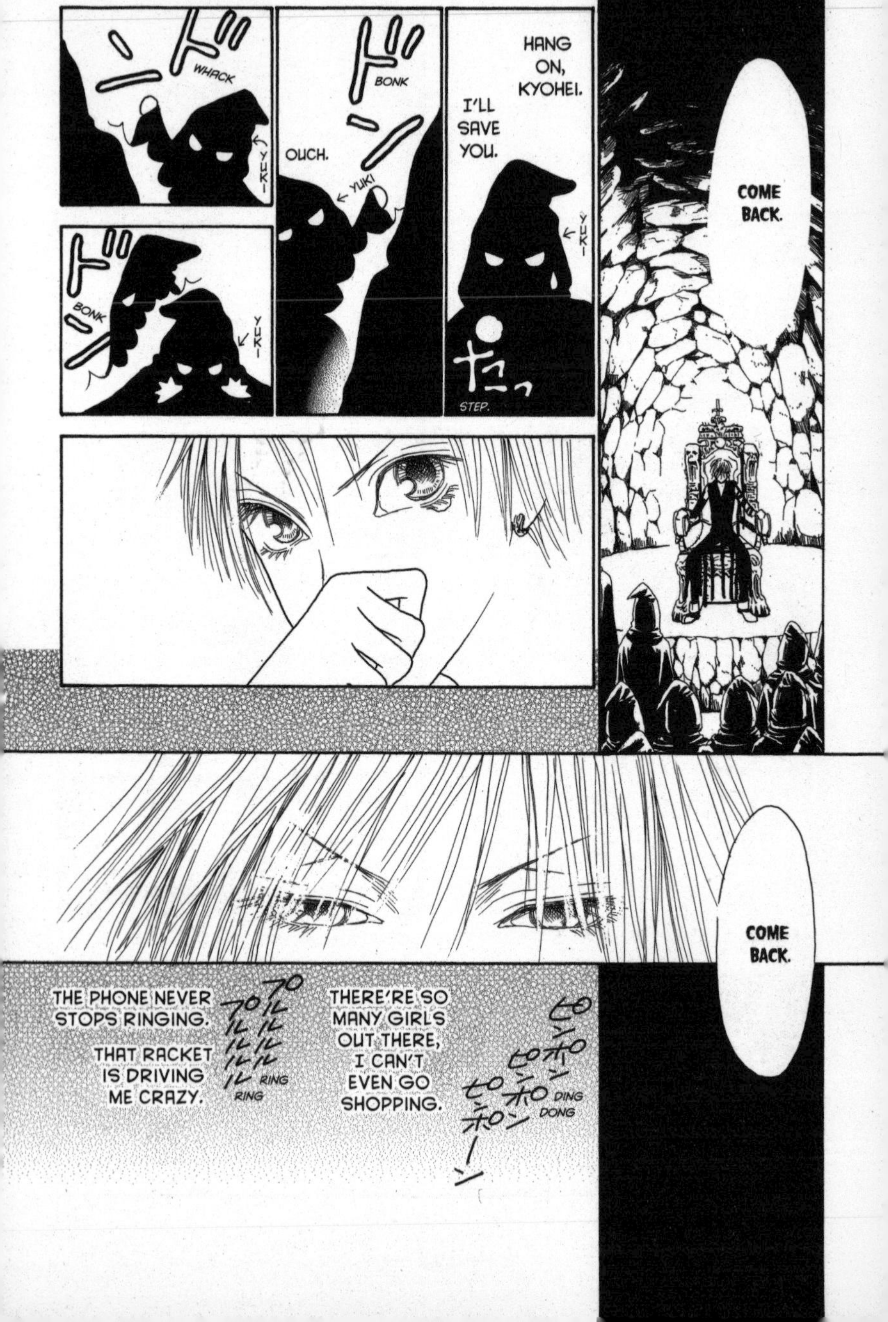
COME BACK.
HANG ON, KYOHEI.
I'LL SAVE YOU.
YUKI
STEP.
BONK
OUCH.
YUKI
WHACK
YUKI
BONK
YUKI
COME BACK.
THERE'RE SO MANY GIRLS OUT THERE, I CAN'T EVEN GO SHOPPING.
DING DONG
THE PHONE NEVER STOPS RINGING.
THAT RACKET IS DRIVING ME CRAZY.
RING RING

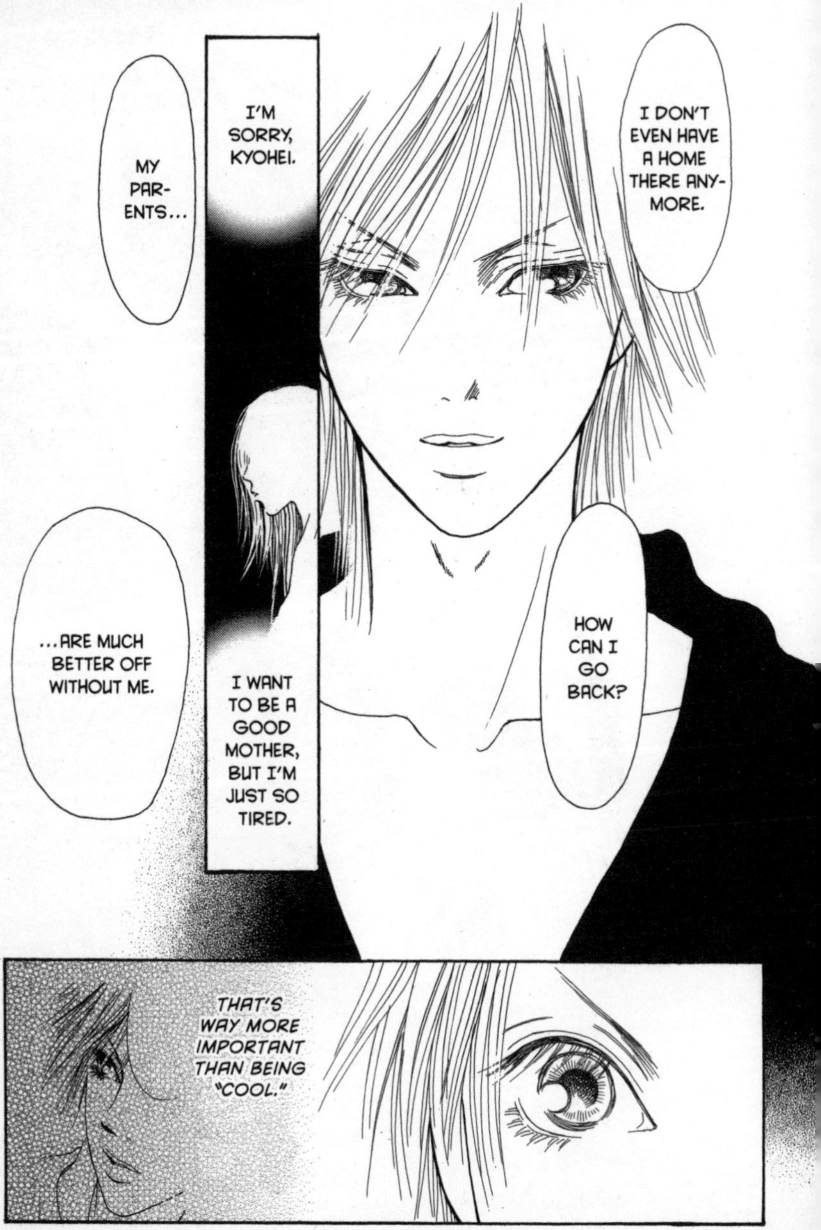
I DON'T EVEN HAVE A HOME THERE ANY-MORE.
HOW CAN I GO BACK?
I'M SORRY, KYOHEI.
I WANT TO BE A GOOD MOTHER, BUT I'M JUST SO TIRED.
MY PAR-ENTS...
...ARE MUCH BETTER OFF WITHOUT ME.
THAT'S WAY MORE IMPORTANT THAN BEING "COOL."

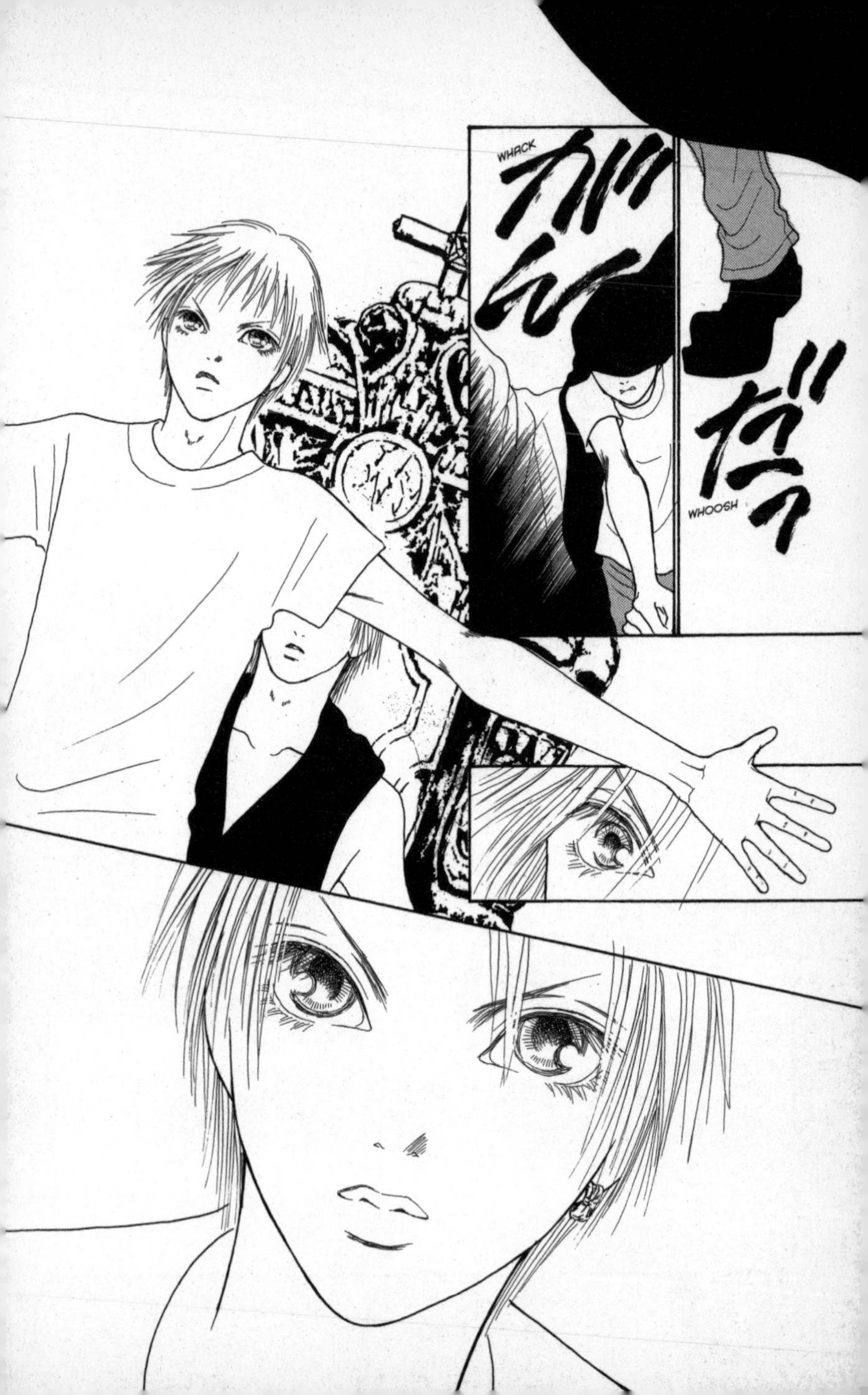
ガバッ
WHOOSH
がんっ
WHACK

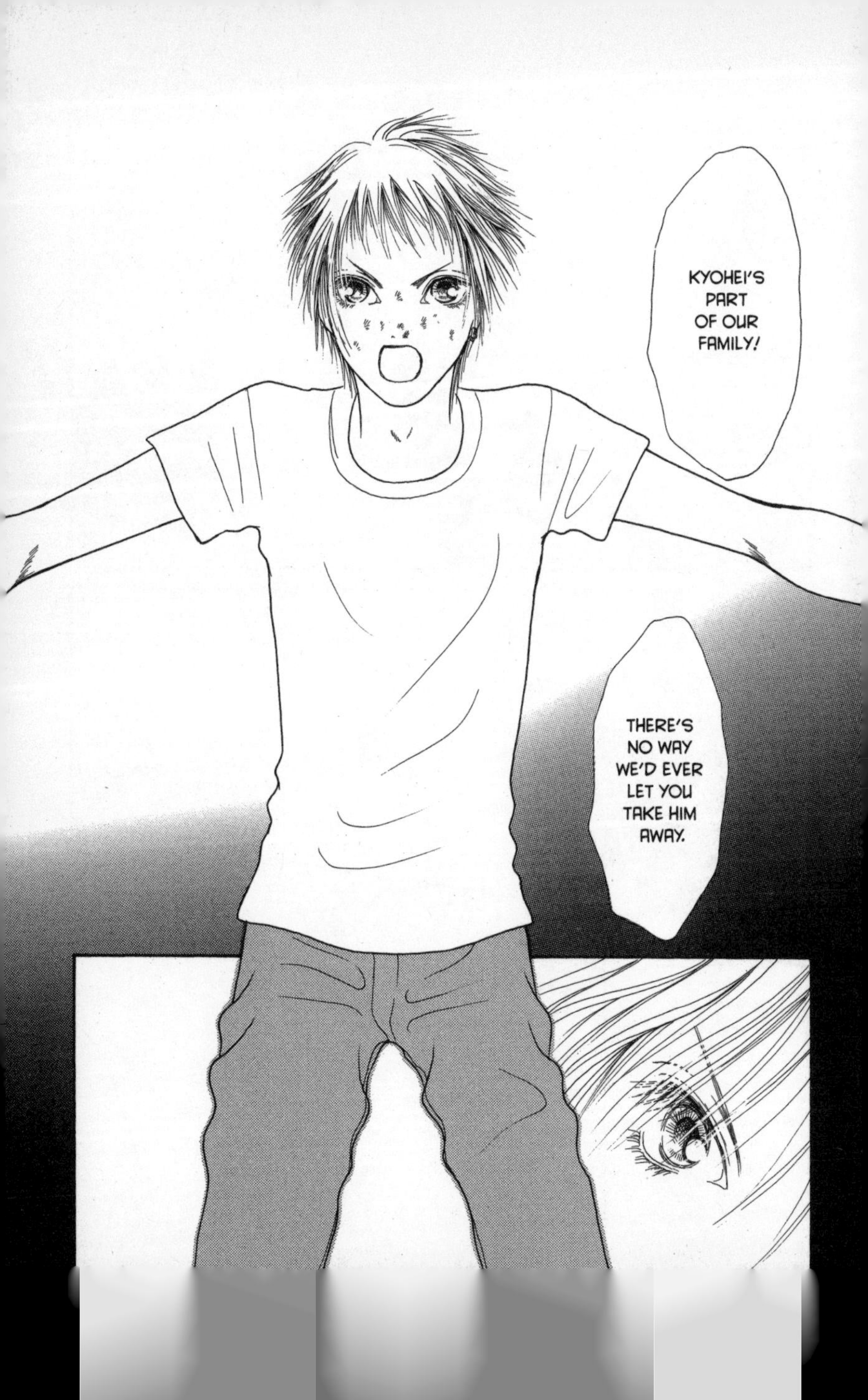
KYOHEI'S PART OF OUR FAMILY!
THERE'S NO WAY WE'D EVER LET YOU TAKE HIM AWAY.

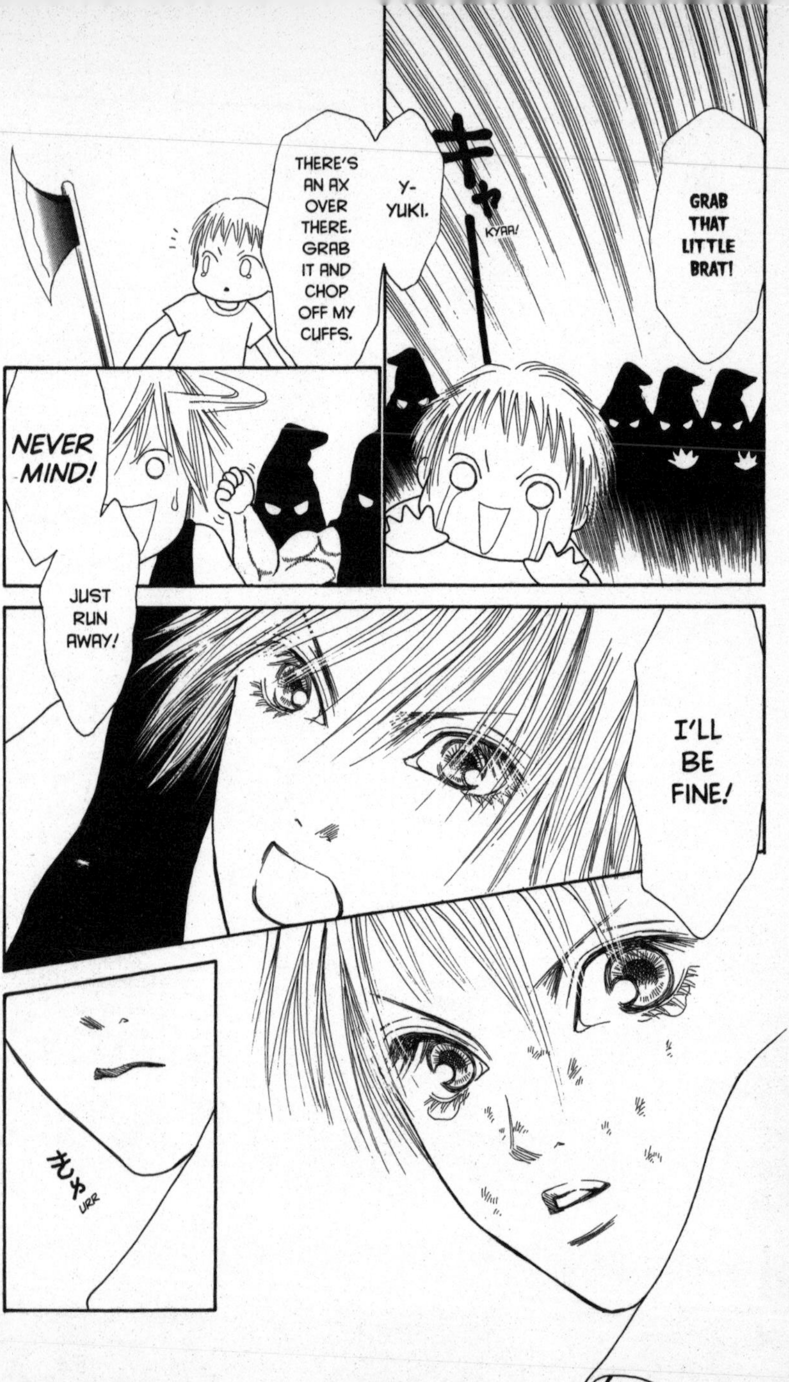
GRAB THAT LITTLE BRAT!
キャ
KYAA!
Y-YUKI.
THERE'S AN AX OVER THERE. GRAB IT AND CHOP OFF MY CUFFS.
NEVER MIND!
JUST RUN AWAY!
I'LL BE FINE!
もゃ
URR

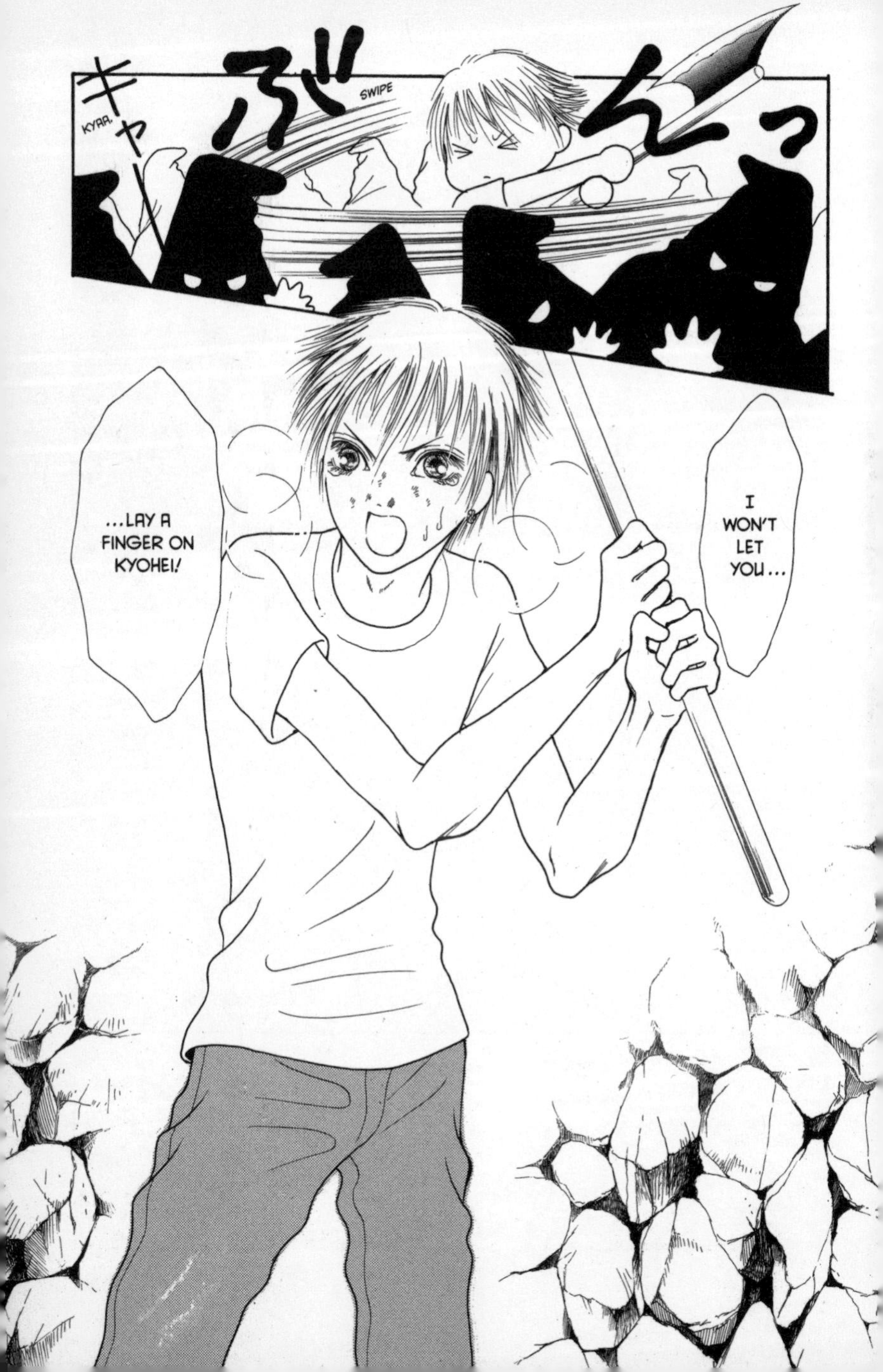
ぶんっ
SWIPE
キャ
KYAA
I WON'T LET YOU...
...LAY A FINGER ON KYOHEI!

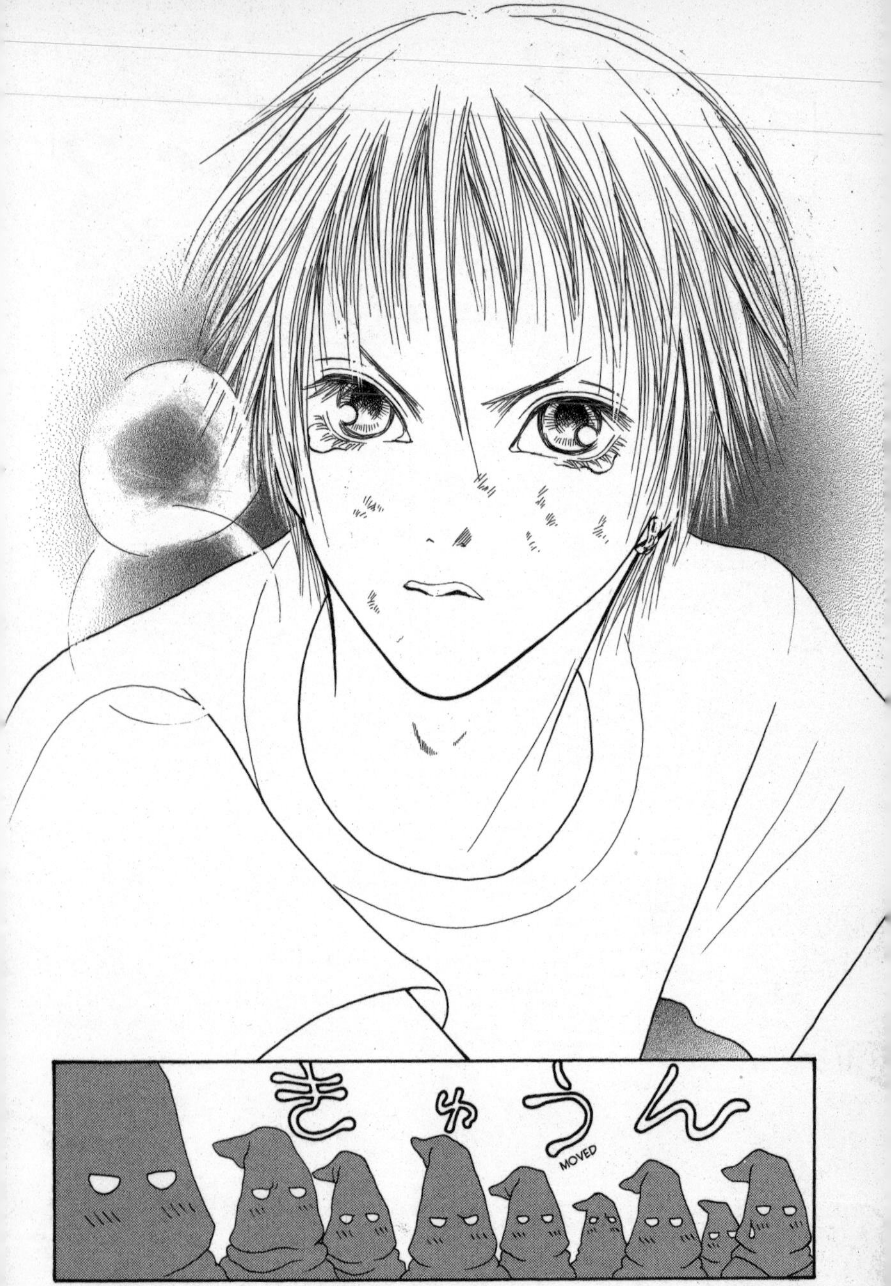
きゅうん
MOVED

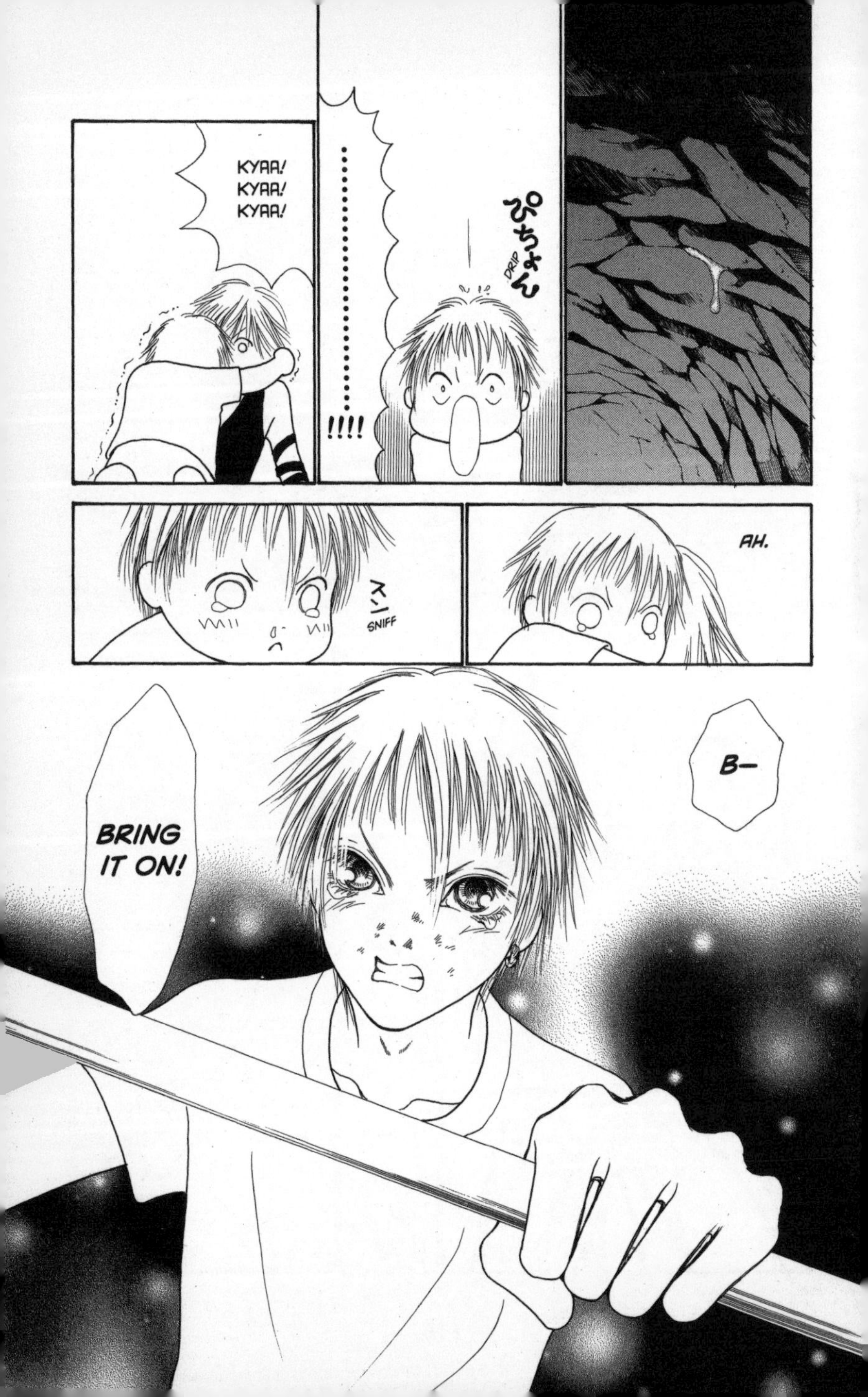
ぴちょん
DRIP
......
!!!!
KYAA!
KYAA!
KYAA!
AH.
スン
SNIFF
B—
BRING IT ON!

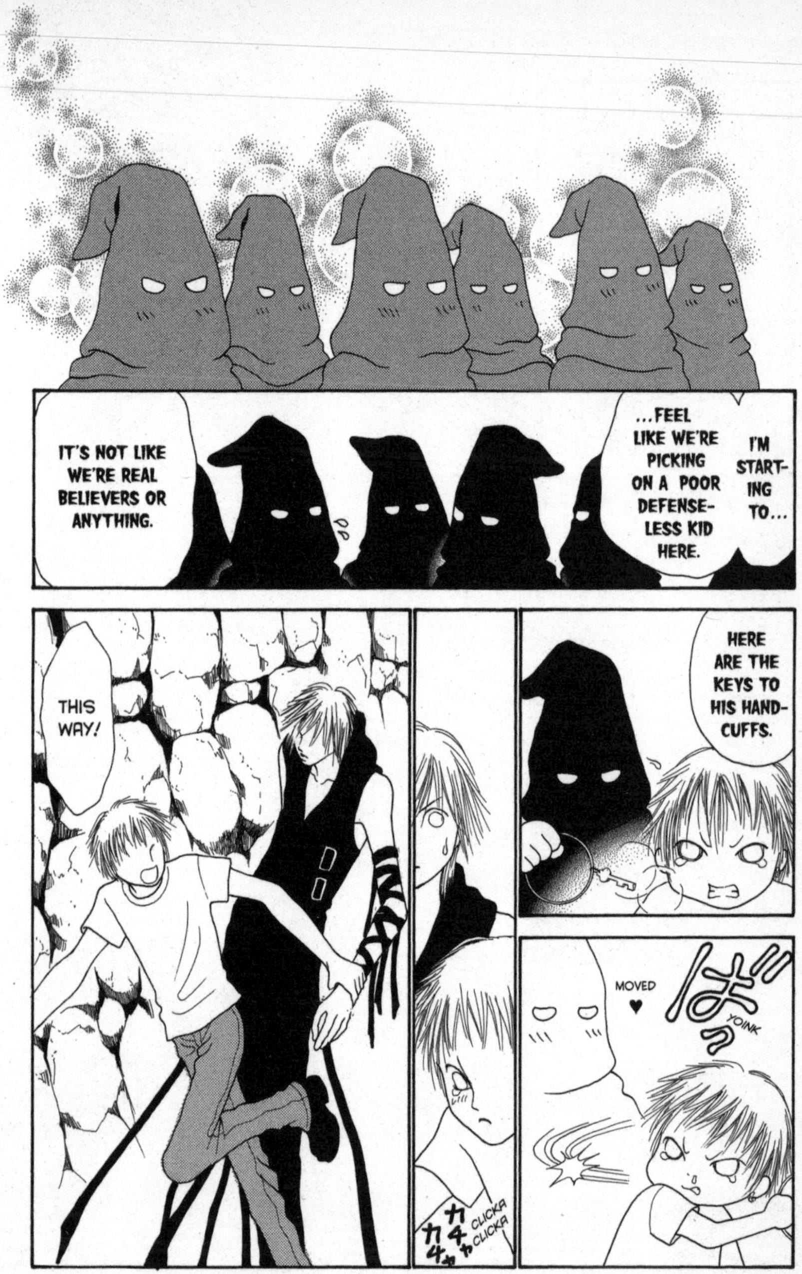
I'M STARTING TO...
...FEEL LIKE WE'RE PICKING ON A POOR DEFENSELESS KID HERE.
IT'S NOT LIKE WE'RE REAL BELIEVERS OR ANYTHING.
HERE ARE THE KEYS TO HIS HANDCUFFS.
MOVED ♥
YOINK
CLICKA CLICKA
THIS WAY!

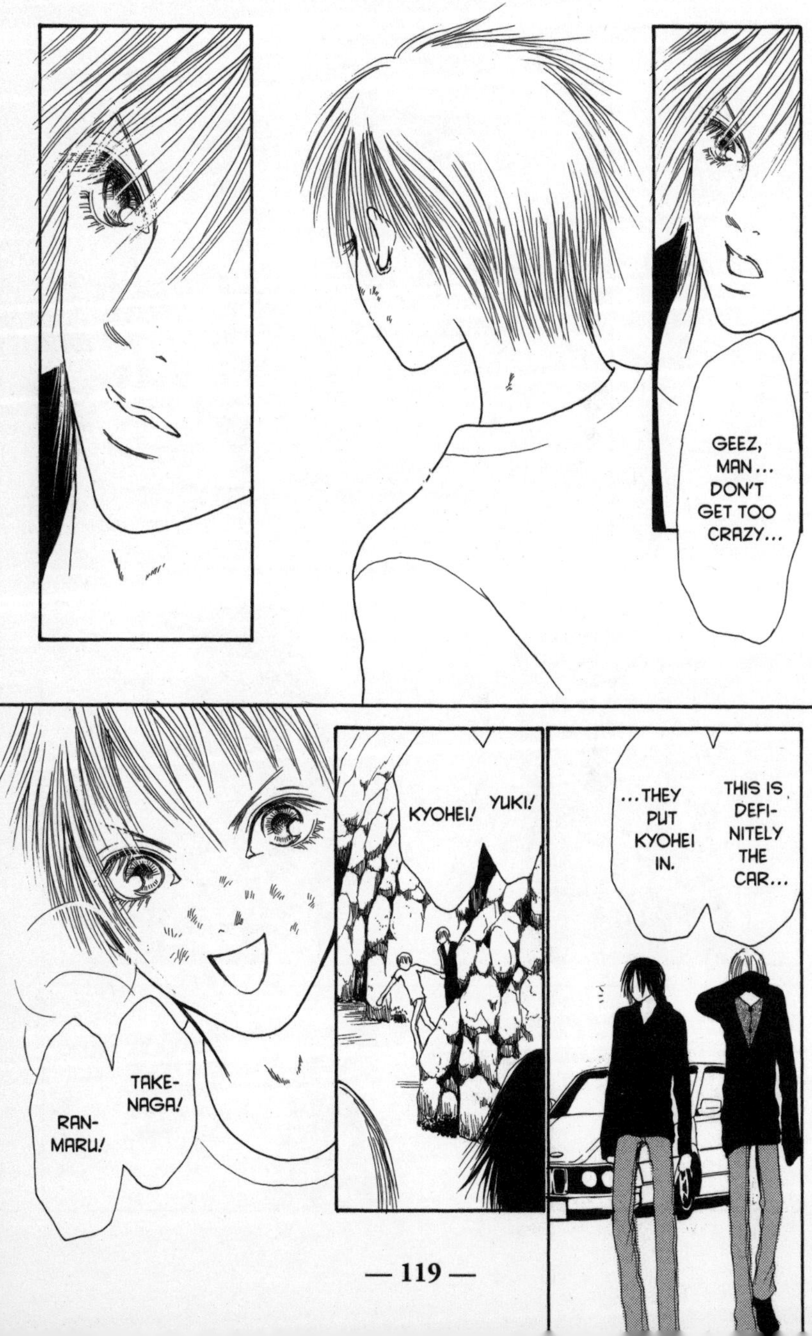
GEEZ, MAN... DON'T GET TOO CRAZY...
THIS IS DEFI-NITELY THE CAR...
...THEY PUT KYOHEI IN.
YUKI!
KYOHEI!
TAKE-NAGA!
RAN-MARU!

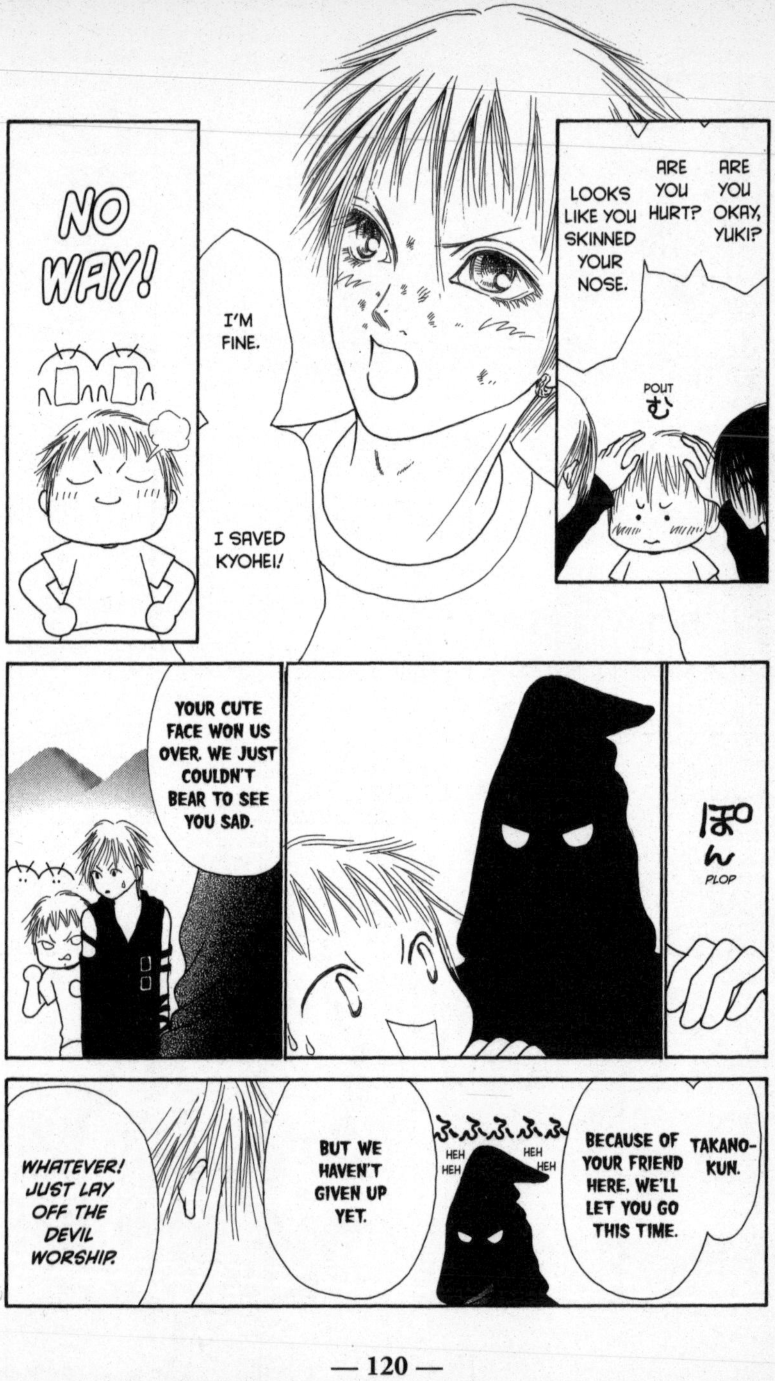
ARE YOU OKAY, YUKI?
ARE YOU HURT?
LOOKS LIKE YOU SKINNED YOUR NOSE.
む
POUT
I'M FINE.
I SAVED KYOHEI!
NO WAY!
ぽん
PLOP
YOUR CUTE FACE WON US OVER. WE JUST COULDN'T BEAR TO SEE YOU SAD.
TAKANO-KUN.
BECAUSE OF YOUR FRIEND HERE, WE'LL LET YOU GO THIS TIME.
ふふふふふ
HEH HEH HEH HEH
BUT WE HAVEN'T GIVEN UP YET.
WHATEVER! JUST LAY OFF THE DEVIL WORSHIP.

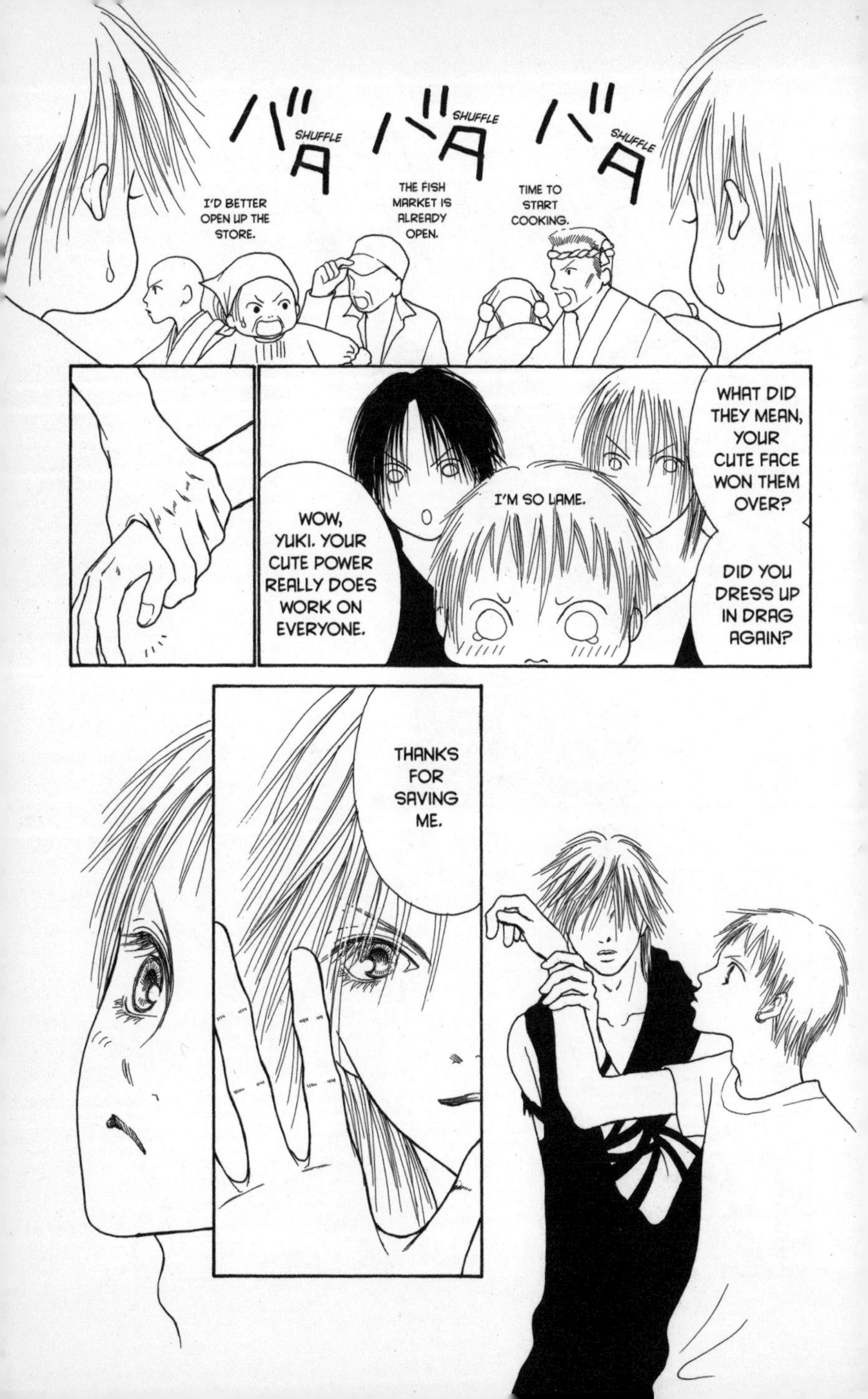

バタ
SHUFFLE
TIME TO START COOKING.
バタ
SHUFFLE
THE FISH MARKET IS ALREADY OPEN.
バタ
SHUFFLE
I'D BETTER OPEN UP THE STORE.
WHAT DID THEY MEAN, YOUR CUTE FACE WON THEM OVER?
DID YOU DRESS UP IN DRAG AGAIN?
I'M SO LAME.
WOW, YUKI. YOUR CUTE POWER REALLY DOES WORK ON EVERYONE.
THANKS FOR SAVING ME.

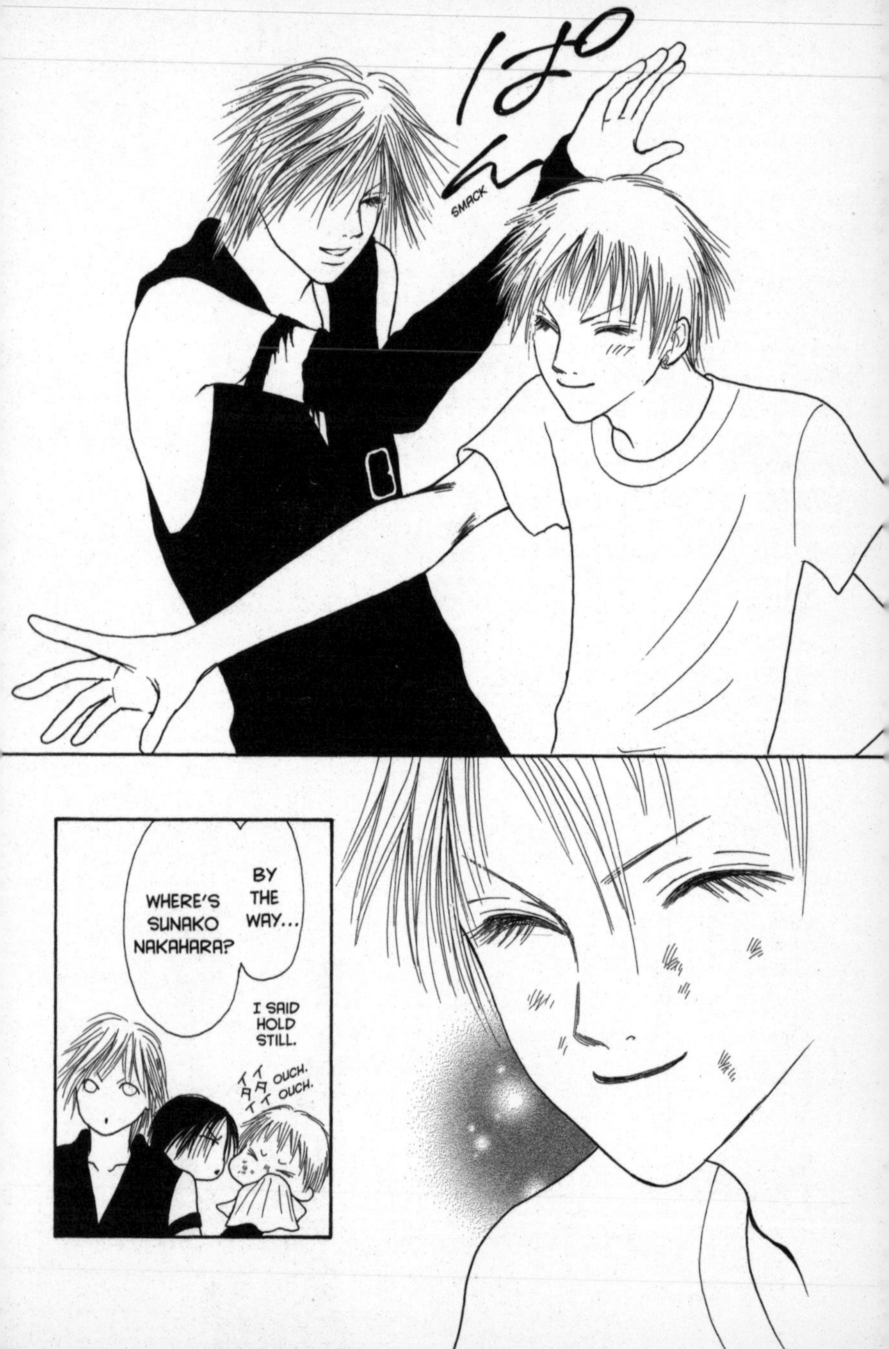
ぱん
SMACK
BY THE WAY... WHERE'S SUNAKO NAKAHARA?
I SAID HOLD STILL.
イタイ OUCH.
イタイ OUCH.

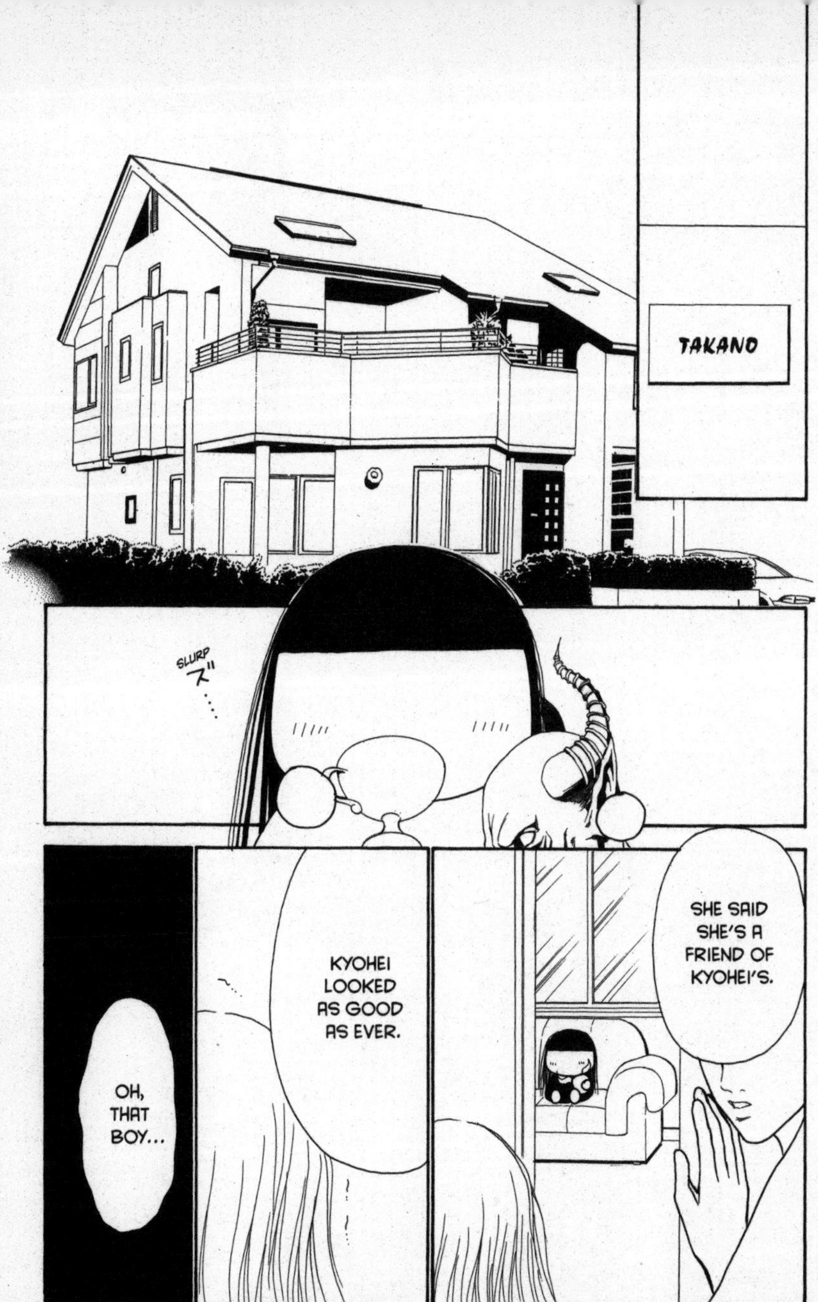
TAKANO
SLURP
ズ"
SHE SAID SHE'S A FRIEND OF KYOHEI'S.
KYOHEI LOOKED AS GOOD AS EVER.
OH, THAT BOY...

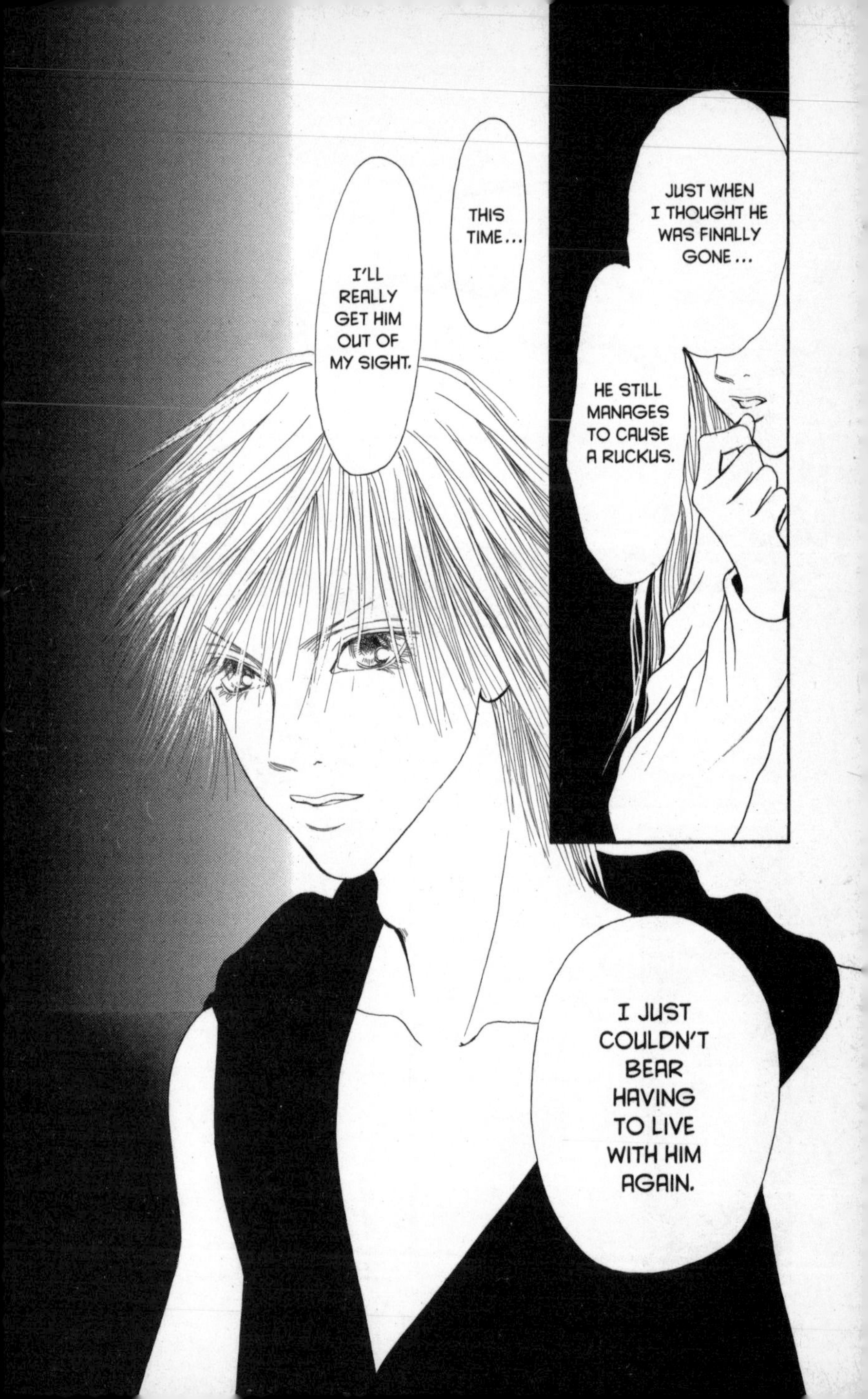
JUST WHEN I THOUGHT HE WAS FINALLY GONE...
HE STILL MANAGES TO CAUSE A RUCKUS.
THIS TIME...
I'LL REALLY GET HIM OUT OF MY SIGHT.
I JUST COULDN'T BEAR HAVING TO LIVE WITH HIM AGAIN.

Eye of the Storm

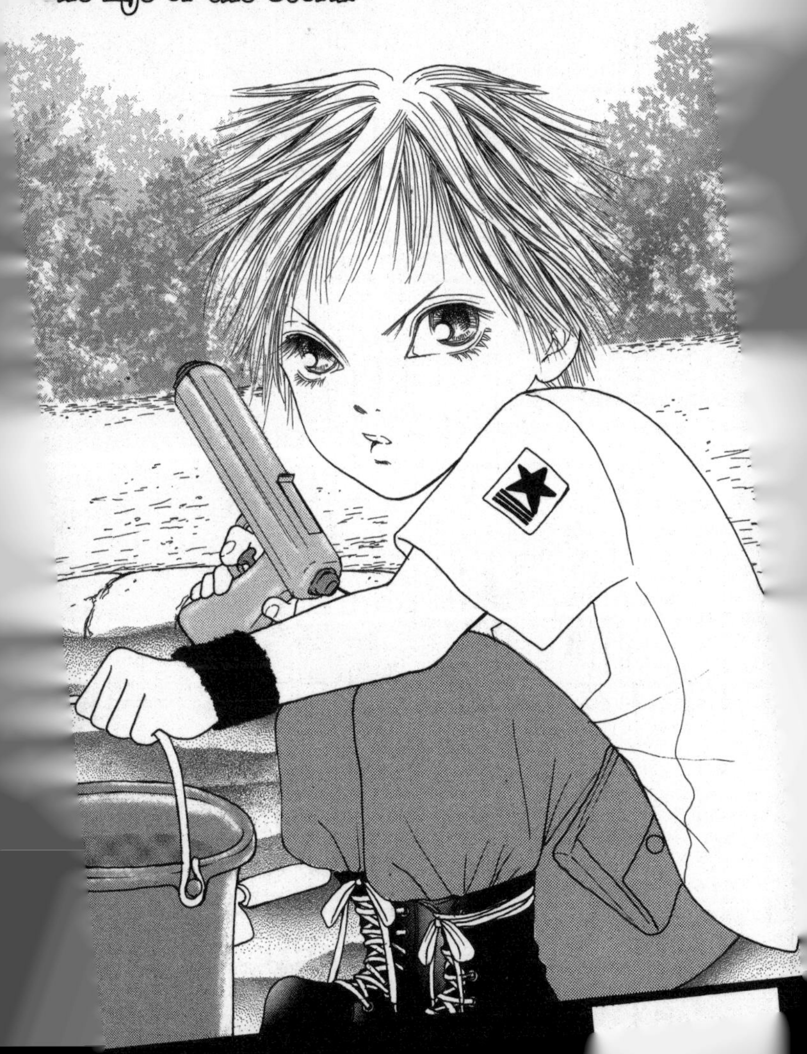

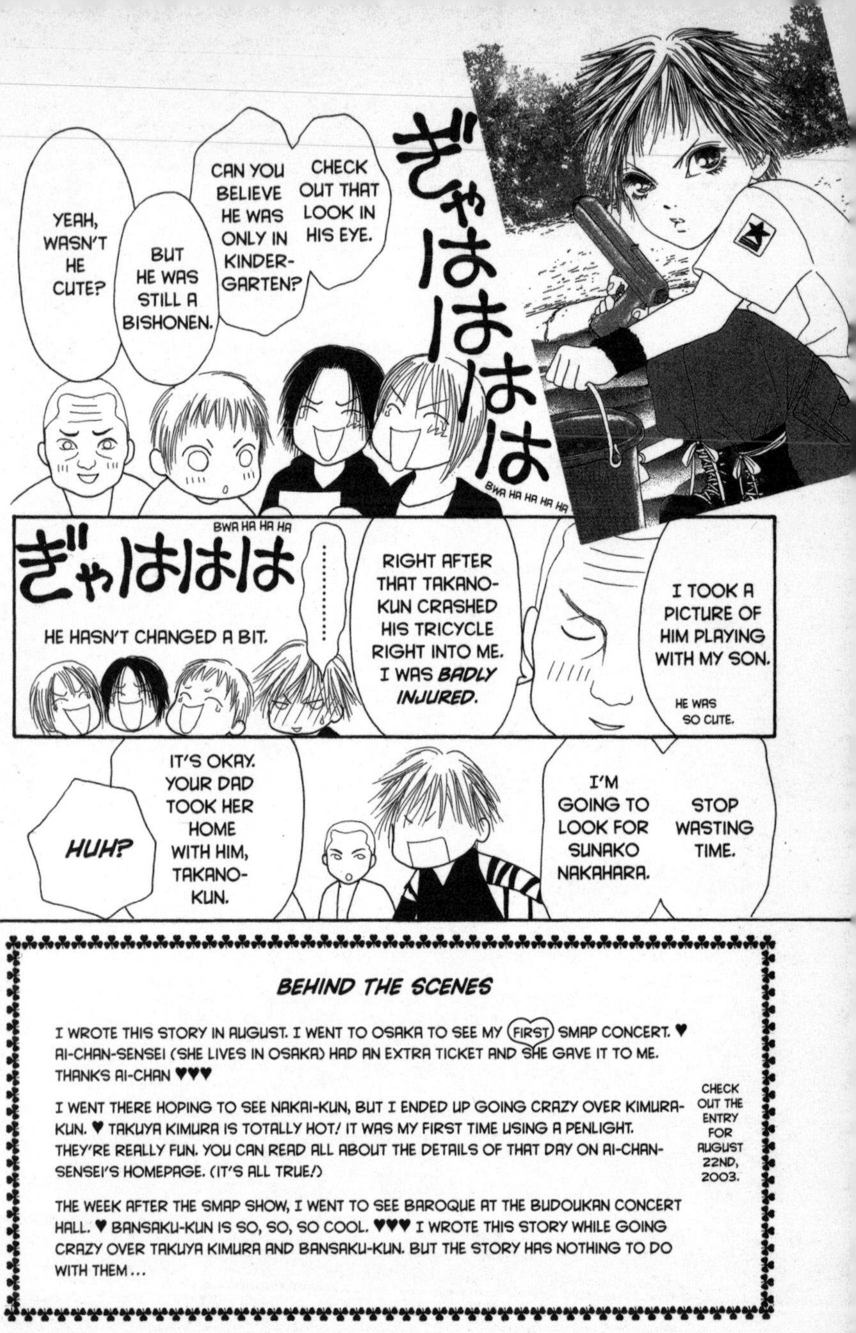
ぎゃははは
BWA HA HA HA
CHECK OUT THAT LOOK IN HIS EYE.
CAN YOU BELIEVE HE WAS ONLY IN KINDER-GARTEN?
BUT HE WAS STILL A BISHONEN.
YEAH, WASN'T HE CUTE?
I TOOK A PICTURE OF HIM PLAYING WITH MY SON.
HE WAS SO CUTE.
RIGHT AFTER THAT TAKANO-KUN CRASHED HIS TRICYCLE RIGHT INTO ME. I WAS *BADLY INJURED*.
......
ぎゃははは
BWA HA HA HA
HE HASN'T CHANGED A BIT.
STOP WASTING TIME.
I'M GOING TO LOOK FOR SUNAKO NAKAHARA.
IT'S OKAY. YOUR DAD TOOK HER HOME WITH HIM, TAKANO-KUN.
HUH?

BEHIND THE SCENES

I WROTE THIS STORY IN AUGUST. I WENT TO OSAKA TO SEE MY (FIRST) SMAP CONCERT. ♥ AI-CHAN-SENSEI (SHE LIVES IN OSAKA) HAD AN EXTRA TICKET AND SHE GAVE IT TO ME. THANKS AI-CHAN ♥♥♥

I WENT THERE HOPING TO SEE NAKAI-KUN, BUT I ENDED UP GOING CRAZY OVER KIMURA-KUN. ♥ TAKUYA KIMURA IS TOTALLY HOT! IT WAS MY FIRST TIME USING A PENLIGHT. THEY'RE REALLY FUN. YOU CAN READ ALL ABOUT THE DETAILS OF THAT DAY ON AI-CHAN-SENSEI'S HOMEPAGE. (IT'S ALL TRUE!)

CHECK OUT THE ENTRY FOR AUGUST 22ND, 2003.

THE WEEK AFTER THE SMAP SHOW, I WENT TO SEE BAROQUE AT THE BUDOUKAN CONCERT HALL. ♥ BANSAKU-KUN IS SO, SO, SO COOL. ♥♥♥ I WROTE THIS STORY WHILE GOING CRAZY OVER TAKUYA KIMURA AND BANSAKU-KUN. BUT THE STORY HAS NOTHING TO DO WITH THEM...

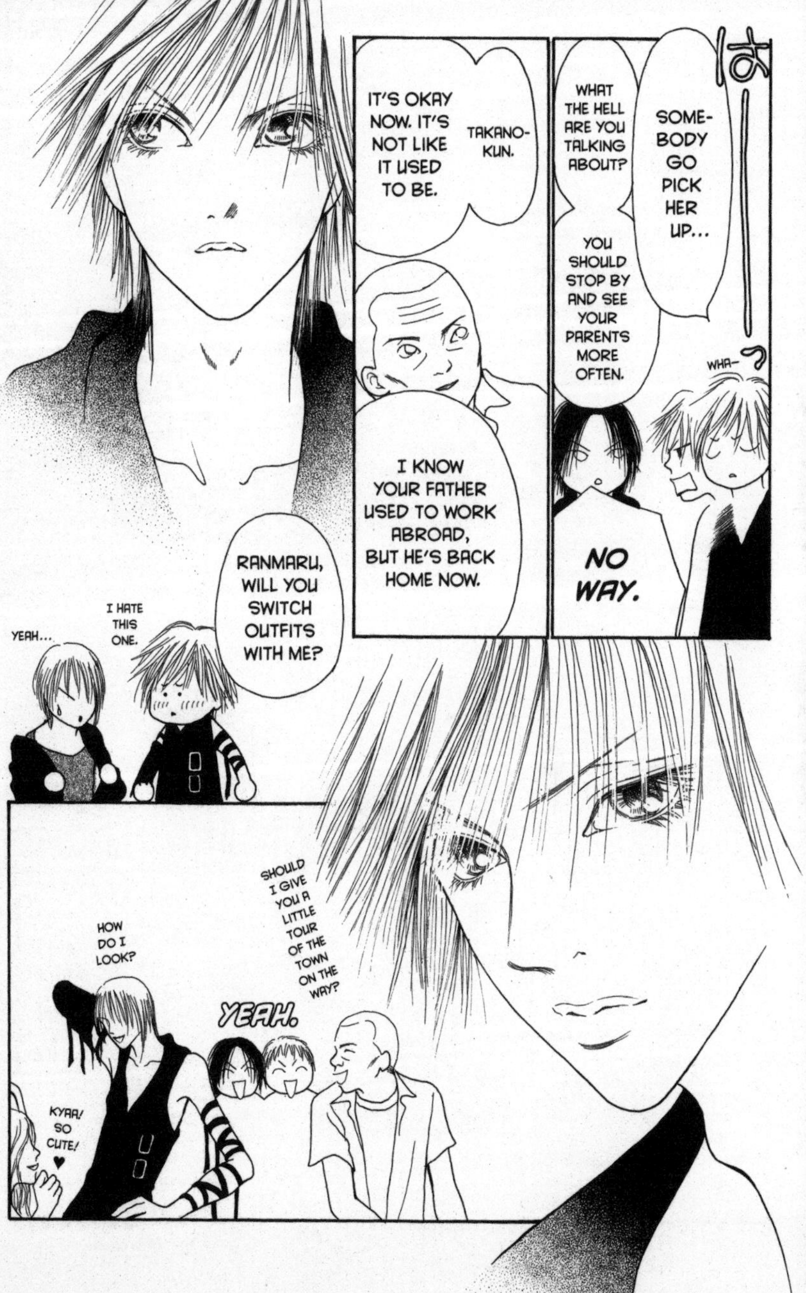
はーっ
SOME-BODY GO PICK HER UP...
WHAT THE HELL ARE YOU TALKING ABOUT?
YOU SHOULD STOP BY AND SEE YOUR PARENTS MORE OFTEN.
WHA-
NO WAY.
TAKANO-KUN.
IT'S OKAY NOW. IT'S NOT LIKE IT USED TO BE.
I KNOW YOUR FATHER USED TO WORK ABROAD, BUT HE'S BACK HOME NOW.
RANMARU, WILL YOU SWITCH OUTFITS WITH ME?
I HATE THIS ONE.
YEAH...
SHOULD I GIVE YOU A LITTLE TOUR OF THE TOWN ON THE WAY?
HOW DO I LOOK?
YEAH.
KYAA! SO CUTE! ♥

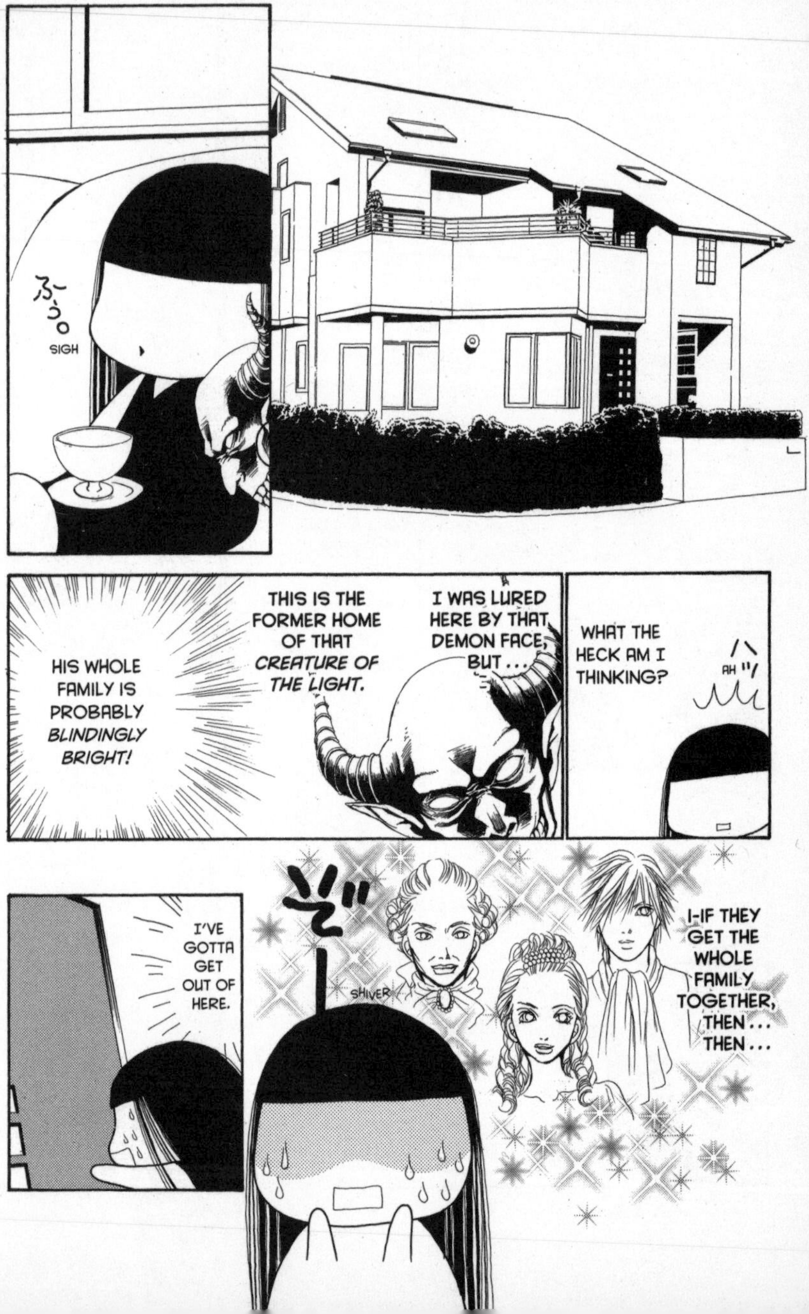
SIGH
AH
WHAT THE HECK AM I THINKING?
I WAS LURED HERE BY THAT DEMON FACE, BUT ...
THIS IS THE FORMER HOME OF THAT *CREATURE OF THE LIGHT.*
HIS WHOLE FAMILY IS PROBABLY *BLINDINGLY BRIGHT!*
I-IF THEY GET THE WHOLE FAMILY TOGETHER, THEN ... THEN ...
SHIVER
I'VE GOTTA GET OUT OF HERE.

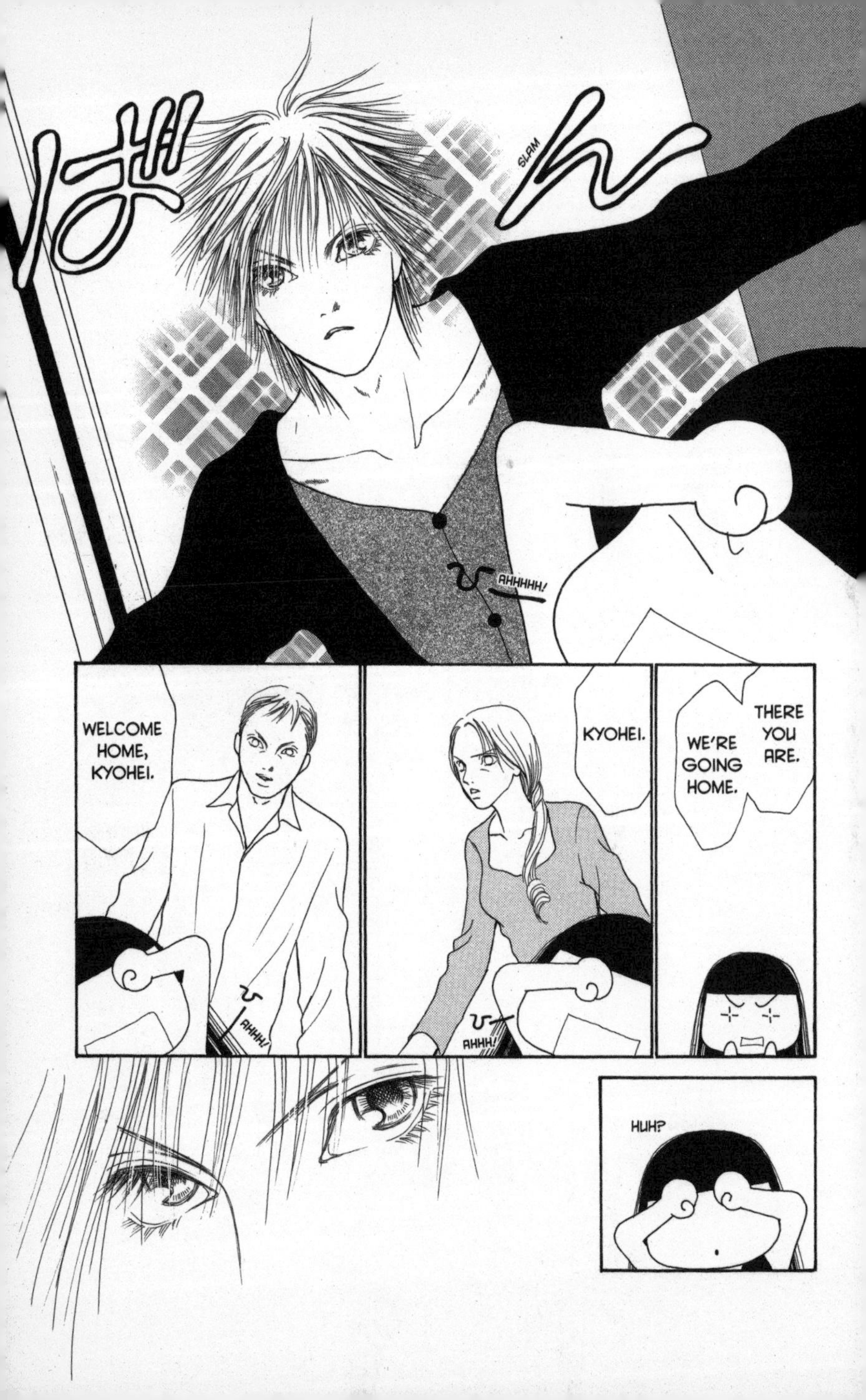

ばん
SLAM
AHHHHH!
THERE YOU ARE.
WE'RE GOING HOME.
KYOHEI.
AHHH!
WELCOME HOME, KYOHEI.
AHHH!
HUH?

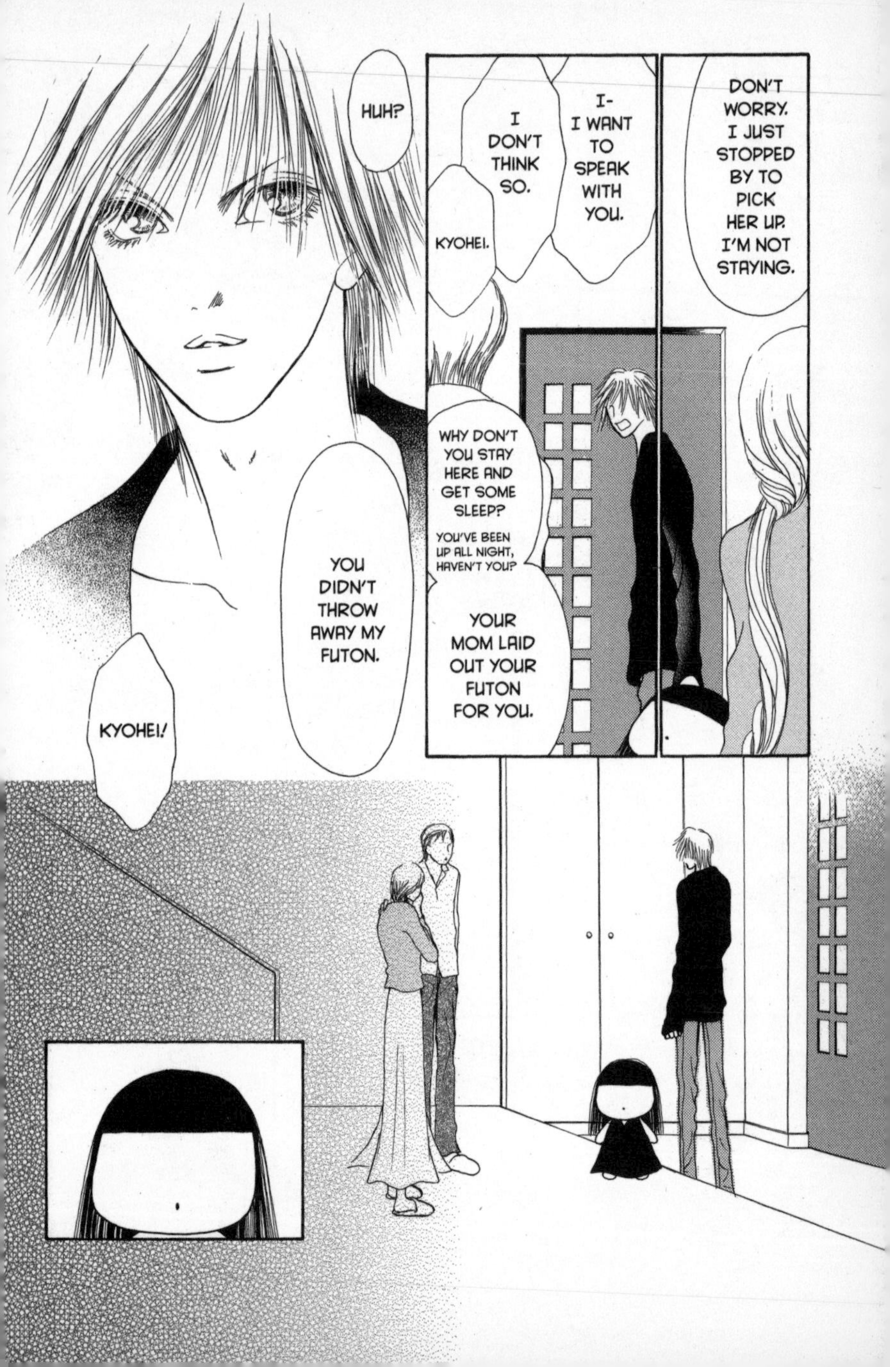
DON'T WORRY. I JUST STOPPED BY TO PICK HER UP. I'M NOT STAYING.
I- I WANT TO SPEAK WITH YOU.
I DON'T THINK SO.
KYOHEI.
WHY DON'T YOU STAY HERE AND GET SOME SLEEP?
YOU'VE BEEN UP ALL NIGHT, HAVEN'T YOU?
YOUR MOM LAID OUT YOUR FUTON FOR YOU.
HUH?
YOU DIDN'T THROW AWAY MY FUTON.
KYOHEI!

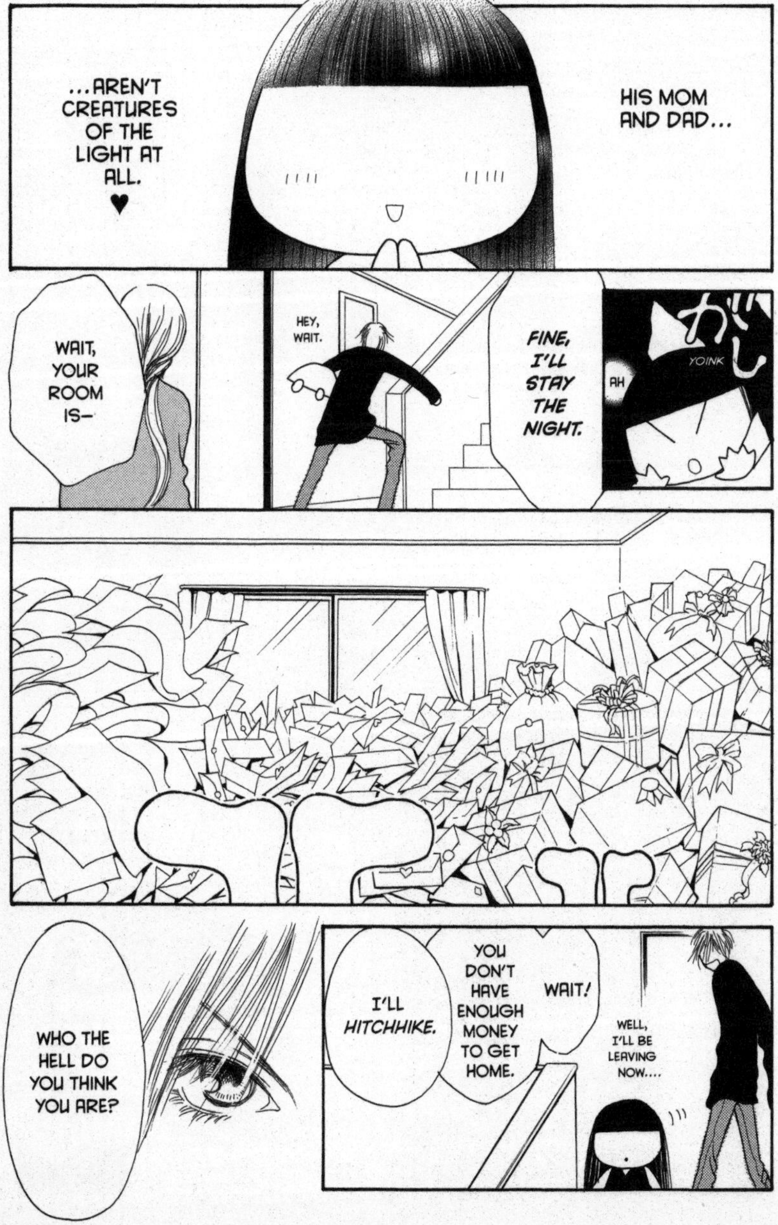
HIS MOM AND DAD...
...AREN'T CREATURES OF THE LIGHT AT ALL. ♥
がし
YOINK
AH
FINE, I'LL STAY THE NIGHT.
HEY, WAIT.
WAIT, YOUR ROOM IS–
WELL, I'LL BE LEAVING NOW....
WAIT!
YOU DON'T HAVE ENOUGH MONEY TO GET HOME.
I'LL HITCHHIKE.
WHO THE HELL DO YOU THINK YOU ARE?

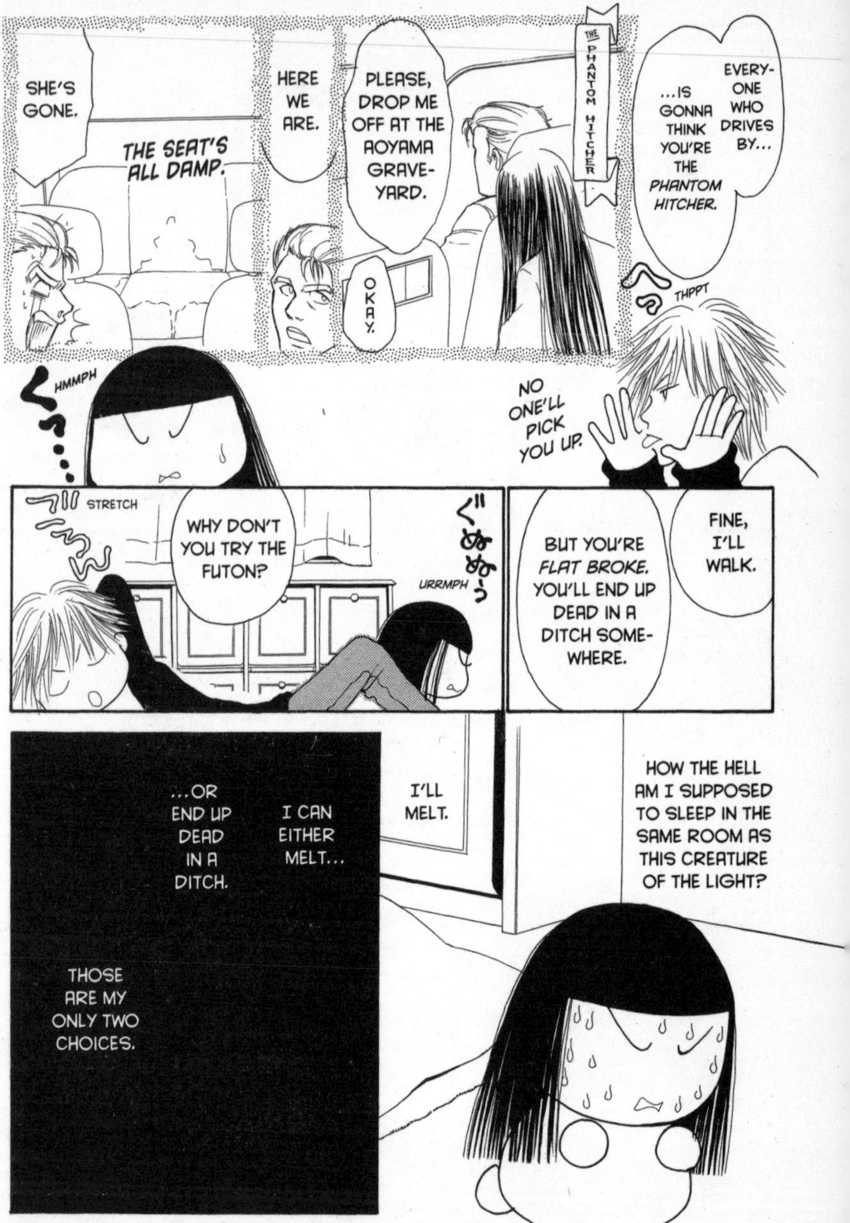
EVERYONE WHO DRIVES BY...
...IS GONNA THINK YOU'RE THE PHANTOM HITCHER.
THE PHANTOM HITCHER
PLEASE, DROP ME OFF AT THE AOYAMA GRAVEYARD.
OKAY.
HERE WE ARE.
SHE'S GONE.
THE SEAT'S ALL DAMP.
THPPT
NO ONE'LL PICK YOU UP.
HMMPH
FINE, I'LL WALK.
BUT YOU'RE FLAT BROKE. YOU'LL END UP DEAD IN A DITCH SOMEWHERE.
URRMPH
WHY DON'T YOU TRY THE FUTON?
STRETCH
HOW THE HELL AM I SUPPOSED TO SLEEP IN THE SAME ROOM AS THIS CREATURE OF THE LIGHT?
I'LL MELT.
I CAN EITHER MELT...
...OR END UP DEAD IN A DITCH.
THOSE ARE MY ONLY TWO CHOICES.

I'LL TAKE DEATH ANY DAY!!!

UM...

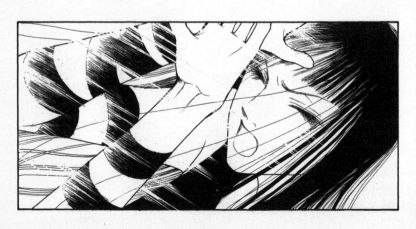

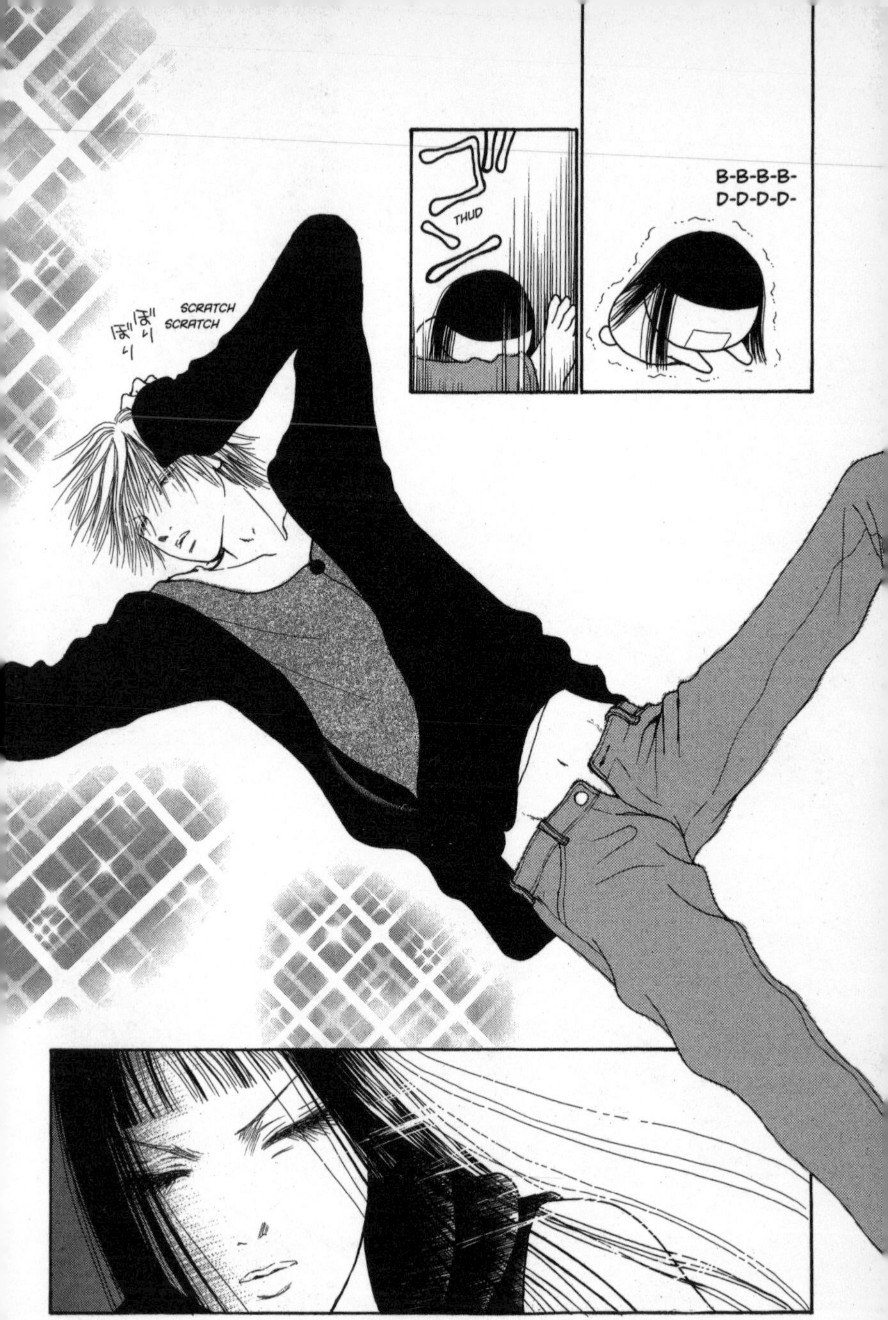
B-B-B-B-
D-D-D-D-
ゴン
THUD
ぼりぼり
SCRATCH
SCRATCH

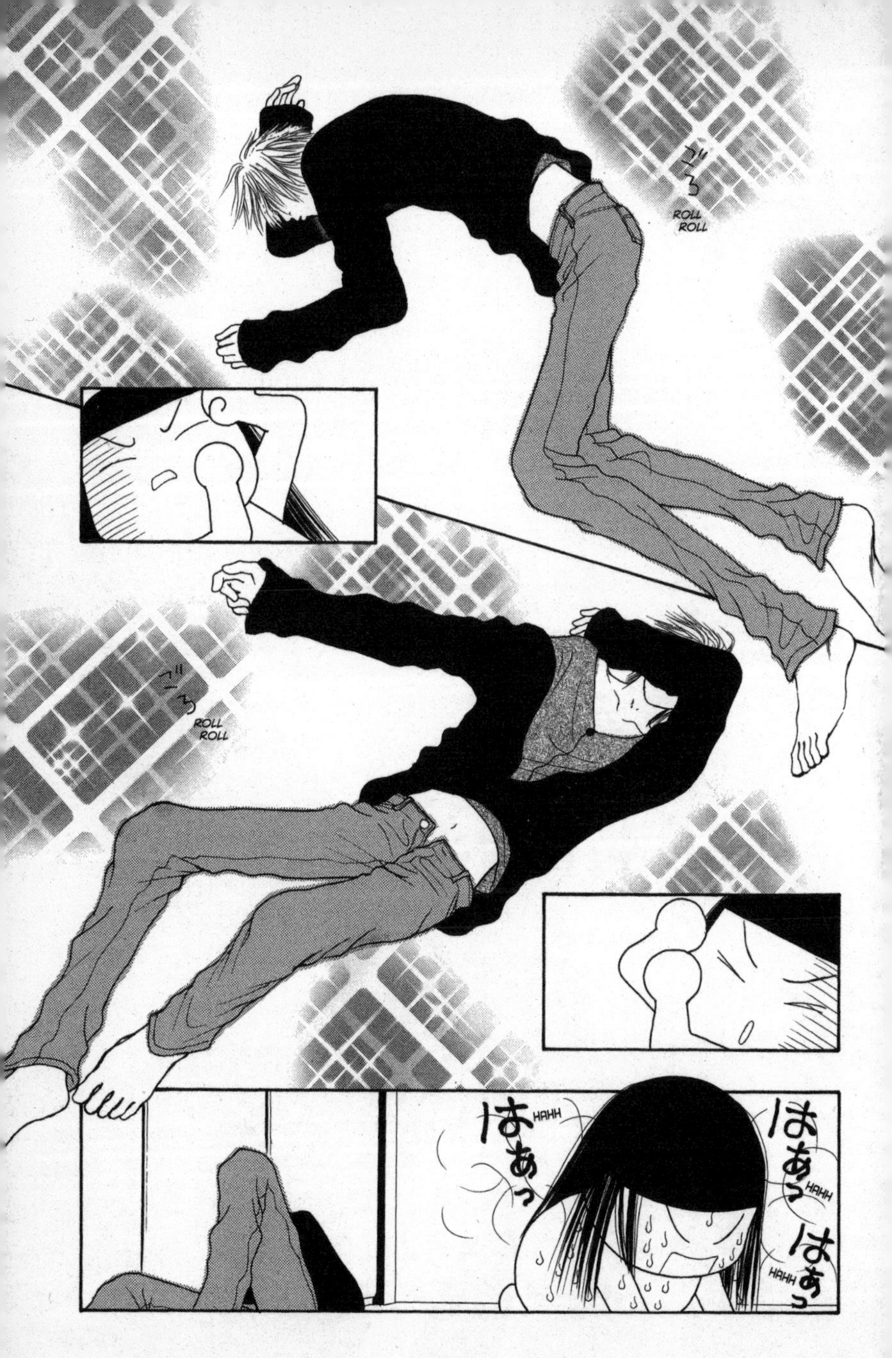
ごろ
ROLL ROLL
ごろ
ROLL ROLL
はあっ
HAHH
はあっ
HAHH
はあっ
HAHH

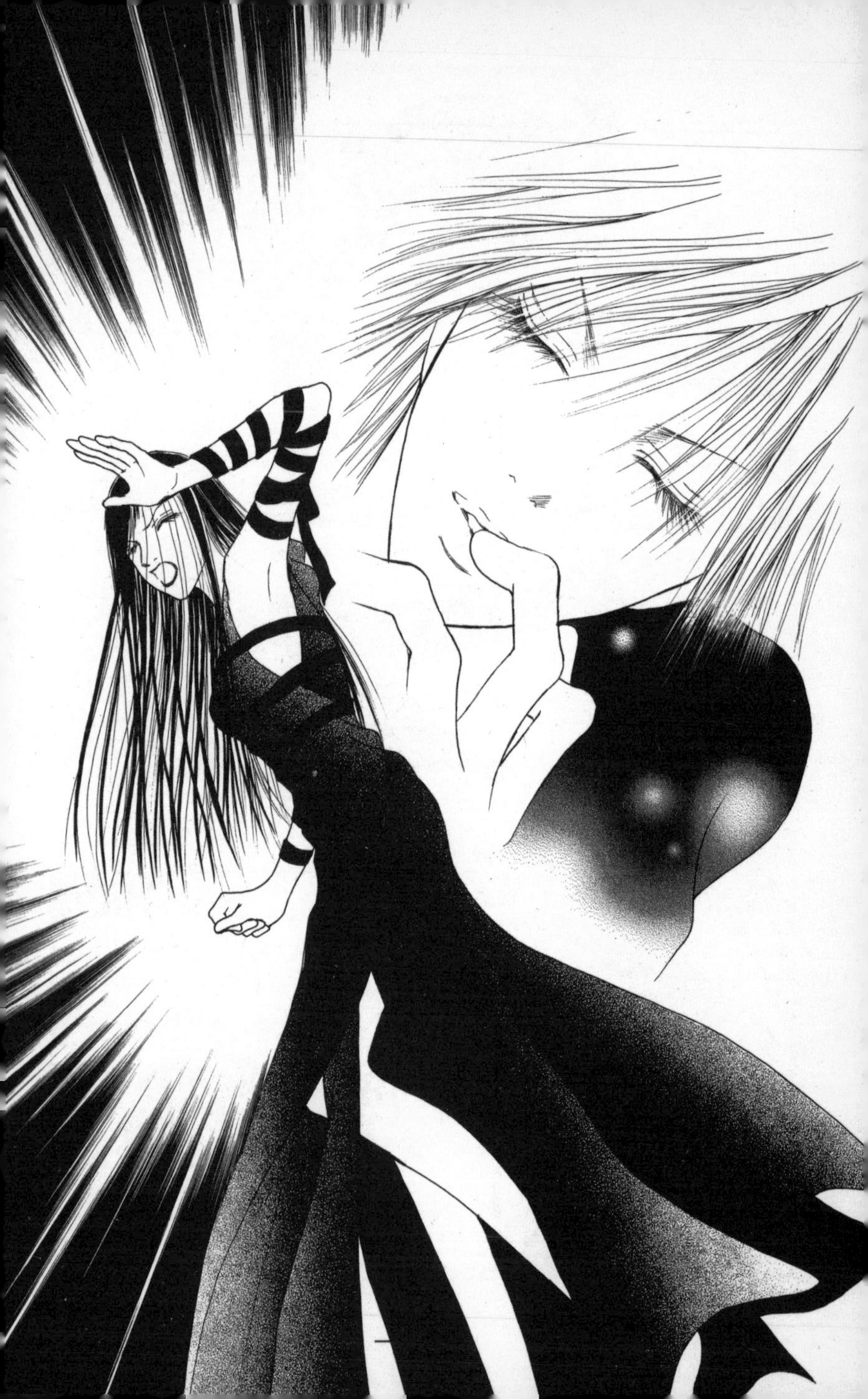

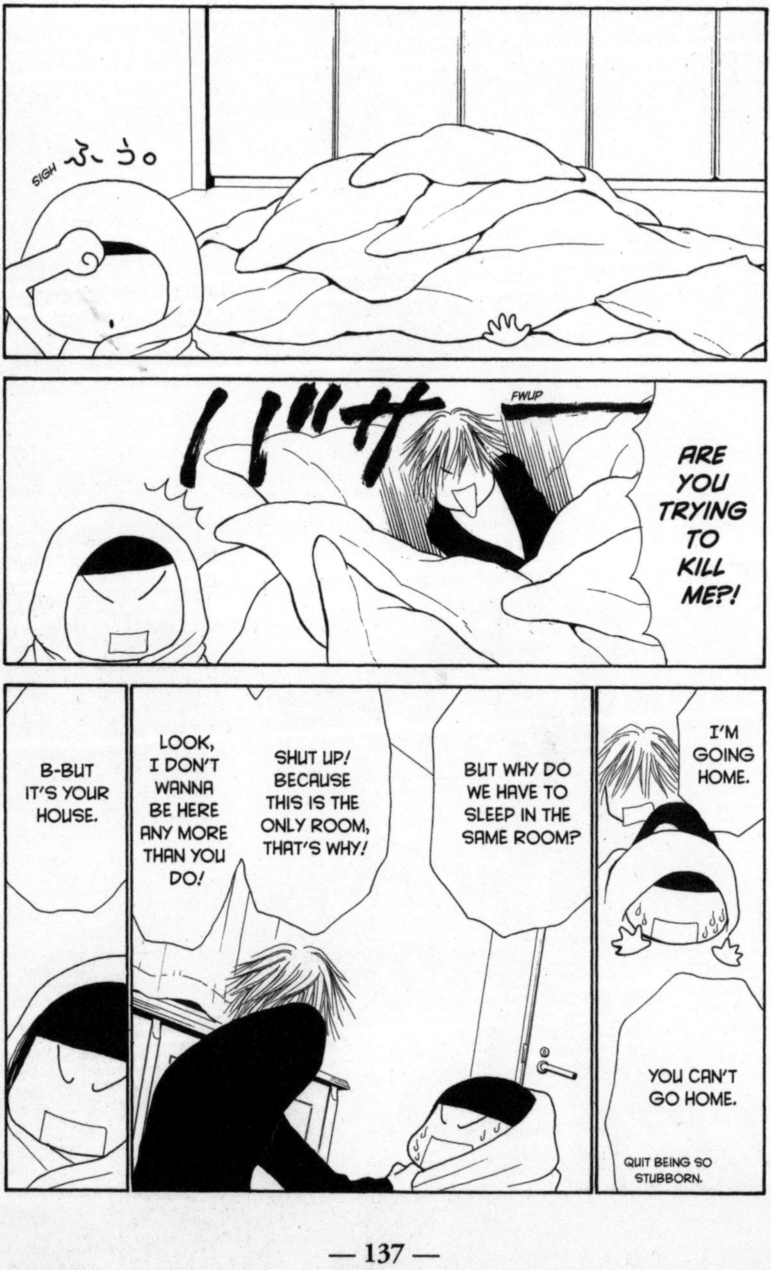
SIGH
ふぅ。
バサ
FWUP
ARE YOU TRYING TO KILL ME?!
I'M GOING HOME.
YOU CAN'T GO HOME.
QUIT BEING SO STUBBORN.
BUT WHY DO WE HAVE TO SLEEP IN THE SAME ROOM?
SHUT UP! BECAUSE THIS IS THE ONLY ROOM, THAT'S WHY!
LOOK, I DON'T WANNA BE HERE ANY MORE THAN YOU DO!
B-BUT IT'S YOUR HOUSE.

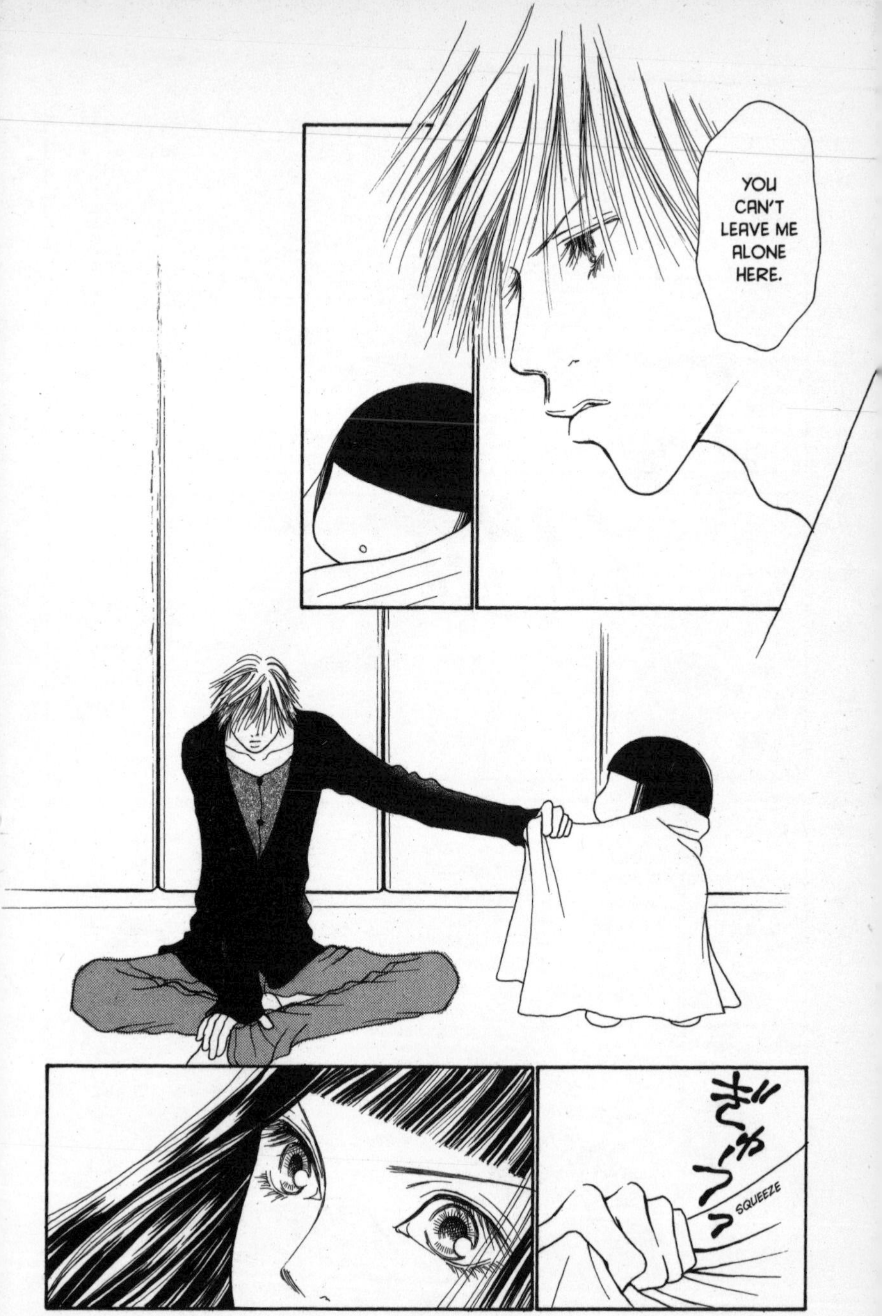
YOU CAN'T LEAVE ME ALONE HERE.
ぎゅっ
SQUEEZE

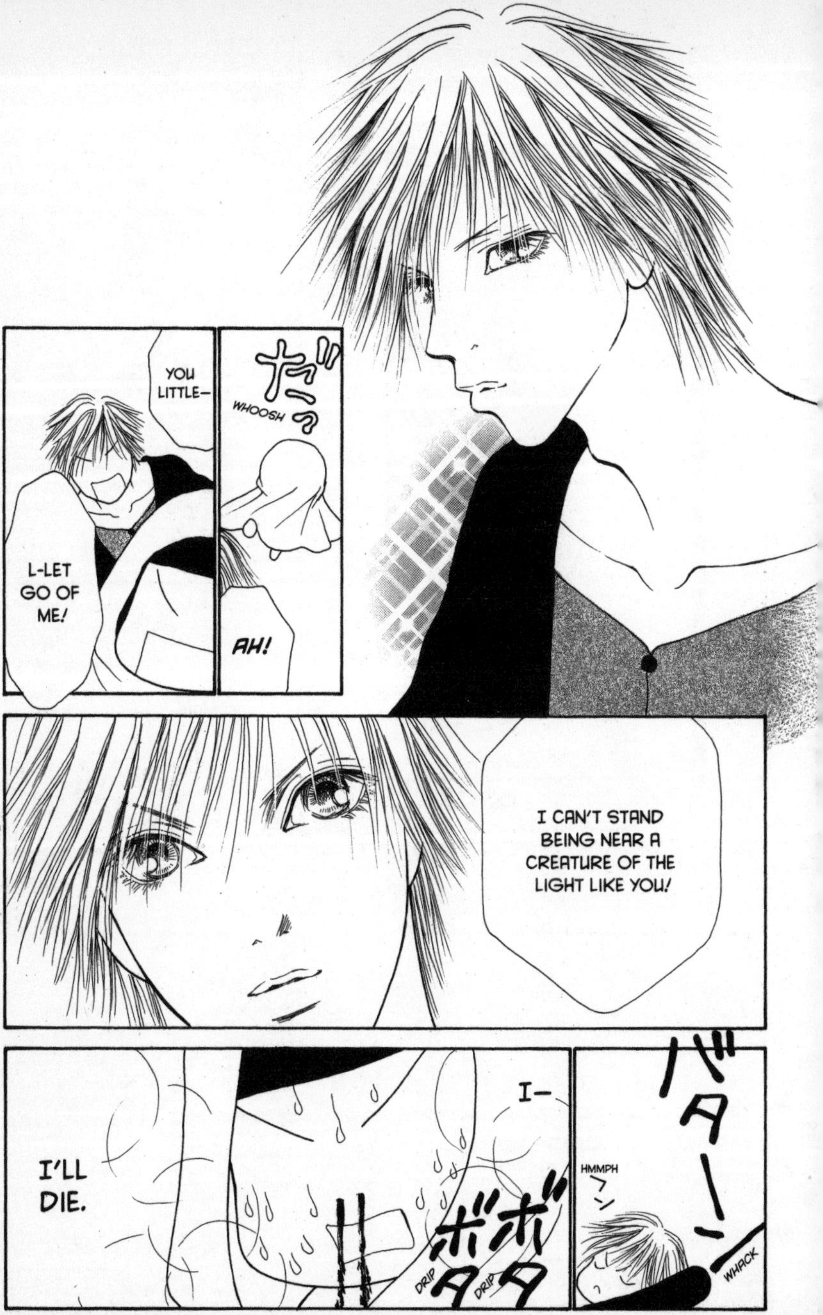
ダッ
WHOOSH
AH!
YOU LITTLE—
L-LET GO OF ME!
I CAN'T STAND BEING NEAR A CREATURE OF THE LIGHT LIKE YOU!
バターン
WHACK
フン
HMMPH
I—
ボタボタ
DRIP DRIP
I'LL DIE.

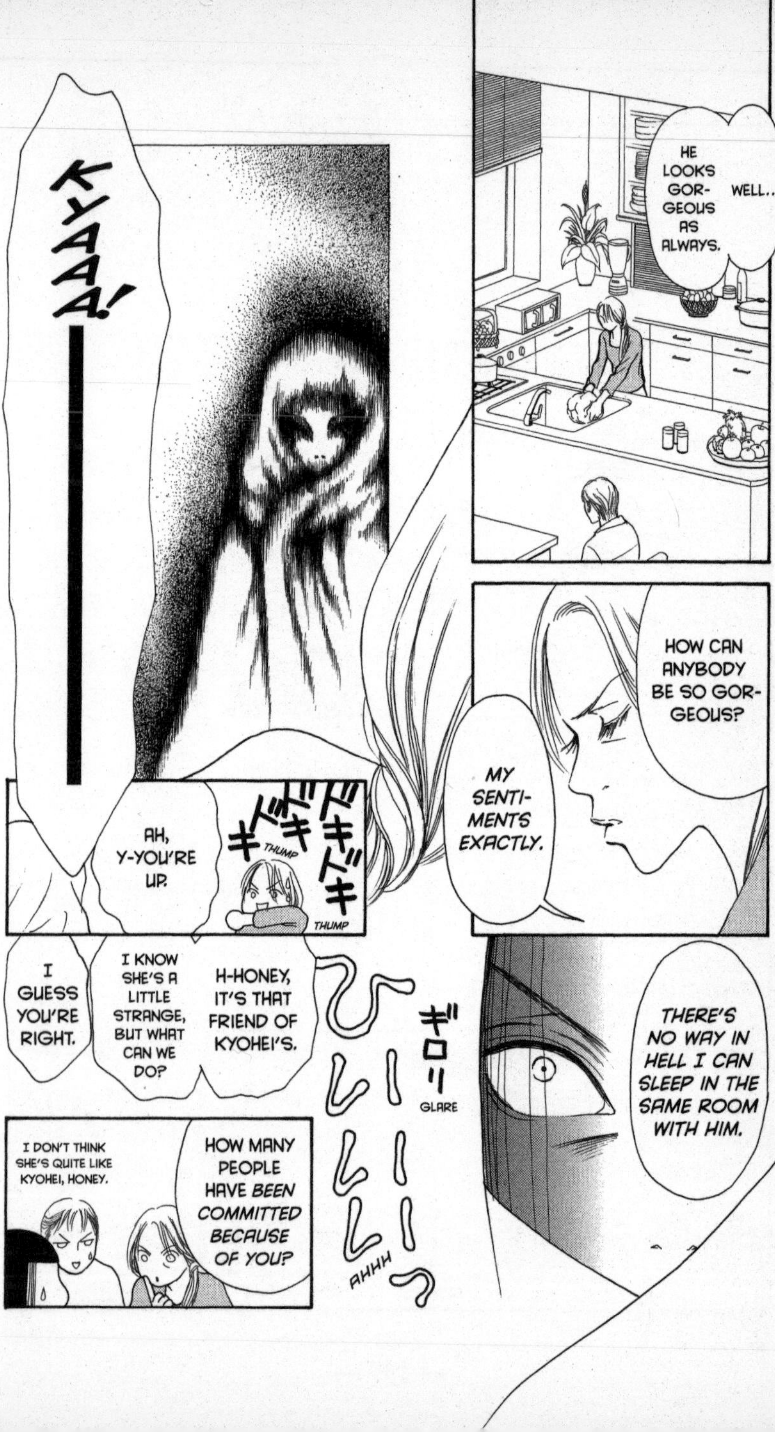

WELL...
HE LOOKS GORGEOUS AS ALWAYS.
HOW CAN ANYBODY BE SO GORGEOUS?
MY SENTIMENTS EXACTLY.
KYAAAA!
ドキドキ
ドキドキ
THUMP
THUMP
AH, Y-YOU'RE UP.
THERE'S NO WAY IN HELL I CAN SLEEP IN THE SAME ROOM WITH HIM.
ギロリ
GLARE
ひ～～～
AHHH
H-HONEY, IT'S THAT FRIEND OF KYOHEI'S.
I KNOW SHE'S A LITTLE STRANGE, BUT WHAT CAN WE DO?
I GUESS YOU'RE RIGHT.
HOW MANY PEOPLE HAVE *BEEN* COMMITTED BECAUSE OF YOU?
I DON'T THINK SHE'S QUITE LIKE KYOHEI, HONEY.

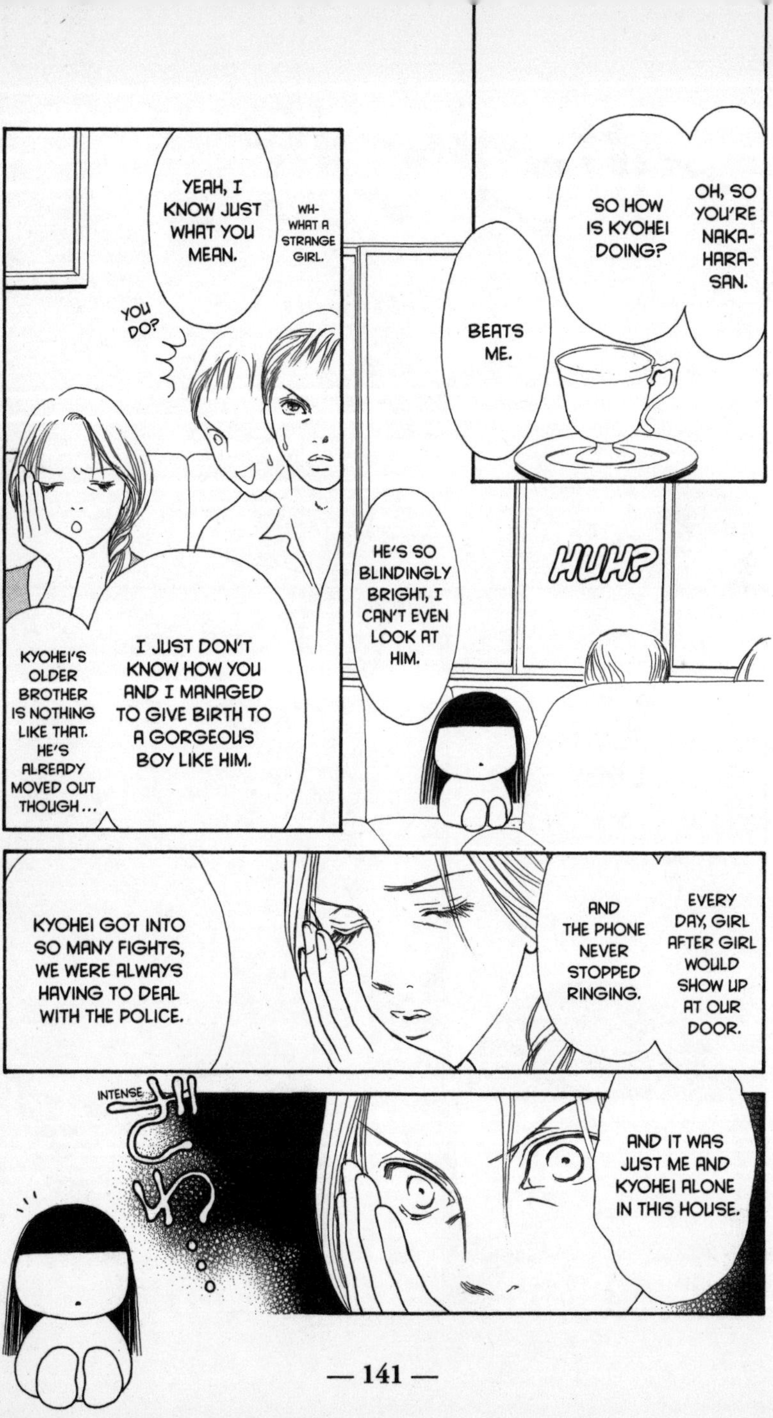
OH, SO YOU'RE NAKA-HARA-SAN.
SO HOW IS KYOHEI DOING?
BEATS ME.
HUH?
HE'S SO BLINDINGLY BRIGHT, I CAN'T EVEN LOOK AT HIM.
WH-WHAT A STRANGE GIRL.
YEAH, I KNOW JUST WHAT YOU MEAN.
YOU DO?
I JUST DON'T KNOW HOW YOU AND I MANAGED TO GIVE BIRTH TO A GORGEOUS BOY LIKE HIM.
KYOHEI'S OLDER BROTHER IS NOTHING LIKE THAT. HE'S ALREADY MOVED OUT THOUGH...
EVERY DAY, GIRL AFTER GIRL WOULD SHOW UP AT OUR DOOR.
AND THE PHONE NEVER STOPPED RINGING.
KYOHEI GOT INTO SO MANY FIGHTS, WE WERE ALWAYS HAVING TO DEAL WITH THE POLICE.
AND IT WAS JUST ME AND KYOHEI ALONE IN THIS HOUSE.
INTENSE

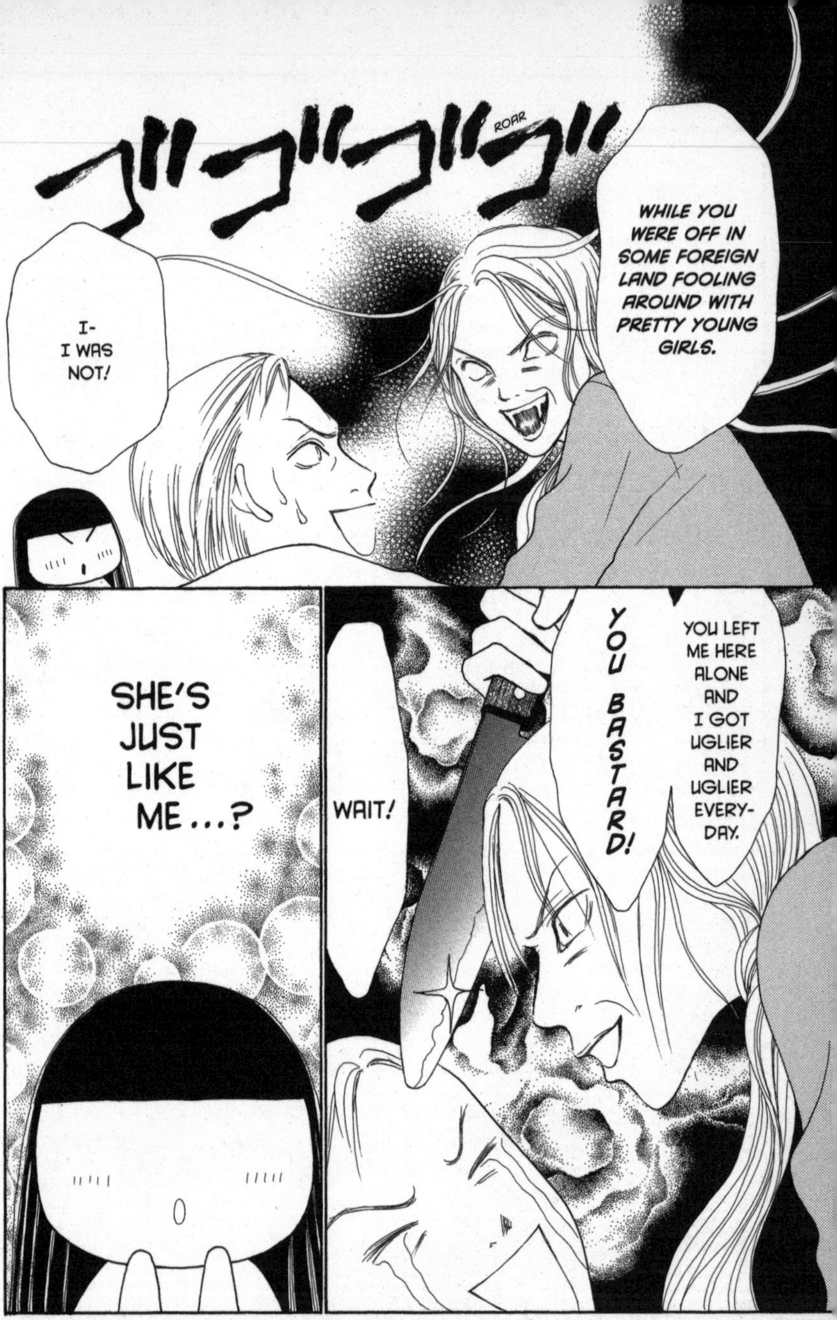
ゴゴゴゴ
ROAR
WHILE YOU WERE OFF IN SOME FOREIGN LAND FOOLING AROUND WITH PRETTY YOUNG GIRLS.
I- I WAS NOT!
YOU LEFT ME HERE ALONE AND I GOT UGLIER AND UGLIER EVERY-DAY.
YOU BASTARD!
WAIT!
SHE'S JUST LIKE ME...?

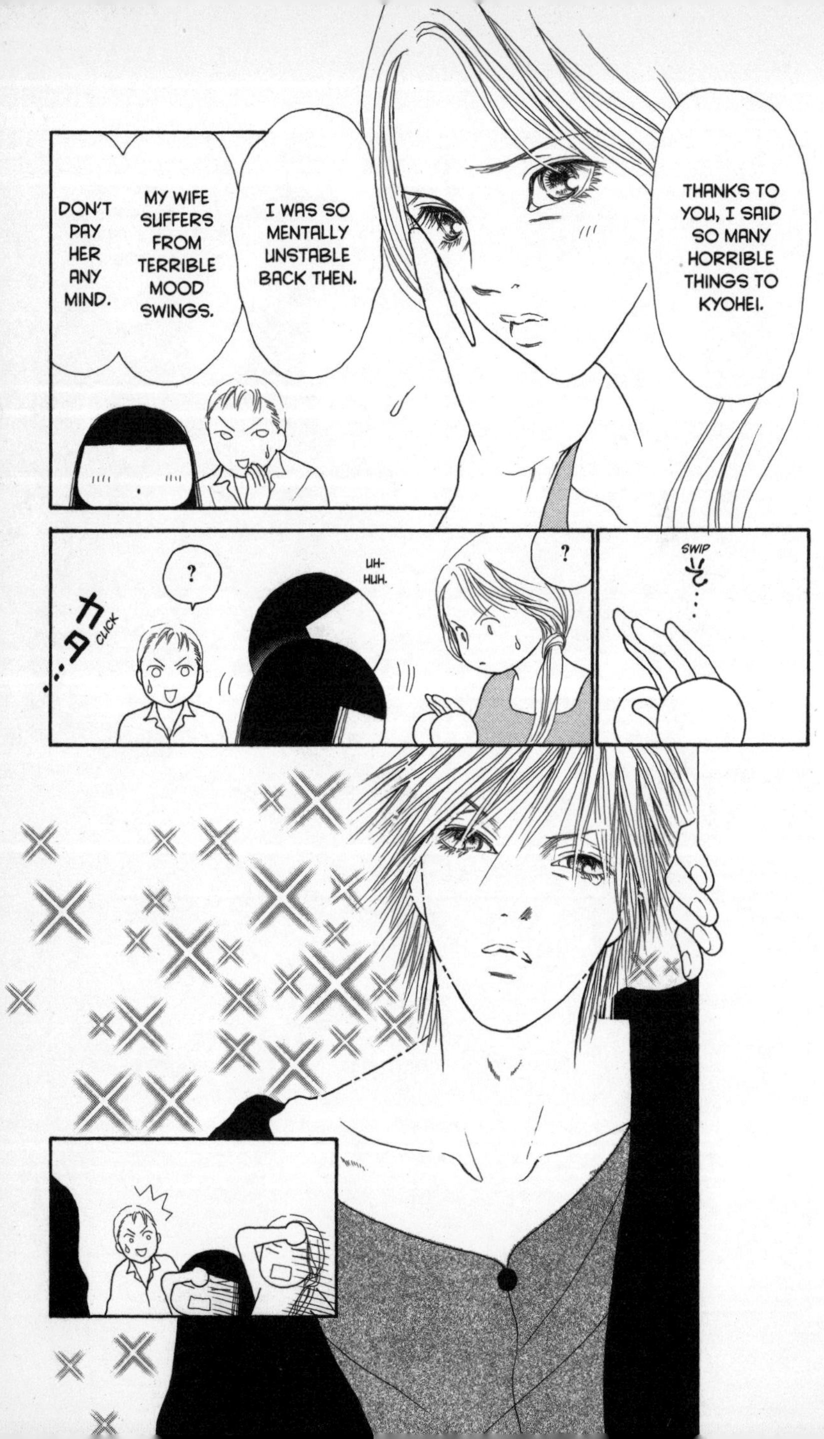
THANKS TO YOU, I SAID SO MANY HORRIBLE THINGS TO KYOHEI.
I WAS SO MENTALLY UNSTABLE BACK THEN.
MY WIFE SUFFERS FROM TERRIBLE MOOD SWINGS.
DON'T PAY HER ANY MIND.
SWIP
?
UH-HUH.
?
カタ...
CLICK

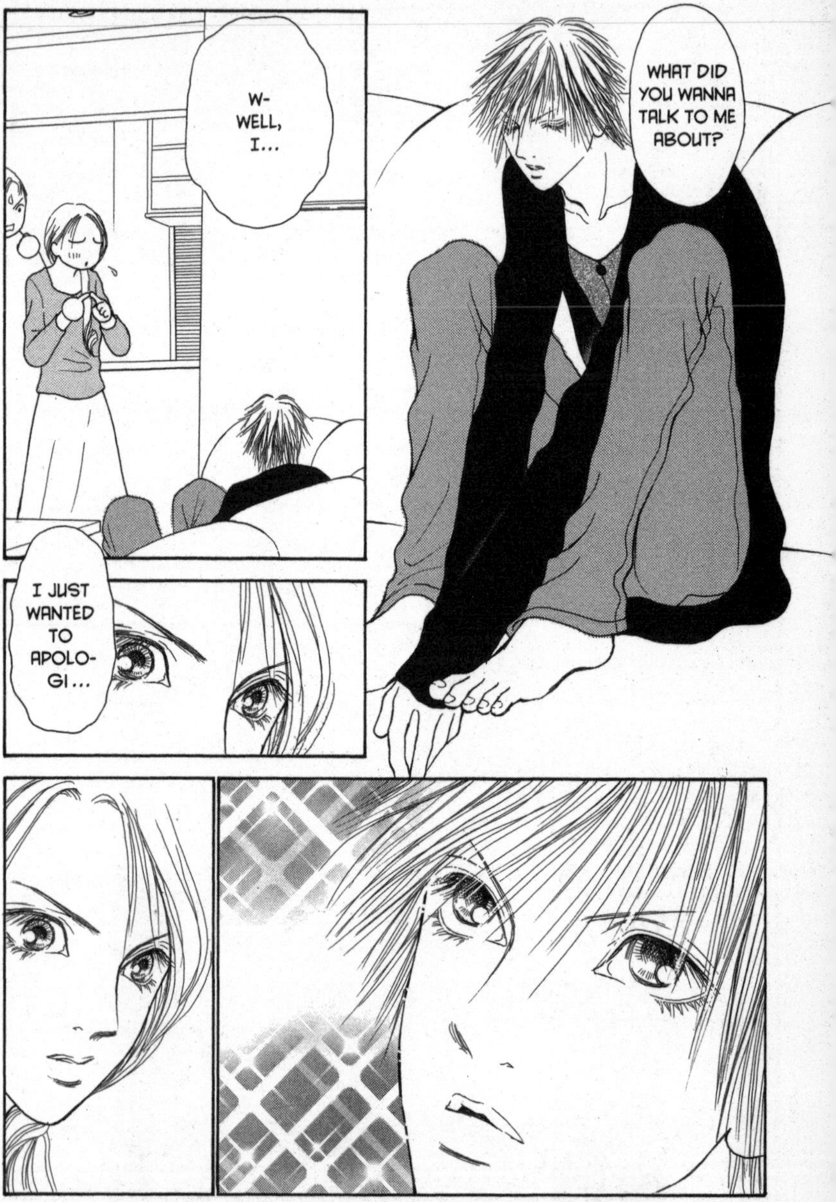
WHAT DID YOU WANNA TALK TO ME ABOUT?
W-WELL, I...
I JUST WANTED TO APOLOGI...

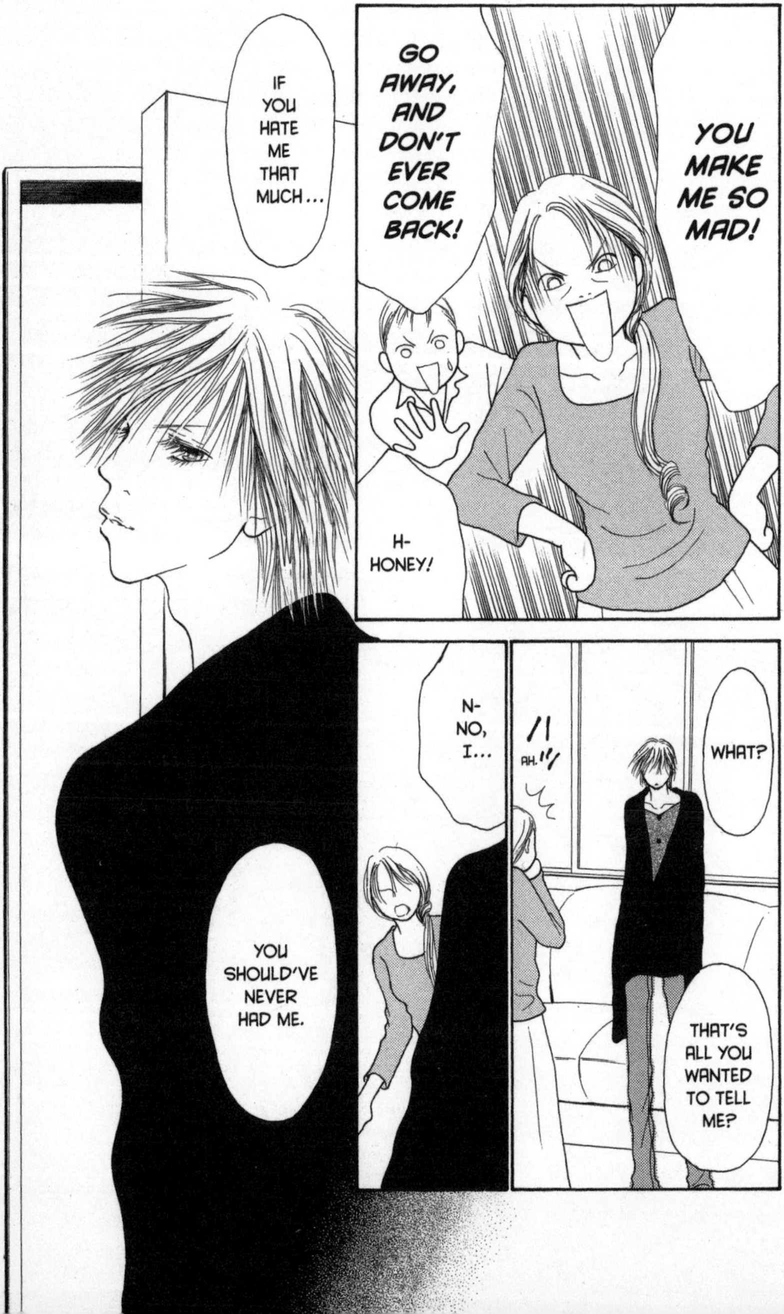
YOU MAKE ME SO MAD!
GO AWAY, AND DON'T EVER COME BACK!
H-HONEY!
WHAT?
THAT'S ALL YOU WANTED TO TELL ME?
AH.
N-NO, I...
IF YOU HATE ME THAT MUCH...
YOU SHOULD'VE NEVER HAD ME.

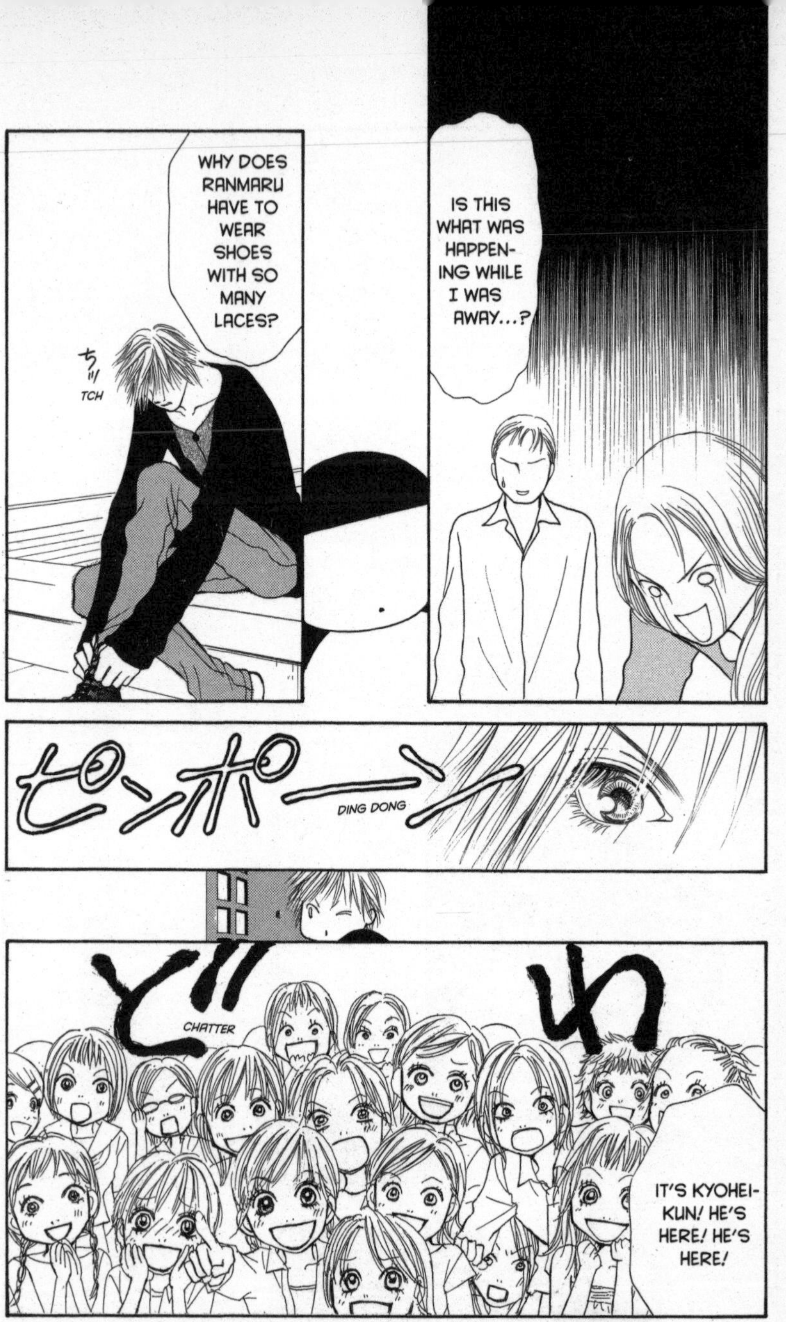
IS THIS WHAT WAS HAPPENING WHILE I WAS AWAY...?
WHY DOES RANMARU HAVE TO WEAR SHOES WITH SO MANY LACES?
ちッ
TCH
ピンポーン
DING DONG
ざわ
CHATTER
IT'S KYOHEI-KUN! HE'S HERE! HE'S HERE!

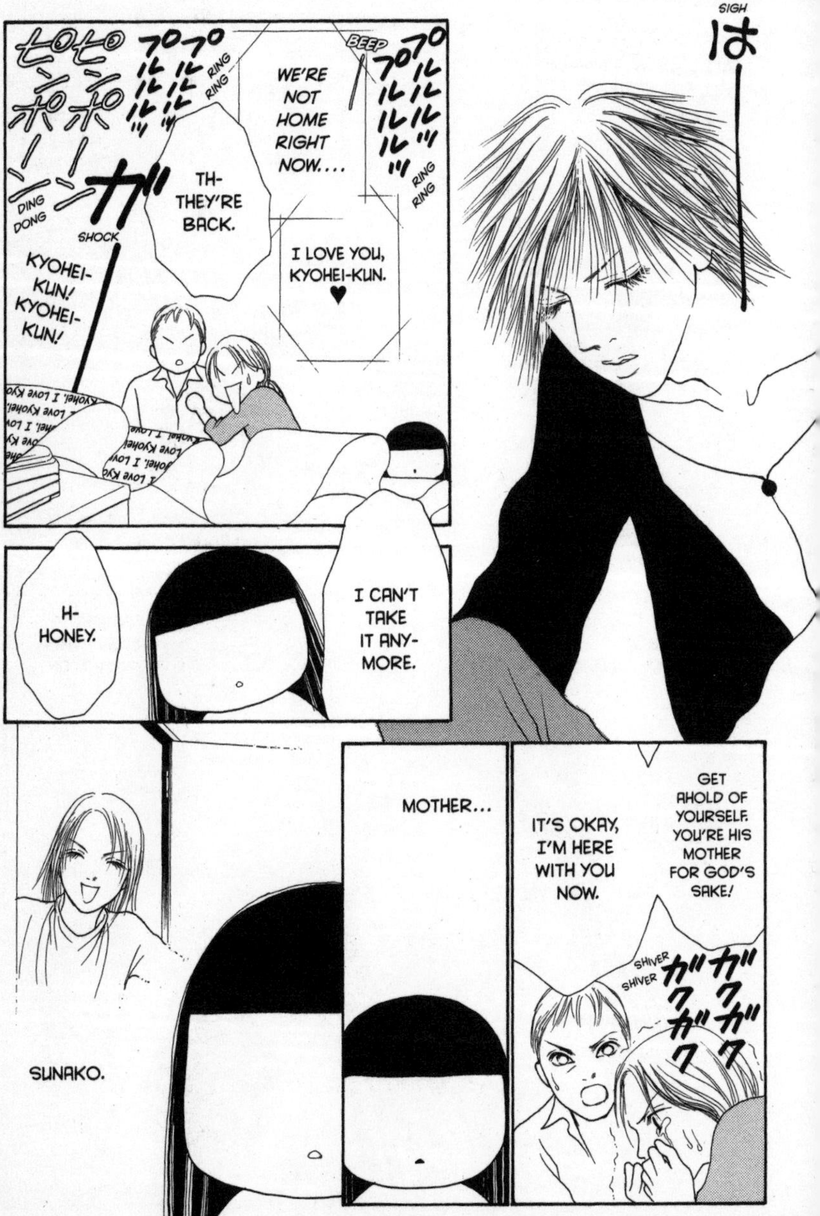
SIGH
はー
BEEP
プルルルッ
RING RING
WE'RE NOT HOME RIGHT NOW....
I LOVE YOU, KYOHEI-KUN. ♥
プルルルッ
RING RING
ピンポーン ピンポーン
DING DONG
TH- THEY'RE BACK.
ガ
SHOCK
KYOHEI-KUN! KYOHEI-KUN!
I CAN'T TAKE IT ANY-MORE.
H- HONEY.
GET AHOLD OF YOURSELF. YOU'RE HIS MOTHER FOR GOD'S SAKE!
IT'S OKAY, I'M HERE WITH YOU NOW.
SHIVER SHIVER
ガクガクガク
MOTHER...
SUNAKO.

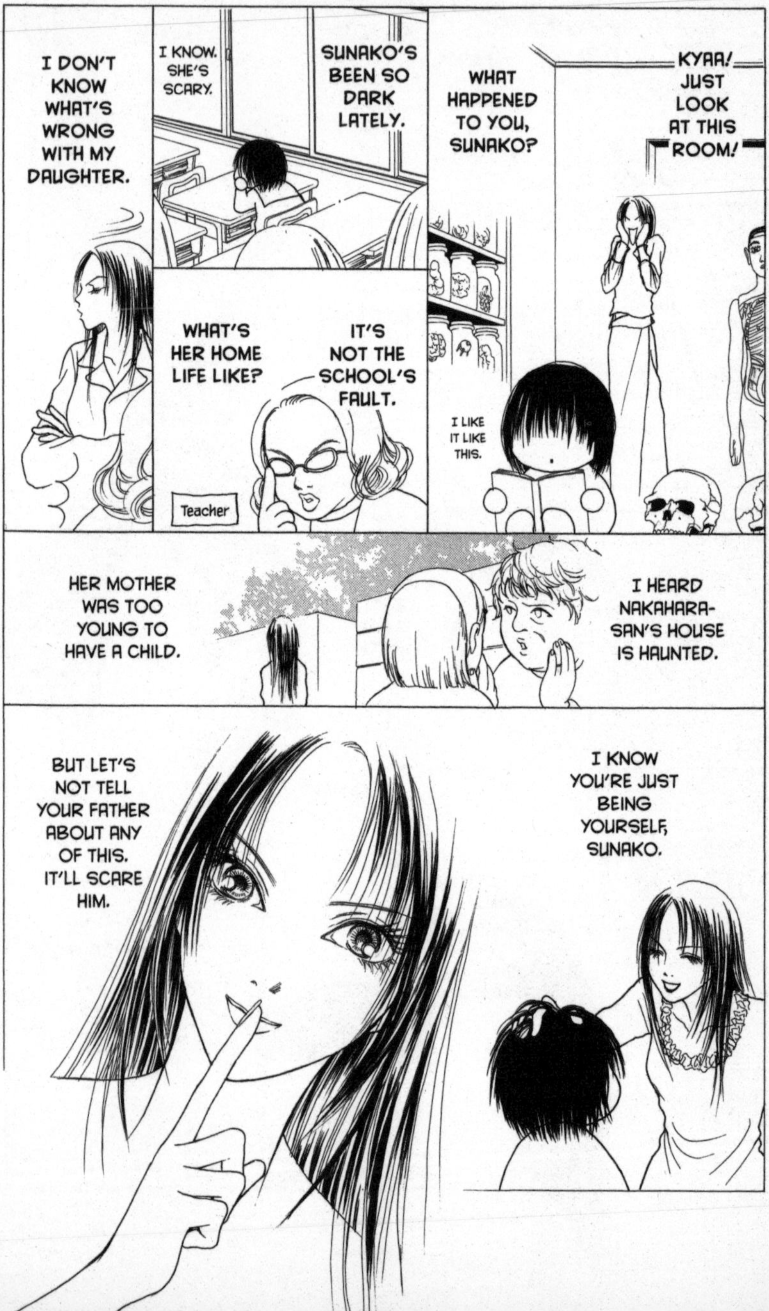
KYAA! JUST LOOK AT THIS ROOM!
WHAT HAPPENED TO YOU, SUNAKO?
I LIKE IT LIKE THIS.
SUNAKO'S BEEN SO DARK LATELY.
I KNOW. SHE'S SCARY.
IT'S NOT THE SCHOOL'S FAULT.
WHAT'S HER HOME LIFE LIKE?
Teacher
I DON'T KNOW WHAT'S WRONG WITH MY DAUGHTER.
I HEARD NAKAHARA-SAN'S HOUSE IS HAUNTED.
HER MOTHER WAS TOO YOUNG TO HAVE A CHILD.
I KNOW YOU'RE JUST BEING YOURSELF, SUNAKO.
BUT LET'S NOT TELL YOUR FATHER ABOUT ANY OF THIS. IT'LL SCARE HIM.

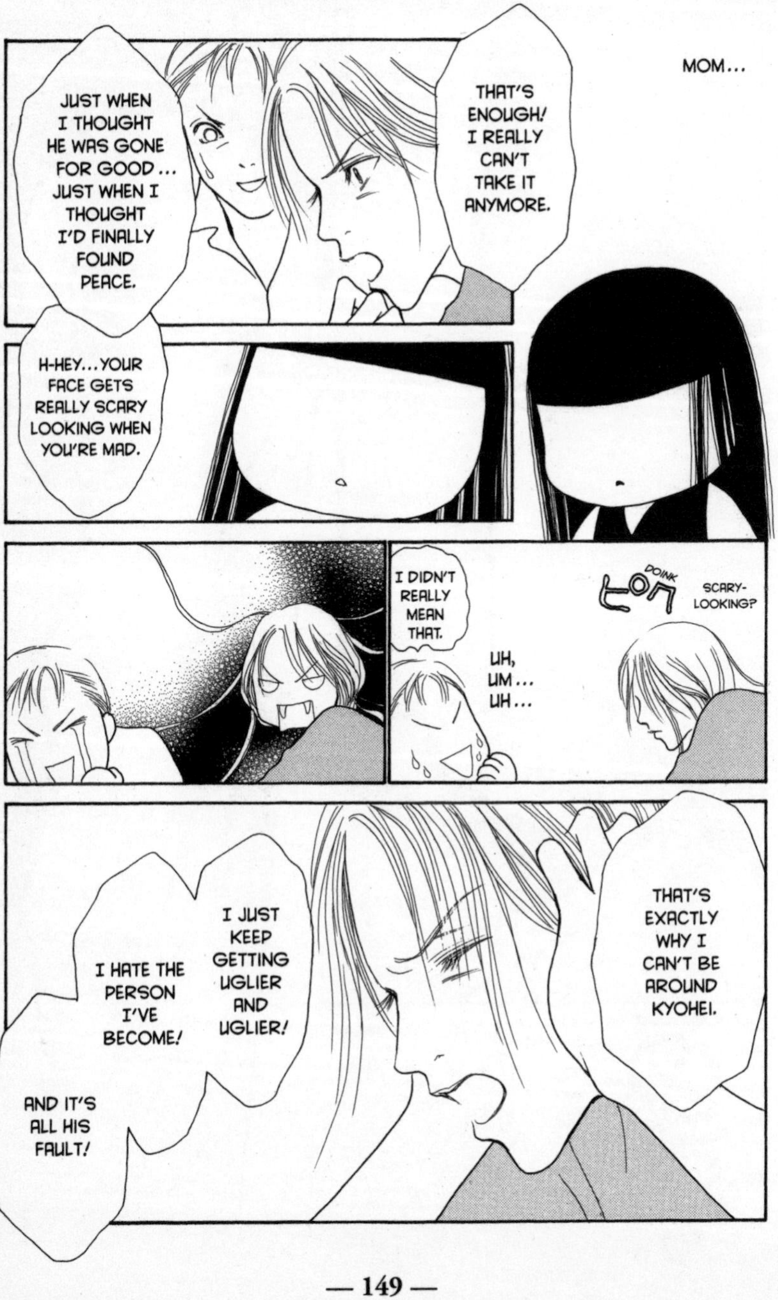
MOM...
THAT'S ENOUGH! I REALLY CAN'T TAKE IT ANYMORE.
JUST WHEN I THOUGHT HE WAS GONE FOR GOOD... JUST WHEN I THOUGHT I'D FINALLY FOUND PEACE.
H-HEY... YOUR FACE GETS REALLY SCARY LOOKING WHEN YOU'RE MAD.
SCARY-LOOKING?
DOINK
UH, UM... UH...
I DIDN'T REALLY MEAN THAT.
THAT'S EXACTLY WHY I CAN'T BE AROUND KYOHEI.
I JUST KEEP GETTING UGLIER AND UGLIER!
I HATE THE PERSON I'VE BECOME!
AND IT'S ALL HIS FAULT!

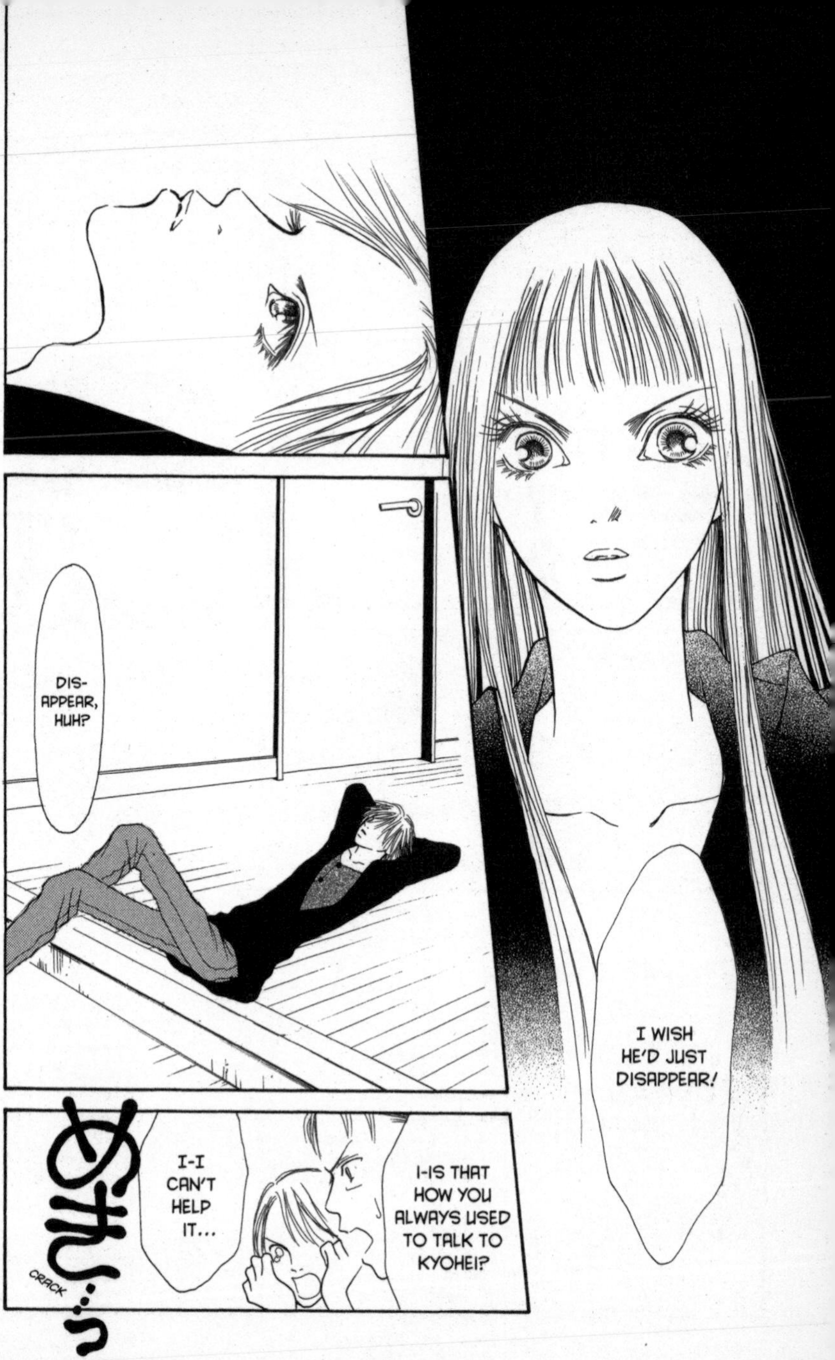
I WISH HE'D JUST DISAPPEAR!
DIS-APPEAR, HUH?
I-IS THAT HOW YOU ALWAYS USED TO TALK TO KYOHEI?
I-I CAN'T HELP IT...
CRACK

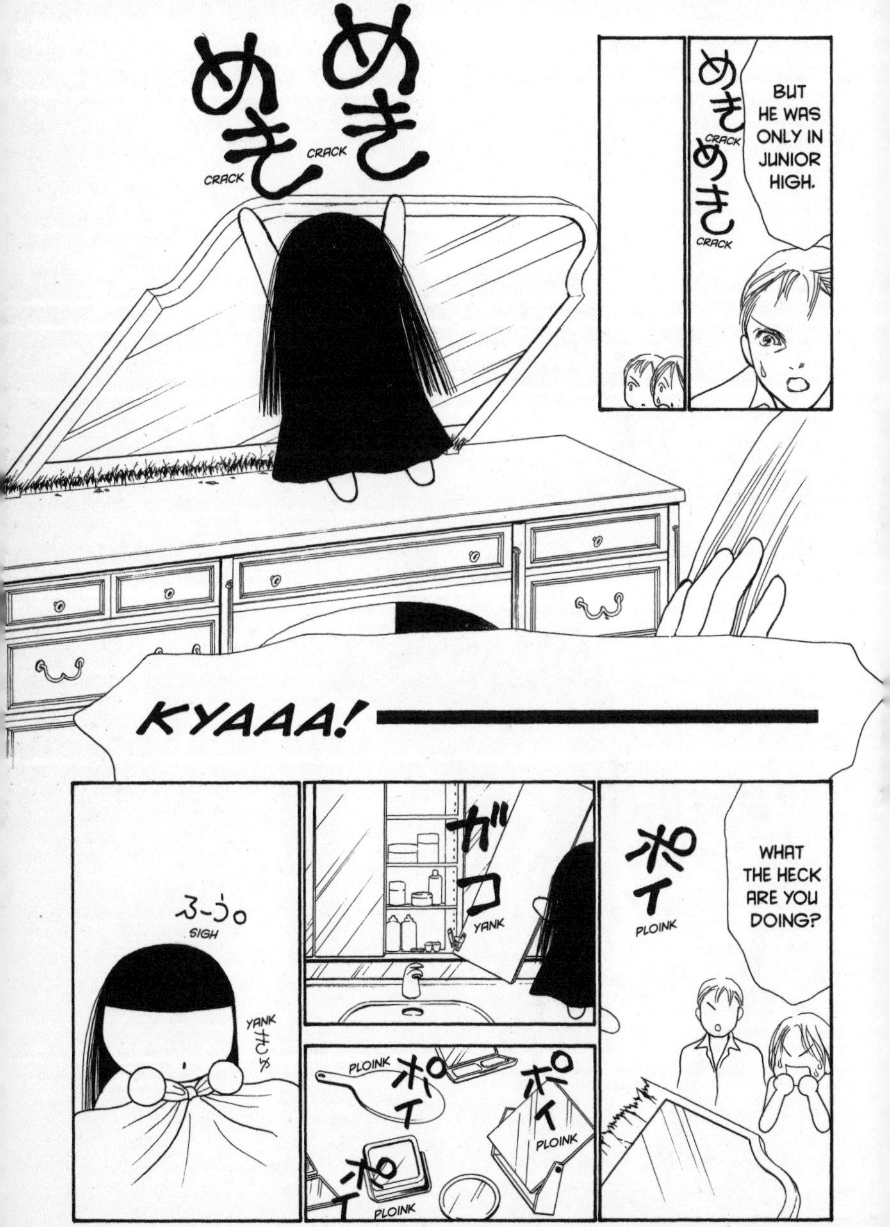

めき
CRACK
めき
CRACK
BUT HE WAS ONLY IN JUNIOR HIGH.
めき
CRACK
めき
CRACK
KYAAA!
ポイ
PLOINK
WHAT THE HECK ARE YOU DOING?
ガコ
YANK
ポイ
PLOINK
ポイ
PLOINK
ポイ
PLOINK
ふーっ。
SIGH
YANK

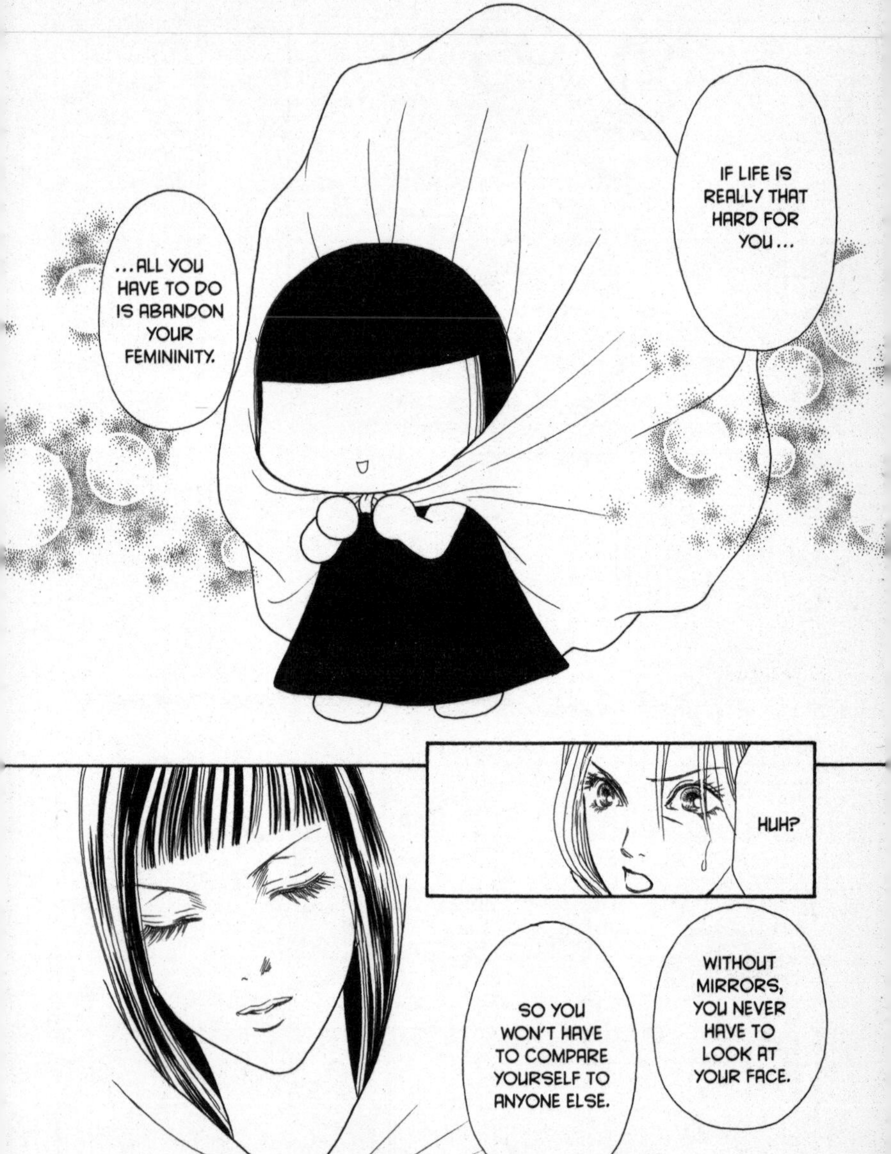
IF LIFE IS REALLY THAT HARD FOR YOU...
...ALL YOU HAVE TO DO IS ABANDON YOUR FEMININITY.
HUH?
WITHOUT MIRRORS, YOU NEVER HAVE TO LOOK AT YOUR FACE.
SO YOU WON'T HAVE TO COMPARE YOURSELF TO ANYONE ELSE.

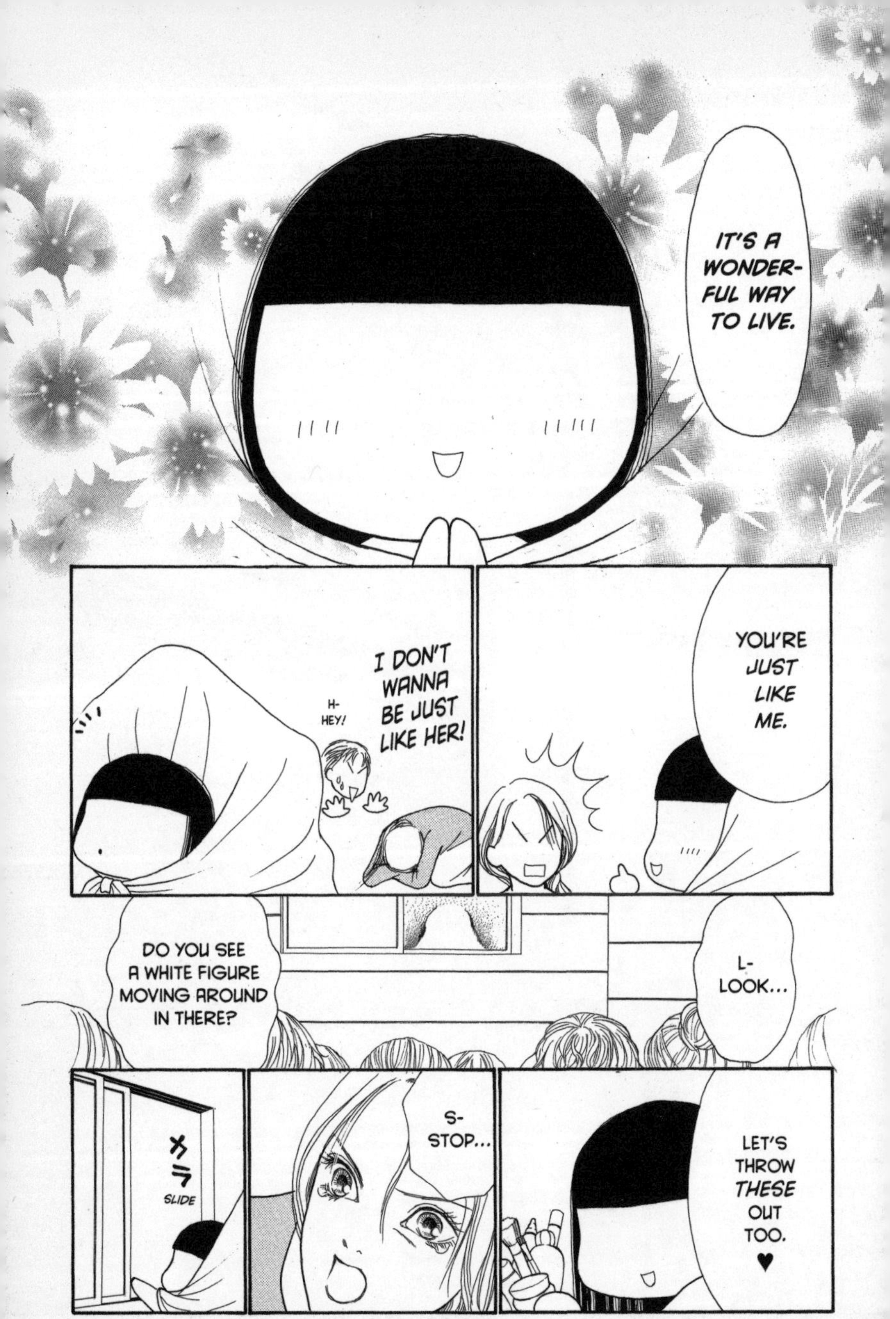
IT'S A WONDERFUL WAY TO LIVE.
YOU'RE JUST LIKE ME.
I DON'T WANNA BE JUST LIKE HER!
H-HEY!
L-LOOK...
DO YOU SEE A WHITE FIGURE MOVING AROUND IN THERE?
LET'S THROW THESE OUT TOO. ♥
S-STOP...
SLIDE

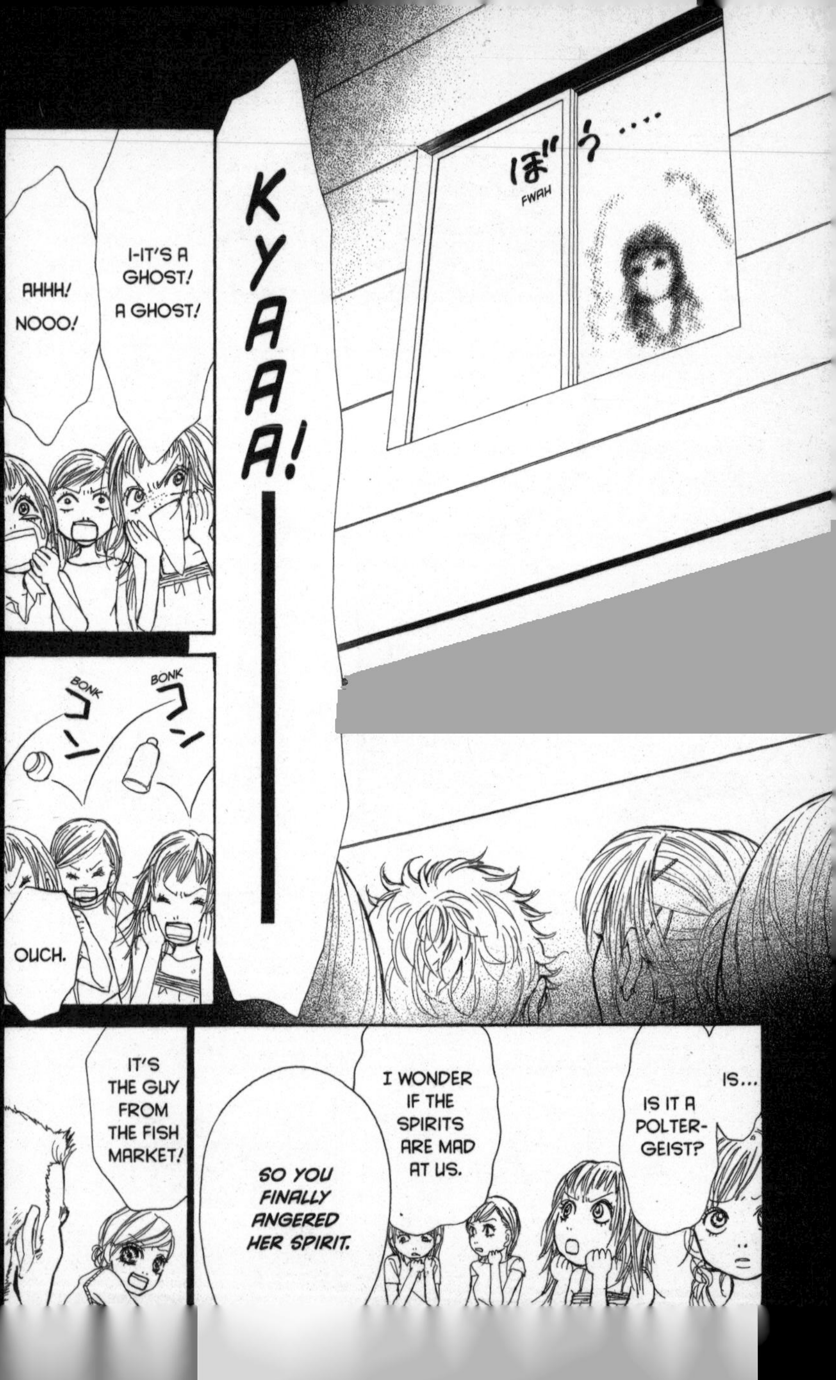
ぼう・・・・
FWAH
KYAAAA!
I-IT'S A GHOST! A GHOST!
AHHH! NOOO!
BONK
BONK
OUCH.
IS...
IS IT A POLTER-GEIST?
I WONDER IF THE SPIRITS ARE MAD AT US.
SO YOU FINALLY ANGERED HER SPIRIT.
IT'S THE GUY FROM THE FISH MARKET!

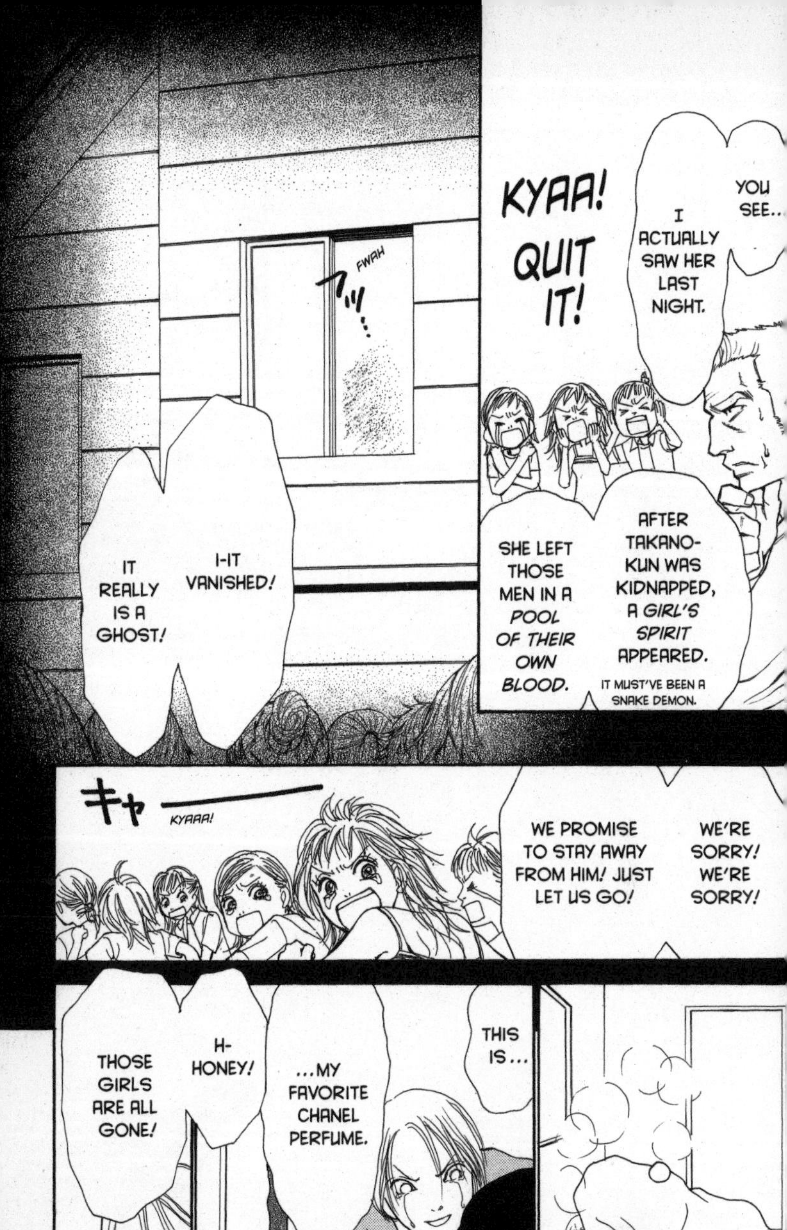
YOU SEE...
I ACTUALLY SAW HER LAST NIGHT.
KYAA! QUIT IT!
AFTER TAKANO-KUN WAS KIDNAPPED, A *GIRL'S SPIRIT* APPEARED.
SHE LEFT THOSE MEN IN A *POOL OF THEIR OWN BLOOD.*
IT MUST'VE BEEN A SNAKE DEMON.
FWAH
I-IT VANISHED!
IT REALLY IS A GHOST!
WE'RE SORRY! WE'RE SORRY!
WE PROMISE TO STAY AWAY FROM HIM! JUST LET US GO!
キャー
KYAAA!
THIS IS...
...MY FAVORITE CHANEL PERFUME.
H-HONEY!
THOSE GIRLS ARE ALL GONE!

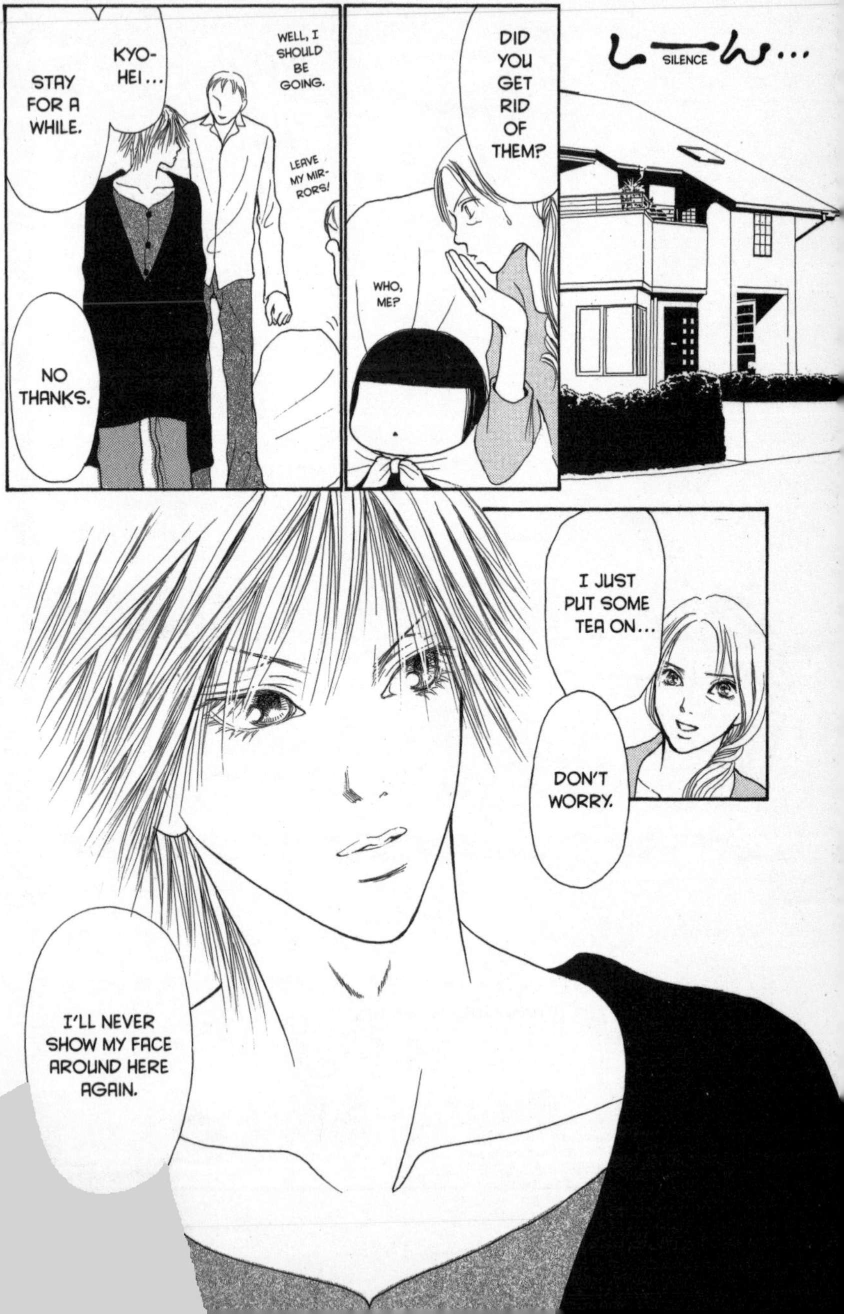
しーん…
SILENCE
DID YOU GET RID OF THEM?
WHO, ME?
WELL, I SHOULD BE GOING.
LEAVE MY MIRRORS!
KYO-HEI...
STAY FOR A WHILE.
NO THANKS.
I JUST PUT SOME TEA ON...
DON'T WORRY.
I'LL NEVER SHOW MY FACE AROUND HERE AGAIN.

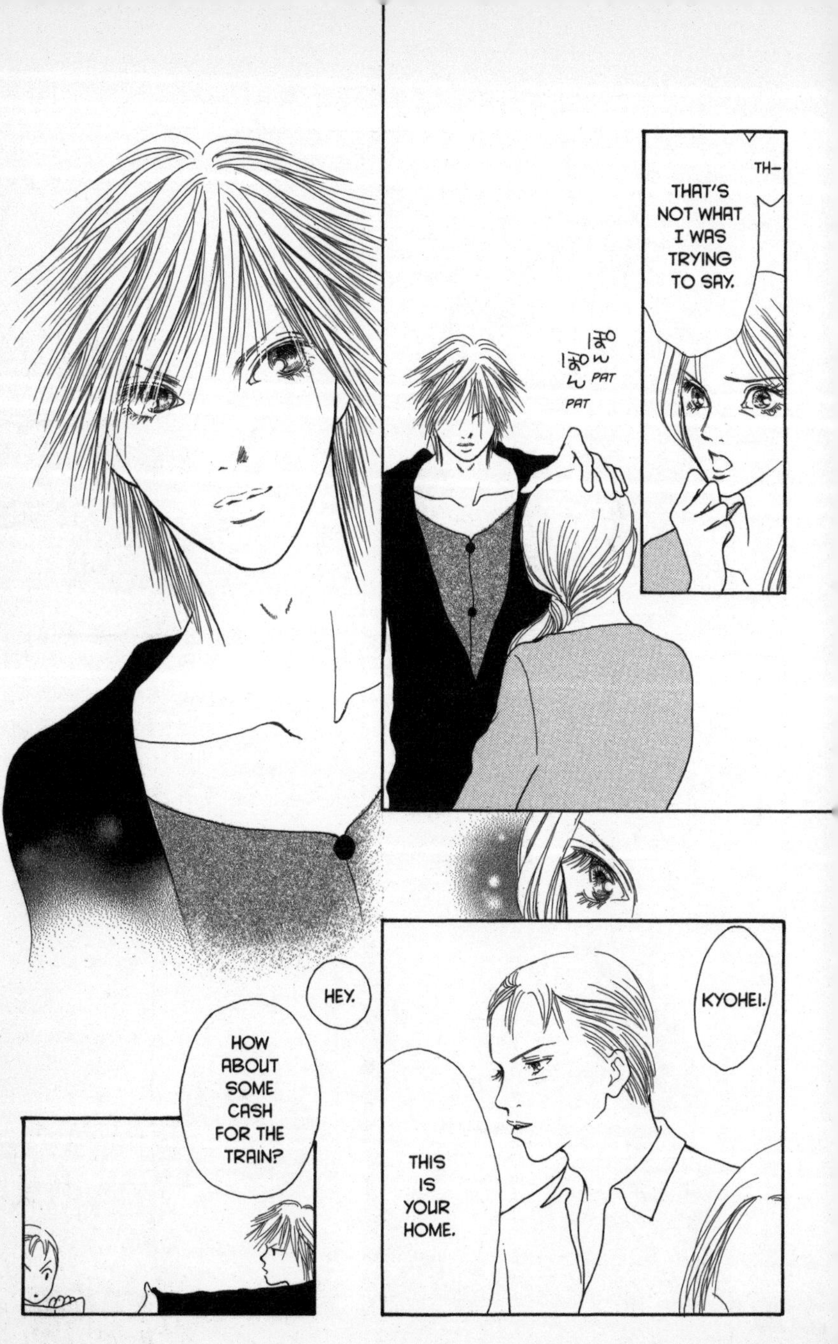
TH—
THAT'S NOT WHAT I WAS TRYING TO SAY.
ぽん PAT
ぽん PAT
KYOHEI.
THIS IS YOUR HOME.
HEY.
HOW ABOUT SOME CASH FOR THE TRAIN?

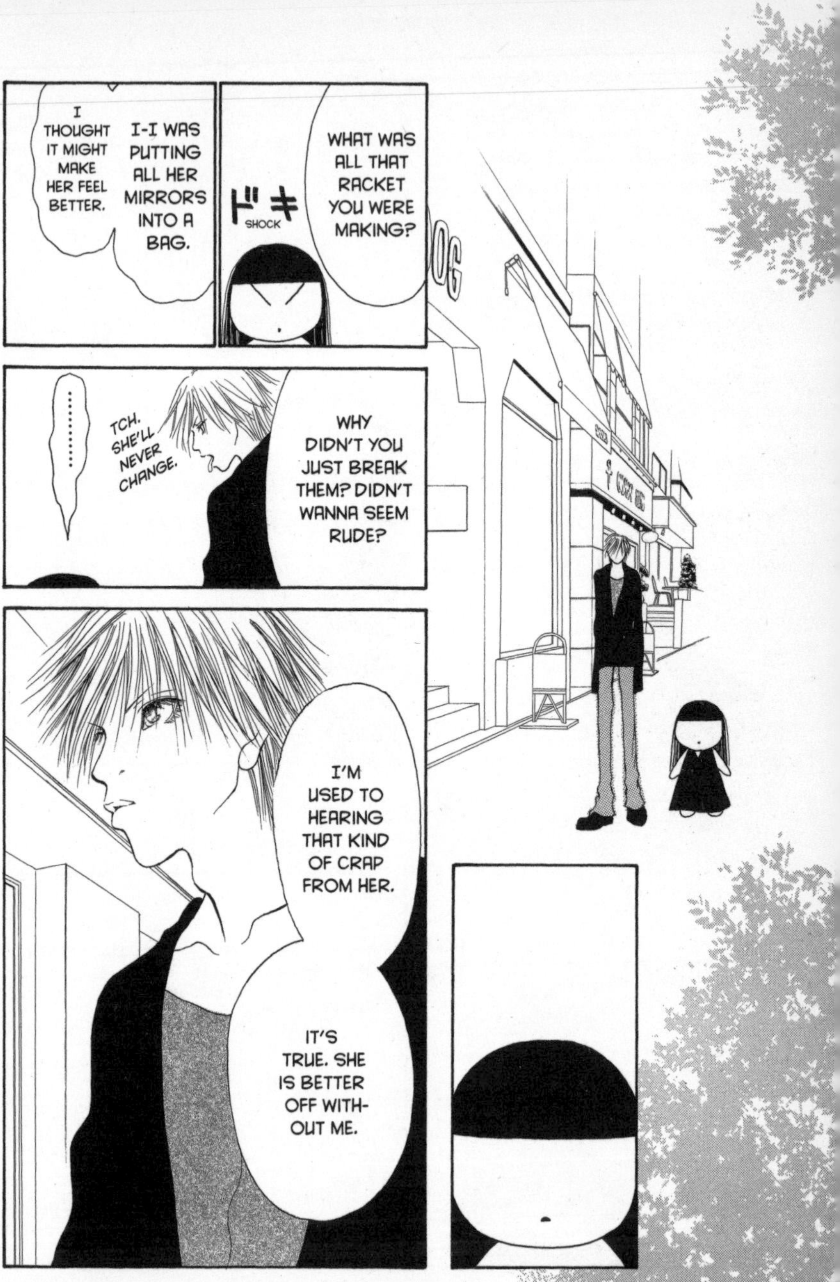
WHAT WAS ALL THAT RACKET YOU WERE MAKING?
ドキ
SHOCK
I-I WAS PUTTING ALL HER MIRRORS INTO A BAG.
I THOUGHT IT MIGHT MAKE HER FEEL BETTER.
WHY DIDN'T YOU JUST BREAK THEM? DIDN'T WANNA SEEM RUDE?
TCH. SHE'LL NEVER CHANGE.
....
I'M USED TO HEARING THAT KIND OF CRAP FROM HER.
IT'S TRUE. SHE IS BETTER OFF WITH-OUT ME.

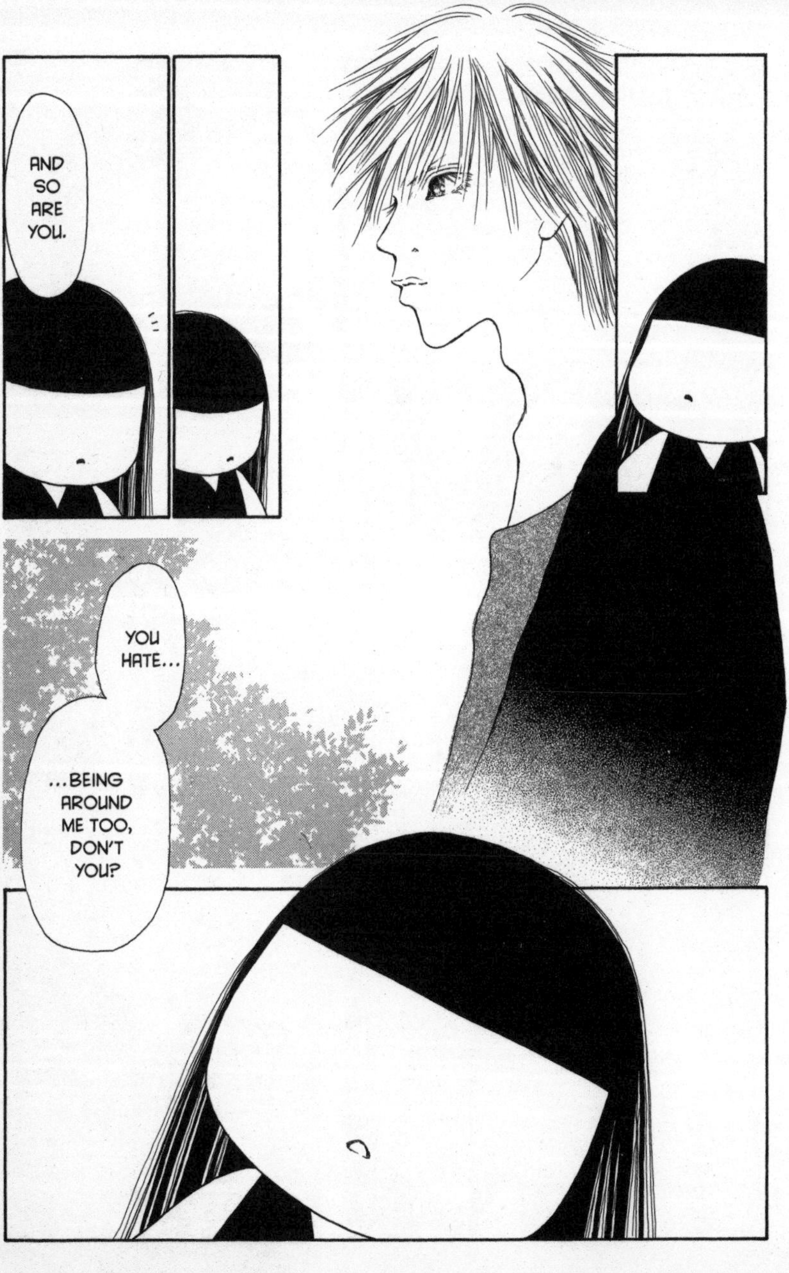
AND SO ARE YOU.
YOU HATE...
...BEING AROUND ME TOO, DON'T YOU?

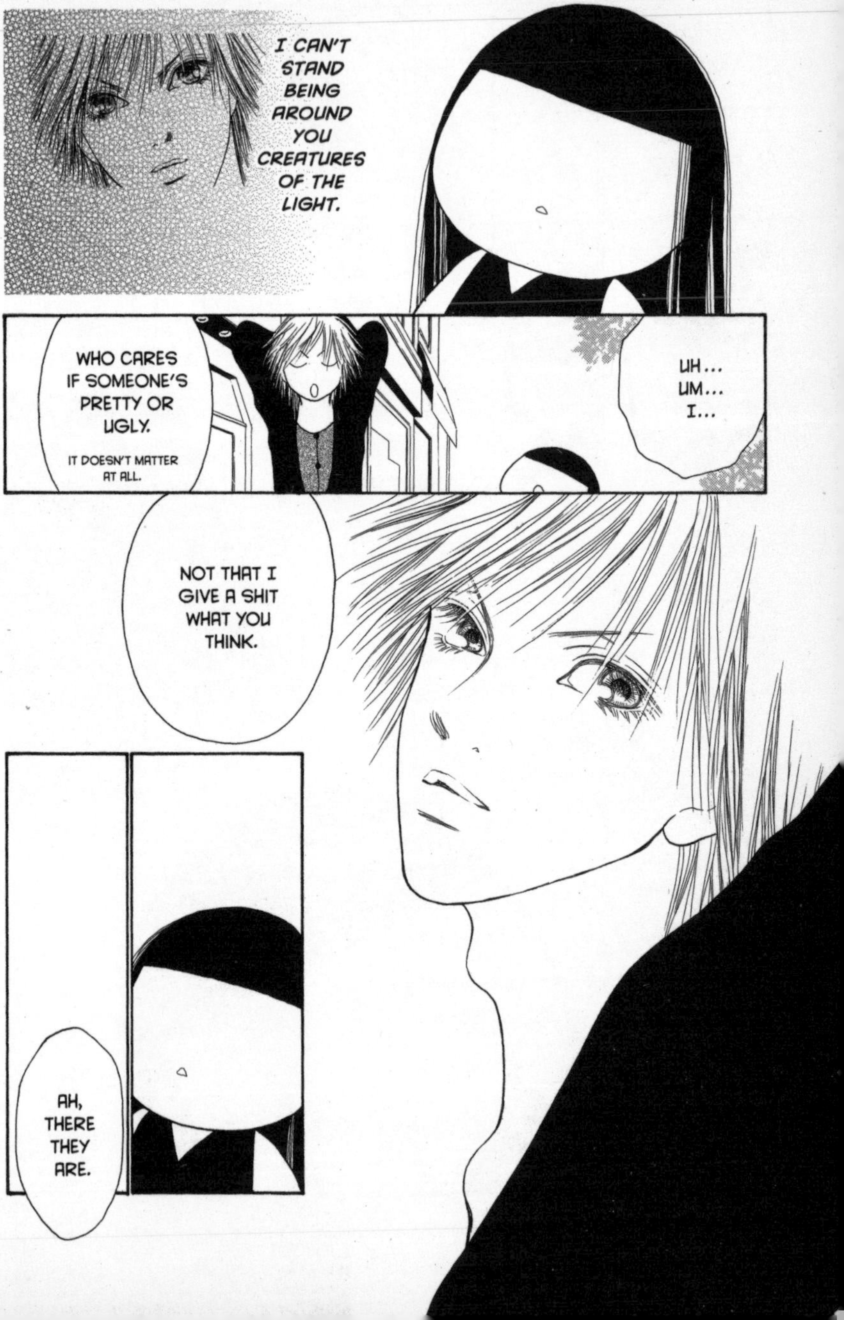
I CAN'T STAND BEING AROUND YOU CREATURES OF THE LIGHT.
UH... UM... I...
WHO CARES IF SOMEONE'S PRETTY OR UGLY.
IT DOESN'T MATTER AT ALL.
NOT THAT I GIVE A SHIT WHAT YOU THINK.
AH, THERE THEY ARE.

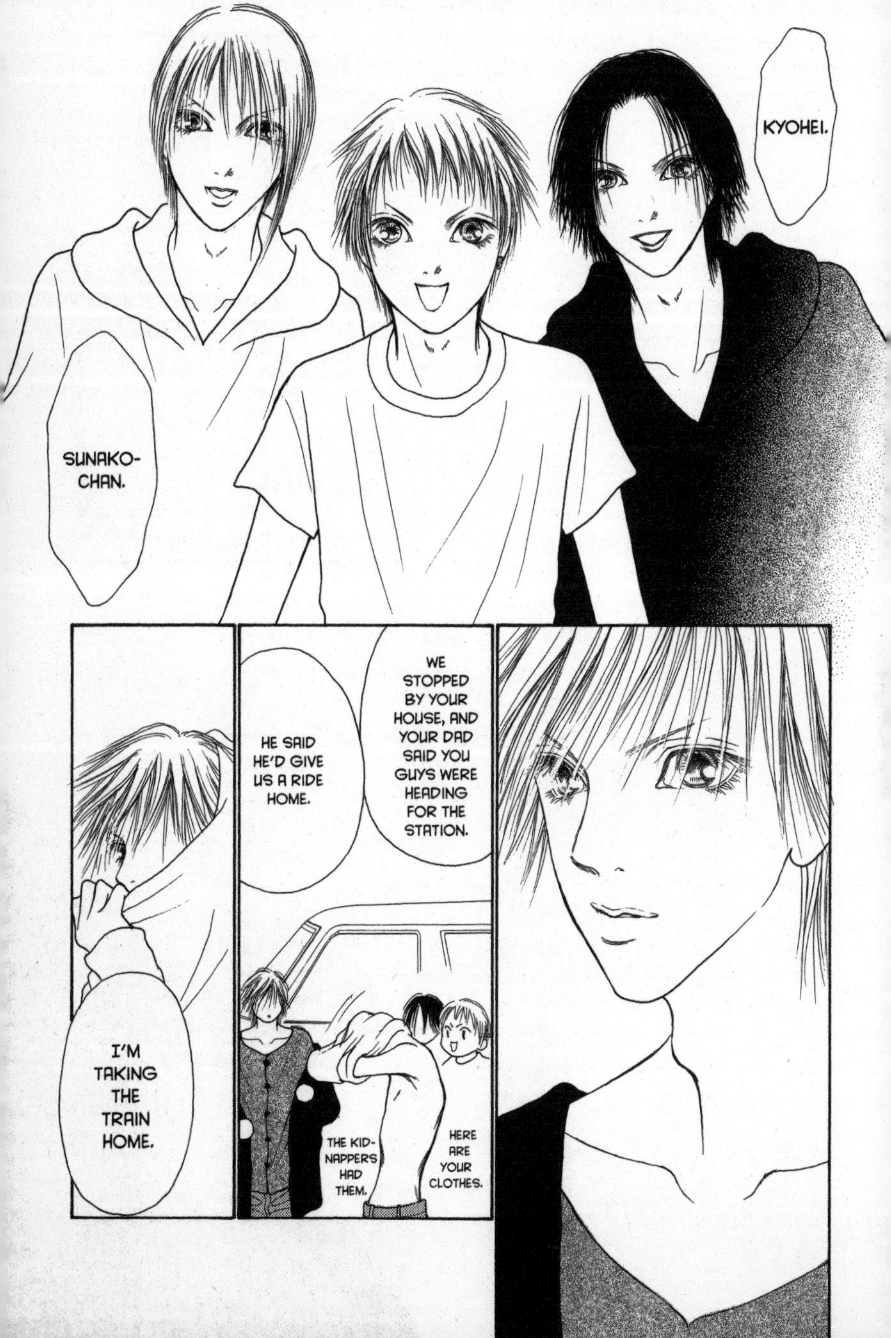
KYOHEI.
SUNAKO-CHAN.
WE STOPPED BY YOUR HOUSE, AND YOUR DAD SAID YOU GUYS WERE HEADING FOR THE STATION.
HE SAID HE'D GIVE US A RIDE HOME.
HERE ARE YOUR CLOTHES.
THE KID-NAPPERS HAD THEM.
I'M TAKING THE TRAIN HOME.

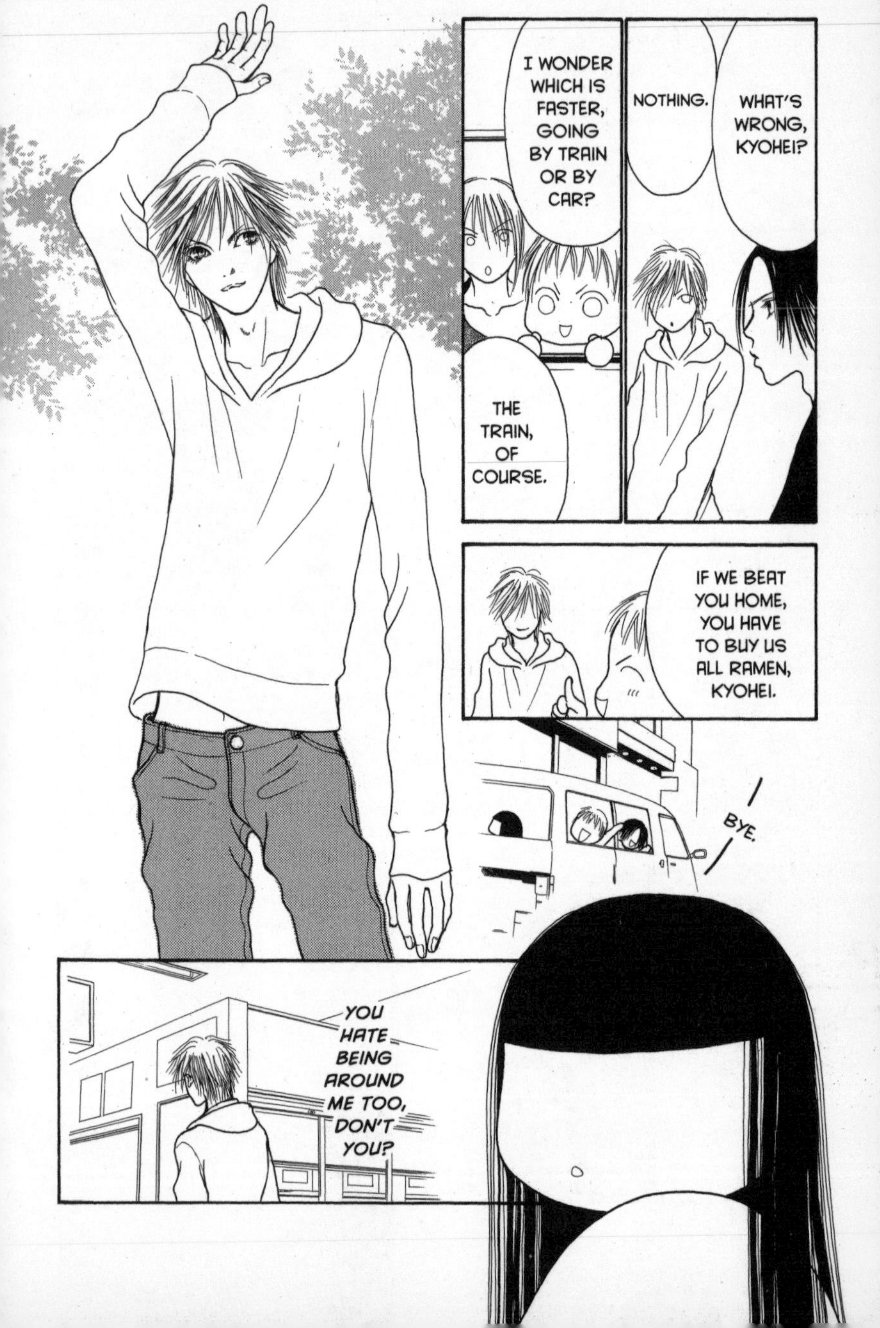
WHAT'S WRONG, KYOHEI?
NOTHING.
I WONDER WHICH IS FASTER, GOING BY TRAIN OR BY CAR?
THE TRAIN, OF COURSE.
IF WE BEAT YOU HOME, YOU HAVE TO BUY US ALL RAMEN, KYOHEI.
BYE.
YOU HATE BEING AROUND ME TOO, DON'T YOU?

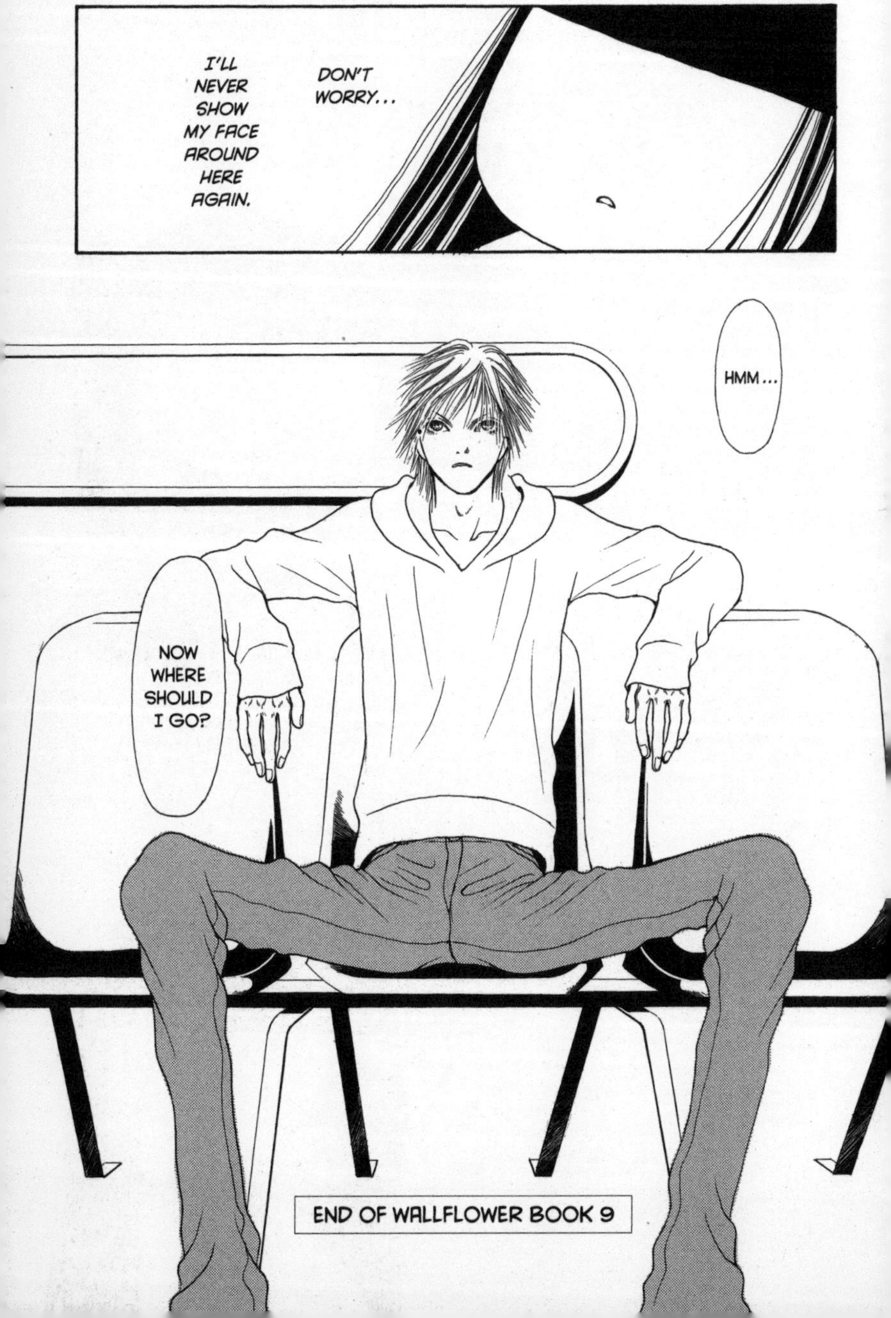
DON'T WORRY...
I'LL NEVER SHOW MY FACE AROUND HERE AGAIN.
HMM...
NOW WHERE SHOULD I GO?
END OF WALLFLOWER BOOK 9

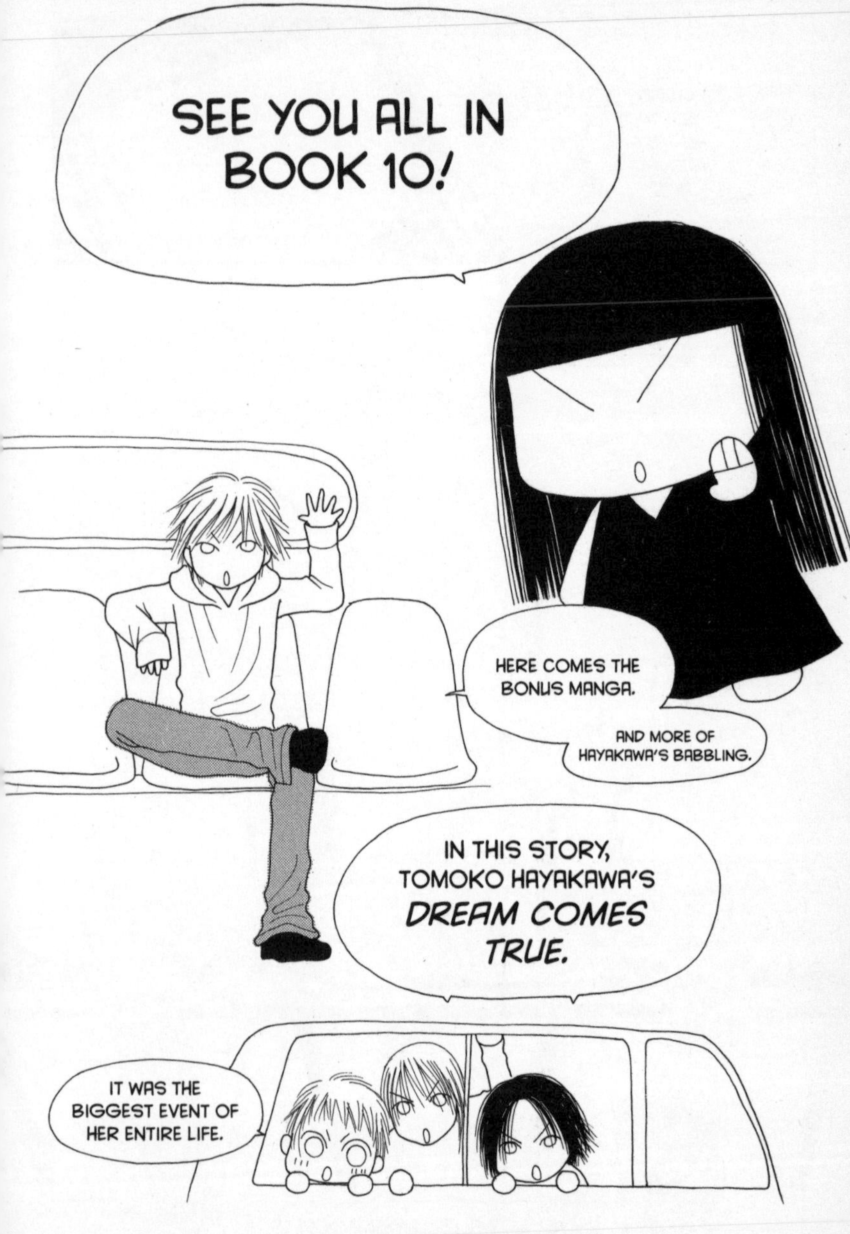
SEE YOU ALL IN BOOK 10!
HERE COMES THE BONUS MANGA.
AND MORE OF HAYAKAWA'S BABBLING.
IN THIS STORY, TOMOKO HAYAKAWA'S *DREAM COMES TRUE.*
IT WAS THE BIGGEST EVENT OF HER ENTIRE LIFE.

TOMOKO HAYAKAWA MEETS KIYOHARU—THE BIG INTERVIEW

I MET KIYOHARU!!!

I GOT AN OFFER TO WRITE A BONUS MANGA FOR THIS ISSUE, BUT I'M A LITTLE NERVOUS ABOUT SHARING THIS EXPERIENCE.

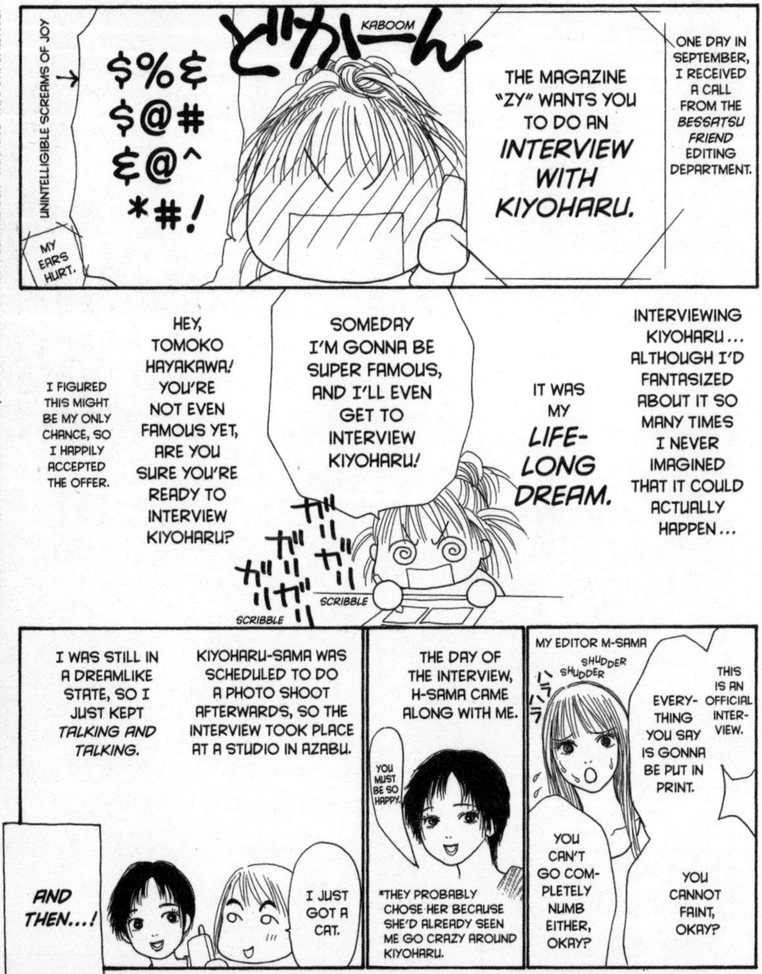
ONE DAY IN SEPTEMBER, I RECEIVED A CALL FROM THE *BESSATSU FRIEND* EDITING DEPARTMENT.
THE MAGAZINE "ZY" WANTS YOU TO DO AN *INTERVIEW WITH KIYOHARU.*
どかーん
KABOOM
$%& $@# &@^ *#!
UNINTELLIGIBLE SCREAMS OF JOY
MY EARS HURT.
INTERVIEWING KIYOHARU... ALTHOUGH I'D FANTASIZED ABOUT IT SO MANY TIMES I NEVER IMAGINED THAT IT COULD ACTUALLY HAPPEN...
IT WAS MY *LIFE-LONG DREAM.*
SOMEDAY I'M GONNA BE SUPER FAMOUS, AND I'LL EVEN GET TO INTERVIEW KIYOHARU!
HEY, TOMOKO HAYAKAWA! YOU'RE NOT EVEN FAMOUS YET, ARE YOU SURE YOU'RE READY TO INTERVIEW KIYOHARU?
I FIGURED THIS MIGHT BE MY ONLY CHANCE, SO I HAPPILY ACCEPTED THE OFFER.
SCRIBBLE
SCRIBBLE
MY EDITOR M-SAMA
SHUDDER SHUDDER
THIS IS AN OFFICIAL INTERVIEW.
EVERYTHING YOU SAY IS GONNA BE PUT IN PRINT.
YOU CANNOT FAINT, OKAY?
YOU CAN'T GO COMPLETELY NUMB EITHER, OKAY?
SHE WAS SERIOUSLY WORRIED.
THE DAY OF THE INTERVIEW, H-SAMA CAME ALONG WITH ME.
YOU MUST BE SO HAPPY.
*THEY PROBABLY CHOSE HER BECAUSE SHE'D ALREADY SEEN ME GO CRAZY AROUND KIYOHARU.
KIYOHARU-SAMA WAS SCHEDULED TO DO A PHOTO SHOOT AFTERWARDS, SO THE INTERVIEW TOOK PLACE AT A STUDIO IN AZABU.
I WAS STILL IN A DREAMLIKE STATE, SO I JUST KEPT *TALKING AND TALKING.*
I JUST GOT A CAT.
AND THEN...!

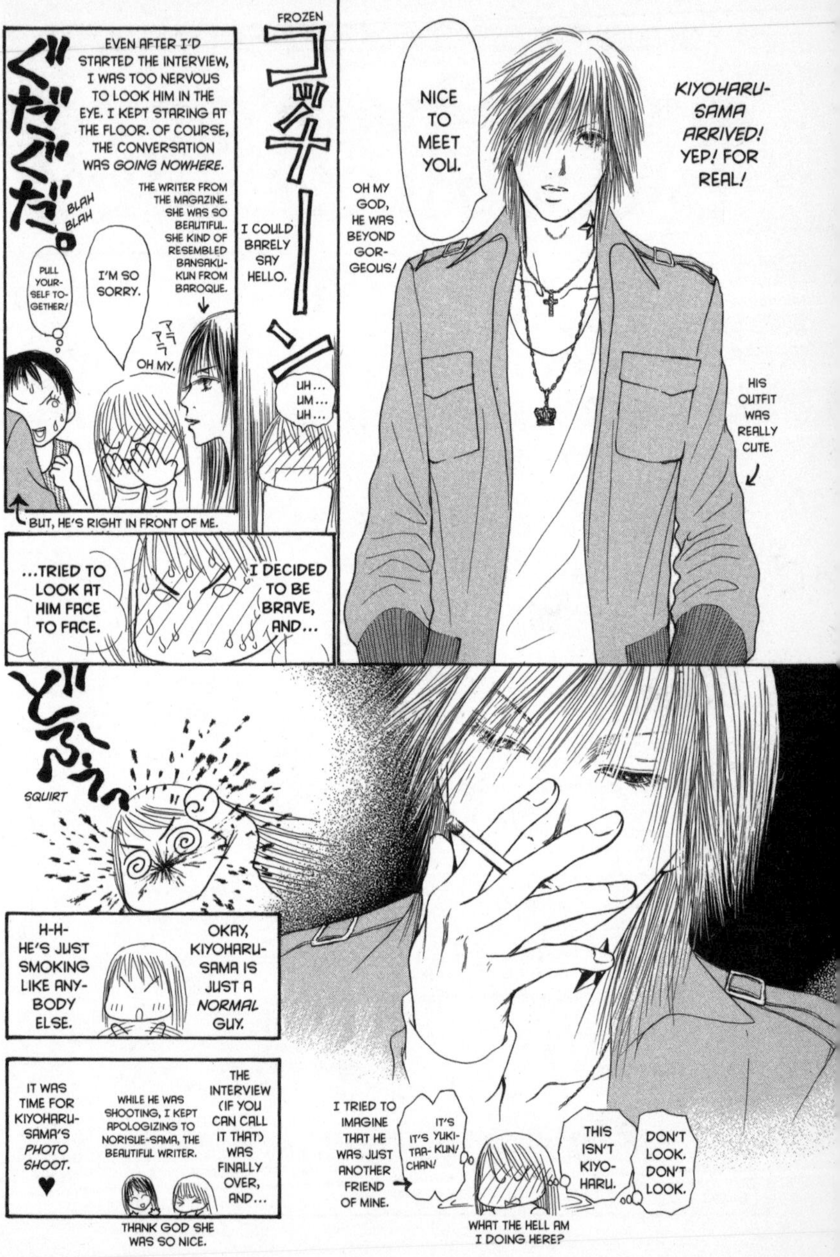
KIYOHARU-SAMA ARRIVED! YEP! FOR REAL!
NICE TO MEET YOU.
OH MY GOD, HE WAS BEYOND GORGEOUS!
HIS OUTFIT WAS REALLY CUTE.
FROZEN
I COULD BARELY SAY HELLO.
UH... UM... UH...
EVEN AFTER I'D STARTED THE INTERVIEW, I WAS TOO NERVOUS TO LOOK HIM IN THE EYE. I KEPT STARING AT THE FLOOR. OF COURSE, THE CONVERSATION WAS *GOING NOWHERE*.
ぐだぐだ。
BLAH BLAH
THE WRITER FROM THE MAGAZINE. SHE WAS SO BEAUTIFUL. SHE KIND OF RESEMBLED BANSAKU-KUN FROM BAROQUE.
アラアラ
OH MY.
I'M SO SORRY.
PULL YOURSELF TOGETHER!
BUT, HE'S RIGHT IN FRONT OF ME.
I DECIDED TO BE BRAVE, AND...
...TRIED TO LOOK AT HIM FACE TO FACE.
DON'T LOOK. DON'T LOOK.
THIS ISN'T KIYOHARU.
IT'S YUKI-KUN/ IT'S TAA-CHAN!
I TRIED TO IMAGINE THAT HE WAS JUST ANOTHER FRIEND OF MINE.
WHAT THE HELL AM I DOING HERE?
SQUIRT
OKAY, KIYOHARU-SAMA IS JUST A *NORMAL* GUY.
H-H-HE'S JUST SMOKING LIKE ANYBODY ELSE.
THE INTERVIEW (IF YOU CAN CALL IT THAT) WAS FINALLY OVER, AND...
WHILE HE WAS SHOOTING, I KEPT APOLOGIZING TO NORISUE-SAMA, THE BEAUTIFUL WRITER.
IT WAS TIME FOR KIYOHARU-SAMA'S *PHOTO SHOOT*. ♥
THANK GOD SHE WAS SO NICE.

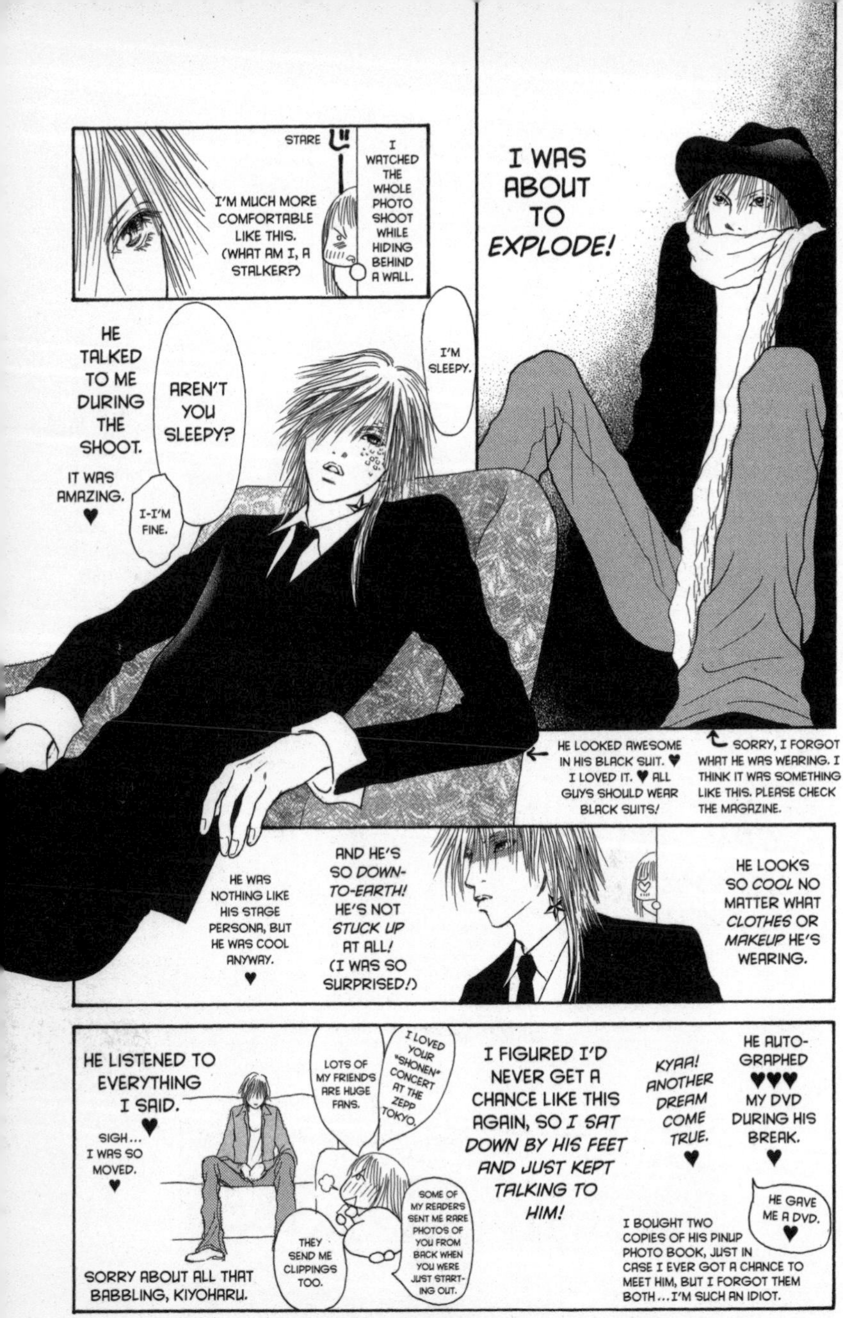

I WAS ABOUT TO EXPLODE!
SORRY, I FORGOT WHAT HE WAS WEARING. I THINK IT WAS SOMETHING LIKE THIS. PLEASE CHECK THE MAGAZINE.
I WATCHED THE WHOLE PHOTO SHOOT WHILE HIDING BEHIND A WALL.
STARE
I'M MUCH MORE COMFORTABLE LIKE THIS. (WHAT AM I, A STALKER?)
I'M SLEEPY.
AREN'T YOU SLEEPY?
HE TALKED TO ME DURING THE SHOOT.
I-I'M FINE.
IT WAS AMAZING. ♥
HE LOOKED AWESOME IN HIS BLACK SUIT. ♥ I LOVED IT. ♥ ALL GUYS SHOULD WEAR BLACK SUITS!
HE LOOKS SO *COOL* NO MATTER WHAT *CLOTHES* OR *MAKEUP* HE'S WEARING.
AND HE'S SO *DOWN-TO-EARTH!* HE'S NOT *STUCK UP* AT ALL! (I WAS SO SURPRISED!)
HE WAS NOTHING LIKE HIS STAGE PERSONA, BUT HE WAS COOL ANYWAY. ♥
HE AUTO-GRAPHED ♥♥♥ MY DVD DURING HIS BREAK. ♥
HE GAVE ME A DVD. ♥
KYAA! ANOTHER DREAM COME TRUE. ♥
I FIGURED I'D NEVER GET A CHANCE LIKE THIS AGAIN, SO *I SAT DOWN BY HIS FEET AND JUST KEPT TALKING TO HIM!*
I BOUGHT TWO COPIES OF HIS PINUP PHOTO BOOK, JUST IN CASE I EVER GOT A CHANCE TO MEET HIM, BUT I FORGOT THEM BOTH... I'M SUCH AN IDIOT.
I LOVED YOUR "SHONEN" CONCERT AT THE ZEPP TOKYO.
LOTS OF MY FRIEND'S ARE HUGE FANS.
SOME OF MY READER'S SENT ME RARE PHOTOS OF YOU FROM BACK WHEN YOU WERE JUST STARTING OUT.
THEY SEND ME CLIPPINGS TOO.
HE LISTENED TO EVERYTHING I SAID. ♥
SIGH... I WAS SO MOVED. ♥
SORRY ABOUT ALL THAT BABBLING, KIYOHARU.

I TALKED ABOUT YOU GUYS TOO!

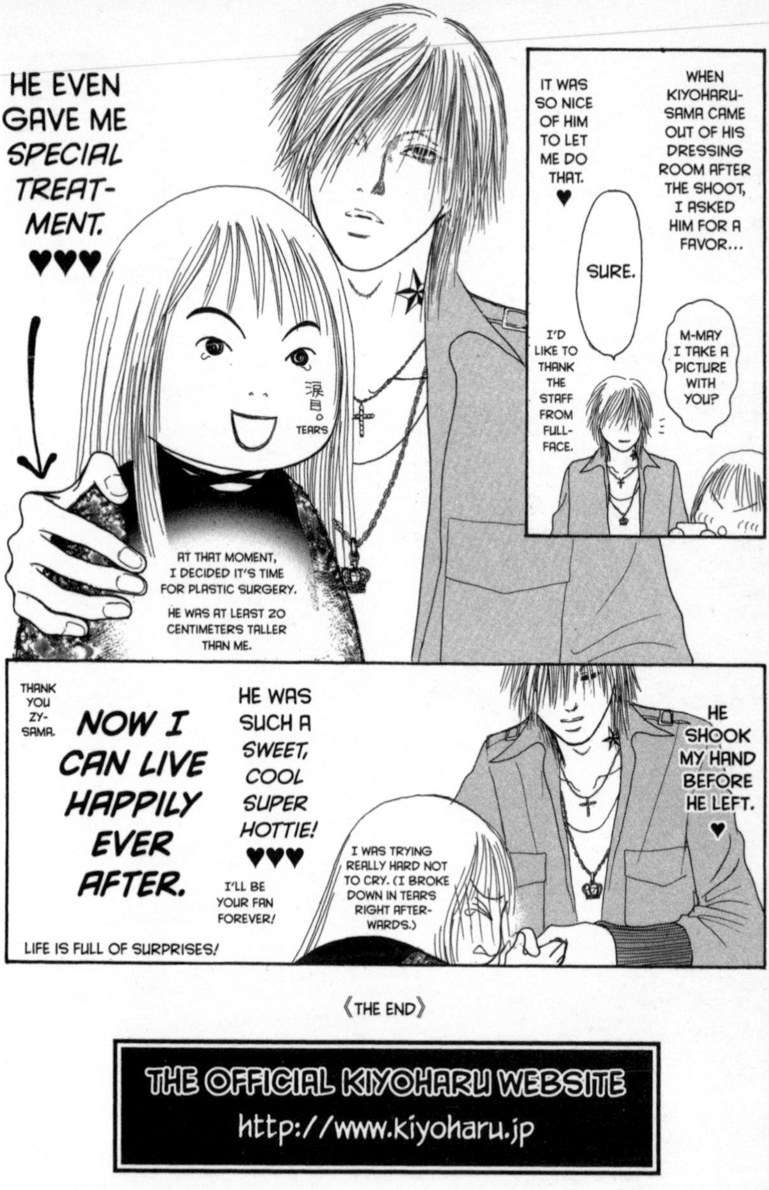

WHEN KIYOHARU-SAMA CAME OUT OF HIS DRESSING ROOM AFTER THE SHOOT, I ASKED HIM FOR A FAVOR...
IT WAS SO NICE OF HIM TO LET ME DO THAT. ♥
M-MAY I TAKE A PICTURE WITH YOU?
SURE.
I'D LIKE TO THANK THE STAFF FROM FULL-FACE.
HE EVEN GAVE ME SPECIAL TREATMENT. ♥♥♥
涙目。
TEARS
AT THAT MOMENT, I DECIDED IT'S TIME FOR PLASTIC SURGERY.
HE WAS AT LEAST 20 CENTIMETERS TALLER THAN ME.
HE SHOOK MY HAND BEFORE HE LEFT. ♥
I WAS TRYING REALLY HARD NOT TO CRY. (I BROKE DOWN IN TEARS RIGHT AFTER-WARDS.)
HE WAS SUCH A SWEET, COOL SUPER HOTTIE! ♥♥♥
I'LL BE YOUR FAN FOREVER!
NOW I CAN LIVE HAPPILY EVER AFTER.
THANK YOU ZY-SAMA.
LIFE IS FULL OF SURPRISES!

《THE END》

THE OFFICIAL KIYOHARU WEBSITE
http://www.kiyoharu.jp

. . . SOME OF THE READERS MIGHT THINK THAT I DIDN'T SOUND NERVOUS AT ALL . . .

BUT THAT'S ONLY BECAUSE I DIDN'T REVEAL EVERYTHING SINCE I KNEW THIS MANGA WAS GONNA BE PUBLISHED IN *BESSATSU FRIEND*. IT WAS ACTUALLY MUCH, MUCH WORSE THAN I DESCRIBED. I WAS GOING CRAZY. I MEAN, WHAT COULD I DO? HE WAS SO GORGEOUS. ♥♥♥ I COULDN'T FIT EVERYTHING INTO FOUR PAGES. I COULDN'T REALLY PORTRAY HIS SEXINESS OR HIS VIBE IN THE DRAWINGS. ESPECIALLY HIS HUSKY, DEEP *VOICE* . . . EVERY SINGLE MOVEMENT HE MADE WAS COOL, AND IT'S NOT LIKE HE WAS TRYING OR ANYTHING . . . THAT MADE HIM EVEN COOLER. ♥

TO THIS DAY, IT STILL FEELS LIKE IT WAS ALL A DREAM.

I WAS ON THE VERGE OF BURSTING INTO TEARS ALL DAY, AND I WAS SAYING TO HAMANO-SAN (H-SAMA) THAT I MIGHT SOB IN THE TAXI ON THE WAY HOME. AND, AS SOON AS I LEFT THE STUDIO, I COULDN'T HOLD IT IN ANYMORE. I DIDN'T STOP CRYING UNTIL I GOT HOME. (THE TAXI DRIVER OFFERED ME A BOX OF TISSUES.) WHEN I GOT OUT OF THE TAXI, APPARENTLY I STARTED CROSSING THE STREET RIGHT THROUGH A RED LIGHT (ACCORDING TO HAMANO-SAMA).

IT MAKES ME CRY JUST THINKING ABOUT IT. I WAS REALLY, REALLY HAPPY. ♥♥♥

I READ THE INTERVIEW IN "ZY" WHEN IT CAME OUT. I WAS SURPRISED, BECAUSE IT TOTALLY LOOKED LIKE A REAL INTERVIEW. IT'S AMAZING WHAT WRITERS CAN DO. I SOUNDED COMPLETELY NORMAL.

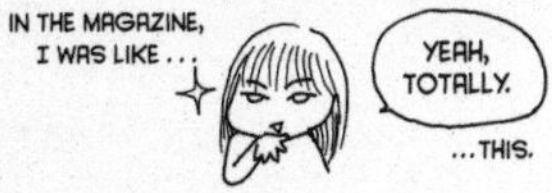
IN THE MAGAZINE, I WAS LIKE . . .
YEAH, TOTALLY.
. . . THIS.

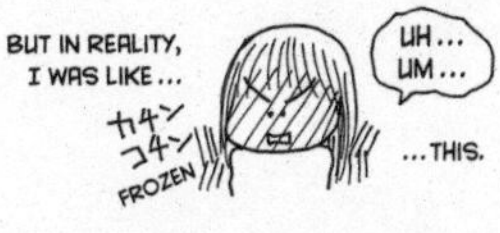
BUT IN REALITY, I WAS LIKE . . .
UH . . . UM . . .
カチン コチン
FROZEN
. . . THIS.

I HAD A CHANCE TO TALK TO THE WRITER A LITTLE BIT, AND I THOUGHT, "THIS JOB WOULD BE A DREAM COME TRUE FOR FANS," BUT THEN I REALIZED THAT NO FAN COULD EVER HANDLE A JOB LIKE THIS. SHE WAS SUCH A COOL LADY. ♥

MY DREAM REALLY DID COME TRUE.

IT MADE ME REALIZE THAT DREAMS CAN ACTUALLY COME TRUE.

. . . NOW I DON'T HAVE ANY MORE GOALS IN LIFE . . . WHAT AM I GONNA DO? I'M CURRENTLY IN SEARCH OF A NEW DREAM.

I'M SERIOUS. MY DREAM REALLY WAS TO MEET KIYOHARU-SAMA IN PERSON . . .

IN SEPTEMBER, ♥ THE SAME MONTH I GOT TO INTERVIEW KIYOHARU-SAMA, ♥ I EXPERIENCED ANOTHER LIFE-CHANGING EVENT.

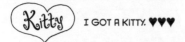

Kitty I GOT A KITTY. ♥♥♥

I KEPT TRYING TO TALK MYSELF OUT OF GETTING A PET, BUT... IT WASN'T QUITE WORKING.

I MEAN, GIVE ME A BREAK. I TOTALLY WANTED A SCOTTISH CAT (OR A POMERANIAN), AND THEN A GOOD FRIEND OF MINE GOES AND GETS ONE AND STARTS TALKING ABOUT IT NONSTOP. (SHE HAD NO IDEA I WANTED A SCOTTISH SO BAD.) I ENVIED HER SO MUCH... (HER CAT IS REALLY SWEET.)

SO I WENT TO SEE SOME CATS, AND I PICKED THE CUTEST ONE OUT (I'M SO PICKY) AND TOOK HIM HOME. HE'S MUCH MORE AGGRESSIVE AND ACTIVE THAN MY FRIEND'S CAT, BUT HE'S JUST ADORABLE. I'M SO IN LOVE WITH HIM. HE BRINGS ME JOY EVERY DAY. ♥

I JUST WISH HE'D LET ME PICK HIM UP.

...HE HATES BEING PICKED UP, BUT HE LOVES TO BE OUT IN THE COLD... HE'S A LITTLE STRANGE.

T TOOK ME TWO DAYS TO DECIDE ON A NAME. ALTHOUGH I HAD A BUNCH OF IDEAS...
SOME OF THE NAMES I CAME UP WITH WERE...
KIYO.
HARU.
AND...
SOME OF THE OTHER NAMES WERE AO AND HAI.
BUT HE DIDN'T REACT TO ANY OF THOSE NAMES.
I WAS JUST KIDDING AROUND WHEN I TRIED CALLING HIM...
TEN.
BUT THEN HE WAS LIKE...
YES?
SO IT WAS DECIDED.
TEN HASN'T MEOWED YET.
WHEN HE WAS LITTLE HE WAS ALL LOVEY-DOVEY. (HE'S NOT LIKE THAT ANYMORE...)
WHENEVER I'D TAKE A NAP ON THE FLOOR...
TAPPA TAPPA TAPPA
ZZZ
HE'S THE SIZE OF MY HAND.
THWUP
HE'D ALWAYS PUT HIS FOREHEAD RIGHT UP AGAINST MINE. ♥
MOVED
CAN HE DO TRICKS?
I WONDER IF HE'LL LEARN ANY BY THE TIME THIS BOOK IS PUBLISHED.
HE LEARNED HOW TO DRINK WATER DIRECTLY FROM THE FAUCET, SO I WANTED TO SHOW MY FRIEND.
READY, TEN?
WAH!
SPLASH
MY FRIEND WAS CRACKING UP.
THIS HAPPENS EVERY ONCE IN A WHILE.
HE'S TRYING SO HARD.

*SORRY, I SUCK AT DRAWING CATS. I HOPE YOU CAN TELL HOW MUCH I LOVE HIM THOUGH...

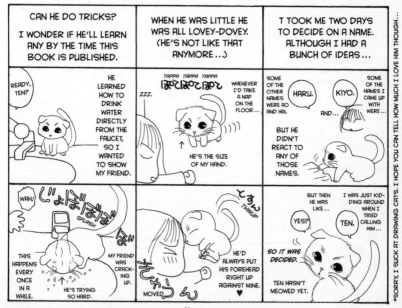

I'VE GOT PLENTY OF "TEN" STORIES I'D LOVE TO SHARE. ♥ ...SORRY, I JUST LOVE MY KITTY SO MUCH...

THANK YOU FOR BUYING KODANSHA COMICS. ♥

EVER SINCE I WROTE ABOUT THE MISTAKE IN BOOK 8,
I'VE BEEN GETTING LETTERS FROM PEOPLE SAYING,
"I BOUGHT THE NEW VERSION." I FEEL BAD. I'M SORRY.
I HAD NO CONTROL OVER IT.
THANK YOU SO MUCH FOR HELPING TO CHEER ME UP.
YOU GUYS ARE GREAT.

"DAMN IT, I WANNA QUIT!" "AAHH, THIS IS TOO HARD!"
WHENEVER I FEEL THIS WAY (THAT'S PRETTY OFTEN THESE DAYS),
I READ YOUR LETTERS, AND THEY ALWAYS HELP MOTIVATE ME.
THEY MAKE ME FEEL 100 TIMES MORE POWERFUL.
I'M REALLY THANKFUL FOR THAT.

I HAVE NO PLANS TO START A WEBSITE, AND I HARDLY EVER
GO ONLINE (SORRY, I CAN'T KEEP UP WITH THE TECHNOLOGY),
SO THE ONLY WAY I CAN HEAR FROM YOU GUYS IS VIA OLD-
FASHIONED LETTERS.

LIKE I'VE SAID MANY TIMES BEFORE, THANK YOU SO MUCH
FOR YOUR SUPPORT. I PROMISE I WON'T LET YOU DOWN.

SPECIAL THANKS

HANA-CHAN	MINE-SAMA
YOSHII	SHIOZAWA-SAMA
ARAKI-KUN	INO-SAMA
IYU KOZAKURA	HAMANO-SAMA
MIZUHO AIMOTO-SENSEI	EVERYBODY IN THE EDITING DEPARTMENT
MACHIKO SAKURAI	

I JUST FOUND OUT THAT YOU'RE GONNA BE WRITING COMMENTS ON THE COVER SLIP FOR THIS VOLUME ...

KIYOHARU-SAMA.

THANK YOU VERY, VERY MUCH.

About the Creator

Tomoko Hayakawa was born on March 4.

Since her debut as a manga creator, Tomoko Hayakawa has worked on many shojo titles with the theme of romantic love—only to realize that she could write about other subjects as well. She decided to pack her newest story with the things she likes most, which led to her current, enormously popular series, *The Wallflower*.

Her favorite things are: Tim Burton's *The Nightmare Before Christmas*, Jean-Paul Gaultier, and samurai dramas on TV. Her hobbies are collecting items with skull designs and watching *bishonen* (beautiful boys). Her dream is to build a mansion like the one the Addams family lives in. Her favorite pastime is to lie around at home with her cat, Ten (whose full name is Tennosuke).

Her zodiac sign is Pisces, and her blood group is AB.

Translation Notes

Japanese is a tricky language for most Westerners, and translation is often more art than science. For your edification and reading pleasure, here are notes on some of the places where we could have gone in a different direction in our translation of the work, or where a Japanese cultural reference is used.

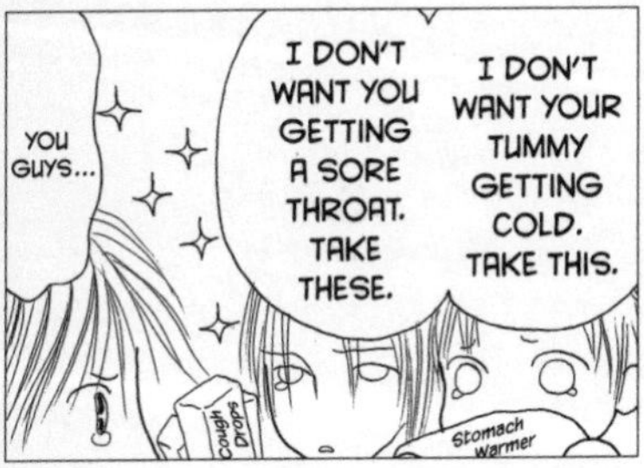
I DON'T WANT YOUR TUMMY GETTING COLD. TAKE THIS.
I DON'T WANT YOU GETTING A SORE THROAT. TAKE THESE.
YOU GUYS...
Stomach Warmer

Stomach warmer, page 15
What Yuki gives Kyohei is a *haramaki*, a kind of stomach warmer. It's a band of cloth worn around the stomach to help keep it warm.

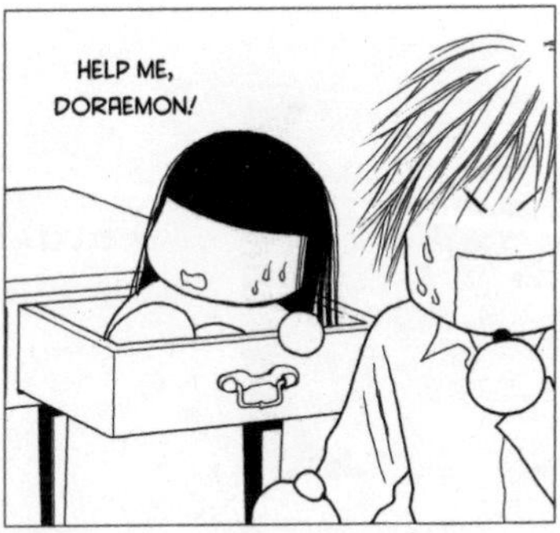
HELP ME, DORAEMON!

Doraemon, page 22
Doraemon is one of Japan's most popular manga/anime characters. He's a magical, catlike creature.

***Okonomiyaki*, page 44**
Okonomiyaki is a Japanese-style pancake filled with various kinds of meat and veggies.

Summers, page 65

Summers is a Japanese comedy group. The guys are also watching them on TV on page 4. The Summers comedians are famous for their ridiculous puns.

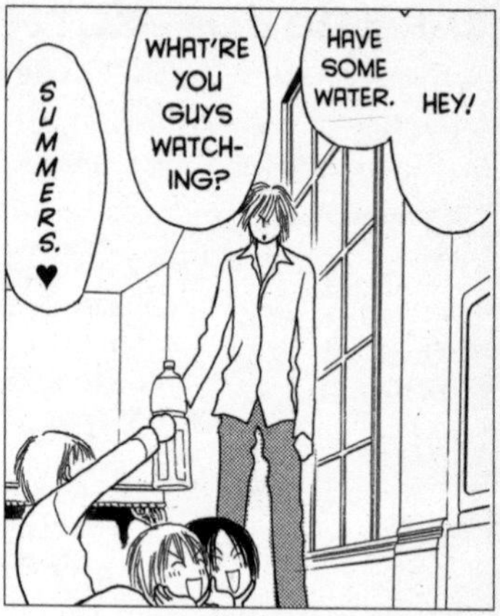
HEY!
HAVE SOME WATER.
WHAT'RE YOU GUYS WATCHING?
SUMMERS. ♥

SMAP, page 82

SMAP is a very popular boy band.

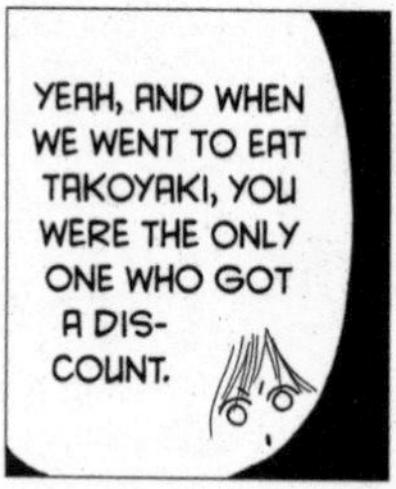
YEAH, AND WHEN WE WENT TO EAT TAKOYAKI, YOU WERE THE ONLY ONE WHO GOT A DISCOUNT.

***Takoyaki*, page 88**

Takoyaki are octopus fritters. They taste much like *okonomiyaki*.

Bishonen, page 126

Bishonen is a term used to describe a cute young guy.

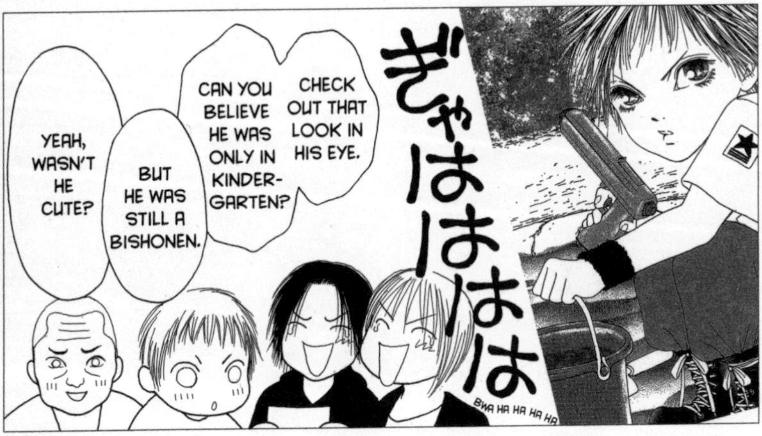
ぎゃははは
BWA HA HA HA HA
CHECK OUT THAT LOOK IN HIS EYE.
CAN YOU BELIEVE HE WAS ONLY IN KINDER-GARTEN?
BUT HE WAS STILL A BISHONEN.
YEAH, WASN'T HE CUTE?

Takuya Kimura, page 126

Takuya Kimura, called "Kimitaku" for short, is a member of SMAP and one of Japan's most popular young male celebrities.

Preview of Volume 10

We're pleased to present you with a preview from volume 10. This volume is available in English now!

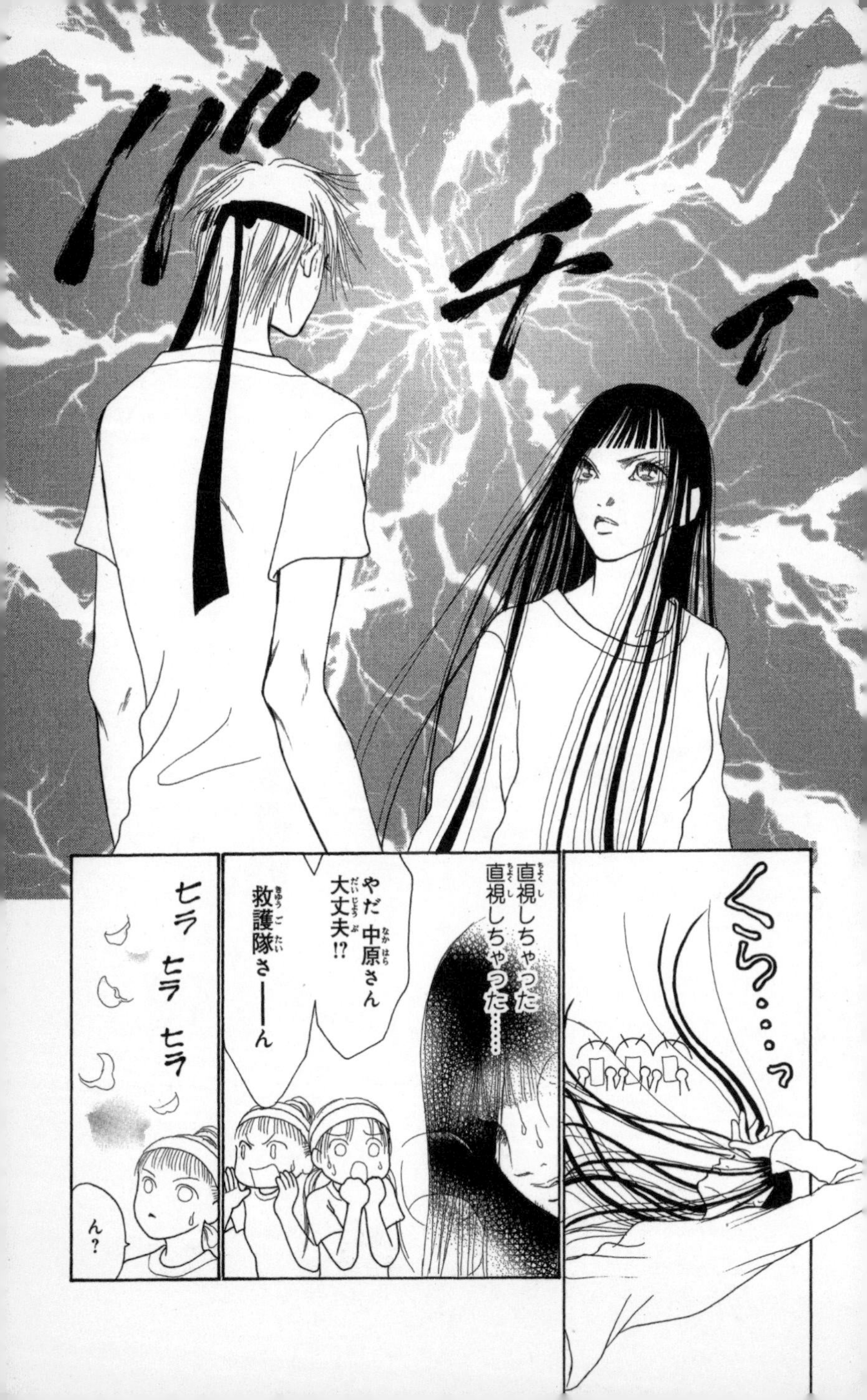
バチィ
くら。。っ
直視しちゃった
直視しちゃった……
やだ中原さん大丈夫!?
救護隊さーーーん
ヒラ　ヒラ　ヒラ
ん?

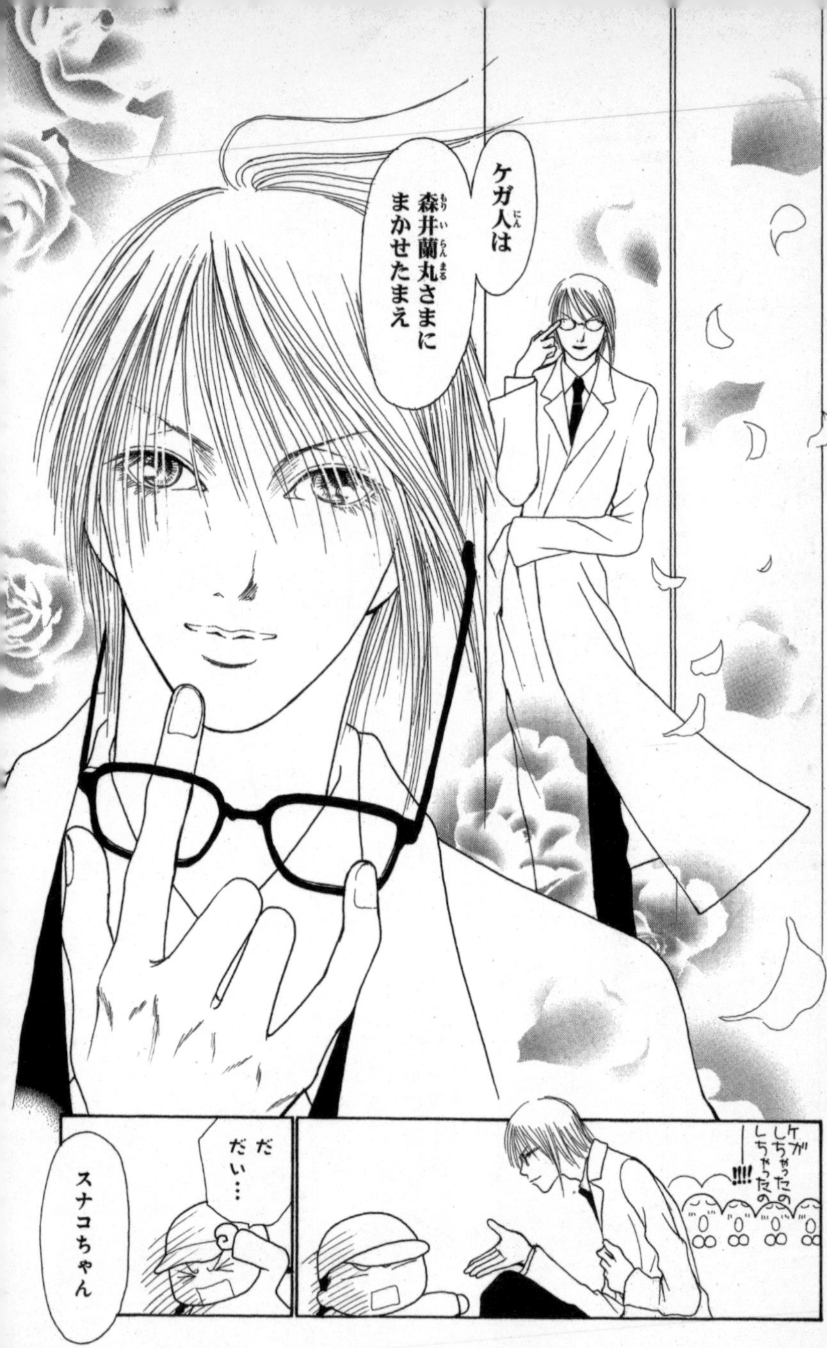
ケガ人は 森井蘭丸さまに まかせたまえ
ケガしちゃったの しちゃったの ー!!!!
だ だい…
スナコちゃん

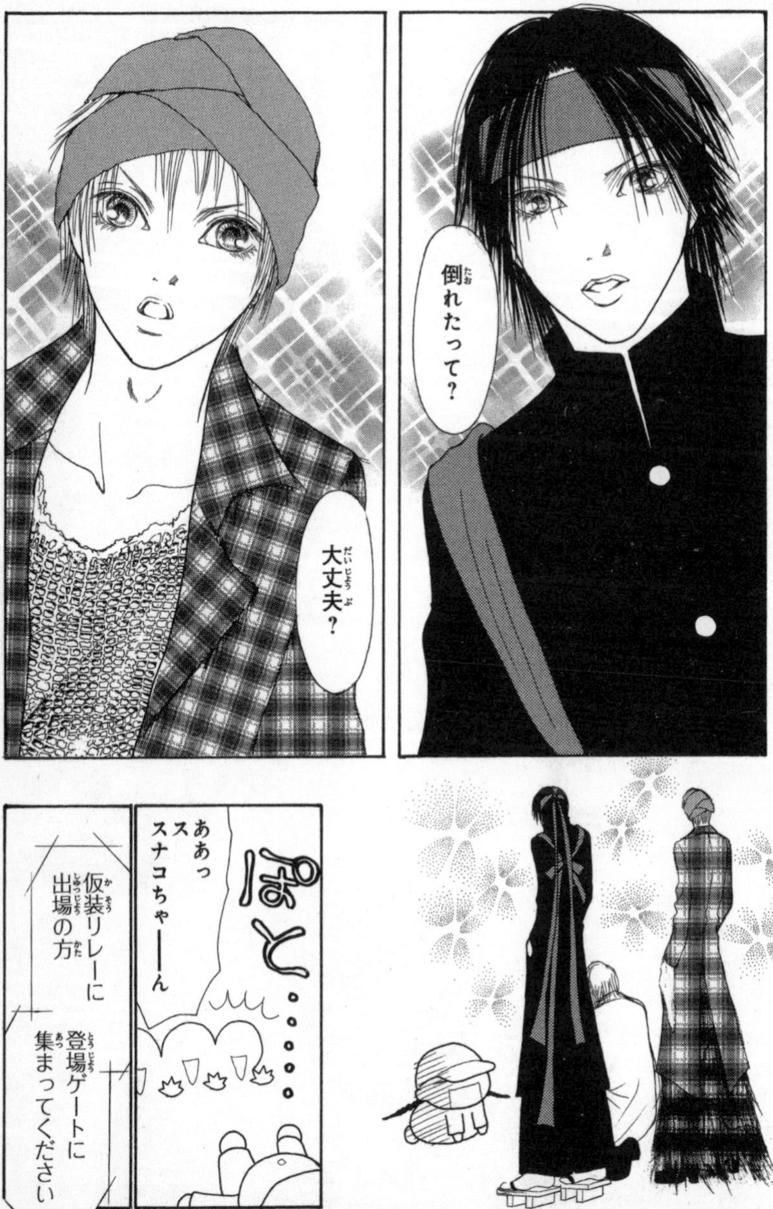
倒れたって?
大丈夫?
ぽと……
ああっ ス スナコちゃーーーん
仮装リレーに出場の方 登場ゲートに集まってください

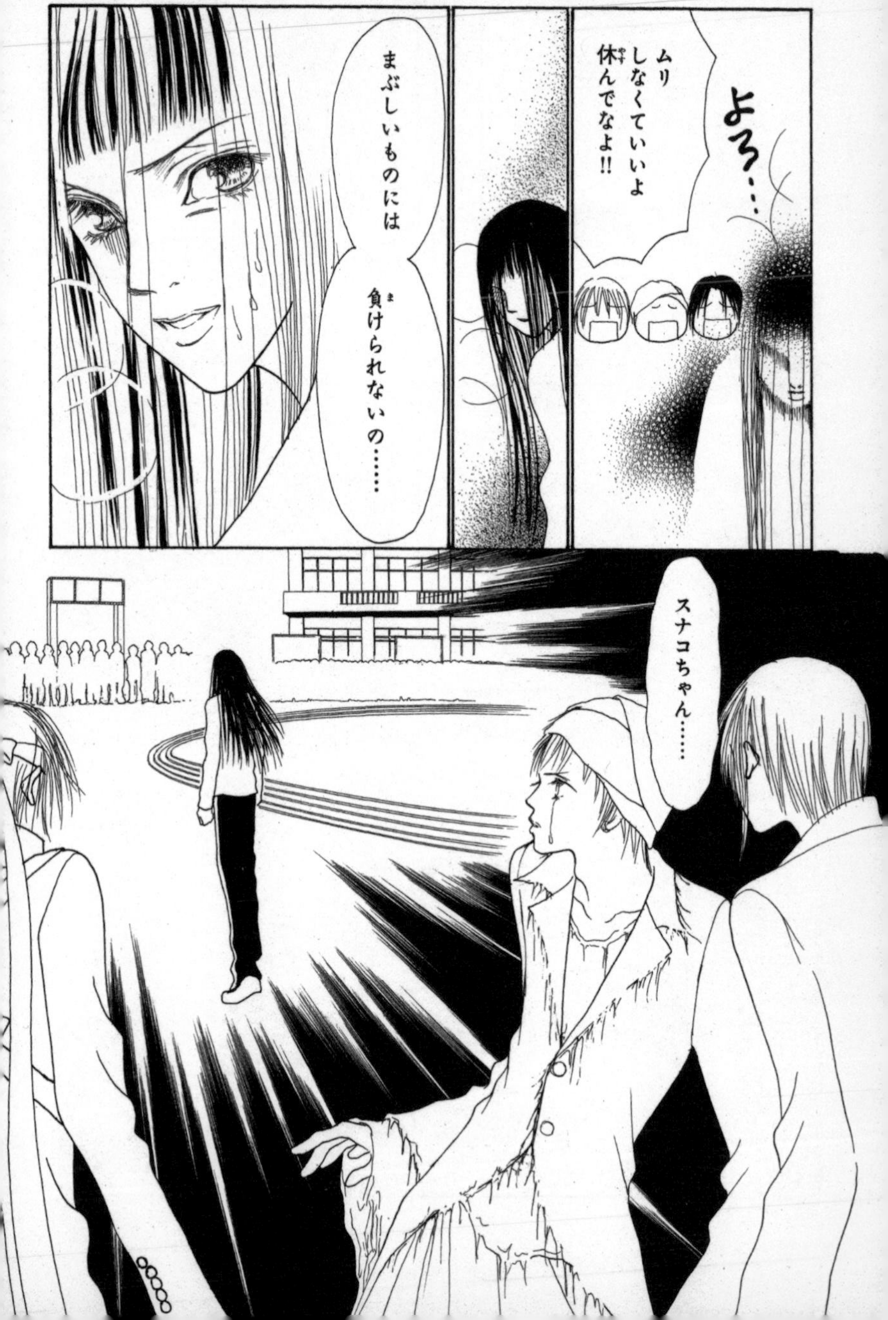
よろ・・・
ムリしなくていいよ休んでなよ!!
まぶしいものには
負けられないの……
スナコちゃん……

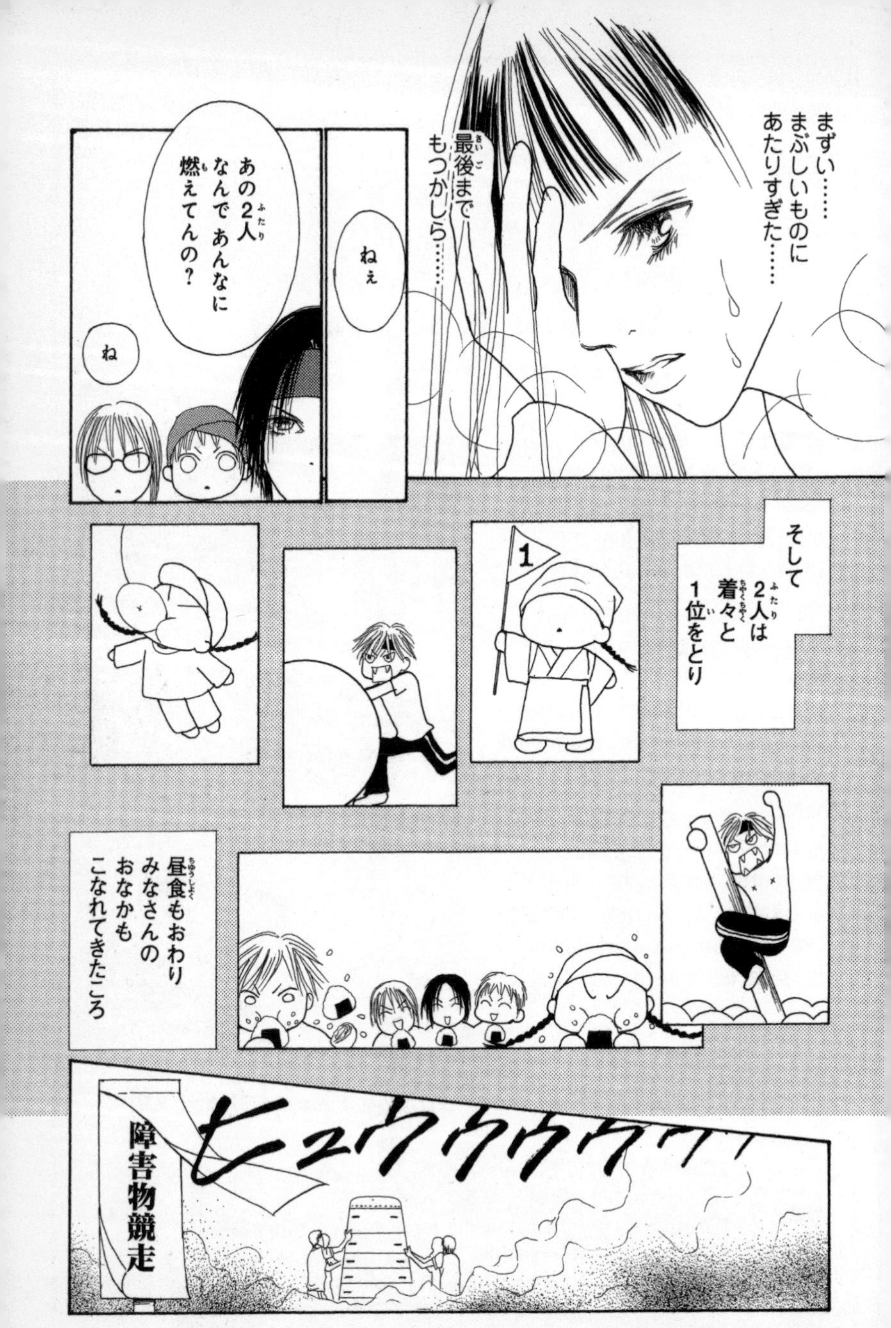
まずい……
まぶしいものに
あたりすぎた……
最後まで
もつかしら……
ねぇ
あの2人
なんであんなに
燃えてんの？
ね
そして
2人は
着々と
1位をとり
1
昼食もおわり
みなさんの
おなかも
こなれてきたころ
ヒュウウウウウ
障害物競走

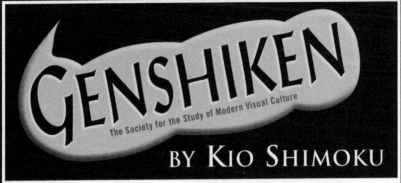

GENSHIKEN
The Society for the Study of Modern Visual Culture

BY KIO SHIMOKU

ARE YOU OTAKU?

It's the spring of freshman year, and Kanji Sasahara is in a quandary. Should he fulfill his long-cherished dream of joining an otaku club? Saki Kasukabe also faces a dilemma. Can she ever turn her boyfriend, anime fanboy Kousaka, into a normal guy? Kanji triumphs where Saki fails, when both Kanji and Kousaka sign up for Genshiken: The Society for the Study of Modern Visual Culture.

Undeterred, Saki chases Kousaka through various activities of the club, from cosplay and comic conventions to video gaming and collecting anime figures—all the while discovering more than she ever wanted to know about the humorous world of the Japanese otaku!

1
Kio Shimoku
GENSHIKEN
The Society for the Study of Modern Visual Culture

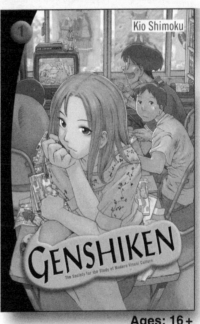

Ages: 16+

Special extras in each volume! Read them all!

DEL REY

VISIT WWW.DELREYMANGA.COM TO:
- **View release date calendars for upcoming volumes**
- **Sign up for Del Rey's free manga e-newsletter**
- **Find out the latest about new Del Rey Manga series**

MY HEAVENLY HOCKEY CLUB

BY AI MORINAGA

WHERE THE BOYS ARE!

Hana Suzuki loves only two things in life: eating and sleeping. So when handsome classmate Izumi Oda asks Hana—his major crush—to join the school hockey club, convincing her proves to be a difficult task. True, the Grand Hockey Club is full of boys—and all the boys are super-cute—but, given a choice, Hana prefers a sizzling steak to a hot date. Then Izumi mentions the field trips to fancy resorts. Now Hana can't wait for the first away game, with its promise of delicious food and luxurious linens. Of course there's the getting up early, working hard, and playing well with others. How will Hana survive?

Special extras in each volume! Read them all!

TOMARE!

止まれ

[STOP!]

You're going the wrong way!

Manga is a completely different type of reading experience.

To start at the *beginning*, go to the *end*!

That's right! Authentic manga is read the traditional Japanese way—from right to left. Exactly the *opposite* of how American books are read. It's easy to follow: Just go to the other end of the book, and read each page—and each panel—from right side to left side, starting at the top right. Now you're experiencing manga as it was meant to be!